The Fourth Gospel in Four Dimensions

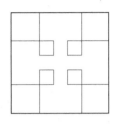

The Fourth Gospel
in Four Dimensions

Judaism and Jesus,
the Gospels and Scripture

D. Moody Smith

The University of South Carolina Press

Published by the University of South Carolina Press
Columbia, South Carolina 29208

www.sc.edu/uscpress

Manufactured in the United States of America

17 16 15 14 13 12 11 10 09 08   10 9 8 7 6 5 4 3 2 1

Library of Congress Cataloging-in-Publication Data

Smith, D. Moody (Dwight Moody)
    The Fourth Gospel in four dimensions : Judaism and Jesus, the Gospels and Scripture /
    D. Moody Smith.
        p. cm.
    Includes bibliographical references and indexes.
    ISBN 978-1-57003-763-4 (pbk : alk. paper)
    1. Bible. N.T. John—Criticism, interpretation, etc. I. Title.
    BS2615.52.S65 2008
    226.5'06—dc22

                                                                        2008024061

This book was printed on Glatfelter Natures, a recycled paper with 30 percent
postconsumer waste content.

To John Painter
Longtime Colleague and Friend

ὑμᾶς δὲ εἴρηκα φίλους

Contents

Preface

In the spring of 1959, before I had passed prelims, my adviser, Professor Paul Schubert of Yale University, asked me what plans I had for a dissertation. I had at least a half-dozen ideas, and spelled them out to him briefly in writing. He read them over and pronounced them good. Then he said, "Now, I tell you what you should do." Although an American citizen, Mr. Schubert was German in upbringing and education. That is the way it works in the German university. The student proposes and the professor disposes.

Rudolf Bultmann's weighty 1941 commentary, *Das Evangelium des Johannes,* in the so-called Meyer series (Kritisch-exegetischer Kommentar über das Neue Testament), was widely known but largely unread in the English-speaking theological world. Bultmann was already a famous figure, not only in New Testament study but also because of his program of demythologizing the New Testament, in theology as well. In his *Theology of the New Testament,* which had been published in fascicles from 1948 to 1953 and translated into English almost immediately (1951–1955), Bultmann placed the theology of the Gospel and Epistles of John after Paul, as the apparent capstone of early Christian theology in what was to become the New Testament. In his treatment of the Johannine writings, Bultmann occasionally referred to his commentary, in which he claimed to have shown that the present state of the text of the Gospel is not original.

Bultmann had subjected the Fourth Gospel to intense scrutiny and analysis and had assigned every bit of it to the author or to one of his sources. He had also made substantial rearrangements in the text, ranging from the transposition of entire chapters to the rearrangement of sentences. Moreover, Bultmann did not lay out the results of this work in the commentary so that the reader could see what these sources looked like. The allegedly original order of the text could be found in the commentary, but there was no key to the location of passages subjected to rearrangement. (This was supplied, however, in the 1971 English translation, *The Gospel of John: A Commentary.*) "What," Mr. Schubert asked, "is going on here? Bultmann is commenting on a text he has himself created!"

My task was therefore first of all to lay out that text and to explain how Bultmann derived it from the canonical one. Bultmann's commentary was not to be translated for more than decade. It existed only in the pre–World War II *Fraktur* German type that has since been abandoned. The work would not be easy, but it would be narrowly defined and would improve my knowledge of German, as well as of the Greek text of the Gospel of John. The dissertation, completed in 1960, was published in 1965 as *The Composition and Order of the Fourth Gospel: Bultmann's Literary Theory.* In that work I was able to trace Bultmann's method of analysis and reconstruction, present his putative sources and the text of the reconstructed Gospel in the original Greek, and offer an evaluation and critique. Bultmann's literary theory about the composition of John, ingenious as it was, could, in the nature of the case, neither be proved true nor falsified. It may be internally consistent, but that does not mean that it is true historically. Moreover, if the unlikely process of composition that Bultmann's theory entails had actually taken place almost two millennia ago, how likely is it that any modern scholarly detective could have uncovered it? In Bultmann's view, the original manuscript of the Gospel was somehow disturbed or disordered, presumably before it was published, and the document was restored in its present form by a later redactor who emended it to include, for example, the sacraments and apocalyptic eschatology.

Perhaps in a postmodern era Bultmann might have simply claimed this reconstruction as his reading of John, which he understood as well as the evangelist who wrote it, and much better than the redactor who had restored and emended it. Be that as it may, Bultmann's grasp of the theology of John's Gospel was acute, and remains unsurpassed in its penetration and comprehensiveness. Yet while he rightly insisted on the indispensability of the Word's having become flesh (that is, human, historical) for John, he was little interested in the possible historical dimensions of the Gospel's narrative or in the concrete historical setting of its origin. At the same time, however, Bultmann's argument that the Gospel, and the Epistles as well, represented a distinct theological tradition, not derivative from Paul or dependent on the Synoptics, merited serious consideration. A similar view was set forth by the leading British scholar of the mid–twentieth century, C. H. Dodd of Cambridge, who also made the Gospel and Epistles of John a lifelong scholarly enterprise. His most important works are, of course, *The Interpretation of the Fourth Gospel* (1953) and *Historical Tradition in the Fourth Gospel* (1963). Like Bultmann, Dodd thought the Johannine writings represented a separate stream of Christian tradition independent of Paul and the Synoptic Gospels, whether or not the author (or authors) of the Gospel (and the Epistles of John) was entirely ignorant of them.

In 1984 the University of South Carolina Press published my *Johannine Christianity: Essays on its Setting, Sources, and Theology.* The title essay of that volume expressed a continuing belief that "Johannine Christianity" is a relatively independent development, that is, not derivative from Paul or the Synoptic

Gospels. As different as Dodd and Bultmann were, they agreed on this important point.

In this connection, a book I first read while still in graduate study seemed to me to be of great importance, namely, P. Gardner-Smith's *Saint John and the Synoptic Gospels* (1938). Gardner-Smith espoused John's independence of the Synoptics and thus influenced his Cambridge colleague Dodd. Shortly thereafter I found Hans Windisch's *Johannes und die Synoptiker* (1926), which had attracted little attention in the English-speaking scholarly world. Windisch granted that John knew the Synoptics, but argued that he wrote his Gospel to displace them because they were inadequate for his purpose. Both addressed the question of why John is so different from the other Gospels, although it nevertheless presents what is obviously an account of the public activity and death of the same figure.

Less than a decade after I had completed graduate study (1968), a thesis that explained John's differences from the Synoptic Gospels and in other matters was advanced by J. Louis Martyn in *History and Theology in the Fourth Gospel*. In Martyn's view John's differences had to do with the importance of "the Jews," who are mentioned so frequently and at important points in the Gospel's narrative. The conflict between Jesus' (also Jewish) disciples who proclaimed him as Messiah or Christ and other Jews, who did not, had fundamentally shaped this quite different and distinctive Gospel. The questions of the role of "the Jews" and the different character or quality of the Fourth Gospel were related, and this seemed to me to be a matter of utmost importance. As they appear in the Fourth Gospel, the Jews are the opponents of the Johannine Jesus and therefore of the Johannine community. How this is to be explained is the burden of Martyn's groundbreaking work.

So the problem of the theological meaning and significance of histories presupposed, or recounted, in the Gospel of John, as well as the relationship of those histories (that is, the historical context of the Gospel of John and the history of Jesus that is narrated), has fueled my interests for most of a career spanning the latter half of the twentieth century and the beginning of the twenty-first. Bultmann afforded the obvious place to begin. In his magisterial *Understanding the Fourth Gospel* (1991), John Ashton devotes "Part I: Questions and Answers" to Bultmann as the pivotal figure. In "Part II: Genesis" (meaning the historical origin of the Fourth Gospel), Ashton turns to the work of Martyn, whom he views as supplying the needed historical matrix missing from Bultmann's treatment. With the publication of his *History and Theology in the Fourth Gospel*, Martyn had set another agenda that most of us have come to regard as crucial and unavoidable. Yet as Ashton observes, the work of Bultmann as a comprehensive interpreter of the basic concept of revelation in the Fourth Gospel has not been surpassed. The essays that constitute the present volume do not fill in the gaps between Bultmann and Martyn, nor were they intended to. They are, however, representative of my effort to play on the same ball field, with similar interests and purposes in view. Yet they do focus largely on matters of history and interpretation that Bultmann and Martyn did not take up or resolve. Questions of history and theology perdure, because they quite obviously arise from the subject matter itself.

All the essays in this volume except one were first published after the appearance of *Johannine Christianity* in 1984, and all but two in the 1990s or thereafter. The one exception is "John's Portrait of Jesus," which originally appeared in *Interpretation* 31 (1977): 367–78. It has been republished more than once. It appears in *Johannine Christianity* (175–89), and reappears in this volume because what I have written there needs to be said in this context, and I cannot say it better. The Johannine Jesus gives long discourses on Christology, but the historical Jesus did not. Five of the essays have not yet appeared in print at this writing: "The Gospel of John in Its Jewish Context"; "The Problem of History in John"; "Jesus Tradition in the Gospel of John"; "Redaction Criticism, Genre, Narrative Criticism, and the Historical Jesus in the Gospel of John"; and "The Historical Figure of Jesus in First John."

Although the individual essays that make up the chapters in this volume were not, for the most part, composed with this book in view, they do reflect a common or coherent viewpoint. Moreover, they deal with related or interlocking issues or groups of issues. There is therefore some overlapping that should prove to be understandable, and this is especially true in chapters that deal with the historical basis of John's narrative of Jesus. Obviously, the data of the text of the Gospel is a given that does not change. In each case a different issue is tackled, a different perspective invoked, or a different, if related, point argued. Obviously, chapter 7, "Jesus Tradition in the Gospel of John," is a comprehensive survey of the landscape and presents the evidence of the Gospel itself, upon which other chapters dealing with this central matter also draw.

James Denton, acquisitions editor for the University of South Carolina Press, has given me much encouragement and help in the production of this book. I thank him as well as his predecessor Barry Blose, who first broached the idea with me. Without them this book would not have materialized. The same goes for my friend, former student, and now, with Robert A. Spivey, my collaborator (*Anatomy of the New Testament,* 6th ed.; Prentice Hall, 2007), Professor C. Clifton Black of Princeton Theological Seminary. He made invaluable suggestions about the arrangement of the book, its title, and the titles of the chapters. Also my friend and colleague Kavin Rowe, now assistant professor of New Testament in Duke Divinity School, has been an unfailing source of help and advice in this and other matters. Jane Allen Smith in asking "Why are you doing this book?" caused me to think twice, as she frequently does. Her questions have always proved to be worth hearing. The answer is that I have addressed issues that should be addressed but remain unresolved or outstanding, whatever may be made of my efforts to resolve them.

The dedication to my friend John Painter marks his retirement from teaching, but certainly not from productive New Testament scholarship. If perhaps I have not cited him sufficiently, it is because I so often agree with him or find him persuasive. In thinking our minds often run parallel, I flatter myself. When we met at a Society for New Testament Studies meeting at the University of Durham, England, where he had done his doctorate with Professor Kingsley Barrett, we discovered we have a common passion for tennis as well as Johannine studies. In his youth John was both a cricketer and a tennis player. In fact, he found himself competing in top junior tennis tournaments in Australia alongside the likes of Kenny Rosewall and Lew Hoad. A serious injury caused him to look in other directions, and the scholarly world of New Testament is much the richer for it. Painter's important contributions to Johannine scholarship include the major study of *The Quest of the Messiah* (rev. ed. 1993), a superb commentary on the Johannine Epistles in the Sacra Pagina series (2002), and the revision of the forthcoming third edition of Barrett's commentary on the Gospel of John. Moreover, his study *Just James,* now in its second edition from the University of South Carolina Press (2004), is the definitive work on the brother of Jesus.

Acknowledgments

The author and the press are grateful to the following publishers:

The Syndics of Cambridge University Press for kind permission to reprint, in revised form, the original version of chapter 2, "John," in *Early Christian Thought in Its Jewish Context,* edited by John Barclay and John Sweet (Cambridge, 1996), pp. 96–111. Copyright © 1996 by Cambridge University Press.

Westminster John Knox Press for kind permission to reprint, in revised form, the original version of chapter 3, "The Contribution of J. Louis Martyn to the Understanding of the Gospel of John," in *History and Theology in the Fourth Gospel. 3rd ed.* (Louisville, Ky. 2003), pp. 1–23. Copyright © 2003 by J. Louis Martyn.

Baylor University Press for kind permission to reprint, in revised form, the original version of chapter 4, "The Problem of History in John," in *What We Have Heard from the Beginning: The Past, Present and Future of Johannine Studies,* edited by Tom Thatcher (Waco, Texas, 2007), pp. 311–20. Copyright © 2007 by Baylor University Press.

E. J. Brill for kind permission to reprint, in revised form, the original version of chapter 5, "John's Quest for Jesus," in *Neotestamentica et Philonica: Studies in Honor of Peder Borgen,* edited by David E. Aune, Torrey Seland, and Jarl Henning Ulrichsen, Supplements to Novum Testamentum 106 (Leiden, 2003), pp. 233–53. Copyright © 2003 by E. J. Brill.

Interpretation: A Journal of Bible and Theology for kind permission to reprint, in revised form, the original version of chapter 6, "The Presentation of Jesus in the Fourth Gospel," *Interpretation* 31 (1977): 367–78. Copyright © 1977 by Union Theological Seminary and Presbyterian School of Christian Education.

E. J. Brill for kind permission to reprint, in revised form, the original version of chapter 7, "Jesus Tradition in the Gospel of John." In *Handbook of the Study of the Historical Jesus,* edited by Stanley Porter and Tom Holmen (Leiden, forthcoming). Copyright © 2006 by E. J. Brill.

William B. Eerdmans Publishing Company for kind permission to reprint, in revised form, the original version of chapter 9, "The Historical Figure of Jesus in 1 John," which appears in slightly different form in *The Word Leaps the*

Gap: Essay on Scripture and Theology in Honor of Richard B. Hays (Grand Rapids, Mich.: Eerdmans, 2008).

Sheffield Academic Press by kind permission of Continuum International Publishing to reprint, in revised form, the original version of chapter 10, "Historical Issues and the Problem of John and the Synoptics," in *From Jesus to John: Essays on Jesus and New Testament Christology in Honour of Marinus de Jonge,* edited by Martinus C. de Boer. Journal for the Study of Religion Monograph Series 84 (Sheffield, 1994), pp. 252–67. Copyright © 1994 by Sheffield Academic Press.

Leuven University Press for kind permission to reprint, in revised form, the original version of chapter 11, "John and the Synoptics and the Question of Gospel Genre," in *The Four Gospels. 1992: Festschrift Frans Neirynck,* edited by F. Van Segbroeck, C. M. Tuckett, G. Van Belle, and J. Verheyden (Leuven: 1992), vol. 3, pp. 1783–97. Copyright © 1992 by Leuven University Press.

Leuven University Press for kind permission to reprint, in revised form, the original version of chapter 12, "The Problem of John and the Synoptics in Light of the Relation between Apocryphal and Canonical Gospels," in *John and the Synoptics,* edited by Adelbert Denaux. Bibliotheca Ephemeridum Theologicarum Lovaniensium 101 (Leuven, 1992), pp. 147–62. Copyright © 1992 by Leuven University Press.

The Society of Biblical Literature for kind permission to reprint, in revised form, the original version of chapter 13, "John and the Synoptics in Light of the Problem of Faith and History," in *Faith and History: Essays in Honor of Paul W. Meyer,* edited by John T. Carroll, Charles H. Cosgrove, and E. Elizabeth Johnson (Atlanta, 1990), pp. 74–89. Copyright © 1990 by Scholars Press.

The Society of Biblical Literature for kind permission to reprint, in revised form, the original version of chapter 14, "When Did the Gospels Become Scripture?" *Journal of Biblical Literature* 119 (2000): 3–20. (Presidential Address, delivered at the 1999 Annual Meeting of the Society of Biblical Literature in Boston, Massachusetts.) Copyright © 2000 by Scholars Press.

William B. Eerdmans Publishing Company for kind permission to reprint, in revised form, the original version of chapter 15, "John, the Synoptics, and the Canonical Approach to Exegesis," in *Tradition and Interpretation in the New Testament: Essays in Honor of E. Earle Ellis,* edited by Gerald F. Hawthorne with Otto Betz (Grand Rapids, Michigan, 1987), pp. 166–178. Copyright © 1987 by Wm. B. Eerdmans.

The Society of Biblical Literature for kind permission to reprint, in revised form, the original version of chapter 16, "Prolegomena to a Canonical Reading of the Fourth Gospel," in *What Is John? Readers and Readings of the Fourth Gospel,* edited by Fernando F. Segovia (Atlanta, 1996), pp. 169–82. Copyright © 1996 by the Society of Biblical Literature.

Part One
John and Judaism

I

The Gospel of John in Its Jewish Context

Why Begin with Judaism?

A half century ago the first question about the Gospel of John would not have been its relation to Judaism. Neither Rudolf Bultmann nor C. H. Dodd, the great mid-twentieth-century interpreters of John, started there. Why not begin with the Gospel of John and Jesus? John, like the other Gospels, purports to be about Jesus. A half century ago, however, one would not have begun with Jesus either. Yet within that time span this also has changed. John is once again coming into its own as a source for Jesus research. Both things have changed, but why one begins with John and Judaism will be the subject of this essay.

Before one presents the Johannine Jesus, or discusses Jesus tradition in the Gospel of John (chapter 7), it is necessary to ask about John and its possibly Jewish originative context. Why should we think such a context is fundamental? Of course, that John should have originated within Judaism is not surprising if the Gospel is about Jesus. Jesus himself was a Jew, as is now universally acknowledged. The so-called third quest of the historical Jesus has unmistakably underscored this fact. For theology, particularly New Testament theology, this means that Jesus' humanity is inseparable from his Jewishness, if it is more than a mere and meaningless abstraction. But was the Judaism of Jesus himself the same as the Judaism portrayed in the Gospel of John? Moreover, was the relationship of Jesus to Judaism the same? Apparently not, but the Dead Sea Scrolls revealed the existence of a Palestinian Judaism with some affinities with Johannine theological language. Yet this fact, although important, did not lead to immediate success in situating John in, or in relation to, Judaism.[1]

In the traditions embodied in Matthew, Mark, and Luke, Jesus appears as a Jew among Jews even as he creates surprise, astonishment, and sometimes anger among some of his fellow Jews.[2] Rarely are "the Jews" singled out in distinction from Jesus, however, because Jesus himself is assumed to be Jewish. The Jews are mentioned only when an evangelist is reflecting his own, later perspective (Matt 28:15; Mark 7:3).

Jesus is said to have begun public activity by proclaiming the imminent advent of the kingdom of God (Mark 1:14–15). Obviously, the realization of God's kingly rule lay in the future, but one could detect in Jesus' own work the signs of its in-breaking and presence (Luke 11:20). For this and other reasons Jesus was an unsettling presence. Jesus represented something new. But that new thing was not at first conceived as the beginning of Christianity as a religion separate from Judaism. In the Gospel of Matthew, perhaps the most Jewish of the Synoptics, Jesus presents himself as one who has come to fulfill scripture, although not necessarily in ways that others would anticipate. He does not reject the biblical law of Judaism, as much as he may dispute with other Jewish teachers how that law should be fulfilled (Matt 5:17–20). It is sometimes said that Jesus radicalized the demand for obedience. Perhaps he did. He certainly did not abandon it. Moreover, there is in Matthew, and in the other Synoptics for that matter, little to suggest that Jesus thought God had sent him on a mission to Gentiles as well as Jews. "I was sent only to the lost sheep of the house of Israel," Matthew adds to Mark's narrative (Matt 15:24; cf. 10:5), but it seems to be the proper understanding of the distinction between "children" and "dogs" in Mark 7:27.

The Apostle Paul, probably Jesus' contemporary although never his earthly companion, gained importance and fame by preaching the good news of Jesus to Gentiles and in effect abandoning the then widespread insistence on their obeying the law. He styled himself the Apostle to the Gentiles, in distinction from Peter and James. Paul, as a Jew, thought of himself as instrumental in making a break with Judaism, not of his own volition but by the call of God (Gal 1:15–17). Paul's move has been called his conversion, but not by Paul himself, who never uses the term *Christian* or *Christianity.* Yet there is good reason that Paul has been thought of as the founder of a Gentile Christian church, forever separate from Judaism. Paul would not have been happy, however, with such a designation or such fame. He saw in his Gentile mission, and in the Gentile churches, a means of bringing his own Jewish brothers and sisters to faith in Jesus Christ, Jesus as the Messiah (Rom 11:13–24), something that was not, however, happening during his own ministry (9:1–5).

Paul is portrayed in Acts (8:3; 9:1–22) as a persecutor of Jesus' followers, a description that accords with his own statements (Gal 1:13, 23). Later, as a missionary for Jesus, he was beaten by his (fellow) Jews (2 Cor 11:24; cf. Deut 25:3). Thus Paul attests, at the very beginning of the Jesus movement within Judaism, that it evoked resistance and hostility, which he had at first, as a Jew, dealt out and then, as a Jewish apostle of Jesus, received. For Paul the parting of the ways had to do with law and custom. Reading Paul's letters and Acts we naturally assume that everything centered on Paul and his mission. Yet this cannot have been the whole story of Christianity's mission and expansion, important as it was.

The Gospel of John

The Johannine literature, particularly the Gospel of John, suggests there was another branch of the Jesus movement (perhaps one of several) that was also grounded in, but separating from, Judaism. Thus the Gospel of John pits the Jews, sometimes referred to as Pharisees, against Jesus the Jew (as he is called in 4:9). Indeed, "the Jews" approach John the Baptist and question him sharply at the beginning of the Gospel's narrative (1:19–28). The fact that John is said to confess, and not deny (v. 25), suggests there is something hostile about the encounter and questioning. John, obviously Jewish, has been sent to Israel (1:31). Obviously, Jews belong to Israel. Israel is made up of Jews. Yet in the Gospel of John the term *Israel* is always used in a positive light (cf. 1:47; 3:10), while the designation *the Jews* usually, although not always, appears in a negative light.

In John 8:31–51 "the Jews" (at first the Jews who have believed in him) and Jesus are locked in mortal opposition to each other. (Yet it is interesting that here the Jews confront Jesus alone, not his disciples.) There would seem to be no possibility of rapprochement between them. Yet earlier "Jews" in Galilee were more perplexed by Jesus than angry with him (6:25–51). But after the horrendous dispute of John 8 "the Jews" are portrayed as having decided to expel from the synagogue anyone who confesses Jesus as the Messiah (9:22). This malevolent intention is repeated at the end of Jesus' public ministry (12:42), and Jesus himself warns his disciples of this and worse as he meets with them at their last supper (16:2). Such statements presume that there were Christ-confessors who did not intend to cease being Jewish. There is something anomalous, and probably anachronistic, about all this. Nothing is said in other Gospels about the disciples of Jesus being in effect excommunicated from Judaism. (Presumably that is what is meant by the technical term *aposynagogoi.*)

There Jesus does not stand over against "the Jews." He stands side by side with other Jews, who are seldom called simply Jews but are identified as Pharisees, Sadducees, scribes, priests, lawyers, or Herodians. Jesus himself is sometimes referred to as a teacher or a prophet. All this makes good sense in a Jewish context. Also, only in John do the Jews seem to be identical with the Pharisees (cf. 9:22 and 12:42), who with the chief priests (who replace the Pharisees in the passion narrative) are the only historically identifiable Jewish groups mentioned. The situation of the Jews in John corresponds to the period after the Roman War (A.D. 70 and later), in which only the interests of the Pharisees survived that holocaust and the identification of "the Pharisees" and "the Jews" made a certain sense.

Interestingly enough, although Jesus is identified as Jewish in John (4:9) and, in the face of the challenge presented by the woman of Samaria, declares that "salvation is of the Jews" (4:22), he himself is never said to be expelled from a synagogue or threatened with such expulsion. This reflects the historical fact that he was not.

The Epistles and Revelation to John

The peculiarity of the state of affairs represented by the Gospel of John is bounded on the one side by the time of Jesus himself, when there was hostility but not with "the Jews," and on the other by the time and setting of the Johannine Epistles, which make no mention of "the Jews." The hostility in the Epistles is directed instead against other Christ-confessors who get it wrong about Jesus. They may confess Jesus (9:22), but they do not confess that Jesus has come in the flesh (1 John 4:2–3). They are docetic heretics. Their confession is worse than useless. It is misleading and corrupting. Yet there is no indication that these opponents are, or ever have been, Jewish. There is, however, an overriding dualism, which seem to require an opposite, or an enemy (if not "the Jews," then the Christ-confessors who make an unforgivable mistake in their understanding and presentation of Jesus).

The Revelation to John, with the Gospel and Epistles, rounds out the traditional Johannine corpus. It is, of course, an apocalypse that reveals secrets, particularly about the future, the return of Jesus and the consummation of the age. At the end the heavenly, exalted Christ says repeatedly that he is coming soon (22:6, 12, 17, 20). The apocalyptic scenario is very different from the Gospel of John. In John also Jesus speaks repeatedly of coming again (14:4), but this coming is now reinterpreted (14:22) in terms of Jesus' continuing presence among his disciples via the Counselor or Advocate (esp. 14:26; 16:12–15).

There is, however, a kind of bridge between Revelation and the Gospel at just this point. The Jesus who is coming soon is the same Jesus who has already spoken from heaven to his disciples on earth (Rev 22:16) in Revelation's seven letters to the seven churches (2–3). John writes the letters (1:4), but what he communicates is a message from the crucified and risen one (1:18) who instructs John what to write (1:19). In every case a synoptic-like saying of Jesus about he who has ears to hear is adapted as, for example, in 2:7: "He who has an ear let him hear what the Spirit says to the churches" (cf. Matt 11:15). Thus between Revelation and the Gospel there seems to be a parallel structure, although the terminology is different. For example, the term *Counselor* or *Advocate* (*paraklētos*), found also in 1 John 2:1, is not used of the Spirit in Revelation. Yet in both cases, Gospel and Revelation, Jesus, who is with God, communicates with his disciples below.[3]

Despite wide differences in terminology, genre, and scenario, there are a number of other points of contact between the Gospel of John and Revelation.[4]

Revelation names as its author a John (1:1 passim), although, paradoxically, the Gospel of John does not. There the author is described as a truthful witness (19:35; 21:24), while the author of 2 and 3 John is the unnamed Elder. At the outset (Rev 1:7) there is a reference to Zech 12:10, the piercing of the (side of) crucified Jesus, elsewhere found only in John 19:37. That the death of Jesus is clearly in view in John 19:37 is made quite explicit. Water and blood flow from Jesus' side. In Rev 1:5 there is also reference to Jesus' (spilled) blood, as his death is also necessarily in view. Revelation, like the Gospel, lays heavy emphasis on witness or witnessing. Jesus is the faithful witness (Rev 1:5): "The testimony of Jesus" (1:9) could be understood as "the witness of Jesus"; "the martyrs of Jesus" (17:6) are Jesus' witnesses; also "the testimony of Jesus" is the "spirit of prophecy" (19:11). Revelation's heavy emphasis on martyrdom and witness is grounded in the fact that *martys* in Greek is both "witness" and "martyr," and John is obviously aware that a pun is intended. Become a martyr in one's witness is also conquering. The disciple who conquers (Rev 21:7; cf. 2:7, 11, 17, 26; 3:5, 12, 21) parallels Jesus, who has overcome, or conquered, the world (John 16:33). Finally, in Revelation Jesus himself is called the Word of God (19:13; 20:4; cf. John 1:1–18 and 1 John 4:1–4).

Moreover, "the Jews" appear in Rev 2:9 and 3:9. Yet they are not truly Jews, although they may claim to be, but are "the synagogue of Satan." Obviously, the synagogue of Satan is not a good thing, but *Jews* is here used in a positive sense. The reader is reminded of Paul's use of *Jew* in Romans (2:17, 28–29; 3:1). A true Jew, or one who is truly a Jew, is a man (or woman) who is obedient to God. Similarly, for Paul in his argument with Peter (Gal 2:14–15) being a Jew counts for something, even though the coming of Jesus has changed the terms on which God's salvation is accessible (cf. Rom 9:1–5). But are these references to Jews and a synagogue of Satan in Revelation closely related to the Gospel of John? Have the Jews who preside over synagogues shown their true colors by expelling the true Jews (in the Gospel of John, "Israelites") who have confessed Jesus? Apparently the followers of Jesus who are here addressed (by the exalted Jesus) are being oppressed by these Jews falsely so-called. I think it quite possible that the Gospel of John and Revelation reflect similar settings in which Christ's confessors are suffering at the hands of their fellow Jews who deny that Jesus is the Christ.[5] It may not be an exact fit, but it is a close one.

The Acts of the Apostles

In the Gospel of John "the Jews" are not followers of Jesus but are usually, with the Pharisees, Jesus' opponents. (Yet some are occasionally portrayed as still contemplating the possibility of belief.) John is usually read as if their hostility is basic throughout the Gospel. Such a complete breach closely parallels what is found in another narrative context, namely, the Acts of the Apostles. Acts, however, describes the emergence of Christianity from Judaism, and even notes that in Antioch, when the gospel was preached to Greeks (presumably Gentiles), the disciples were first called Christians (11:26). Obviously, such disciples were no longer thought of—nor did they think of themselves—as Jews.

At the end of Acts 12, after the release of Peter from prison and the death of his nemesis Herod, the scene shifts fully to Antioch and the narration of Paul's missionary work begins. Only in Acts 15 do we read that the apostles and elders, including Peter, gather again in Jerusalem, before James, to decide whether converts must be circumcised and charged to keep the law of Moses as Pharisaic believers were still insisting (15:5). The decision is basically negative, so that the mission of Paul and Barnabas is vindicated (cf. Gal 2:1–10). The reader then learns of Paul's further missionary work (16:1 until his arrest in Jerusalem in 21:27–36), and after that of his hearings and speeches before Roman as well as Jewish authorities as he moves from Jerusalem to Rome, where the narrative ends. Thus, after chapter 12, Acts is an account of Paul's mission and his defense of it as Apostle to the Gentiles. We do not learn much about what is going on among Christians or churches in other places. We do, however, learn that there are still "thousands" of law-abiding followers of Jesus in Jerusalem who advocate circumcision and obedience to the law for all true disciples of Jesus and suspect Paul because he does not (21:20–21). The Jewish authorities are now Paul's opponents (24:1–8) although they recognize his Jewish origin. Their hostility is mortal, because they seek his death (Acts 25:2–3). One is reminded of Jesus' dire forecast in John 16:2.

The Book of Acts, read critically, gives a historically plausible portrayal of the mission and expansion of Christianity. Obviously Luke does not describe everything that was going on within the first generation. In fact, that would have been impossible. Does Acts represent an unbiased portrayal? Obviously it does not. If postmodernism has taught us anything, it is to suspect any claims for such a portrayal, ancient or modern. Acts, however, deals with real people and events. That impression is not false, as a comparison with the only sources certainly contemporaneous with the events, Paul's letters, shows. The data of Acts and Paul do not always agree, which suggests not that Acts or Paul is valueless historically, but that they are dealing with the same or related data.

We have briefly canvassed through the Synoptic Gospels, Acts, Paul, and the Johannine writings, looking at the use of *Ioudaioi*, "Jews." It is a striking fact that the term occurs nowhere else in the New Testament. It is not found in the Catholic Epistles (including the Johannine), Hebrews, or the Pauline Pastorals. Neither does it occur in Ephesians, Philippians, 2 Thessalonians, or Philemon. Its most significant occurrences are in the Gospel of John, some of Paul's letters (especially Romans), and the Book of Acts.

How do the Johannine writings, particularly the Fourth Gospel, fit in? Do they "fit in"? It has often been presumed that the Johannine writings came in the aftermath of the situation described in Paul's letters and Acts. That is, with respect to the Jewish-Christian issue specifically, they presume and reflect the position attained at the end of the line of development (*Entwicklungslinie* or trajectory) reflected in Paul's letters and described in Acts. But do they? Or do they represent a separate, related but independent, line of development?

If they represent the end point of such a development, "Judaism" would scarcely be the proper beginning point for a book on John's Gospel. That issue would have been settled. If, however, there was a distinctly Johannine line of development, Judaism may well be the place to begin. In the former case, it has seemed appropriate to treat John, particularly the Gospel of John, in the context of the development of Christian theology within the apostolic or New Testament period as its last chapter.[6] To what Christian theological issues or situation was John then addressed? As different as Edwyn Clement Hoskyns's commentary and Ernst Käsemann's monograph are, to name two important works of the mid–twentieth century, they were written on the basis of the same or similar premises. John is a theological document and its place is to be sought within inner-Christian theological developments.[7] Bultmann, however, noticed that John, although in many respects similar or parallel to Paul, was nevertheless independent and not based on a specifically Pauline foundation.[8] He even recognized that it reflected a historical break with Judaism.[9] But all three, Hoskyns, Käsemann, and Bultmann, viewed John's Gospel as first and foremost an expression of Christian theological interests.

History and Theology According to Martyn

Significantly, J. Louis Martyn's groundbreaking work is entitled *History and Theology in the Fourth Gospel*, with history coming first.[10] Theology is certainly not irrelevant for Martyn, but it is grounded in the history of the Johannine disciples of Jesus and of Jesus of Nazareth. In other words, the Gospel of John is the fruition of a history going back toward, and originating with, Jesus. This premise is perhaps obscured by the fact that Martyn's work concentrates on the "Community of the Beloved Disciple," to use the language of Martyn's long-time Union colleague Raymond E. Brown.

Exegetically, this is the so-called upper level of Martyn's two levels. Whether one speaks of a community, a circle, or a school, the same reality is in view.[11] It is premised on the belief that there is a distinctly Johannine line of development within early Christianity that is related to, but not dependent on, other manifestations represented in the New Testament.

At this point the relationship of John to the Synoptic Gospels comes into play. It is not obvious that John used, or was dependent upon, the Synoptic Gospels. Gardner-Smith argued in favor of John's independence many years ago.[12] Independence does not necessarily imply ignorance, but John's basis or beginning point is scarcely Mark's narrative, as is obvious in its account of Jesus' public ministry. At the same time Mark's version, on which Matthew and Luke are based, is constructed more on the basis of literary and theological interests than of historical knowledge.[13] Either through necessity or conscious intention the Fourth Evangelist chose to go his own way. Efforts to explain John's narrative on the basis of the Synoptics vary widely because of a lack of points of control, except in the passion narrative. Within the Synoptic "canon" they are many and profuse. In the case of John and the Synoptics they are few and diffuse, if not abstruse.

It is not a coincidence that Martyn's approach is allied with the work of his doctoral student Robert T. Fortna.[14] Fortna's simple narrative Gospel, the reconstructed Gospel of Signs, provides the basis for later theological developments. The Gospel of Signs is a missionary tract composed within a Jewish context. It contains no polemic against "the Jews" because it is an inner-Jewish pamphlet seeking to demonstrate that Jesus is the Messiah. In it elements of Davidic messianic expectation combine with a similarly Jewish, but rival, expectation of a prophet like Moses.[15] Such expectation may seem off-beat, but it is nevertheless Jewish. That there was no single form of Jewish messianic expectation is now generally acknowledged. To what extent, however, have New Testament scholars, most of whom are not expert in postbiblical Judaism, allowed themselves nevertheless to be overly influenced by the messianic expectation formulated in the Synoptic Gospels, Acts, and Paul? John's messianic expectations obviously include the performance of signs, analogous to those performed by Moses. That Moses performed signs to authenticate his divine commission is of course a commonplace of the Exodus tradition.

In any event, Martyn has in view a Johannine line of development and community that perdured through time. The closely related Johannine Epistles followed the Gospel of John. Quite possibly the Revelation to John preceded the Gospel, as C. K. Barrett once proposed.[16] Martyn's adoption of Fortna's proposal of a Gospel of Signs signals his recognition that the Gospel of John was not composed by one author at one sitting, so to speak, but was composed over time. He cites Barnabas Lindars to the effect that "the Fourth Gospel began life as separate homilies."[17] Yet there is a pervasive unity about the Fourth Gospel, despite the problematic character of its narrative at many points. The implied author speaks the same theological language and projects the same literary style throughout. Marvelous and tightly woven discourses, conversations, and narratives are juxtaposed in an order that is generally intelligible, but sometimes moves by fits and starts. Chapter 21 appears to be an afterthought, although it sheds light on, as well as adding to, what has already been written. Jesus' Farewell Discourses seem to end at 14:31, but then continue for another three chapters (15–17). Chapter 6 might fit better before chapter 5, rather than after as it now stands. So Martyn projects two levels, that of the Johannine church and its earlier tradition, which is based on Jesus tradition, represented by the Gospel of Signs. There may be more than two levels, but there are at least two. Both are in conflict with (other forms of) Judaism.

Luke wrote a Gospel, a narrative of Jesus' ministry and death, culminating in his resurrection. Then he composed a second volume, which presents the life and mission of the postresurrection church. One can think of John as presenting both together as a kind of layer cake. The Gospel period, the Jesus period, was of course followed chronologically by the period of the postresurrection church. Luke does the reasonable thing and presents them in the conventional chronological order. John tells the story of Jesus in terms provided by the later Johannine church, while at the same time telling the church's story in terms of the ministry of Jesus.[18] As Jesus was threatened and died, so the church lives under the threat of suffering and death. Luke's history, or biography and history, is history in the conventional sense, instantaneously recognizable as such, even now as then. John's Gospel is different, but, given the hermeneutical key, can be opened and read as history, John's and Jesus'.

The order of presentation of the present volume reflects a belief that Martyn's construal of the origin and character of the Fourth Gospel affords the best perspective on its nature and meaning. Although a genius, the Fourth Evangelist was not a theological Lone Ranger. If his Gospel looks like a maverick Gospel,[19] it looks like one to us rather than to him.

It is a Gospel that reflects the postresurrection Johannine Christian church's break with Judaism, its parent religion. That break occurred before the Gospel was written and published in its present form. In the Farewell Discourses that break is presupposed, and the Gospel's interest is focused on the problem created by Jesus' absence and his failure to return in the manner anticipated. Yet Jesus has returned, in the presence of the *paraklētos,* the Holy Spirit, and continues to guide and protect his followers. The Jews reappear finally in the passion narrative to accuse Jesus before Pilate, the representative of Roman authority. Both there abdicate their authority. The chief priests declare they have no king but Caesar (19:15), and Pilate, having three times declared Jesus innocent, capitulates to them, then mocks them by having Jesus crucified as "Jesus of Nazareth, the King of the Jews."

John is rooted in circles of disciples who were Jews. Probably some of them were already disciples of John the Baptist, called only "John" in the Fourth Gospel. This John, unlike Jesus' own disciples, always understands who Jesus is and gets it right about him. The Gospel of John departs from the other Gospels in portraying the Baptist as sending his own disciples over to Jesus (1:35–42).[20] Does this John provide the link between the Fourth Gospel and the Qumran community? Later Jesus himself is baptizing alongside, and in apparent rivalry with, John (3:22–23, 26; 4:1–2). Jesus is baptizing more people than John.

Although this may show Jesus' superiority, it is within the Gospel recognized as a problem: not Jesus, but his disciples, baptized (4:2). Yet there is no account of Jesus' disciples baptizing in the other Gospels.[21] Once the supposition that John is later is abandoned, a picture of this Gospel's Jewish roots emerges more clearly.

Since the publication of the first edition of Martyn's *History and Theology in the Fourth Gospel* (1968) and Brown's commentary in the Anchor Bible series, as well as his *Community of the Beloved Disciple,* exegetes working on the Johannine literature, particularly the Fourth Gospel, have in increasing numbers acknowledged the Fourth Gospel's roots in Judaism. Who are "the Jews" in the Gospel of John? For Bultmann they are surrogates for unbelievers generally.[22] Although Bultmann acknowledged some early Jewish roots of the Gospel, he made little of them as he distilled from the Gospel a complex literary development. With the publication of Martyn's book, however, eyes began turning in the direction of "the Jews."[23] Already Wayne A. Meeks's important dissertation and monograph, *The Prophet-King* (1967), had found the roots of Johannine Christology within Judaism.[24] Not long after, his groundbreaking article "The Man from Heaven in Johannine Sectarianism" (1972) employed Martyn's work also to advance a sociological analysis and explanation of the Johannine dualism.[25]

Resistance to Martyn's thesis has tended to center on the role of the *Birkath ha-Minim,* as if his case stood or fell with the wording, character, and dating of that text, which exists in manuscripts no older than the tenth century. As has been observed, however, Martyn's thesis is not dependent on the *Birkat ha-Minim* per se, but at most on a state of affairs it represents.[26] John Ashton made this point in his magisterial *Understanding the Fourth Gospel,* as he paired Martyn with Bultmann as providing the satisfying historical analysis of the origins of John's Gospel, something that Bultmann's insightful theological treatment lacked.[27] Thus John's relationship to Judaism has, since the initial publication of *History and Theology in the Fourth Gospel* in 1968, become a continuing and dominant issue. A Louvain Conference was dedicated to "Anti-Judaism and The Fourth Gospel," and the papers delivered there published as a book.[28] Any such discussion must now deal with the historical issues, as this book does. Thus we have begun with Judaism and the Gospel of John.

The following chapter (chapter 2) presents John's understanding of Judaism. Our thesis is that John rejects, but does not misrepresent, a Judaism of the first century. The objections raised against the Johannine Jesus are, given presuppositions based on monotheistic faith, perfectly understandable. They may be shared by many Christians, ancient or modern, especially those who espouse a Christology from below.

Chapter 3 is a more detailed discussion of the importance of Martyn's *History and Theology in the Fourth Gospel,* which put Judaism at the forefront in the discussion of John's origins. It first appeared in a Festschrift for Martyn and in emended form as the introduction to the third, revised edition of *History and Theology in the Fourth Gospel* (2003).

Martyn's thesis that the Gospel of John embraces two levels (that of the evangelist and his community and that of the Jesus tradition) is subject to recurring questioning and criticism, as is the hypothesis of a Johannine community distinct from other forms of early Christianity. They are obviously linked.

As to a Johannine community, one might ask whether it would be preferable to refer to a Johannine church. In fact, *community* (*koinōnia*) is a distinctive and important term in 1 John (1:3, 6, 7; cf. 2 John 11). *Church* (*ekklēsia*), the generic term, is first and most widely attested in the Pauline corpus and then in Acts. It is found only in 3 John 6, 9, 10 within the Johannine Epistles, although it frequently occurs in the letters to the seven churches in Revelation (chapters 1–3). Of course, the seven letters are sent to seven churches, including the church at Ephesus, which obviously constituted a circle or community of churches that has every reason to be described as "Johannine." The Apocalypse was written by a prophet named John. Among the Gospels, *ekklēsia* occurs only in Matthew (16:18; 18:17). In John, however, the concept of the unity of the disciples appears in the Allegory of the Vine (15:1–8) and is emphasized in Jesus' final prayer (17:20–23). Jesus' unity with his disciples and their consequent union with each other is a central Johannine theological theme, found also in Paul, of course, but expressed differently ("body of Christ"). The concept is not uniquely Johannine, but it is reasonable to suppose that it defined an empirical Johannine community. Thus the rupture of that community reflected in such passages as 1 John 2:18–27 is particularly heinous. It does not follow, however, that the Johannine community was out of touch with other churches. In Ephesus it could scarcely have been totally isolated.

Martyn's thesis of two levels is now also subject to question, particularly by colleagues who maintain that it is too neat or that there may have been more than two levels. In response it is worth observing that Martyn may have become a victim of his own rich, if historically informed and disciplined, historical imagination. Martyn writes dramatic, even suspenseful, prose. His narrative keeps the reader on edge like no other piece of serious New Testament scholarship I know. It matches, and may even be inspired by, Bultmann's *Theology of the New Testament,* in which the author frequently poses questions to himself and to the reader.

Martyn questions himself: "At this point caution is necessary [John 7:30]. Have we not overstepped the bounds of probability? The drama may indeed reflect two levels *in general.* But do we not press the case too far if we take *these* developments as reflections of *actual* events in John's milieu?"[29] Martyn's answer is that they do reflect such events. In a 1969 review of *History and Theology in the Fourth Gospel* I wrote that "Martyn's approach has the advantage of being grounded upon the obvious fact that there is something going with the Jews in the Fourth Gospel."[30] Yet for most exegetes that was not at the time so obvious—that is, that "the Jews" might provide a historical open sesame. Martyn made it seem probable by the courage of his historical imagination. Thus for good reason his work became a watershed in the study of the Fourth Gospel. Can we know as much as Martyn purports to know about the specifics of inner-synagogue dramas that led to the expulsion of Christ-believers? Quite possibly not, but we would never have paid attention if Martyn had not been so bold as to suggest the details.

2

Judaism in the Johannine Context

Does the Gospel of John Misrepresent Judaism?

The question of the Jews, or Judaism, in the Gospel of John has been investigated and revisited many times. This intense interest is based on at least two factors: first, the recognition that this Gospel originated within Judaism or at the nexus between Judaism and what was to be called Christianity; second, the awareness that the mutual antipathy between Jesus and the Jews, which grows throughout the Gospel and reaches its climax in the trial before Pilate, makes John seem an anti-Jewish, if not anti-Semitic, Gospel.[1]

Both factors have emerged into prominence largely since the World War II. The discovery of the Dead Sea Scrolls, and particularly the Community Rule, in 1947 led to the realization that the distinctive language and conceptuality of the Fourth Gospel was not foreign to first-century Palestine, and certainly not to Judaism.[2] This realization in turn implied that the frequent references to the Jews in the Fourth Gospel should be taken as somehow related to its origin and purpose. Yet those references are mostly quite hostile, and in the aftermath of the Holocaust sound dreadfully anti-Semitic. Sadly, passages in the Fourth Gospel have stimulated and encouraged Christian anti-Semitism. In all probability, they were occasioned by contemporaneous tensions and disputes, and the evangelist could scarcely have imagined the uses to which his text would be put. Yet a text is inseparable from its interpretive community, and thus much depends on how the church receives and understands the Fourth Gospel, what issues it is understood to address, and what purpose it serves. What is the axis or historical basis of interpretation?

Obviously, John knows, or purports to know, a great deal about Judaism. Most commentators now agree that the Fourth Gospel reflects conditions after the Roman War rather than during the time of Jesus. All the sects or parties of Judaism save the Pharisees have disappeared. *Jews* and *Pharisees* seem to be interchangeable terms. The temple is acknowledged as the central site and institution of Jewish religion, yet there are hints the temple has been destroyed

(2:19; 4:21; 11:49). Scribes, who are prominent in the Synoptic Gospels, have completely disappeared from the scene.

Although Jesus himself says that salvation is of the Jews (4:22), John's treatment of Judaism is hardly an appreciative one. More often than not the Jews or Pharisees appear in a bad light, if only because they oppose Jesus, the perfect protagonist who always appears in the positive light of God himself. Nevertheless, it is worth asking whether in the Gospel of John Judaism is accurately represented and whether its beliefs and practices are fairly treated. It is my thesis that, although the Jews are obviously not treated sympathetically, what they believe or stand for is not misrepresented. The problem with the Jews seems to be that, by definition, they do not believe in Jesus.

Yet things are not always that simple. The evangelist is quite aware that Jesus himself was a Jew (4:9), the son of Joseph from Nazareth (1:45–46), as was John the Baptist, as were Jesus' disciples, one of whom was an acquaintance of the high priest (18:16). Nicodemus (chapter 3), a Pharisee, teacher of Israel, and ruler of the Jews, cannot at first comprehend Jesus, but later returns to defend him (7:50–52), and finally to bury him, with Joseph of Arimathea, who because of "the Jews" is a disciple in secret (19:38–39). Presumably Nicodemus also falls into this same category: he may be a believer, but not a confessor. The same may be said of many Jewish leaders (12:42) whose failure to confess Jesus is, however, reprehensible. They fear the Pharisees, who are unalterably opposed to Jesus, and their fear reveals that they love human praise more than the glory of God (12:43). Repeatedly in the public ministry of Jesus the Jews are described as divided about Jesus and some believe in him (7:12,31; 10:4; 11:45), which, in the evangelist's view, is exactly what they should do.

Moreover, a crowd is portrayed as asking Jesus, "What must we do to perform the works of God?" (6:28). Jesus' answer, "Believe in the one God has sent," summarizes the whole Johannine theology or soteriology. The question, at least at this point in the dialogue, reveals an openness to Jesus as well as a popular Jewish attitude: the Jew wants to do God's will, that is, to perform the works of God. All crowds are obviously not the same in John, but later in the Gospel the Pharisees denounce a crowd who do not know the law as accursed (7:49)—perhaps a typical attitude toward "the people of the land." Apparently this is the same crowd, or part thereof, that earlier affirmed Jesus as prophet or Messiah (7:40–41f.). Still earlier in the same scene the Jews (also known as Pharisees) have asked about Jesus, "How does this man have so much learning, when he has never been taught?" (7:15). Their question apparently betrays a profound suspicion. Later (7:20) the crowd is portrayed as hostile, but this is not typical. More characteristic of popular sentiment is the wonder-struck "No man ever spoke as this man," uttered by the officers or temple police, whose view is immediately contrasted with that of the authorities, or Pharisees, who denigrate them (7:46–47).

The Pharisees represent the post-70 perspective of a rabbinic Judaism that was coming into being even as Judaism and what would become Christianity were defining themselves over against one another. The mutual exclusivity that since the first century has characterized the relationship between Judaism and Christianity is uncannily prefigured in the Gospel of John. At the same time, what even these Jews believe is not denigrated or rejected. To a considerable extent John shares their belief. But exactly how, or in what sense, the Jews believe is fundamentally affected by the fact that they do not believe in Jesus. Thus, for example, they believe that scripture is the word of God, but they emphatically do not believe that scripture is about Jesus. By the same token, they believe that God created all things, but not through the agency of the pre-existent Christ. Of course, John believes that scripture is finally about Jesus (5:46) and that God created all things through the incarnate *logos* (1:1–3). Significantly, John's presentation of creation presupposes the Genesis account and can be viewed as a kind of commentary upon it.[3] There is then more than a general agreement that the created world is the work of a divine agent.

Situating John in Relation to Judaism

When shortly after World War II the newly discovered Dead Sea Scrolls turned the attention of scholars to the Gospel of John and raised again the question of its Jewish provenance, the views of some earlier scholars were confirmed. For example, Adolf Schlatter (1930), H. Odeberg (1929), and William Wrede (1903) had in the earlier part of this century and by different routes come to the conclusion that John was a fundamentally Jewish Gospel, or one fully engaged with Judaism.[4] Thus, when in the late 1960s Raymond E. Brown and J. Louis Martyn independently suggested that the threat of expulsion from the synagogue (John 9:22; 12:42; 16:2) was related to the *Birkath ha-Minim,* the Blessing of the Heretics of the Eighteen Benedictions, the scholarly fields were, so to speak, already ripe for harvest (cf. John 4:35).[5]

Martyn's ingeniously worked out proposal for reading the Gospel of John on two levels, that of Jesus and that of the Johannine church (which originated within the synagogue), may give too many hostages to fortune to win universal acceptance in its intricate detail. Whether the *Birkath ha-Minim,* the Twelfth Benediction, was formulated or reformulated during the 80s of the first century to identify followers of Jesus with a view to expelling them from the synagogue, as Martyn argued, has been the subject of heated debate. Nevertheless, the Gospel itself reflects a fear (9:22; 12:42)—and the alleged reality (16:2)—of expulsion from the synagogue, which must be an important aspect of its life-setting. That the *minim* and the *notzrim* of the Cairo Geniza formulation of the *Birkath ha-Minim* have something to do with early Jewish Christians remains likely.[6] Thus, despite reservations in many quarters, Martyn's boldness has won very broad assent to the general proposal.[7] John is now read against a

Jewish, rather than a Hellenistic or general Christian, background. Actually, Martyn made little of the Scrolls. Nor did Wayne A. Meeks, who at the same time proposed a distinctly Jewish provenance for important aspects of Johannine Christology.[8] Yet it is probably accurate to say that the Scrolls created a scholarly ambience in which proposals to read John against a Jewish background would command a wide, and ultimately favorable, hearing.

The Gospel of John and Anti-Semitism

This Jewish reading of the Gospel of John coincidentally follows World War II and the Holocaust. That the Jews appeared as the enemies of Jesus, and Judaism as the enemy of Christianity, is inevitably seen in that light and, indeed, in the light of a long history of the persecution of Jews in nominally Christian societies. The Constantinian era, in which the church rather quickly went from being the persecuted to becoming the persecutors, hovers in the background. That some early Christians were in fact persecuted, perhaps even killed (John 16:2), by their fellow Jews is, of course, no justification for subsequent pogroms, as Martyn himself notes. Such mortal antagonisms are a part of a long history of murderous religious hostility and persecution that continues today, in the East as well as in the West, and from which no major religion is entirely guilt-free.

Understandably, morally sensitive Christians have been made uneasy by the role the Jews play in the Fourth Gospel, for with some reason they see there the roots of this history of persecution and counterpersecution, of which the Holocaust was the horrific culmination. That it all may have begun with Jewish persecution of Christians, or—more accurately—with persecution of Christ-confessing Jews by other Jews, is very small comfort indeed. One wonders whether such considerations may have figured in the way Bultmann dealt with "the Jews" in the Fourth Gospel. In his commentary, written in pre-Holocaust but already anti-Semitic Nazi Germany, he maintains that "the Jews" function as surrogates of the world in its rejection of Jesus.[9] In other words, they are not really Jews, or at least their Jewishness is not the principal point.

It is worth recalling that Bultmann himself was a supporter of the Barmen Declaration of 1934 and a member of the explicitly anti-Nazi Confessing Church. Moreover, Bultmann was also on record in his scholarly writings to the effect that both Jesus and Paul were Jews and should be understood as such. Bultmann's 1936 article "Jesus and Paul" was written in explicit response to the Nazi ideologist Alfred Rosenberg, who had claimed that Jesus was not really a Jew, but that he had in effect been Judaized by Paul and the early church.[10] The article shows why it is impossible to drive such a wedge between Jesus and Paul. In his earlier (1930) article on Paul, Bultmann begins with the fact that Paul was deeply Jewish.[11] It is, of course, the premise of Bultmann's *Jesus and the*

Word (English translation 1934) that Jesus is to be understood within Judaism, albeit as a revolutionary figure.[12]

In the aftermath of the Holocaust, the Second Vatican Council revised and restated its understanding of the Roman Catholic Church's relation to Judaism, and in its Declaration on the Relationship of the Church to Non-Christian Religions specifically renounced the once widely held view that all Jews, or all Jews contemporary with Jesus, should be held responsible for his death.[13] The view that they should be has, unfortunately, some basis in the New Testament (for example, in Matt 27:25: "His blood be on us and on our children"), as well as in the Fourth Gospel, where in the trial before Pilate "the Jews" insist, against Pilate's wishes, that Jesus be put to death (19:12–16). Such texts have understandably led to the charge of deicide against Jews.

Nevertheless, by "the Jews," the evangelist did not mean all Jews, not even all those in Jesus' day or even in Jerusalem, but principally the chief priests and Pharisees (cf. 18:3), with the Pharisees apparently assuming authority alongside the chief priests. Yet such a refined and nuanced reading awaited modern historical-exegetical insights, and it is understandable that precritical readers and readings saw in such texts, naïvely assumed to be historical accounts, the wholesale condemnation of Jews and Judaism. As Eldon Jay Epp has put it: "The attitude toward the Jews that finds expression in the Fourth Gospel . . . co-acted with the extraordinary popularity of that Gospel so as to encourage and to buttress anti-Semitic sentiments among Christians from the second century CE until the present time."[14] According to Rosemary Ruether, the Jews in John "are the very incarnation of the false, apostate principles of the fallen world, alienated from its true being in God." She continues: "Because they belong to the world and its hostile, alienated principle of existence, their instinctive reaction to the revelation of the spiritual Son of God is murderousness (John 8:20, 44)."[15]

The Johannine Portrayal of Judaism

Against the background of the Jewishness of the Fourth Gospel and the anti-Jewishness stimulated or confirmed in many Christian readings, we now look more closely at the Johannine portrayal of Judaism per se, encapsulated as it is in what the Jews are said, or assumed, to believe and do. Is the Judaism of the Gospel of John a caricature or straw man? Insofar as it is not, to what extent does John actually presuppose Jewish assumptions or beliefs?

That John reflects and even shares Jewish belief in the God of Abraham, Isaac, and Jacob is apparent. In what sense this is or is not the same God John worships is a question that is really up for debate throughout the Gospel, but it is obvious that the Fourth Evangelist believes that those who confess Jesus properly believe in the God of Israel and thus in Israel's scripture. *Israel* and

Israelite are always used in a positive sense (1:31, 47, 49), and Jesus is hailed as the one about whom Moses and the prophets wrote (1:45). "Salvation is of the Jews," who worship what they know (4:22).[16] The point does not need belaboring.

The biblical story of God's role in creation and the history of Israel is presumed. God, is, of course, Creator, albeit through the Word (1:1–3). Yet the role of the Word in creation closely parallels the creative role of wisdom in Proverbs (8:22–31) and the other wisdom books (Sir 1:4–10; Wis 7:22). As has often been observed, John employs a wisdom Christology (cf. 1 Cor 1:24), which allows him to articulate the role of Christ in creation. (Martin Scott's 1992 monograph on wisdom in John has an interesting feminist dimension, and is also in other respects a worthwhile contribution to the background of Johannine christology.[17]) Likewise, it is obvious that the opening words of the Gospel intentionally parallel Genesis (cf. John 1:1–5 with Gen 1:1–4), where in the beginning God creates by speaking, if not through the Word, and separates light from darkness.

That God called a people, Israel, who claimed Abraham as their forefather is likewise presumed (John 8:33–58). The vitriolic debate of John 8 portrays Jesus, as well as the Jews or Jewish believers, assuming that their sonship to Abraham is not only a historic fact (v. 37), but a good thing (v. 37–40). That the Jews seek to kill Jesus does not call this fact into question, but nullifies its positive theological significance for them. Yet even as Jesus seems to put distance between himself and Abraham by calling him "your father," he declares that "Abraham rejoiced that he would see my day; he saw it and was glad" (v. 56). (That Abraham is alive before God agrees with the word of Jesus in Mark 12:26–27).

In controversy with other Jews about sabbath observance John says matter-of-factly that circumcision is from the fathers, not from Moses—seemingly correcting Jesus, if Jesus is not to be understood as correcting himself (7:22). Is it significant that there is no polemic against circumcision per se, but that it appears in an apparently positive light? (Interestingly, among the Gospels the noun *circumcision* appears only in the Gospel of John; the verb is, however, found in Luke 1:59 and 2:21). Circumcising a male child on the sabbath may be necessary to fulfill the law calling for circumcision on the eighth day (Lev 12:3), which overrides the sabbath prohibition. Jesus, arguing from the lesser to the greater (7:23), nevertheless honors both circumcision and the law. Of course, that Jesus says "you circumcise a male on the Sabbath" implies this is something that Jews, not Christians, do. Yet the narrative, in which Jesus is engaged in heated debate, calls for Jesus to couch his statement in these terms; for him to say "we circumcise" would have been unnatural at this point. A split between Jews and Christians is then suggested, but circumcision itself does not seem to be a matter of controversy, as it was in the Pauline churches.

The work of Moses and the exodus traditions are presumed in John 3:14–15 as well as in John 6:25–51. In the latter case the fact of manna in the wilderness is not disputed, but whether it is truly the bread of God. Here John expresses a supersessionist theology, but without denying the factuality of the work of Moses. Rather, he presumes it. Yet what Moses did does not suffice; to have eternal life one must eat the flesh and drink the blood of the Son of Man (6:52–58).[18] (Thus Abraham and the prophets died—8:52—but are alive in Christ.) Likewise, that the law was given through Moses is expressly said (1:17; 7:19) and its origin is presumed to be God. The law is not the commandments of a false God, but of the one true God. Thus not only the exodus but also the Sinai tradition is presupposed as true and, in a qualified sense, valid.

Although Jesus can refer to the law as "your law" (8:17), he seems to believe that the law should be maintained (cf. 10:34–35).[19] There is little evidence of debate over the validity of the law in the Johannine community, or even between the community and others. Of course, Jesus gives his disciples the new commandment to love one another (13:34; cf. 15:12–14), which can be viewed as superseding the law. The love command (cf. Lev 19:18) is presented elsewhere in the New Testament as the fulfillment or summation of the law (Gal 5:14; Rom 13:8–10; cf. Matt 22:37–40). Whether John presupposes Paul, or Matthew, or an earlier Christian tradition is a good and debatable question, and one that is relevant at this point. Does the new commandment displace the old? If John presupposes Paul, Matthew, or traditions parallel to them, this is evidently not the case. Yet even if John does not presume them, and is read on its own terms, the commandment's newness need not refer to its unprecedented character, but rather to its definitive promulgation by Jesus (cf. 1 John 2:7–8). In any event, the love commandment does not intrinsically contradict biblical law, but may rather be an expression of its essence. John also manifests knowledge of the law's specific content: so every male is to be circumcised (7:22–23; cf. Lev 12:3); the sabbath is to be observed (5:10; 9:16; Exod 20:8), although how it should be may, as we have seen, be debated (7:22–24). John clearly believes Jesus does not violate the sabbath law. Of course, to agree that he does not one must accede to the Johannine Christology (5:17–18). Moreover, the law requires a fair hearing for the accused (7:51; cf. Deut 1:16–17); in a trial two witnesses are needed (8:17; cf. Deut 9:15).

Jesus himself may be above or beyond the law (1:17); but when his opponents pose the alternative of being disciples of Moses rather than of Jesus (9:28), one should not jump too quickly to the conclusion that John would have accepted it. The unavoidability of that alternative is precisely the position of the opponents of Jesus and the Johannine community. In John, Jesus is above the law in the sense that he is the purpose and goal of the law (cf. Rom 10:4). He is the arbiter of the meaning of the law. Moses, the human author of the law, after all wrote about Jesus (1:45; 5:46–47). Such an interpretation of

Moses, and of the law, is, of course, precisely what is at stake in the Fourth Gospel. Did Moses write about Jesus? Does the law point ahead to Jesus as its fulfillment? "By no means," the Johannine Jews answer. For John that is precisely why they misunderstood everything.

Yet the Jews cannot be convinced on the basis of their own hermeneutical premises. Thus exegetical debate on the basis of those premises is futile as far as John is concerned.[20] Although Nicodemus approaches Jesus in a quite positive and affirmative mode, acknowledging that Jesus is a teacher sent from God and apparently willing to engage him in friendly conversation (3:2), he is seemingly brushed rudely aside: unless one is born from above that person cannot see the kingdom of God (3:3). Jesus will not converse with Nicodemus on terms the latter assumes are shared. Something like a paradigm shift or conversion is required. Still, John clearly knows those terms. For example, John knows the tradition that the Messiah is to be of the lineage of David and from Bethlehem, David's city (7:42; cf. 2 Sam 7:12–13; Mic 5:2), but this tradition is ascribed to members of the Judean crowd who reject Jesus because he does not fulfill this expectation. Why does John not correct them? Does he not know the tradition of Jesus' own Davidic lineage and birth in Bethlehem? Or does he find this tradition irrelevant to his fundamental christological point that Jesus' origin is God and that he, uniquely, has come down from heaven (3:13; 6:38)? He is the only-begotten of God (1:18).

Yet that Jesus is the Messiah, in that he fulfills traditional hopes and expectations, is clearly understood. In fact, as Messiah he is expressly called the King of Israel (1:49), and in no other Gospel's passion narrative does the question of Jesus' kingship, and its nature, loom so large as in John. That Jesus' kingship is not of this world (18:36) means that traditional messianic hopes are being reinterpreted, but not abandoned. That elements of the expectation of a prophet like Moses (Deut 18) infiltrate John's messianic conception is quite probable.[21] Why else would the Messiah be expected to perform signs like Moses' signs before Pharaoh? (Of course, the Davidic Messiah was not expected to perform miracles.) Such Mosaic expectation corresponds to John's interest in Samaria and Samaritans as well. The Samaritan *Taheb* was to be a prophet like Moses, not the Davidic Messiah.[22] While traditional messianic hope is obviously reinterpreted in John, such reinterpretation obviously begins within the ancient traditions themselves, and is not, so to speak, a Christian operation solely.

That this hope looks toward Jesus' reign as Messiah is therefore obvious, although the nature of this reign has been reconceived. By the same token, the traditional Jewish and primitive Christian eschatological expectations are presumed. God raises the dead and holds judgment (5:19–29; cf. 11:24). This is a future event. Of course, God has given this judgment into the hands of the Son of Man (5:27; cf. Matt 25:31–45; Mark 8:38). In the Synoptics it is still future. In John it is already taking place. Indeed, that the future eschatological events are occurring or have occurred is the recurrent theme of the farewell discourses.

Since John knows and affirms biblical history, Jewish scriptures, messianic hopes, and eschatological expectation—while reinterpreting them—it should not surprise us to find that he takes a similar stance with respect to temple and cult. John knows that Judaism is concerned with questions of purification (2:6; 3:25; 11:55; cf. 19:31, 42), and he does not disparage this concern. Moreover, Jesus appears in Jerusalem, as a good Jewish male should, not only at Passover but also at other Jewish feasts (2:13; 5:1; 10:22; 11:55–57), which become occasions for his self-manifestation and teaching (cf. 18:20). Indeed, Jesus appears in Jerusalem at Passover at the very beginning of this Gospel and cleanses the temple (2:13–22). Although Jesus appears in the temple at the end of the other Gospels, only in John does his whole ministry seem to center about the temple. Interestingly, the closest parallel is in Luke-Acts where the infant Jesus is presented in the temple (Luke 2:22), the boy Jesus questions the teachers in the temple (2:46), and Jesus' disciples in Jerusalem gather at the temple after his ascension (Acts 2:46; 3:1).[23]

It is not too much to say that John respects the temple. The chief priests and Pharisees worry lest the temple be destroyed by the Romans (11:48), and their worry is understandable, if misplaced. Jesus tells the vendors to stop making his father's house a marketplace (2:16; cf. Zech 14:21) and his disciples remember (v. 17): "Zeal for your house will consume me" (Ps 69:9). Although we are then told that when Jesus speaks of the dissolution of the temple he is really talking about his own body (2:22), the earlier statements clearly refer to the earthly, Jerusalem temple. Not a word is said against the temple itself, in some contrast to the statement of Stephen (Acts 7:47–50). Of course, Jesus' body replaces or displaces the temple (2:22; cf. 4:22–24), as the prologue has already hinted (1:14), as Jesus becomes the site of God's definitive and final revelation.[24] This should not surprise the knowledgeable exegete, however, because it is exactly what one would expect. Jesus stands in relation to the temple somewhat as he stands in relation to the law. They are both true and valid vehicles of God's revelation to Israel, and with God's sending of his Son they testify to him in the sense that both appear as his forerunner, even as John the Baptist is. The law can now be read as Moses' testimony to Jesus. Jesus, as God's dwelling place, succeeds the temple, but Jesus does not destroy the temple (cf. Mark 14:58; 15:29). In all probability that had already happened when John wrote. But the temple's destruction does not mean that God has no dwelling place. God had already come to dwell in Jesus, and Jesus would dwell among his followers, through the Spirit, forever.

In *The Gospel and the Land*, W. D. Davies acutely observes that in John "there is a deliberate presentation of the replacement of 'holy places' by the

Person of Jesus."[25] John's concern with the land, or the temple, is not territorial, but theological or christological, and his own interpretation of the significance of the land would therefore be unacceptable to contemporary Jews. Yet it would be immediately recognizable to them. In other words, they would recognize and acknowledge the accuracy of the data without for a moment accepting its interpretation. This is so obvious it is easy to overlook. Jerusalem is as much the center of the Fourth Gospel as it is of Israel's cultic and national identity. Of course, the temple is the center of Jerusalem. The Samaritans are an alienated and despised group. According to tradition, Bethlehem is to be the birthplace of the Messiah. Nazareth is a Galilean village of little or no account. The traditional evaluation of locations descends from Jerusalem to Nazareth, but in John's book Jesus arises from Nazareth to supersede Jerusalem, its temple and authorities. The places are altogether familiar, but the precedence is reversed.

The sense of familiarity, but also of reversal or rejection, is reminiscent of the Qumran Scrolls. For the Essenes of Qumran the map was familiar, but in need of radical transformation or redrawing. The temple could not be holy while presided over by an illegitimate priesthood. Implied throughout the Qumran documents, as in the Fourth Gospel, is the question of whether one will choose to join a new covenant and community in which such transformation is effected or promised. In neither case, however, is the vantage point, the point of observation, detached or remote. The degree of tension is commensurate with the intensity of involvement.

By way of contrast, the perspective on Judaism encountered in the contemporary pagan documents collected by Menahem Stern is external and the attitude uninvolved.[26] Although there were positive evaluations of Judaism in antiquity (for example, Hecataeus of Abdera and Numenius of Apamea), denigration and misinformation are plentiful. Apion repeats the rumor that the Jews kept a golden ass head in the sanctuary of the temple and relates the slanderous story of how Antiochus Epiphanes found in the temple a Greek who was being fattened in order to be consumed by the Jews, presumably in one of their orgies.[27] Tacitus, who was possessed of a good bit of information about Israel and Judaism, gave an entirely secular interpretation or construction of the exodus tradition.[28] There is a curious but real analogy between the perspective of Tacitus and that of a modern historicism, which as a methodological principle would explain the exodus on terms other than the theological ones chosen by the biblical narrator. In sharp contrast, John, like the Essenes of Qumran, accepts this theological interpretation of Israel's history. That, in John's view, Jesus Christ as the pre-existent Word and Son of God was prior to that history (and in this sense took precedence over it in that he was its beginning as well as its goal) does not for a moment alter its reality and significance. This is a fundamental fact not appreciated by ancient gnostic and some modern interpreters of the Gospel of John.

Jesus Christ belongs, and is intelligible, only in his Jewish and biblical context, while at the same time an adequate assessment of who he is sheds a radically new light on that context, causes it to be viewed differently, but does not destroy or negate it. It is in the interest of the evangelist not to destroy or negate Judaism, but to remain in dialogue with it. Thus although "the Jews" have a deadly hostility toward Jesus, Nicodemus, a ruler of the Jews, remains open to him (3:2; 7:50–51), even though at the end his attitude and deeds (19:39) are ambiguous, and perhaps ambivalent, as the sharp disagreement of modern exegetes itself suggests. John holds traditional Jewish messianism and his own distinctive Christology in creative tension. (The latter is, of course, based upon earlier Christian belief and tradition.) C. K. Barrett aptly characterizes John's theological method, which comprehends his understanding of the relationship of the Gospel to Jewish tradition: "Christianity and Judaism stand side by side, linked uneasily by a unique similarity and a unique dissimilarity to which John has given pointed expression."[29] On the one hand, that John's portrayal of Judaism is thoroughly colored by his theological judgments goes without saying. On the other, John's is a recognizable portrayal of Judaism, as a comparison with Tacitus or Apion clearly shows.

3

The Stressful Tension between Judaism and the Johannine Jesus

Revisiting and Evaluating J. Louis Martyn's Classic Proposal

In the decades immediately after World War II, the study of the Gospel and Epistles of John was dominated by theological questions, a state of affairs that was appropriate enough, for the controlling issues of the Johannine literature are clearly theological. The sharpest debates had to do with the historical setting and its bearing on the theological issues. In fact, J. Louis Martyn's contribution lies precisely in the determination of that historical setting and its impact on the interpretation of Johannine theology, particularly in the Gospel. He called into question the view that the most relevant historical setting was Hellenistic, gnostic, or Christian by proposing that the primal context of Johannine thought was Jewish, or Jewish-Christian.[1]

Johannine Interpretation in the Decades after World War II

The dominant modes of Johannine interpretation in the postwar decades were rooted in research going back much earlier. Fittingly, the era's two most notable scholars, in Great Britain and Germany respectively, capped lifetimes of scholarship with *magna opera* on the Fourth Gospel: Rudolf Bultmann with his magisterial commentary;[2] C. H. Dodd with his two weighty books on the interpretation and historical tradition of the Gospel.[3] A third work should perhaps be put alongside them—namely, Edwyn Clement Hoskyns's *The Fourth Gospel*.[4] A kind of exegetical "Unfinished Symphony," it was brought to completion and published by Hoskyns's colleague Francis Noel Davey. In order to see Martyn's contribution in perspective, it will be useful to characterize each of the three, for in their approach and assessment of the issues they represent alternatives that differ, while sharing certain important presuppositions. All set the problem of Johannine interpretation against a horizon of Christian or more general religious or existential theological concerns.

Dodd's work was based on his wide-ranging and deep research in the Hellenistic cultural and religious world, as well as his appreciation of Judaism, its traditions and scriptures. *The Interpretation of the Fourth Gospel* (1953) set the Gospel of John against a wide range of Hellenistic and Jewish backgrounds, which Dodd deemed more or less relevant for its understanding. While Dodd saw important connections with Judaism, and particularly the Old Testament, he was satisfied to characterize the intended audience of the Gospel as those intelligent, literate, and religious readers who were fairly numerous in the Hellenistic world. Interestingly enough, Dodd did not dismiss the tradition of apostolic authorship, although it becomes quite clear in *Interpretation* that he placed little or no stock in it. That is, it was wholly unnecessary to the perspective and approach that work represents. The situation may have changed just slightly with *Historical Tradition in the Fourth Gospel,* for in that book Dodd clearly intends to trace the Johannine tradition, whether in written or oral form, to its historical roots. Moreover, he is strongly disposed to view it as standing in a significant and positive relation to Jesus himself. Nevertheless, he does not rest his case on apostolic authorship, but rather he analyzes the text with a view to establishing its traditional, and putatively historical, roots. Interestingly enough, the Johannine tradition's rootage in Jesus himself would be congruent with Dodd's view of Jesus' own realized eschatology. Thus the Fourth Gospel represents, not a development or departure from Jesus, but rather the fundamental eschatological perspective of Jesus, albeit dressed out in more hellenized form.

The hellenized form of the Fourth Gospel is roughly equivalent in meaning or import to its universal scope. Its message is adapted to cultured, literate readers with religious interests, be they Jew or Greek. Whether in Palestine, Athens, Alexandria, or Rome, the intended reader would understand and feel the appeal of the Gospel of John. Specific historical circumstances of the Gospel's setting are less important than general religious and cultural relevance and affinities in Dodd's view.

To a remarkable extent the same can be said of the equally influential perspective and theological interpretation of Bultmann.[5] Of course, Bultmann had a quite specific and distinctive view of the Gospel's historical origin and literary development. Its origin lay close to the same baptist circles in Syria or Palestine from which John the Baptist emerged. In fact, the sign-source of the Gospel may have first been used as a missionary tract among disciples of John the Baptist, and the evangelist himself may have once followed John. These early baptists seem to have been heterodox Jews, from whom (or in near proximity to whom) the Mandaeans later developed or emerged. The Mandaean sources, with their dualism and terminological affinities with the Johannine literature, became for Bultmann extremely important documents for understanding the milieu and meaning of the Gospel and Epistles of John. The Mandaeans—whose name, of course, means "knowledge" (or gnostic)—provide the gnostic connection of the Fourth Gospel. One should recall, however, that the Gospel of John was written not to embrace or affirm a gnostic point of view, but rather to oppose it. It remained for his student Ernst Käsemann to espouse a much more positively gnosticizing interpretation of the Fourth Gospel. Of course, Bultmann assumed that the traditional view of Johannine authorship had long since been shown to be problematic. In fact, the ecclesiastical redactor of the Gospel was the first to equate the Beloved Disciple with the evangelist.[6]

While Bultmann's historical and literary theories are amazingly specific and detailed at some points, much more so than Dodd's, they too are at the service of a higher theological interpretation that tends to be universal or universalizing. The connection through Mandaeism with a largely hypothetical early oriental gnosticism developing at the fringes of Judaism is the key to this process. Bultmann, drawing upon the work of his student Hans Jonas, understood historic gnosticism to enshrine a classic understanding of existence as alienation, embodied in its typical dualism. It is this understanding of existence that is overcome in the Christian gospel as presented by John. The gnostic mythology becomes the vehicle for the Christian message. By the same token the Jews, who appear throughout the Gospel as Jesus' opponents, are not real, historic Jews, but symbolize unfaith's rejection of Jesus. Bultmann acknowledges almost incidentally that their presence in John may be rooted in a synagogue-church conflict.[7] Nevertheless, the Gospel of John can be properly read and understood without knowledge of its specific historical setting and purpose. At the same time, however, the Gospel can be appreciated in its theological purity only if Bultmann's various literary reconstructions are followed. Otherwise, one encounters a Gospel somewhat diluted, even corrupted, by later accretions and especially rearrangement accomplished by a process of ecclesiastical editing.[8]

Hoskyns differs from the interpretations of Dodd and Bultmann in that he placed the Gospel's development from beginning to end against a Christian background. That is, John knew, if not the Synoptic Gospels, certainly the traditions they contain, and his purpose was to bring to the forefront their central and essential theological meaning and significance. Crucial for Hoskyns was the theological commensurability of John with the Synoptics, indeed, with the other major New Testament witnesses also. This is the test of the Gospel's theological appropriateness and validity. Thus, not surprisingly, Hoskyns emphasized the indispensability and importance of the historical revelation of God in Jesus Christ for the evangelist. Fundamentally, Hoskyns agreed with both

Bultmann and Dodd in this respect, although each exegete conceived of this historical dimension and emphasis on the incarnation in his own distinctive way.

In setting forth the meaning of John's Gospel in the context of the earliest development of Christian dogma—that is, within the New Testament period —Hoskyns adopted a mode or horizon of interpretation most amenable to the classical Christian understanding of the document. Already, at the end of the second century, Clement of Alexandria spoke of John, in relation to the others, as a spiritual Gospel. The sixteenth-century reformer John Calvin, at the beginning of his commentary, characterized the Gospel of John as the key to the proper understanding of the others. In fact, making due allowance for the differences of historical understanding and circumstance, one could truthfully say that Hoskyns's perspective and commentary stand directly in the legacy of both Clement and Calvin, as well as many other Christian interpreters before and since. John embraces and brings to articulation the essence of catholic Christianity as it is found elsewhere in the New Testament and in other early Christian witnesses. Thus, in effect, John is perceived as paving the way for the kind of New Testament or biblical theology to which Irenaeus gave expression toward the end of the second century.

It is worth noting at this point that the obverse of Hoskyns's position on the place of the Johannine Gospel in the development of early Christianity is not represented by Dodd or Bultmann so much as by Käsemann, whose *Jesu letzter Wille nach Johannes 17* appeared more than two decades later.[9] In fact, the works of Käsemann and Martyn appeared at about the same time. Moreover, Martyn had studied with Käsemann in the 1950s. Interestingly, like Hoskyns, Käsemann saw the Fourth Gospel as a response to, or development of, distinctly Christian theological concerns or issues. He, too, attempted to place the Fourth Gospel in the history of early Christianity by analyzing the character and thrust of its theology. But there the similarity to Hoskyns ends. Whereas Hoskyns saw in John the paragon of what might be called orthodoxy in the development of dogma, presumably toward the end of the first century, Käsemann had already, since his famous article "Ketzer und Zeuge," been accustomed to viewing the evangelist—or Elder, as he styled him—as both heretic and witness.[10] Far from representing the direction in which orthodox church doctrine would move, John was naively docetic, suspect in orthodox circles—if unfairly so—for its gnostic leanings. Only by human error and the providence of God did the Gospel eventually find its way into the Christian canon of holy scripture. Yet, despite the suspicion in which it once stood, Käsemann values John highly for its uncompromising emphasis on Jesus Christ as God's word, set forth at a juncture in church history when the Christian gospel might easily have been overwhelmed or obscured by a suffocating ecclesiasticism and sacramentalism.

Bultmann's interpretation of John against a gnostic background lives on in Käsemann, but in drastically altered, it not inverted, form. No longer is John's kerygma to be demythologized in terms of an understanding of existence. Now the word of the quasidocetic Christ calls human beings to uncompromising allegiance to himself, making claims that put his own humanity in question and that can only be described as dogmatic. Ironically, John's Spirit-inspired Christology and ecclesiology in time came to undergird an ecclesiastical orthodoxy in which church office and sacrament tended to rein in, and perhaps override, freedom of the same Spirit.

Martyn's Proposal and Contribution

Just when the stage might have seemed set for a battle royal between Käsemann and his allies and the more orthodox position represented by Hoskyns, the terms on which such a discussion could go forward were radically questioned by the original, insightful, provocative contribution of Martyn's *History and Theology in the Fourth Gospel*.[11] In setting John against a Jewish, rather than a Christian, background, Martyn had predecessors. But he rightly gets credit for a sea change in Johannine studies for somewhat the same reason that the Wright brothers got credit for the airplane. Others may have gotten off the ground, but Martyn—like the Wright brothers—achieved sustained flight. To extend the metaphor, his vehicle may not have been perfect, but it has proven good enough to maintain itself and to stand correction.

This is not the place to summarize Martyn's position. That has been done often enough, with variations on the theme, by myself and others. Suffice it to say that Martyn, unlike the dominant interpreters antecedent to him, took seriously the tension and hostility between "the Jews" and Jesus as the key to the historical life-setting and purpose of the Gospel of John. His entire proposal is based on two fundamental assumptions or insights. First, the prominence of the Jews and their hostility to Jesus and his disciples likely represents a genuine historical setting (that is, it is not an exercise in theological symbolism). Second, this historical setting can scarcely be that of Jesus and his actual, original disciples and opponents.[12] Therefore, one is not only justified, but also impelled, to look for a historical setting and state of affairs corresponding to the nature and direction or thrust of the Gospel's tensions and conflict. Martyn is actually invoking the modern, form-critical principle that the Gospels bear testimony primarily to the life-setting in which they were produced, and only secondarily to their subject matter.

As is well known, Martyn finds the major key to that setting in the thrice-repeated reference to the expulsion from the synagogue of those who confess belief in Jesus (9:22; 12:42; 16:2), and more particularly in the evangelist's statement that "the Jews had already agreed that if anyone should confess him to be Messiah, he would become an excommunicate from the synagogue."[13]

This agreement is traced to the Jamnian Academy under the leadership of Gamaliel II (80–115 C.E.) and to the reformulation of the Twelfth Benediction of the Eighteen (*Shemoneh Esre*) by the legendary Samuel the Small. According to Martyn, this malediction against Nazarenes (Christians) and Minim (heretics) was used to smoke out followers of Jesus in the synagogue service, for they could not in good conscience recite it, much less lead it. Martyn daringly reconstructs a dramatic scene in which the Christ-confessor would be identified and excluded. His reconstruction is based principally on *Berakoth* 28 (see also *y. Berakoth* 8a) of the Babylonian Talmud (54; see also 61), and secondarily on such data as the instances in Justin's *Dialogue with Trypho* (16, 110) in which Jews are said to curse in their synagogues all who believe in Christ (16) or to expel Christians from their property (110).[14] *Berakoth* 28 describes how making a mistake on the Twelfth Benediction brings down upon the reader the suspicion of being a Min, and suggests, but does not say, that the recitation of the Benediction was intended as a test for heretics, possibly Christians. Martyn's dramatic reconstruction has made his thesis all the more alluring, as he evokes the synagogue and city of the evangelist.[15]

Wayne A. Meeks, who has made his own distinctive contribution to the definition of a Jewish milieu for John, has noted the difficulty of establishing some aspects of Martyn's thesis and rightly observes that the Twelfth Benediction has become a kind of red herring of Johannine scholarship.[16] For one thing, it is unclear that within the first century the Jamnian Academy had the kind of general authority that Martyn's thesis attributes to it. For another, the date of the Twelfth Benediction is uncertain, and since Martyn first published, a number of scholars have strongly contested the view that it was composed as early as the 80s of the first century. In the third place, there is not direct or unambiguous evidence that the Benediction was formulated for the purpose of smoking Christians out of the synagogue or that it was ever actually used in that way. It should be added, however, that despite Meeks's reservations about the specifics of Martyn's thesis, he is far from dismissing it as unfounded and is inclined to believe that the evidence Martyn has adduced on the Johannine side bespeaks some such controversy as Martyn has proposed. Moreover, his hesitations with regard to the rabbinic and other evidence on the Jewish side do not amount to a rejection, but to a series of cautions.[17] Meeks would prefer to think of a linear development in which the promulgation of the *Birkath ha-Minim* was a culmination rather than the beginning point of a development, a position that Martyn does not regard as devastating to his own.[18]

Nevertheless, in the revised edition of *History and Theology in the Fourth Gospel* Martyn sees no reason to retreat from what is from any point of view a murky swamp in which his opponents' views can be grounded no more securely than his own. The evidence is itself incomplete and demands a coherent theory if one is to make sense of it. In fact, he earlier on declared that the correlation between the *Birkath ha-Minim* and the expression "to be put out of the synagogue" is one of the relatively secure points in the history of the Johannine community.[19] Meeks's assessment, like that of other experts, is typical: "Louis Martyn's ingenious 'two-level' reading of John 9 and other conflict stories in this Gospel has been widely accepted in its general outline if not in all its details."[20] Meeks's discussion of the Johannine community makes clear that he himself is a part of this general consensus, although he would make some qualifications and introduce some important nuances. As many questions as one may have about the daringly bold formulation of Martyn's thesis, it is difficult to reject the evidence and Martyn's construal of it as without foundation.

Perhaps the issues have become exacerbated in view of Martyn's belief that John 16:2, when linked to the Jews' mortal opposition to Jesus in the Gospel, suggests that some Johannine missioner (or missioners) had been put to death by Jews as a beguiler (*mesith*). At this point the possible implications of Martyn's thesis for modern Jewish-Christian relations are obvious enough, although Martyn himself has been careful to keep the discussion on the plane of historical investigation and to make clear that his findings have no direct implications of modern interfaith relations in the sense that they could legitimately be used by anyone for or against anyone else. About 16:2, Martyn writes:

> In light of the fact that the horrible and heinous and centuries-long persecution of Jews by Christians has sometimes been "justified" by the theory that the Jews did the first persecuting, it is understandable that a number of Christian interpreters have wished to see this verse as a reference to the persecution of Christians not by Jews, but by Roman authorities. Yet the Greek word rendered "act of (worshipful) service" refers elsewhere in the New Testament to Jewish worship; and the other experience referred to in this text, excommunication from the synagogue, points to the action of Jewish authorities. Modern relations between Christians and Jews are not helped by an antihistorical interpretation of Biblical texts.[21]

To leave the impression that Martyn's work on John was mainly accomplished by the publication of one book, as important as it may be, would be misleading. Martyn's 1957 Yale Ph.D. dissertation, "The Salvation-History Perspective in the Fourth Gospel," was in large part a study of the historical setting of the Gospel, in which he found the key in the role played by "the Jews." As in *History and Theology in the Fourth Gospel*, Martyn argues that the original setting of the Fourth Gospel (or its antecedent tradition) was the synagogue, in which followers of Jesus incurred the hostility of their fellow Jews. One sees here already even the imaginatively constructed dramatic scenes in and around the synagogue that appear in *History and Theology in the Fourth Gospel*.

What is missing is any reference to the *Birkath ha-Minim* on the Jewish side. Thus while the relevance of *aposynagogoi* is noted, it plays a somewhat less important role than in the book. Nevertheless, the indications of setting in the Gospel led Martyn to look for a corresponding situation in post-70 Judaism, which in his further research he finds in the promulgation of the Twelfth Benediction.

Shortly after the publication of this major book, Martyn presented "Source Criticism and Religionsgeschichte in the Fourth Gospel" to the first Gospels Seminar of the Society of Biblical Literature (November 1969) and also before the Pittsburgh Theological Seminary Festival on the Gospels.[22] In that paper he correlates his own thesis with Robert T. Fortna's source criticism (see below), with side glances at the works of Käsemann and Meeks in particular. His subsequent book *The Gospel of John in Christian History* (1979), which draws together with some revision essays offered in the years intervening, appeared earlier in the same year as the revised edition of *History and Theology in the Fourth Gospel*. In these essays Martyn advances three separate but related theses. He proposes that the evangelist has suppressed the identification of Jesus with Elijah found in his source. He analyzes the so-called *Ascents of James* in the Pseudo-Clementines and shows how it reflects a Jewish-Christian synagogal setting with real affinities and relationships to that of the Fourth Gospel. Finally, he draws together his earlier work by presenting "Glimpses into the History of the Johannine Community." In this essay, as well as the one on Elijah, Martyn's basic agreement with, and appropriation of, the source criticism of Fortna is very much in the forefront.[23]

Although Fortna was Martyn's student at Union Theological Seminary, his work had an independent beginning point. Fortna undertook a source-critical analysis of the Fourth Gospel on the basis of convictions growing out of his careful and detailed study of earlier source theories, particularly Bultmann's. Initially forgoing theological criteria, which are easily suspect of being subjective, and stylistic criteria, which are at least initially indecisive, Fortna undertook a careful study of the text of the Gospel, looking for telltale contextual traces of an author's annotating or supplementing an earlier text. It was Fortna's belief, which he tested by exegetical analysis, that the evidence of such redactional use of an earlier source could best be explained on the basis of a rather simple two-layer hypothesis, *Grundschrift* (original source) and later redaction and elaboration. As it turned out, the *Grundschrift* was discovered primarily in the narrative portions of John (signs and passion) and the evangelist's elaborations, not surprisingly, in the discourses that follow or are interlarded among the narrative portions.

Fortna's source theory might have become one of a rather large library of such efforts, which might—but need not—be true, had it not been integrally related to such an overall view as has been worked out by Martyn. The Gospel of Signs in the Martyn-Fortna proposal becomes the evangelistic tract that formed the basis of the missionary efforts by believing Jews in synagogues. That it consisted of miracles and passion corresponded perfectly with Martyn's scenario, for precisely the miracles are signs demonstrating the truth of the claim that Jesus was the prophet-Messiah. Moreover, the death of the messianic claimant would of necessity have been dealt with in the context of the synagogue, where it caused offense, and belief in the resurrection could not be assumed. That the miracles of Jesus are not signs in the Synoptics, but only in John, further strengthens the linkage of Fortna's source analysis with Martyn's overall theory. While Martyn's thesis does not require Fortna's source-critical results precisely, it does require some cogent explanation of how the content of the Gospel of John, particularly the narrative content, is linked to the synagogue controversy. Fortna's work supplies that link, and Martyn has continued to regard it as essentially correct. Moreover, it has the virtues of coherence and plausibility. The Johannine narratives do not seem to be drawn from the Synoptic Gospels. At the same time they stand out from the rest of the Gospel and, on Fortna's reading, form a coherent whole.

Interestingly, as Martyn builds upon the essential correctness of Fortna's source-critical work, so Fortna now views Martyn's thesis as congruent with his own work. This is evident in his later book, in which he writes: "I find highly persuasive the detailed reconstruction of Martyn in his *History and Theology,* in particular his proposal that expulsion of the Evangelist's Christian community from the synagogue has occasioned many of the differences between source and extant Gospel."[24] Nevertheless, Fortna indicates that his own focus continues to be on the texts themselves, particularly on the theological shifts that can be observed between the Gospel of Signs and the Gospel of John.

Less explicit, but no less intriguing, is the question of the relationship of Martyn's thesis about Jamnia and the Gospel of John to his Union colleague W. D. Davies's proposal, in the 1963 study *The Setting of the Sermon on the Mount,* linking the Gospel of Matthew to the sequence of events that led to the emergence of the Jamnian Academy or College.[25] Suffice it to say that the parallels are broad and general, but both Martyn and Davies see the respective Gospels as Christian responses to a crisis brought on by the retrenchment of Jewish thought and life that "Jamnia" represents. While for Martyn John is more a crisis document than is Matthew for Davies, the latter nevertheless rests his case on the view that Matthew was a Christian response, and an alternative, to Jamnia. Thus its halakhic character. In fact, it was Davies who first described how the Twelfth Benediction might have applied to, or been used against, Christians who were seeking to remain within the synagogue. Obviously, Davies and Martyn share similar views of when the *Birkath ha-Minim* was composed (in the

80s) and where its focus and purpose lay, as Martyn acknowledges. Davies's book antedates Martyn by five years, but while there are affinities and points of contact, Martyn does not deal with Davies's thesis. By the same token, although Davies could not have taken account of Martyn when writing *The Setting of the Sermon on the Mount*, to the best of my knowledge he did not later comment on Martyn's thesis regarding the Johannine community in any formal way.

The question of such relationships is more than a matter of a possibly interesting scholarly connection, for substantive issues are involved. Can it be that such different Gospels arose out of parallel or closely related circumstances? If one Gospel arose out of the post-Jamnian rivalry between Judaism and the movement that was becoming Christianity, is it likely that the other did as well? It is not impossible to think that they both did, especially in view of the fact that they would represent different sorts of encounter and response. But just the differences posited are intriguing.

Although, as we have observed, Martyn does not deal with or react to Davies's thesis, in a most significant observation he points out that in John, Jesus refuses to engage in argument with his Pharisaic opponents on their terms. That is, he eschews midrashic debate on terms laid down or presupposed by Jewish opponents.[26] (Nevertheless, John is convinced that scripture, rightly understood, supports his cause.) Just such midrashic debate would seem to be what Matthew was engaged in, albeit in a different, narrative genre. From Davies's standpoint, Matthew undertakes debate with post-Jamnian, Pharisaic Judaism on terms they largely share. With John it is precisely the case that the most crucial terms are *not* shared. John 7:40–42 illustrates the point well. Does John not know Matthew or Matthew's (and Luke's) tradition of Jesus' birth in Bethlehem, which is set forth precisely and explicitly as the fulfillment of Old Testament prophecy (Mic 5:1–3) and Jewish expectation? Or if he knows, does he simply pass it up because he does not want to engage in debate while conceding this common ground? Whatever one makes of John's relation to Matthew, his silence is telling. It is possible to maintain that John expects the reader to know Matthew and to appreciate the irony of the Jews' ignorance. If so, the evangelist is quite subtle on this point, and never reveals to the unknowing reader (or modern scholar!) that he is engaging in such subtlety. In any event, he chooses not to point out the Jews' (or the disciples') failure to understand, as he does elsewhere (such as in 2:21–22). In fact, Martyn's assessment of John's rejection of a common basis for midrash seems to fit this pericope perfectly. Of course, we cannot here attempt to resolve this exegetical issue, much less the problem of John's relation to the Synoptics. But the question of how to understand John 7:40–42 points up how fruitful a discussion over these matters between Martyn and Davies (from the standpoint of their respective positions) might have been.[27]

The Continuing Influence of Martyn's Work

Perhaps Martyn's closest and longest scholarly and collegial relationship has been with Raymond E. Brown, who was Davies's successor at Union Theological Seminary. Already in his Anchor Bible commentary, the first volume of which was published two years before Martyn's work appeared (but too late to influence it) and before they were colleagues, Brown had suggested that John's Gospel was written after and as a response to the situation of expulsion from the synagogue, brought about by the publication of the Twelfth Benediction of the *Shemoneh Esre*.[28] Of course, Brown's suggestion, which was quite important to him in fixing the date and establishing the purpose of the Fourth Gospel, was not developed in the detail and with all the nuances of Martyn's proposal. Nevertheless, Brown continued to work on the matter in conversation with Martyn, but in some ways also independently of him. Brown extended his analysis and description of the setting and development of the Johannine literature backward to the Beloved Disciple (and ultimately Jesus) and forward to the Epistles and their relationship to the Gospel (first in his *Community of the Beloved Disciple* and more definitively in his Anchor Bible commentary on the Johannine Epistles.)[29] For Brown, as well as for most other interpreters, the letters of John reflect a different, presumably later, setting in which the sharp conflict with representatives of the Jews has given way to other problems.

It would be misleading, however, to leave the impression that Brown simply accepted Martyn's construction of the historical setting of the Gospel and moved on to deal with the letters. His view of the origin of the Gospel is in some ways more complex than Martyn's and in other ways different. Already in the first volume of his commentary Brown had set forth the thesis that the Gospel arose in five stages of composition, beginning with the earliest oral preaching and culminating with the present canonical text, which is the product of editing by a hand later than the evangelist's. In *The Community of the Beloved Disciple,* Brown refined, and complicated, his thesis of Gospel origins as he discerned various interests, such as the Samaritan mission, conservative Jewish Christians, and apostolic (Petrine) Christians, each playing a role at different points in the development of the Gospel. Thus as Brown developed his own reconstruction, it differed from Martyn's in more than one respect. But while the series of literary stages seems more complex, it is actually also more comprehensive. Martyn is concerned only with Fortna's Gospel of Signs, the *Grundschrift,* and the subsequent controversy that leads ultimately to its expansion into the Gospel we now know. (Thus there are three stages against Brown's five.) But Martyn actually deals only with the middle of the spectrum of development as Brown sees it and not at all with a putative development from Jesus to the original Johannine tradition or with any final redaction of the Gospel and the publication of the letters.

In addition, Brown saw the initial conflict between Christ-confessors and Jewish authorities as breaking out over theological issues at a point at which Samaritan Christian influence began to assert itself in the Johannine community. For Martyn the tensions arose as the Johannine preacher(s) vigorously prosecuted the mission to other Jews, whether through the Gospel of Signs or otherwise, and threatened to draw increasing numbers of synagogue members to belief in Jesus. Only subsequently did doctrinal considerations—that is, ditheism (John 5)—become the paramount issue. Brown apparently sees the tensions arising precisely with the introduction of a "high" Christology that appears to threaten monotheism and under the influence of the Samaritan Christian element of the Johannine community. The differences between Martyn and Brown are of less weight than the agreements, but they are not insignificant. Obviously, they reflect both the collegiality and the independence of two longtime friends and colleagues, even as they set an agenda for further discussion.

Just as Brown, the leading commentator on the Gospel of John in North America, found himself in basic agreement with Martyn's thesis, something similar was happening across the Atlantic. In 1978 C. K. Barrett brought out a considerably revised and expanded version of his commentary, long regarded as the standard English-language commentary on the Greek text.[30] Barrett did not manifest much agreement with divergent views (the independence of John from the Synoptics; the close relationship of John and Qumran) that had gained increasing support since the initial publication of his commentary. But he tacitly acknowledged that research had advanced in at least one significant respect, for he indicated his basic agreement with Martyn's view of the circumstances of origin of John's Gospel. It was initially the product of the sharp disputation and hostility within the synagogue between Christ-confessors and other Jews. The influence of Martyn's thesis on Barrett's actual commentary is less pervasive than one might expect, but that is in large part a function of the character of the commentary as a series of erudite and exceedingly useful notes on the Greek text. Nevertheless, Barrett's agreement with Martyn's basic thesis was significant in itself, and also as an indication of which way the winds of informed scholarly opinion were blowing. (It should be noted, however, that Barrett had already suggested the possibility of a link between the Gospel and the *Birkath ha-Minim* in commenting on 9:22 in the first edition of his commentary.)[31]

Scholarly work, of course, advances but often reflects Martyn's influence at a quite fundamental level and in interesting ways. For example, the monograph of Klaus Wengst, *Bedrängte Gemeinde und verherrlichte Christus,* takes for granted the basic correctness of Martyn's proposal and proceeds to move beyond it in determining the geographical site and place of origin of the

Johannine community and Gospel.[32] In a brief allusion to the matter of place of origin, Martyn had more or less dismissed the traditional site of Ephesus, but had left the door open for Alexandria.[33] Now Wengst, on the basis of research principally in Josephus and rabbinic sources, proposes Batanea (the present Golan Heights) as the locus of the community that produced the Gospel of John. His reasoning actually begins from Martyn's thesis, as he asks where in the latter part of the first century one would find an area in which Jews were the dominant, but certainly not the only, group. It would be an area in which the designation "the Jews" would be intelligible as indicating one religious and cultural grouping over against others. Wengst argues that in such an area expulsion from the synagogue would involve genuine social, religious, and perhaps economic penalties or loss. Perhaps it goes without saying that only after 70, and especially outside Palestine, would synagogue membership be the decisive mark of Jewish identity. Wengst believes, moreover, that connections and communications can be traced between Judaism in the Transjordanian highlands and Jamnia in the period soon after the Roman War. All this involves a considerable amount of inference from sources not intended to supply such information—the Gospel of John included! The thesis is, however, quite plausible, as Meeks had already observed.[34] Although it may fall into that rather large body or category of research that presents conclusions that are possible and plausible without being demonstrably true, Wengst's monograph nevertheless demonstrates how fruitful and seminal Martyn's work has been in stimulating further creative investigations.

Other instances of Martyn's influence could easily be multiplied. I shall mention only two other works. Jerome S. Neyrey, in *Ideology of Revolt: John's Christology in Social Science Perspective,*[35] seems to assume as generally correct a picture of the conflict setting of John's Gospel as Martyn has portrayed it. On that basis he then pursues his own new and distinctive analysis. Similarly, David Rensberger, *Johannine Faith and Liberating Community,*[36] moves forward on the basis of Martyn, indicating his own position even as he accurately describes the present state of scholarship on the Gospel: "Subsequent studies have fully confirmed the rightness of this [Martyn's] basic insight. While few have accepted Martyn's delineation of the action behind the Fourth Gospel in all of its details, the fundamental conception that he outlined has been elaborated in a variety of directions and has become the cornerstone of much current Johannine research."[37] Thus Meeks can say confidently and rightly: "The rupture between the followers of Jesus and 'the Jews' is at the center of attention. It has manifestly shaped the Johannine groups' language and their perception of the world. These features of the Johannine universe have become so widely recognized in recent scholarship that there is no need for me to rehearse the evidence."[38]

Needless to say, not all recent Johannine research has followed Martyn's lead. Quite legitimately, new questions are raised, and the Gospel of John is approached from fresh perspectives. Typical of the subsequent literary-critical or narratological approach is R. Alan Culpepper's *Anatomy of the Fourth Gospel: A Study in Literary Design,* a groundbreaking work as far as the Gospel of John is concerned.[39] In that Culpepper deliberately refuses to regard the Gospel of John as a window for looking beyond the text into some atextual historical reality, whether the Jesus the text describes or the community that produced this highly distinctive account of him, he would seem to run counter to Martyn's work. Yet, Culpepper explicitly indicates that his purpose in this regard is heuristic rather than eristic. That is, he is not disavowing historical research on its relevance, but simply setting it aside for the time being to take another tack.

In fact, Culpepper's earlier *Johannine School* was quite congenial with Martyn's perspective and approach, and the results of *Anatomy of the Fourth Gospel* may be as well. Culpepper's literary analysis of John as such does not, of course, stand or fall with whether or not it makes John conform to anything beyond the document itself. Quite the contrary. Yet, when one reads Culpepper with Martyn in mind, some remarkable convergences or congruities appear. The implied readers of the Gospel need not be actual, ancient, historical readers. Nor need the implied author reflect, or address himself to, such an actual historical setting or crisis as Martyn posits. Yet, Culpepper's analysis of the implied author's role and interest, as well as those of the implied readers, actually fits rather well a historical situation in which a threatened or oppressed community (Wengst) draws upon its perception of its founder and master to find resources to face the present threat. Although the symbolic role of the Jews as foes of Jesus' disciples, not to mention Jesus himself, need have had no genuine historical counterpart, the existence of such referenced historical counterparts is certainly not excluded by viewing the Gospel from a literary-critical perspective, as Culpepper has done.

It would be unfair to Culpepper's worthwhile project to imply that its value lies in confirming Martyn's contribution. But just the fact that by pursuing a different goal, from a different perspective, and with different methods, Culpepper has produced an analysis of John's Gospel that is in many respects congruent with Martyn's historical reconstruction is something that needs to be considered carefully in further historical investigations, whatever may be done on the literary-critical side.

Postscript for the Third Edition of Martyn's *History and Theology in the Fourth Gospel*

As the title *History and Theology in the Fourth Gospel* indicates, Martyn's classic volume has two major and interrelated foci, issues of an essentially historical sort, and issues more clearly theological in nature. Both remain at the center of Johannine research and writing, although discussion of Martyn's work has focused primarily on its historical dimensions.

History

A year after the original publication of the essay that constitutes the bulk of this chapter, John Ashton's magisterial *Understanding the Fourth Gospel* appeared.[40] Ashton saw in the work of Bultmann and Martyn the two major pillars or benchmarks of Johannine scholarship in the twentieth century. Bultmann had rightly identified the theological issues and bearing of the Fourth Gospel, but had not set them in a credible historical context that could be documented from outside the Gospel itself. That task was left to Martyn, who saw that "the Jews" of the Fourth Gospel were more than theological symbols. They were real actors who figured importantly in the generation of this Gospel and needed to be identified. It remained for Martyn to flesh out who these actors were. In Ashton's judgment Martyn had performed this task in the most convincing way possible. Whereas Bultmann's John hung in the air and its Jews were ciphers for unbelief, Martyn gave the Gospel a home and identified its Jews as real people.

Most New Testament exegetes working on the Gospel of John and the history of early Christianity have found Martyn's basic thesis persuasive, principally because it makes the narrative text of John understandable. Why are "the Jews" so central, and why is expulsion from the synagogue an issue? Most rabbinic experts who have turned their attention to Martyn's arguments have, however, remained unpersuaded (see above, n. 18). I cited a number of these scholars earlier (Kimelman, Katz, and Schäfer, 8, n. 17). Now, in turning his attention to this issue, Daniel Boyarin has vigorously advanced the case against Martyn's appropriation of the Twelfth Benediction, the benediction against heretics, to illumine the Johannine setting from the Jewish side.[41] Boyarin's position is that no such version of the benediction as Martyn proposed existed sufficiently early as to have played a role in Johannine origins. Nor was there a Jamnian magisterium with the authority to promulgate such excommunications. This issue is vexed, and the claim that the benediction played a role in Johannine origins is, on any accounting, subject to doubt. Ashton's observation is, however, still relevant: "But the plausibility of the hypothesis depends on the light it sheds on the Gospel; and, in any case, Martyn's reading of ch. 9 is not *built upon* his interpretation of the Eighteen Benedictions; at most it is buttressed by it."[42]

Historically viewed, this assertion is true. After having postulated the role of *aposynagogos* in the development of the Fourth Gospel in his unpublished doctoral dissertation (Yale, 1957), Martyn discovered what he thought was its Jewish counterpart. But that came later in *History and Theology in the Fourth Gospel* (1968; see above, pp. 33–34). Alternatively, it is conceivable that expulsions from the synagogue occurred (or were threatened), but were prior to, and perhaps even unrelated to, the formulation of the Twelfth Benediction. In some sense, the Twelfth Benediction and rabbinic statements made about it work to explain Johannine origins. The original identity of the *minim* and *notzrim* in the one version of the Twelfth Benediction hit upon by Martyn is at best unclear, as is its date. Could the setting of John's Gospel explain such a statement? Martyn's thesis, whether justifiable or not, needs to be viewed as an effort to illuminate the benediction, and ancient rabbinic statements about it, as well as the origin of the Gospel of John. Moreover, Martyn has not only reconstructed the hypothetical synagogue controversy from within the Fourth Gospel. He has also carefully studied the Pseudo-Clementine literature and cogently argued that it presents an inner-synagogue situation similar to what lies behind the Gospel of John.[43]

Some exegetes who have rejected Martyn seem to read his thesis in the following way: The hypothetical Jamnian authorities, "the Jews," are the heirs of the Pharisees, who opposed Jesus, and, indeed, the Pharisees and "the Jews" in John are interchangeable. These Jamnian authorities rejected the claims made for Jesus and, in the 80s, instituted the synagogue ban so as to expel from synagogues everywhere Jews who believed that Jesus was the Messiah. Thus the sundering of Christians and Jews, which has endured to this day, was the product of Pharisaic Jews, the opponents of Jesus and of the Johannine community, as well as the architects of the rabbinic Judaism that has shaped all Judaism, particularly Orthodox Judaism, down to the present. Obviously such a construal is subject to question at a number of points. That the rabbis of Jamnia exercised such control toward the end of the first century may be improbable. (That they were *of a mind* to exercise such control is a different, but not unrelated, matter. That *some of them* were of a mind to exercise such control is again a different, but not unrelated matter.) Thus Martyn's position can be caricatured as maintaining that a monolithic rabbinic Judaism expelled all Jews who believed in Jesus so that they were forced to become something else, presumably Christians, and thus began to refer to their erstwhile (Jewish) opponents as "the Jews." Although this approach may be a caricature of Martyn's position, it is not a falsification, but a statement of it bereft of any nuance or qualification. Taken in this way, this stance also may make a Jewish establishment seem responsible for the separation of Christians who would have gladly remained in the synagogue.

Let us assume for the moment that no *monolithic* Jewish establishment existed at the time John's Gospel was composed or developed. Was there anything on the Johannine side, aside from messianic claims about Jesus, that would have incensed their Jewish coreligionists and led to expulsion and separation from the synagogue? Even a casual reading of John 5 suggests there was, for Jesus is given every opportunity to issue a disclaimer when he is said to make himself equal to God (5:18). But instead of seizing a loophole, John's Jesus does just the opposite, using the occasion to promote his equality with God, and the only disclaimer is that the Father has shown him what to do, which is what God himself is doing. Jesus' statements about himself and his role fly in the face of traditional biblical monotheism. For good reason, Ashton suspects, as did Raymond Brown, that such claims about Jesus preceded and precipitated expulsion from the synagogue, and understandably so.[44] (Martyn placed expulsion from the synagogue before, rather than after, the introduction of such a Christology.)

Martyn's thesis about Johannine origins has not been so significant because it has explained every aspect of that process satisfactorily, or in detail. Rather, it holds out greater promise for such explanation than any comparable theses. (On Martyn's own premises plenty of room is available to see two sides of this story, the Jewish as well as the Jewish-Christian, as doubtless there were.) This is why it has changed the landscape so much. It has encouraged us to look in a new direction in our quest for the key to unlocking the secrets of how this strangely different Gospel began.

In recent years interest has shifted back in the direction of literary function and theological bearing of "the Jews" in John's Gospel. But those whose interests are centered there often embrace some version of Martyn's thesis as a kind of historical basis. For example, Francis J. Moloney, whose interests are literary but also fundamentally theological, doubts the connection of synagogue expulsion with the *Birkath ha-Minim* and Gamaliel II in the 80s of the first century. Yet he takes the event of separation to have been real and historically important.[45] Something similar seems to be the case in Adele Reinhartz's *Befriending the Beloved Disciple*.[46] The revival of scholarly concerns about anti-Judaism in the Fourth Gospel, which gave rise to such significant expressions as the 2000 Louvain Conference, doubtless owes much to Martyn's thesis. In one of the volumes emerging from that meeting, *Anti-Judaism and the Fourth Gospel*, Martyn is still the most frequently cited figure. Every author but two cites him, usually at the outset of the essay. Although Martyn's goal was first of all exegetical and historical, as well as theological, his thesis doubtlessly has in important ways shaped the broader discussion. That broader discussion is important, as Martyn would readily acknowledge, but historical issues have a certain necessity and priority. As Martyn has succinctly and sharply put it: "Modern relations between Christians and Jews are not helped by an antihistorical interpretation of Biblical texts."[47]

Theology

Weighty and crucial as the historical issues are, it would be a mistake to allow any preoccupation with them—that of the Twelfth Benediction, for example —to shift the focus away from Martyn's major theological contribution, the reading of John's Gospel as a two-level drama. We can say, indeed, that in John's dramatic narrative the Word's becoming flesh has created a truly new history, one that stretches into the present without leaving the past. Thus, the retrospective character of the narrative, which, theologically speaking, is the work of the Paraclete. In characterizing Martyn's interpretation of John, I have remarked elsewhere, "the narrative operates at two levels, that of Jesus himself and that of the Johannine Christians and community. To elucidate John's theology means not to destroy his narrative, but to show how its theological emphases arose from and relate to the emergence of that community. "[48] In a word, the theology of the Fourth Gospel bears a distinctly communal stamp, arising from the certainty that the true narrative of Jesus is the story of who he was among his disciples and who he is, as he continues to give life itself to the Johannine community.[49] Yet an anonymous evangelist gave this Gospel a distinctive character and earned for himself the title John the Theologian. If Paul was the first Christian theologian, this John was the second. Yet Paul wrote no gospel narrative. that John did is a matter of theological, as will as historical, importance. As for John the Evangelist, faith and theology continue to be rooted in the story of Jesus. Moreover, the story of Jesus continues to be recapitulated in the stories of his followers.

Part Two

John and the Historical Jesus

4

The Problem of History in John

The Gospel Narratives as History at Two Levels

Christian faith's interest in history is, and always has been, fueled by the historical fact claims of the New Testament itself. Modern historical criticism has, of course, raised serious questions about those claims, and these questions are nowhere more acute than in the case of the Fourth Gospel. My own interest in the Gospel of John grew up alongside an equal interest in the quest of the historical Jesus, particularly the presentation and critique of Albert Schweitzer. In Schweitzer's great work the Gospel of John plays no role. It is laid aside as theology rather than history, despite its apparent fact claims (19:35; 21:24).

Rudolf Bultmann's commentary on John's Gospel might have seemed to provide an alternative to Schweitzer's dismissal of it. Bultmann correctly saw that the historicity of Jesus was crucial in John, but only his "thatness," not his "whatness." According to Bultmann, John's affirmation that the Word became flesh (1:14) is essential for Johannine, or for any, Christology. Yet the Johannine portrayal of Jesus is for the most part a Christian theological construction. One might say that for Bultmann John is, within the New Testament, the final step, and the right step, in the development of a proper Christology. As such it represents an inner-Christian theological development, not dependent on Judaism or on the historical figure of Jesus. Yet matters could not come to rest there, as a new generation of exegetes raised fresh questions about history and the Gospels.

As a graduate student, one of the first things I read in Paul Minear's New Testament Theology seminar at Yale in the fall of 1957 was James M. Robinson's noteworthy monograph *The Problem of History in Mark,* whose full significance I did not grasp at the time. Nor did I think to ask whether there is a comparable problem of history in John. A little over a decade later, however, J. Louis Martyn was to publish his groundbreaking study *History and Theology in the Fourth Gospel* (1968; 3rd ed., 2003).[1] For Martyn the problem of history in John was the problem of the history and conflicts of the Johannine community. The Jesus of that history was the Jesus present by means of the Spirit-Paraclete to that community. The Fourth Gospel's narrative moves at two levels, that of the Johannine community or church in its struggle against (other) Jews who do not accept Jesus as the Messiah and, underneath so to speak, the *einmalig* (onetime) level of Jesus or the old tradition about Jesus and his ministry. Martyn did not dismiss the *einmalig* level. Indeed, it is essential to his thesis. But he focused on the other, higher level in the two-level drama, whose ultimate unity was vested in the work of the Paraclete.

Nevertheless, John is a narrative of Jesus' ministry. Like the Synoptics it begins with the appearance of John the Baptist and ends with the passion narrative. Moreover, the narrator says "We have beheld his glory" (1:14), and Nathanael is told that he will see "the angels of God ascending and descending on the Son of Man" (1:52). The piercing of Jesus' side (19:34) has been seen by the true witness, who is apparently the source of this Gospel (21:24). Does not the Fourth Gospel deserve to be taken seriously for what it claims to be?[2]

Moreover, 1 John emphasizes as strongly as the Gospel the importance of Jesus as a real, historical figure, but the Epistle seldom, if ever, figures in discussions of this issue. Yet the Epistle's prologue (1:1–3) emphasizes even more than the Gospel's (1:1–18) the visibility, audibility, and tangibility of the word of life. If in 1 John 1:1–3 the Gospel's prologue is in view—and 1 John's prologue would otherwise make little sense—Jesus himself is in view. Moreover, Jesus keeps reappearing in this letter, even when his name is not explicitly called. There is continual reference to "the beginning" (*archē*) throughout the document. True, the Jesus who died and is now the Paraclete/Advocate with the Father (2:1; cf. John 13:34) presides over the scene. But at the same time he is inseparable from his historical past.

This is evident as soon as his commandments come into view. It is not just a matter of keeping commandments, however, but walking as that one (masculine singular) walked (2:6). The one whose walk is to be emulated is obviously Jesus. If this were not clear enough already, there is a telling play on the "new commandment" which Jesus issues in the Gospel of John (13:34). When an old commandment replaces the new commandment (2:7) it is described as the one which you had from the beginning, obviously from Jesus himself ("the word that you have heard").

The importance of Jesus as a real human being is underscored by the condemnation of christological heresy in 4:1–3. Who is from God (or "of God") and who is not? Obviously, the crucial criterion is confessing that Jesus has come in the flesh, which means as a real human being. Denial of the humanity of Jesus is the heresy that has divided the community (see also 2:18–25). Interest in the historical figure of Jesus is not academic. The interest is not in history per se, but in doctrine, and the doctrine depends on the historical reality of a human being.

First John makes clear what the Word's becoming flesh (John 1:14) means. The Epistle is more explicit on this point than the Gospel, although it is a proper interpretation of the Gospel, for which the humanity of Jesus is a basic ingredient. Rarely is Jesus spoken of as the son of Joseph in the Synoptic Gospels, but Philip introduces him to Nathanael as Jesus son of Joseph from Nazareth (John 1:45). After Jesus has referred to himself as the bread from heaven (6:41), the Jews, who are apparently his fellow Galileans, say "Is not this Jesus, the Son of Joseph, whose father and mother we know? How does he now say 'I have come down from heaven'?" Jesus is a human being whose natural origins are known. His claims, taken literally, are inconceivable, and therefore presumably false. But they are not to be taken literally. They must be demythologized, as the evangelist has demythologized the myth of the descending and ascending redeemer. For Gospel as for Epistle the humanity and historical reality of Jesus are basic.

Of course, historical skepticism about John's portrayal of Jesus did not begin yesterday. That the Johannine Jesus is preaching the gospel of the post-resurrection church has been apparent to most exegetes since the rise of historical criticism. Moreover, we are asked to believe that Jesus gave sight to a man blind from birth and raised from the dead a man who had been dead for four days. Really? Jesus' supernatural power is too much in evidence for Bultmann's modern man or woman.[3] Yet such power is already manifest in the synoptic Jesus. John only enlarges it or goes out of his way to call attention to it. Here, as in other cases, John makes what is latent in the Synoptics patent or explicit.

Obviously, in John, Jesus' deeds of power (NRSV; RSV's "mighty works") become signs, which they are not in the Synoptics. Yet even there they are more than humanitarian acts; they signify Jesus' mission as a commission from God. They betoken the in-breaking rule of God (Matt 12:28; Luke 11:20), as they likely did for Jesus himself and for his followers. They have a latent christological function.

The sayings of Jesus in John are another matter, in that Jesus talks Christology quite explicitly and debates his role with his opponents, although this does not happen in the Synoptics. In Mark, for example, the question about Jesus' mission and role lurks constantly in the background and moves the narrative forward. In John it is answered at the beginning, and the narrative therefore lacks the same movement. The question is only who will accept Jesus' claims and who will not. This is an excellent example of what is latent in the Synoptics being patent in John. Although the anachronistic character of the Johannine Jesus' preaching has long been recognized, significant progress has been made in setting the character and content of his speech in the context of a conflict with Judaism, or better, within Judaism, about the validity of the emerging church's claims for Jesus. Moreover, as the Gospel itself makes clear, the continuing revelation of Jesus, through the ever present Jesus speaking to his church, is the work of the Spirit or Paraclete, which Jesus himself promised (John 14:25–26; 16:12–15).

John's historical value as a source for Jesus or genuine Jesus tradition is, of course, closely related to the question of John and the Synoptics. The Synoptics are favored over John for obvious reasons. In the Synoptics Jesus is recognizably human; in John he is not. He is, rather, God striding across the earth, or that is the predominant impression. But however that may be, the resolution of the question of John and the Synoptics is not the necessary a priori for addressing the problem of Jesus tradition in the Gospel of John.[4] There are various positions on the question of John and Synoptic Gospels that may tilt the answer to the Jesus tradition question one way or the other, but they do not necessarily decide it.

Take for example the view that John knew and used one (usually Mark) or more of the Synoptics. One may decide that the historical substance of John is derived from the Synoptics and any departure from them is a product of John's apologetic or theological interests. This is an arguable position, and has been set out by Maurice Casey.[5] Frans Neirynck, in contrast, argues that John knew and used all the Synoptics, but as far as I know he has not suggested that because of this the Fourth Gospel can contain no historical data not found in the others. Similarly, Mgr. de Solages believes John knew the Synoptics, but he argues that where John differs from them it is likely more accurate historically.[6] The author is, in his view, John the Beloved Disciple, who knew because he was there.

Yet the position that John is independent of the Synoptics as enunciated by P. Gardner-Smith and developed by his Cambridge colleague C. H. Dodd is quite congenial with the historical value of John. Dodd himself certainly thought so, and his masterful *Historical Tradition in the Fourth Gospel* is as impressive an effort to demonstrate that as one can imagine.[7] If John does not use the Synoptic Gospels, what are his sources? Dodd favors oral tradition. (Bultmann had argued for a sign source and a passion source; Fortna was to advocate a Gospel of Signs.) In any event, as Gardner-Smith and Dodd saw, John's independence opens the door to its historicity.

Yet the earliest gospel evidence from outside the New Testament shows that independence of the Synoptics does not necessarily imply historicity. Do any of the apocryphal gospels that we know, albeit mostly in fragmentary form, seem to be based upon Mark (or the Synoptics)? Apparently they are not, and therefore they are at least in this sense independent. Yet they are for the most part patently fictional (although elements of old tradition may underlie the

Gospel of Peter at a few points and the *Gospel of Thomas* may contain independently transmitted sayings). In fact, a three-gospel canon seems to have formed around Mark, and it suppressed the development of other Gospels. Its only lasting rivals were the Gospel of John and in some circles in the fourth century and later the *Diatessaron*. The *Diatessaron* was, of course, a compilation of the canonical four. John, like all gospels outside the Marcan canon, largely went its own way, but followed a general gospel (but not necessarily the Marcan) outline or structure.

Recent investigation and discussion of the synoptic problem suggest that while the two-or four-document hypothesis is as good as we can do, synoptic relationships may be more complex. If that is the case, and it may be, any relationship among all four Gospels, and perhaps others, would, in the nature of the case, be even more complex. To make any conclusion about history or historical tradition in John dependent on its resolution would likely be tantamount to postponing it indefinitely.

I deal elsewhere with the question of Jesus tradition in John more extensively than is possible here.[8] Yet it will be useful to look at a few representative instances: first, several in which John contradicts or differs from the Synoptics; and, second, a few in which John differs from Matthew and Mark while agreeing with Luke.

Obviously, in John Jesus' ministry is spread over as much as three years, certainly more than two (three Passovers; 2:13; 6:4; 11:55), while in the Synoptics it is limited to one year—really less than one (one Passover; Mark 14:1). Moreover, Jesus is frequently found in Jerusalem and Judea, while in the Synoptics he does not go there until the end. While one may scarcely speak of demonstration or proof, in principle the Johannine version is more probable, particularly since the synoptic version is based solely on Mark, whose framework owes as much or more to theology than to history. Yet the Marcan account of the growing impact of Jesus and opposition to him suggests a period of more than one year rather than less. Even in Mark there are suggestions that Jesus has spent more time in Jerusalem, probably prior to his final visit. At his arrest he alludes to a period of time spent teaching in the temple ("day by day"; Mark 14:49). He seems to have made previous preparation for his entry into Jerusalem (11:1–6) and for the room for the Last Supper (14:12–16). Both pericopes can be viewed as Marcan compositions intended to portray Jesus' advance, presumably supernatural, knowledge. In fact, we cannot be sure that this is the case. (Incidentally, it is strange if John had been following Mark that he omitted these scenes that so fully correspond to his view of Jesus' knowledge and power.) Possibly both scenes bespeak Jesus' longer or previous presence in Jerusalem. Moreover, it is altogether likely that Jesus went up to Jerusalem regularly; not only for Passover but other feasts (cf. John 5:1; 7:2).

Both John and the Synoptics portray Jesus' ministry as beginning with John the Baptist, but with striking differences. In the Synoptics Jesus' encounter with John, during which he is baptized, is separate from the account of the calling of disciples, the brothers Peter and Andrew and James and John, from their work as fishermen (Mark 1:16–20 par.) on the Sea of Galilee. Jesus commands; they follow. They seem to follow only because Jesus commands and without any prior knowledge. In John the similar account of their encounter does not mention baptism, but instead has John send his disciples to Jesus. Disciples of John become disciples of Jesus. That is a more plausible historical scenario than Mark's, if less dramatic. Although in John's version Jesus is shortly thereafter declared to be Messiah (1:41), Mark's is theologically pregnant. Jesus has only to command and his would-be disciples obey.

In all the Gospels John reappears, but only in the Fourth Gospel is Jesus portrayed as conducting a ministry alongside the Baptist. Mark has John's work end with his imprisonment before the ministry of Jesus begins (1:14), in what appears to be a neat, theologically motivated, compartmentalization. John goes out of his way to emphasize Jesus' superiority to John the Baptist (1:15, 30), yet he depicts Jesus and John baptizing in a kind of rivalry (3:22, 26; 4:1). Although this portrayal is promptly corrected (4:2), the correction seems to be a sort of afterthought in which it is stated that not Jesus himself, but only his disciples, baptized. But that is also something found in no other Gospel. Throughout this Johannine scene the statements of Jesus and John bear all the marks of later theological reflection, but the data about their relationship are in all likelihood historical, despite their absence from the Synoptics.

John's differences from the Synoptics, particularly Matthew and Mark, are often accompanied by peculiar contact or affinities with Luke. This is nowhere more evident than in the trial of Jesus before the Sanhedrin, which is entirely missing from John, although a place has, so to speak, been marked for it with the mere mention of Jesus' being taken to and from Caiaphas the high priest (John 18:24, 28). Instead there is a brief and theologically inconsequential hearing before Annas (18:13–14, 19–23). At the same time, Mark's lengthy and theologically weighty account of Jesus' formal trial before the Sanhedrin (14:53–64), in which witnesses are sought and heard, a confession under questioning is made by Jesus, and a verdict rendered, is missing from John. Remarkably, Luke, who is clearly using Mark in his rendition of the Sanhedrin scene, omits just these juridical elements (22:66–71). In Luke it is no longer a trial. The historical difficulties of the Marcan trial account have long been observed, by commentators both Jewish and Christian. It violates a number of stipulations governing a capital trial laid out in the Mishnaic tractate *Sanhedrin*. Did it happen? The simpler Johannine account of a hearing before Annas does not present comparable difficulties and is more likely historical.

Ironically, on John's accounting one such difficulty could be removed. The evening of Jesus' arrest and arraignment is not Passover itself, a high holy day on which the trial and other events as recounted in Mark (and Matthew) are scarcely conceivable, but the day previous. John states and reiterates that Jesus' death occurred the afternoon before Passover rather than the day after (18:28; 19:14, 31, 42: cf. 13:1). Has John changed the date so that Jesus dies as the Passover lambs are slain? Despite John 1:29 and 36, as well as 19:36, this is not noted in John. That is, the slaughtering of the lambs while Jesus is dying is not explicitly mentioned. Moreover, in John Jesus' death is not explained in terms of the sacrificial cult, the temple altar, as it is in the Words of Institution of the Lord's Supper, which are, of course, found only in the Synoptic Gospels and Paul. The differing Johannine chronology relieves the historical problems created by the Synoptic accounts, and does not really support clear and explicit Johannine theological themes.

On this point of divergence there is not a Lucan parallel to John, but there are others. The trial scene, of course, stands out. But in the death scene also Luke and John agree in omitting the so-called cry of derelictie (Ps 22:2; Mark 15:34; Matt 27:46). Luke, clearly following Mark, has Jesus say instead, but in the same "loud voice," "Father, into thy hands I commit my spirit" (24:46). In John, not obviously following Mark, Jesus says only, "It is finished," but the narrator adds, "and bowing his head he gave over the spirit." *Spirit* figures in both John and Luke. So in pericopes that are found in all four Gospels, Luke often diverges from Mark and Matthew where John does. To give another example, John's account of the calling of the disciples differs from Mark (and Matthew), as we observed, and Luke also differs radically (Luke 5:2–11; cf. the similar story, John 20:1–14), although in a different manner. Matthew and Mark have two feeding narratives; Luke and John only the feeding of five thousand. Only Luke and John report speculation over whether John the Baptist was the Messiah (Luke 3:15; John 1:20). While John does not report Jesus' baptism at all, Luke barely mentions it after it has occurred, and does not describe the act (Luke 3:21).

If there is any dependence between John and Luke, which way does it run? Is it likely that John, who is not following Mark, even if he knew Mark, would have elected to go with Luke at some points, having both before him (or knowing both)? Or is it more likely that Luke, who used Mark, would have been influenced by an alternative (Johannine?) account that differed at many points? I think the latter is more probable. The cry of derelictie is a relevant instance. Unquestionably, Luke is following Mark. John, whether or not he knew Mark, is not. How is it that Luke and John agree both in the deletion of the cry and its replacement with a reference to the spirit, whether Jesus' or God's? Which way does dependence go? The answer is not a given, but the conclusion that

Luke is swayed from his dependence on Mark by his knowledge of John, or a John-like narrative, is both plausible and inviting. Luke would have changed a statement about Jesus' death (John 19:30; "gave up his spirit" or "expired") into an appropriate word of a dying martyr, after which he similarly "expired" (Luke 23:46; using the verbal rather than John's nominal form of *pneuma*). Of course, Johannine priority does not necessarily imply historicity, but again opens the door for it.

Is there a problem of history in John? There is little doubt that there is. The problem of the historical setting of John is a problem of history that is as near resolution as it ever has been. Jesus stands over against the Jews. Who are these Jews? For that matter, who is this Jesus? Most exegetes would now agree that he is not the historical Jesus. Why is he opposed by "the Jews" when he and his disciples are themselves Jews? Why should Jesus' would-be disciples fear expulsion from synagogues? Or why should they even think of such a thing? The answer to these and similar questions lies in the reconstruction of the setting of the Fourth Gospel in, or at the edge of, a Judaism that rejects the claims of Jesus' (still Jewish) followers, who have been, or anticipate being, rejected themselves ("put out of the synagogue"). They want to remain Jews, but as it is turning out, they will not. The reconstruction remains hypothetical, but fits the data of the text remarkably well. This is why it has been gaining ground among knowledgeable exegetes.

What about the historical figure of Jesus in the Gospel of John? That John's Jesus is not the same as the historical figure of early-first-century Galilee is clear enough, although he may sometimes be glimpsed through the Johannine lens. But when we ask about Jesus tradition in John, that is a different issue. What is at stake in this case is old tradition and quasihistorical data. In this chapter I aim to survey the territory, indicate the issues involved (for example, John and the Synoptics), suggest how they play out with regard to this issue, and point to evidence for Jesus tradition, in the sense of data pertinent to the historical ministry of Jesus, in the Gospel of John.

We began by setting Martyn's *History and Theology in the Fourth Gospel* alongside Robinson's *The Problem of History in Mark,* with the intention of discussing the problem of history in the Fourth Gospel. It may be worthwhile now to look again at Robinson on Mark to take stock of any parallel between his work and Martyn's on John. (In a small seminar on Mark at the University of Zurich in the academic year 1963–64, Professor Eduard Schweizer in discussing some feature of Mark would sometimes ask what it was reminiscent of, and the answer would usually be "das Johannesevangelium.")

Robinson's presentation is set against the context of the then current Continental discussion, which pivoted about the exegetical and theological work of Bultmann. Although an active partner in that discussion, Robinson set forth a position on Mark that ran counter to Bultmann's theological position and interests. Robinson emphasized that Mark speaks for a community (or church) for which history and historicity were important. Historicity was more than the punctiliar moment in which one encounters and accepts the kerygma. Such social and historical conceptions about Mark as Robinson proposed thus ran counter to Bultmann's theological perception and program. Because of this, Robinson conjectures—I think correctly—that Mark (and the Synoptics generally) are relegated to a relatively minor role in Bultmann's classic *Theology of the New Testament*.[9]

For Robinson the history of the Marcan community recapitulates the history of Jesus. Mark "sees Jesus and the Church engaged in the same cosmic struggle against the same demonic force of evil."[10] Moreover, "since the Church sees its history founded in Jesus' history, it can witness to and explain its religious experience better by writing the history of Jesus as the Messiah than by describing its own religious life."[11] Could not the same be said of John?

If so, there is a significant analogy between the problem of history in John and the same problem in Mark. In both the evangelist tells the story of his community while at the same time telling the story of Jesus' ministry. If this were not the case, neither Gospel would have been written. There is a real and important parallel. Of what does Mark remind us? Obviously, "das Johannesevangelium." At the same time there are quite obvious differences between John and Mark. Their eschatological perspectives are different, as Robinson's treatment of Mark makes clear. Until the passion narrative they apparently drew upon different traditions. In John Jesus preaches the gospel about himself, which Mark also shares without putting it on the lips of Jesus. Mark is closer to the historical figure of Jesus than is John, although no less committed to a theological perception of him that affects the way he shapes and structures his Gospel. It is all the more remarkable then that at just those points where the Fourth Gospel differs from Mark and the other Synoptic Gospels John's version is often preferable historically. There is a "problem of history in John" not unlike that in Mark. Mark presents problems when evaluated historically, but greater problems when history is left out of account. The same is true of John. For all their differences Mark and John are obviously about the same protagonist. Not only is he named Jesus, but he is also a Galilean Jew who carries out his mission within the boundaries of biblical Israel. He teaches; he performs healings and other extraordinary miracles; he goes to Jerusalem to face death. What Mark obviously believes about Jesus, John puts on Jesus' lips.

Both John and Mark are extraordinary biographies. They are extraordinary in two senses: first, because of claims made for the protagonist; but, second, because the nature of those claims has fundamentally shaped the character and context of the narration. The crowning and most significant event of his life was his death, but it was not the end. He rose from the dead. At least that is what the authors of these unique documents believed, and they represent groups of followers who were equally convinced. Their differences seem to fade before these common factors.

5

John's Quest for Jesus

The Pastness of the Present Jesus

The Quest of the Historical Jesus is the title given to the English translation of Albert Schweitzer's great book *Von Reimarus zu Wrede.*[1] It has become the name of the search for the real (that is, historical) Jesus in modern New Testament scholarship. We thus now have the Old Quest, the New Quest, and the Third Quest. All are products of modernity (if not postmodernity) and have no parallel in antiquity, or so we historians and exegetes think. There was in antiquity no "disinterested" quest for Jesus. But we have learned recently—if we did not already know—that no quest was ever "disinterested."[2] There are various interests, some more appropriate than others.

The Gospel: Finding Jesus in the Present

Today, as in antiquity, Jesus has found people. He has found George W. Bush, Jane Fonda, and my sister-in-law, among others—and not least Schweitzer himself ("He comes to us as one unknown, as of old, by the lakeside, he came to those men who did not know who he was. He says the same word: 'Follow thou me.'"). In antiquity he found, first of all (or "last of all") Paul of Tarsus. There is a sense in which the priority always lies, or lay, with Jesus. "You did not choose me but I chose you," says Jesus in John (15:16). Yet this does not mean people do not—did not—also seek Jesus (John 1:38–39). John Painter has written an important book about the quest motif and quest stories in the Gospel of John.[3] Jesus seeks and finds people, but they also quest for him. This is a theological motif, but it also has a historical basis, one that may be quite ancient.

The very production of Gospels bespeaks an interest in who Jesus was, that is, in a quest. I think this is true of Matthew and even Mark, although they do not express it. In Matthew, of course, Jesus is Emmanuel, "God with us" (1:23), and he promises to stay with his disciples to the end of the age (28:20). But because he is who he is, and will be who he will be, who he *was* is important, both theologically and historically. If Jesus Christ is the same yesterday, today, and forever (Heb 13:8), who he was is an essential part of who he is. We (exegetes and historians) may agree that in the Gospels there was an uncritical merging of Jesus' *was-ness* with his *is-ness,* but this does not necessarily mean who Jesus was had been forgotten or deemed of no importance. When Paul speaks of Jesus' having been rich, and for our sakes becoming poor (2 Cor 8:9), or of his humbling himself and becoming obedient to death (Phil 2:8), does he not reflect knowledge of who Jesus was and what his ministry was like?

I just said "even Mark" bespeaks such a historical interest. The beginning of the good news of Jesus Christ the Son of God (Mark 1:1) may be John the Baptizer, or it could be Jesus himself. In any event, the fact that Mark tells this story—what becomes the basic narrative—of Jesus' ministry must be of fundamental importance for understanding what Mark is about. The beginning of the good news is this story. Or the beginning is John the Baptizer whose activity is the first episode of this story of Jesus' ministry.

When we turn to the presumably later Gospels of Luke and John, the historical interest becomes explicit. Luke tells us several important things in his brief preface (1:1–4): First, he has had predecessors, and is not the first to write such a narrative. (We know Mark, but were there others?). Second, he himself was not an eyewitness. Third, he has conducted a thorough investigation. Fourth, and finally, this historical narrative will apparently confirm the Christian instruction that Theophilus has received. Luke actually reinforces the view, now long held by Christians, that the historical truth of the narrative is somehow basic to its theological truth. What is implicit in Mark's and Matthew's undertaking to write a Gospel now becomes explicit. Indeed, what here becomes explicit is already implicit in Paul's "He died for our sins according to the Scriptures" (1 Cor 15:3). Something happened that naturally evokes a narrative.

When one turns to the Gospel of John, the same interest appears, if in different form. In the prologue John writes, "We have beheld his glory" (1:14), and for John the glory of Jesus is already present to the eyes of his followers in his historic ministry (2:11), even though they cannot comprehend it. Beyond that, as in Luke, the historical dimension is attested by the work or position of the author. The disciple whom Jesus loved is the one "who is testifying to these things" (or "who bears witness concerning these things") and "who has written these things" (or "who has caused these things to be written"). He represents, and testifies to, a community: "We know that his witness is true" (21:24). The Gospel then concludes with the author's, or narrator's, concession that this Gospel does not contain everything Jesus did and his rumination about how much space it would take to hold the books that would be filled if a complete account of Jesus' ministry were given (21:25). The same witness also appears earlier at the foot of the cross, to attest the piercing of Jesus' side and the efflux of water and blood (19:35). The historical interest of Luke thus finds its counterpart in John.

Both these later Gospels make this interest, and its theological importance, quite obvious. There is, nevertheless, a major difference: Luke, although confident of the accuracy of his narrative, makes clear that he himself was not an eyewitness, but rather dependent on their testimony. The Gospel of John, on the other hand, claims to be based on the eyewitness of one person in particular, the disciple whom Jesus loved: John, according to later tradition. (The Gospel itself never names this disciple; he remains anonymous.) No Gospel makes as strong or as specific a claim. Ironically, Luke, who is one or two steps removed from the eyewitness generation seems to most of us much closer to the historical figure of Jesus than the narrator of the Fourth Gospel. I think that is actually the case. Jesus proclaimed God's will for human beings, spoke of the advent of the kingdom of God, taught in parables, healed the sick, cast out demons, debated with scribes and Pharisees about matters other than his role and dignity. This characterization agrees with Mark and Matthew, but not so much with John, whose portrayal of Jesus and his ministry, while embracing the broad outlines of the Marcan narrative, is different in many respects, large and small. In John Jesus talks about himself: he talks Christology.

But even as John assures the reader of the sufficiency of the Gospel's witness, a different concern comes into view: not how the church can reach the Jesus of the past, but how the Jesus of the past, and future, is, or can be, present to the church. The Fourth Evangelist ("John" for convenience's sake) surely believes that Jesus is present to his church. I do not think that he believes Jesus can be produced by literary or theological sleight of hand. Still, John has a purpose and a project: to show how, despite the doubts and apprehension of his disciples, Jesus intended and accomplished his purpose of returning to his disciples after his death and departure from them.

Unlike Luke, John does not write a narrative about Jesus followed by a narrative of the church. His narrative ends with the resurrection, and also the ascension of Jesus, which coincides with his resurrection rather than following it (or concluding it) as in Luke. John's narrative, while it is about Jesus, also portrays the historical situation of his own church, which is opposed by some Jews, particularly Pharisees, who reject the claims made for Jesus. Let me give the example made famous by J. Louis Martyn.[4]

In John's depiction of the giving of sight to the man born blind (chapter 9), the Jews and Pharisees are named interchangeably as the opponents of Jesus, and particularly of the healed man, who insists on the reality of what Jesus had done for him. Meanwhile, his parents decline to answer the crucial question of the Jews for fear of being put out of the synagogue as followers of the Christ (9:22; "the Jews" have agreed to put Christ-confessors out of the synagogue). Martyn has convincingly argued that a piece of old Jesus tradition, which tells of his healing of a blind man, has been developed in terms of the controversies of John's own day. Jewish opponents of the Johannine church are in effect excommunicating other Jews who believe that Jesus is the Messiah of Jewish and biblical expectation. The opponents of Jesus merge with the church's opponents, and even the figure of Jesus merges with that of the early Christian preachers. Thus Martyn speaks of two levels in the Gospel of John, that of the old tradition, putatively Jesus, and that of the Johannine church. Whether or not John has analyzed these two levels as we do, he obviously believes that the two levels of conflict and struggle are fundamentally the same. Thus rather than telling the story of Jesus and then the story of the church, as Luke does, John imposes the one upon the other. We might say that in doing so John distorts history. If he were to think in these terms, John might, contrariwise, insist that instead history is clarified, because the two levels are two (historical) stages of the same struggle.

John does not believe that Jesus' presence in the conflicts of his followers is something he himself has accomplished simply by his literary or theological cleverness. It is a real state of affairs corresponding to the church's postresurrection experience. Of course, prior to Jesus' death, ascension, and resurrection, the disciples could scarcely know what was in store for them, despite the fact that in the farewell discourses Jesus had already told them.

In fact, a principal question of the discourses is raised by Jesus' telling his disciples, in response to Peter's question ("Lord, where are you going?"), that he is going where Peter cannot follow until "afterward"—that is, after Jesus' own death and resurrection (13:36). But this language is enigmatic to Peter, as it will be to the disciples throughout the discourses, even when they think they understand (16:29–32). Jesus' initial statements then deal with the question of how the disciples will continue in Jesus' dwelling place with the Father (14:1–4). Not surprisingly, these words are perennial favorites at Christian funeral services, and with some reason, but they actually introduce a basic theme of the farewell discourses: Jesus' continuing presence with the disciples. Thomas plays a key role in evincing the disciples' ignorance (14:5): "How can we know the way?"[5] Jesus then makes his famous response, "I am the way, the truth, and the life. No one comes to the Father except through me" (14:6). We may read this and assume there were many ways to God the Father, and Jesus has closed the others off. Jesus and John's hearers would have assumed there was no way except the one opened by Jesus. Jesus then continues by assuring the disciples that they know the Father through knowing him, Jesus (v. 7), but their perplexity continues (vv. 8–14) as Philip asks, "Show us the Father." So Jesus eventually issues the first promise of the (another) Paraclete, translated Advocate (NRSV) or Counselor (RSV), the Spirit of truth (14:15–17).

Only the Gospel of John calls the Spirit of truth or Holy Spirit (14:26) the Advocate or Counselor. The Greek word is *paraklētos* (in English, "Paraclete"), which can be translated either way. "Lawyer" is also a possible meaning. The lawyer pleads for his client ("Advocate") or counsels his client ("Counselor"). In 1 John 2:1 Jesus himself is called our Advocate (Paraclete) with the Father. That application to Jesus is apparently in view when Jesus speaks of another Advocate, that is, the Spirit of truth. In view of the Spirit-Paraclete's actual function according to the Gospel, "Counselor" seems to me the better translation.[6] The Spirit of truth or Holy Spirit counsels the disciples. Indeed, the Spirit-Paraclete is the form of Jesus' presence with them. He speaks for Jesus and to the church.

After promising the Spirit-Paraclete,[7] Jesus reverts to more widely known, traditional eschatological forms of speech: "I will not leave you orphaned; I am coming to you. In a little while the world will no longer see me, but you will see me " (vv. 18, 19). Soon thereafter Judas, not Iscariot, asks Jesus how he will reveal himself to the disciples and not to the world (v. 22). Judas's question recognizes that traditional eschatological expectation is being revised. Jesus' coming is not to be a public event. Jesus' presence with his disciples is somehow contingent on their keeping his commandments (v. 21), his words (v. 24), but there is more to it than that. Once again Jesus speaks of the Paraclete, now identified as the Holy Spirit, who will be the means of Jesus' active presence in the community of his disciples, teaching them "all things" and reminding them of what Jesus has said (14:25–26).

One thinks back to 2:22, after Jesus' word about his resurrection that concludes John's temple-cleansing scene: "When therefore he was raised from the dead, his disciples remembered that he had said this; and they believed the scripture and the word which Jesus had spoken" (2:22). Also the conclusion of the triumphal entry scene (12:12–19), with its citation of Ps 18:25–26 and Zech 9:9: "His disciples did not understand this at first; but when Jesus was glorified, then they remembered that this had been written of him and had been done to him" (John 12:16). Moreover, after Jesus' mysterious saying about thirsting and drinking (7:37–38), the evangelist comments: "Now this he said about the Spirit, which those who believed in him were to receive; for as yet the Spirit had not been given, because Jesus was not yet glorified" (John 7:39). What is now being said in the concluding discourses has been anticipated during Jesus' public ministry. But later on, the disciples' continuing anxiety over Jesus' departure is reflected in Jesus' reassuring word: "Nevertheless I tell you the truth: it is to your advantage that I go away, for if I do not go away, the Counselor will not come to you; but if I go, I will send him to you" (John 16:7).

With Jesus' departure the disciples will be closer to, not farther from, Jesus, but they cannot yet appreciate this fact. Yet the importance of the advent of the Spirit-Paraclete cannot be overstated. The Paraclete, the Spirit of truth, has a continuing revelatory, as well as a reminding and reassuring, function: "he will guide you into all truth" (16:13). Obviously, he will tell the church things Jesus has not yet told the disciples: "you cannot bear them now" (16:12). But these new things will not be discontinuous with Jesus: "he will take what is mine and declare it to you" (v. 14). Nevertheless, there will be further words of Jesus, which he did not utter during his historic ministry, but which will be delivered to the church through the Spirit.

When one reflects on it, this is an astounding assertion and claim. With good reason one asks how much of the Gospel of John itself is a fulfillment of this promise. What we have been reading here corresponds to the character of the Gospel of John, particularly the words ascribed to Jesus. As far as we can tell through comparison with the Synoptics, there are numerous words of Jesus in John that go back to old tradition, if not Jesus himself (for example, 12:25–26; cf. Mark 8:34–35 et par. Matt 16:34 and Luke 17:33). (In many cases, however, these sayings do not seem to be derived directly from the Synoptics, although scholarly opinions differ.) Much, however, of what is ascribed to Jesus is unparalleled in the Synoptics, or in any other document we know. Moreover, most of these words, including the farewell discourses themselves, speak directly to the situation and needs of the Johannine church in the postresurrection period. In the long run Christians generally have found in these words Jesus' direct address to themselves. To a large extent the words of the Johannine Jesus are Spirit-inspired words, and are to be taken seriously as such. They are misconstrued if taken as self-consciously conceived means of expressing the evangelist's theology. They deserve to be taken at face value as words of the exalted Christ speaking through the Spirit.[8]

As Martyn maintained, the Spirit-Paraclete is the key to the two levels of John's witness, the once-upon-a-time (*einmalig*) and the level of the Johannine church.[9] The Paraclete brings the two together and is the mode or means of Jesus' speaking to the church. The Paraclete warrants the claim within the church that its situation and that of Jesus are fundamentally the same. Therefore, words of Jesus spoken to his situation may now be directed to the church, and new words of Jesus may be, and are, forthcoming as new situations arise: "He will glorify me, because he will take what is mine and declare it to you" (16:14). What the Spirit declares in the name of Jesus is the revelation of God to the church: "All that the Father has is mine. For this reason I said he will take what is mine and declare it to you" (16:15). So through the Fourth Evangelist and under the aegis of the Spirit, Jesus continues to speak. As Schweitzer concludes: "He says the same words, 'Follow thou me!' and sets us to the tasks which he must fulfill in our time. He commands, and to those who obey him, whether wise or simple, he will reveal himself in the tranquility, the toils, the conflicts, which they will live through in his fellowship, and as an inexpressible mystery they will experience who he is." Ironically perhaps, the same Schweitzer who dismisses the Gospel of John as a historical source here sounds quite Johannine. Perhaps it is not irony, but rather that Schweitzer, like the Fourth Evangelist, has heard Jesus speaking. No wonder then that in these almost poetic lines he falls into a rhythmic cadence, a Johannine mode of speech!

We see here the establishment of a Spiritual authority, but one that does not actualize itself in the community apart from Jesus, who in his own historical moment has been seen and heard. Jesus is the basis and criterion. Yet such spiritual authority already implies a charismatic office or prophetic ministry in the church. When we turn to Revelation and the Johannine Letters we can see something of its effect.

The Epistles: Finding Jesus in the Past

When we compare the Gospel with the Epistles, there are, as interpreters have long observed, many similarities, not only in vocabulary and style, but in specifically theological language. They come from the same theological and presumably ecclesiastical circles, if not from the same author.[10] True, the First Epistle lacks the same theological depth, and sharpness, that we find in the Gospel. It is sometimes perplexing, and one wonders whether the author himself was perplexed. Or, as some have seriously suggested, perhaps he had grown old and somewhat less articulate!

However that may be, and we shall not attempt to decide the question of authorship, there is a common theological ground (*Mütterboden*) on which Gospel and Epistles are based. They come from the same school or circle of churches.[11] Yet there are differences. For one thing, the setting or situation is apparently different. The Jewish opponents of Jesus—probably also the opponents of the Johannine church—have disappeared. That is, the opponents are not—I would say no longer—"the Jews," but heretical Christians, whose confession or theology is not only inadequate but dangerous. Their heresy has to do with their view of Jesus, and this in turn is related to the somewhat different perspective on Jesus in the Epistles, particularly 1 John, as compared with that of the Gospel. In the Gospel the presence of Jesus to the church is an urgent need and, for the evangelist, a reality. In the Epistle there is a renewed emphasis on Jesus as a figure of the past. To put it another way, the problem is no longer occasioned by the absence of Jesus, but by his spiritual presence, or at least by what is said about him with the authorization of the Spirit.

Before turning to the Epistles, however, we should consider the Revelation to John, particularly the so-called letters to the seven churches of chapters 2–3. That the author of Revelation is the same as the evangelist or the Elder of the letters (2 and 3 John) is generally, and I think correctly, denied by critical scholarship. (Interestingly, however, only in Revelation does the author call himself John.) The differences in language, literary style, and theology are all too great. Yet there are points of similarity: for example, the emphasis on witness and witnessing (testimony and testifying); the portrayal of Christ as the Word of God

(Rev 19:13); Christ's or his followers' "conquering." (Jörg Frey has once again made the case—I think convincingly—for Revelation's relation to the Johannine school.[12]) For our purposes the most significant connections are found in these letters to the seven churches of Asia.

At the outset John of Patmos sees the heavenly, exalted Son of Man, who announces the messages to be written to each of the angels of the churches. Yet each of these messages is at the end described as "what the Spirit is saying to the churches." So these seem to be messages from Christ delivered in writing to the angels of the seven churches, who presumably deliver their respective messages to the churches themselves. The I-words throughout the letters also make it clear that these are messages of the exalted Jesus Christ himself.[13] It is he who says, "Behold, I stand at the door and knock" (3:20). Yet the whole process is described as the Spirit's speaking to the churches. Thus the heavenly Son of Man, Christ, and the Spirit are very closely associated, if not identified. What is promised from the Paraclete in the Gospel seems to be fulfilled in what is now happening among the churches of Asia Minor (although the Spirit is not called *paraklētos* in Revelation). The message is, or has become, one of ethical exhortation, encouragement, and warning. There are clear hints at the existence of doctrinal problems (for example, "the deep things of Satan" in 2:24; cf. 2:25 and 2 John 9), but in Revelation these do not yet seem central. In 1 and 2 John, however, heresy of a christological sort is the crucial danger.

We can draw some lines of connection among the Gospel, Revelation, and the Epistles. These lines cannot be demonstrated, but they seem quite probable. So how do they connect? What picture can be drawn? First of all, in Revelation and 1 John (probably also 2 John), we see signs of Christian prophets at work—not all, however, on the right side. John of Patmos is himself such a prophet (1:3; 22:18–19), a role that the wicked Jezebel also claims (2:20). (Perhaps it is significant that the Jezebel of Rev 2:20 styles herself a prophetess, even as she leads the church of Thyatira astray.) In the Fourth Gospel such prophets are not explicitly named, but the Paraclete, the Holy Spirit, gives utterance to words of Jesus, either by way of reminder or extending into the present (and future) what Jesus said in the past or would say were he present. Such words were presumably uttered by prophets. As we have noted, such prophets are not mentioned in the Gospel, even as the Spirit-Paraclete is not mentioned in Revelation or the Epistles. Although the Spirit is not called *paraklētos* in 1 John, the exalted Christ is (2:1): "We have an Advocate [*paraklētos*] with the Father." "Thus when the Paraclete is first mentioned in the Gospel, we hear of "another Paraclete" (or Advocate; 14:16), whom the Father will send on Jesus' petition. It may be, as we shall observe, that there are reasons why in 1 John *paraklētos* is used only of Jesus.

If in the Gospel there is no mention of Christian prophets, Jesus himself is called a prophet (4:19; 6:14). While this title may be inadequate for Johannine

Christology, it is not erroneous, and the followers of Jesus recapitulate his ministry (20:21). Perhaps such Christian prophets are not yet mentioned because John presents the disciples as they were during Jesus' historic ministry. They lack postresurrection knowledge and have not assumed the roles they will later play. Yet the role of the Christian prophet in the postresurrection Johannine community was likely a large one. If the Spirit-Paraclete was to pronounce words of Jesus, someone must actually have done the speaking if the words were to be heard throughout the community. Probably the best evidence for the existence of such words of Jesus is the Gospel of John itself. (We have already noted such words in Rev. 1–3, and in 2 Cor 12:8–9 Paul speaks of receiving a word from the Lord.) Virtually all the words of Jesus "sound" Johannine although a number have synoptic parallels. For example 12:25 has the typical Johannine cadence and terminology: "He who loves his life loses it, and he who hates his life in this world will keep it for eternal life." Yet it has impressive synoptic parallels, not only in Mark (8:34 par.), but also in Q (Matt 10:39; Luke 17:33). It has, therefore, triple attestation. One can imagine this is a traditional saying of Jesus of which the Spirit-Paraclete has reminded the community. In contrast, Jesus also says: "I am the way, and the truth, and the life. No one comes to the Father except through me" (14:6). This sounds, and is, quite Johannine and is, moreover, without significant synoptic parallels. One can imagine that this is a Spirit-inspired word originating with the postresurrection, exalted Jesus. This saying suits, and speaks to, the situation of the Johannine church in its conflict with the synagogue. Jesus makes sweeping revelatory and salvific claims for himself, which fit that situation. Those who reject Jesus (that is, the Johannine community's proclamation of Jesus) cut themselves off from God.

Such sayings have often been regarded as theological, literary creations of the evangelist, or his community/church. Perhaps one can too easily imagine the learned theologian sitting at his desk with other Gospels, documents, and fragments of tradition before him, which he regards as inadequate. So he shapes them to suit his needs or creates sayings that will make the theological points that need making. All the time he is thinking: "If I put them on the lips of Jesus everybody will have to acknowledge them." Then they will be authoritative. Possibly, but such a scenario is as improbable in antiquity as it would seem to be today. Are not these words of Jesus more intelligible as Spirit-inspired prophetic words delivered with self-authenticating authority and power, probably within a church whose worship was charismatic?

The portrayal of Jesus promising to send the Spirit-Paraclete also forms an intelligible background for what we read about the work of prophets inspired by the Spirit in Revelation and the Epistles of John. Is the Gospel of John therefore earlier than Revelation and the Epistles? I think so, at least in the case of the Epistles, which seem to presuppose something very much like the Gospel, although they do not quote it.[14] As for Revelation, I do not know. Although ancient tradition puts it late in the first century, in the period of the Emperor Domitian, this is less than certain. It could be earlier, and also earlier than the Gospel of John.[15] Certainly its futuristic eschatology suggests a time earlier than the Gospel, reflecting an urgent apocalyptic expectancy (for example, 22:20) that the Gospel modifies or corrects (cf. John 11:25; 14:22; as well as 21:23).

In the farewell discourses of the Gospel Jesus speaks to disciples who cannot yet understand him because they have not yet attained the postresurrection, eschatological knowledge they will have when Jesus is glorified and they have received the Spirit (7:39). Thus Jesus says things that he understands and the reader who is a Johannine "insider" can understand. But the disciples are not yet in a position to understand. One might say that John has created a literary fiction in the sense that he has portrayed the disciples as they would have been before the glorification of Jesus and Jesus as he was after his glorification. (Actually this is an example of the two levels in John.) In the Revelation to John, however, we see the process the Gospel presumes as future actually at work. That is, Jesus and the disciples are in the same time frame. The exalted Christ speaks words to the churches that are delivered by the Spirit with the help of the prophet who writes these things down. The work of the Spirit is then a factor of fundamental importance holding the Johannine books together. Yet the Gospel, Epistles, and Revelation represent different perspectives, problems and issues.

In Revelation the Spirit is not named the Paraclete, but appears to fulfill the function or role of delivering words of Jesus. In the Epistles also the Spirit-Paraclete is not mentioned and neither is anything said about such a role. Jesus himself is the Paraclete or Advocate. In fact, the Spirit plays a somewhat different role in the Epistles, although the doctrine or concept is there (see 1 John 3:24, 4:13), doubtless corresponding to the experienced reality of the community. Probably the anointing that teaches and provides knowledge is the Holy Spirit (2:20, 27).[16]

In 1 John the abiding of Jesus with believers is contingent upon their obeying his commandments (3:23), as in the Gospel (for example, 14:13–21). The Spirit is then the source, or channel, of the believer's assurance (3:24). So 1 John clearly knows the Gospel or at least its substantive theological content with respect to the Spirit. This knowledge is certainly present, and its importance not denied. Yet the principle and practice of spiritual authority has led to a problem, which is articulated in 1 John 4:1–6. Before getting into that, however, it is important to note that the discussion of the problem that has arisen is framed within an acknowledgment of the work of the Spirit, called in the Fourth Gospel the Paraclete, of course.

Whether or not 1 John knows the Gospel in its present, canonical form, a similar concept of the work of the Spirit is assumed, and this seems to be the basis of the warning given in 4:1–6. The situation addressed here is clear enough. First, the false prophets who have gone into the world are mentioned (4:1). Apparently they utter words that they claim to be Spirit-inspired, but in the author's view only those who confess Jesus Christ come in the flesh are inspired by the Spirit of God (v. 2). Those who do not make this confession are not of God (v. 3). Rather, they give utterance to the spirit of the Antichrist (v. 3) and of error (v. 6). How does one distinguish? By their doctrinal content, of course.[17] The false prophets who are inspired by the spirit of the Antichrist or of error apparently do not confess that Jesus is come in the flesh (v. 2). Thus they do not confess Jesus (v. 3). There is an alternative (v. 3) reading: "does away with Jesus" or "dissolves Jesus" (*luei*) which is attractive, since it implies the docetism that is evidently the issue here, but is not strongly attested and is probably not original.[18]

In 2 John also the same christological issue is raised and here the denial that Jesus has come in the flesh is explicitly said to be the work of deceivers who have gone out into the world (v. 7). Such a person is the deceiver and the Antichrist. Whether 1 John or 2 John is the earlier, the setting or problem situation seems on the face of it to be the same.

Despite the fact that the term *Antichrist* (*antichristos*) is often used to designate the manifestation of the traditional eschatological enemy of God and the Messiah, it actually occurs only in these two Johannine letters in the New Testament, and aside from the passages just noted, only in 1 John 2:18 and 22.[19] In 1 John 2:18–27 his role as the eschatological enemy is made clear. The Antichrist is the one who denies Jesus as the Christ (2:22). It does not say "denies Jesus has come in the flesh," although that is probably meant (as in 2 John 7). Jews, indeed, everyone except the early Christians, denied that Jesus was the Christ—if they thought about the matter at all. A specific confession, or lack of confession, by a specific person or party is apparently in view. The emphasis falls on Jesus rather than Christ: "that *Jesus* is the Christ."

That such a denial of the fleshliness, and therefore the humanity, of Jesus is in view is supported by the prologue of 1 John, which is obviously modeled on the prologue found in the Gospel.[20] As is now commonly observed, "the beginning" (*ap' archēs,* 1:1) is no longer the primordial beginning, but as is immediately evident, the beginning of the Christian tradition, namely, Jesus. Clearly 1 John echoes the Gospel as the Gospel echoes Genesis, but the narrowing down upon Jesus is evident, particularly if this statement is to be understood in light of 4:2–3 and 2 John 7, as it should be. (This interpretation may be circular, but sometimes circularity makes for good interpretation rather than bad.) "What we have heard, what we have seen with our eyes, what we have looked at and touched with our hands" is not a pre-existent word, or even the word of historical revelation in general, but the Word made flesh (John 1:14). What is next said about the life which was with the Father being revealed (v. 2) alludes to the Gospel's prologue; but then to have seen and borne witness points to the historic manifestations of Jesus, as does the subsequent reference in verse 3 to having seen and heard.

As the letter takes an ethical turn the meaning of this beginning in the prologue becomes even clearer (2:3): "Now by this we may be sure that we know him [Jesus] if we obey his commandments." Again, the indissoluble connection of knowledge of Jesus and obedience to him echoes the farewell discourses of the Gospel (14:18–24). Then there is a specific reference to Jesus' commandment that differs strikingly from the Gospel's: "Beloved, I am writing you no new commandment, but an old commandment which you had from the beginning; the old commandment is the word which you have heard" (1 John 2:7). Yet this "old commandment" is also new (1 John 2:8): "Yet I am writing you a new commandment, which is true in him and in you, because the darkness is passing away and the true light is already shining." The author plays upon "old and new," because he and his readers clearly know the new commandment found in the Fourth Gospel (13:34; 15:12). But it has now become important to say first of all that it is old. Why?

Because it comes from Jesus himself. "Whoever says, 'I abide in him,' ought to walk just as he walked" (2:6), that is, "in his steps" (cf. 1 Pet 2:21). The old commandment is the one the followers of Jesus have had from the beginning (ap' archēs again), which they have heard (1 John 2:7). The commandment is of course to love one another (3:11): "For this is the message you have heard from the beginning, that we should love one another." This summation picks up on the initial statement of 1:5: "This is the message we have heard from him and proclaim to you, that God is light, and in him there is no darkness at all." Walking in the light is walking as Jesus walked (2:6), following his example, as well as obeying the command of love: "We know love by this, that he laid down his life for us—and we ought to lay down our lives for one another" (1 John 3:16; cf. John 15:12). Not to follow Jesus' command is to walk in darkness (1:6), no matter what one may say or claim (2:9–10): "Whoever says, 'I am in the light,' while hating a brother or sister, is still in the darkness. Whoever loves a brother or sister lives in the light. Jesus' commandment is "that we should believe in the name of his Son Jesus Christ and love one another, just as he has commanded us" (3:23). In this last statement the subject is really God, but the command clearly comes from Jesus, so closely do God and Jesus coincide—in the Epistle even more than in the Gospel. (No wonder commentators cannot agree on whether the antecedent of a pronoun in 1 John is Jesus or God!)[21] At this point (3:24) the Spirit is mentioned as the one who assures believers of their abiding—in Christ and God. Then follows the warning we have just dealt with about false prophets and the spirit of error (4:1–6).

Later there is a second affirmation of the work of the Spirit (4:13)—"By this we know that we abide in him and he in us, because he has given us of his Spirit." These positive Spirit words frame the warnings about false prophets and their claims. But finally, John returns to the historical Jesus. "And we have seen and testify that the Father has sent his Son as the Savior of the world. Whoever confesses that Jesus is the Son of God, God abides in him, and he in God" (1 John 4:14–15 RSV). Note the emphasis on having seen and testifying. One could say instead of "testify," "bear witness." I like "bear witness," for it implies in English, as it seems to have in Greek, that one sees and reports on what one has seen. Thus in the RSV translation of John 1:34, John (the Baptist) says, "And I have seen and have borne witness that this is the Son of God." Or even in the prologue (1:8): "He was not the light but came to bear witness [NRSV "testify to"] the light." Again in 3:11: "Truly, truly I say to you, we speak of what we know, and bear witness to what we have seen" (RSV). In 1 John the apostolic seeing and testifying means reporting on what one has seen.

Perhaps it has now become evident why the Spirit is not called *paraklētos*, the Paraclete, in 1 John. That title is reserved for Jesus, the exalted Jesus who pleads to the Father (2:1). He is the Jesus of the past, who has been seen, and of the present, but now he is with the Father. (The same construction, *pros* with the accusative, is used in 1 John 2:1 and John 1:2: "The Word was with God.") The idea of advocacy is clearly present, but place is also important, as in the Gospel. Jesus Christ the righteous is still with the Father. What he did and said and continues to do are of utmost relevance. But what he had to say to the church he has already said to his disciples. It is essential that he be remembered and obeyed and that his reality and word not be distorted. Thus the author of 1 John declines to bestow the title of Paraclete (Counselor or Advocate) upon the Spirit, or anyone else. (The evangelist of course knows that Jesus was the original Paraclete, for in 14:16 he introduces the Spirit of truth as another Paraclete.)

In this connection, we should observe that 1 John does not quite close the circle we have attempted to draw here. Nowhere in 1 John (or in the Johannine Epistles) is it said that the prophets in question give utterance to words of Jesus himself. Obviously, the prophets who do not confess that Jesus has come in the flesh (1 John 4:3; 2 John 7) claim the authority of the Spirit, and therefore of God, and presumably of Jesus Christ. If we are on target so far, there is a common charismatic milieu and dimension of the Gospel, Revelation, and Epistles of John. But only in the Gospel and Revelation is Jesus himself represented as speaking through the Spirit. This is promised in the Gospel and attested in

Revelation, but missing in the Epistles. I do not know why it is missing in the Epistles, particularly 1 John, but one can make an educated guess.

Possibly the epistolary author simply does not know, or know of, such Spirit-conveyed words of Jesus. Yet if they are charismatic phenomena characteristic of the Johannine community, this would seem unlikely. Probably he was familiar with the Spirit-inspired utterance of such words. Why then would he not mention them? Although they were a part of his community's worship and practice, he sees a danger inherent in them. Rather than denounce the practice itself, he denounces the false doctrine that has been produced. At the same time he also withholds the title Paraclete from the Spirit, reserving it for Jesus, who *is* our Advocate *with* the Father and *was* present with us. The effect would have been to put the brakes on such Spirit-inspired production of words of Jesus, which nevertheless belonged to the history, tradition, and practice of his community, on which his own theological understanding was based. Thus it became important for him to reiterate that Jesus' command, to love one another, was old, as well as new—that is, it goes back to the earthly Jesus and was delivered during his historic ministry.

John's quest for Jesus has a dual focus, the present and the past. In the Gospel emphasis lies on the present, that is, the presence of Jesus in the church. In the Epistles, especially 1 John, emphasis returns to the past. In the Gospel there is ample evidence that the presence of Jesus is regarded as an extension of his past historical reality. John takes seriously the factuality of Jesus and the trustworthiness of the witness on which the Gospel is based. The question is how does the past reality of Jesus, and the witness to him, extend into the future and thus into the church's present. What are the limitations? Are there criteria? There must be. In 1 John doctrine becomes an essential criterion or test of whether Jesus, or the Spirit of truth, is speaking.[22] This is put succinctly in 1 John 3:23: "And this is his commandment, that he should believe in the name of his Son Jesus Christ and love one another, just as he commanded us." Thus for 1 John particularly, while faith is believing *in*—trusting—there is also an irreducible kernel of believing *that*. There is a givenness of revelation that follows from its historical character. Who Jesus is cannot be separable from who Jesus was, even as who he was can never be isolated from who he is to the believer, and even to the historian. John seems to know this. Moreover, believing, to be meaningful, is inseparable from obeying.

There is then a real and significant sense in which the Epistles, particularly 1 and 2 John, emphasize the continuing necessity of turning again and again to the past, to what was, from the beginning, namely Jesus, in order to understand Christian revelation. To understand is then to obey: to obey Jesus and in doing so to obey God.

We began thinking about the so-called quest of the historical Jesus, a modern undertaking, but one that finds some ancient precedent. Such quests, whether ancient or modern, are seldom, if ever, without some agenda, often theological. Perhaps the Fourth Gospel's approach to Jesus is too self-assured— or Spirit-assured—to best be described as a quest. Moreover, the Fourth Evangelist claims to have a witness, or to be a witness worthy of great confidence. It is of course of fundamental importance to him that the word became flesh and dwelt among us (1:14 RSV).[23] Yet for John the pressing issue is how the pre-existent and glorified, exalted Jesus imposes himself on the present, on us. Fundamentally, the answer is given in the coming of the Spirit-Paraclete, as we have seen. This John presses Jesus into the present and (from Jesus' perspective) the future.

If 1 John is later than the Gospel, as I, along with many commentators, suspect, its author seems deliberately to ignore this process. The Jesus who is, and will be, is still subject to the Jesus who was. The evangelist would not, of course, have denied the was-ness of Jesus, but his interest was shifting forward. The epistolary author, however, wants to emphasize the continuing and normative function of who Jesus was. Thus the new commandment is also the old commandment which the disciples, the church, have had from the beginning (1 John 2:7–8).

There has been in the history of Christianity, as already in the New Testament, a predisposition to look back, to the beginning, for criteria and norms. "The old is better," says Jesus in Luke 5:39 according to some manuscripts. Probably that is not the original reading, but it reflects a classic Christian theological disposition. Finally Jesus is the norm against which what follows— even the claim to speak in Jesus' name—must be judged. Getting back to Jesus is not as easy an undertaking as one might think, or hope. More than two centuries of Jesus research have taught us that. But the impulse to turn back toward Jesus is a very ancient one, one that is reflected in the Johannine literature. While the Gospel sees Jesus in the present, and Revelation sees him in the future as well, 1 John insists on his pastness. The quest of the historical Jesus— or should I say the original Jesus?—has an obvious New Testament basis.

Obviously this fact does not warrant everything that has happened under the aegis of "the Quest" or of "Jesus research." It does, however, make it understandable theologically. And it should not surprise us that we can detect theological agendas at work. On the one hand, I suppose no "purely historical" quest will be willing to admit to such a theological agenda. On the other, no Christology can dispense with any or all historical agendas. Faith in Jesus looks to the past, as well as the present and future.

6

John's Portrait of Jesus

Jesus Portrayed as Talking Christology
in John's Narrative

It is the genius of the Fourth Evangelist to have created a Gospel in which Jesus as the representative of the world above visits and really lives in this world without depriving it of its verisimilitude and without depriving life here of its seriousness. We speak of the presentation of Jesus rather than Johannine Christology. Obviously, christological teaching is implied, and even uttered, in the Fourth Gospel; Jesus teaches about himself. But to speak of Christology is already to put oneself one stage away from the Johannine presentation. Christology is second-order language about Jesus. John's Gospel is a first-order presentation of Jesus. It is not without significance that John wrote a gospel, and thus presented the story of Jesus, and not a theological tract. He does not talk about Jesus, but purports to describe how Jesus acted and talked about himself.

Jesus in John and in the Synoptics

Because John does this, his work invites comparison with other Gospels, especially the Synoptics. (Whether by coincidence or not, no surviving noncanonical gospel extant in its entirety presents a narrative of Jesus' ministry, although such gospels existed.) In making this comparison one inevitably faces the question of whether John wrote with knowledge of any or all of the other Gospels which have been canonized. Yet whether one decides pro or con, and even if he does not decide at all, he will find the comparisons and contrasts illuminating on both sides.

Jesus has been described as a healing, teaching, and suffering Messiah,[1] and in all four Gospels he appears as a Messiah who performs miracles, teaches, and dies. Yet it is not correct to characterize the Jesus of John's Gospel as suffering, nor are his miracles best described as healings. Jesus is certainly designated a teacher in John, yet his teaching is not, and by its nature could not be, understood by his interlocutors. It is a teaching which can, however, be understood by the Christian reader. Although Jesus' suffering is not emphasized in the synoptic passion narratives, the passion predictions describe his death as suffering, and certainly Mark underscores suffering as characteristic of Jesus' ministry. John, however, does no more than hint that Jesus' death involves him in the suffering which the Synoptics strongly suggest. The differences between the Johannine and synoptic portrayals of Jesus' miracles, teaching, and death are in large measure the differences between John and the Synoptics, and the distinctive features of the former become all the clearer when set in contrast with the latter.

The miracles of the Fourth Gospel are, in contrast to the Synoptics, referred to as signs.[2] Other miracles of Jesus which are not recounted are also called signs in this Gospel (2:23; 20:30). As such they point to Jesus as one sent from God and are acknowledged outside the immediate circle of his disciples (3:2). They have the express function of raising the question of who Jesus is and suggesting an answer. Those who are impressed by his signs do not for that reason only know who Jesus really is (3:2ff.), but they are on the right track. Those who want to reject Jesus are reluctant even to credit the authenticity and actuality of his signs (chapter 9). Faith in the Gospel of John is not simply belief in miracles, whether or not it was that in the source or traditions from which the Johannine miracle stories were drawn. Nevertheless, Jesus' miracles can only be understood as events credited as historical which perform a positive function in the theology of the Fourth Gospel.[3] One can infer from their prominence that the miracle stories are taken up or recounted in the first instance because they aptly put the question of Jesus' identity (and thus create the possibility of genuine faith), not because the author wished to correct their erroneous theology. This use of miracles in John thus differentiates it from the Synoptics, although there is a sense in which the miracle stories of those Gospels perform a similar function. This is especially true of Mark. But what is explicit in John (that is, the relationship of miracles to faith) is only implicit in Mark. Moreover, Mark more than John sets a question mark over the validity of miracles as propaedeutic to faith. This is especially true if Peter's confession of Jesus' messiahship, which Jesus all but rejects, is seen as the expression of a popular view of Jesus.

Be that as it may, the miracle tradition which John employs is itself quite different from that found elsewhere. It is often pointed out that none of the demon exorcisms common to the Synoptics is found in John. Perhaps even more astonishing is the fact that no Marcan healing narrative has a Johannine parallel, although there are three or four Johannine stories of a similar sort. The one healing story which has a clear synoptic parallel, that of the ruler's son, is found in Matthew (8:5–13) and Luke (7:1–10) only and is therefore a Q miracle, something of an anomaly. The Johannine miracle stories with clear Marcan parallels are not healings (6:1–15; 6:16–21). Thus one may say that the miracle traditions of Mark and (therefore also of Matthew and Luke), particularly the healings, are not found in John, while the healing miracles of John are also not found in Mark. For that matter, only four miracle stories in John qualify as healings, that is, only a fraction of the number found in Mark or in the Synoptics generally.

Jesus is repeatedly called rabbi or teacher in the Fourth Gospel. In fact, *rabbi* is said to mean teacher (1:38). Somehow the knowledge that Jesus was a teacher, or that he taught, so prevalent in the Synoptics, is still alive in John. But in John, Jesus' teaching has a very narrow focus. As we have noted, he teaches about himself and that teaching is distinctly Christian. While there may be, and likely are, authentic sayings of Jesus in the Johannine discourses, the content, as well as the style, of his teaching can scarcely be historically authentic. Efforts to explain the Johannine Jesus' teaching as essentially authentic historically, whether by invoking the Qumran parallels or not, often end up appealing to well-worn hypotheses of a secret or esoteric teaching found only in John.[4] Such theories, reminiscent of the ancient Gnostics, can scarcely withstand critical scrutiny.

Quite apart from the christological content and emphasis, which is so dominant in the Gospel of John, one finds there another peculiarity. Aside from his discourses and disputes about himself and his own role, Jesus utters no teaching whatever during his public ministry. Only after he has withdrawn with his disciples, his own, does Jesus offer instruction regarding the conduct of life. Even then his instructions lack specificity. Rather, he commands his disciples to love one another as he has loved them (13:34–35). The character of his love for them, and therefore of the love to which they themselves are enjoined, is spelled out further in John 15:12–13. But such specificity as may be found there has to do only with the extent of love—it is to be limitless in its self-giving—not with concrete ways of living and acting in the world. Even 1 John, which dwells upon the necessity of love, does not elaborate upon the nature of love by referring to exemplary instances of loving acts.[5]

The richness, color, specificity, concreteness, and variety which characterize the teaching of Jesus in the Synoptic Gospels are by and large absent from John, as is his apparent willingness and intention to teach anyone who would listen the demands and will of God in view of the near advent of his kingdom. We have no parables, no pronouncement stories in John; therefore, we have none of the brief epigrammatic sayings which are so characteristic of the synoptic Jesus. Neither can much of Q or of the didactic elements of Mark, M, or L be found. Instead, the Johannine Jesus expounds Christology and argues with his theological opponents, the Jews.

Any suffering of Jesus at his death can at most be imputed to the Fourth Gospel on the basis of other sources. In John, Jesus goes to the cross by his own volition and by his own decision. He decides when the hour for his departure in death has arrived, or rather he alone knows when the Father has decreed that his hour has come. He lays down his own life; no one takes it from him (10:18). In John, Jesus' death is his glorification, not his humiliation.[6] No narrative typifies this more than the Johannine account of his arrest (18:1–11). There is no anguish of Jesus just preceding it. Gethsemane is at most alluded to in 12:27. Instead, Jesus seems to direct his own arrest even as later he will direct his own death (19:28–30). Jesus does nothing, and nothing happens to him, by chance; and this is nowhere more evident than in the account of his death, whether in the passion narrative proper or in the many references and allusions to it throughout the Gospel. In his conversation with Pilate at his trial, Jesus explains what is going on, in contrast to the Synoptics in which he remains silent throughout. Perhaps it is too much to say that Jesus interrogates Pilate, rather than Pilate interrogating Jesus; yet it is nevertheless clear that Jesus, not Pilate, is in control of matters. Indeed, Jesus' own steadfast purpose is contrasted, probably quite deliberately, with Pilate's uncertainty.

By way of summary, in John as in the Synoptics Jesus appears as miracle worker and teacher as well as the one destined for death. Yet in contrast with the Synoptics the Jesus of John performs miracles expressly to signify who he is. Such works are not acts of compassion—only a few are healings—nor are they manifestations of the in-breaking eschatological power. The Johannine Jesus' teaching is explicitly, and rather narrowly, christological, lacking the diversity and specificity of the Synoptics. Not surprisingly, then, the tragic dimensions of Jesus' death, his own anguish and suffering in the face of it, are largely absent in John. He dies as man is scarcely known to die. If in Mark Jesus utters a cry of dereliction and in Luke a pious prayer, in John Jesus marks the end of his own earthly ministry and work with the imperious pronouncement "It is finished."

It should be possible to account for the obvious and significant differences in this broadly similar portrayal of Jesus, but this is not easy to do, as the history of the discussion of the problem clearly shows. Traditionally, it has been suggested that John knew the other Gospels and intended to deepen or supplement their presentation. Some critical scholarship, working on similar premises regarding the relationship of John to the Synoptics, arrived at the view that John intended not to supplement but to supplant the other Gospels.[7] Subsequently, the assumption that John knew the Synoptics at all was seriously called into question.[8] Certainly it is now no longer possible to assume that John's differences from the Synoptics can be accounted for by recourse to his alleged intention to augment or to alter them. If he knew one or more of them, he did not regard them as authoritative scripture. They were more or less at the periphery of his consciousness. The shape and character of the Fourth Gospel were apparently determined by other factors.

At this point it is relevant to indicate the hermeneutical issue raised by the question of John's historical relationship to the other Gospels. Whether or not the Fourth Evangelist wrote with knowledge of the Synoptics, and whatever his intention with respect to them, the church ultimately accepted John's Gospel as a part of the canon of scripture alongside and in conjunction with the Synoptic Gospels. Therefore, the interpretation of the Fourth Gospel in its original purpose and intent is one thing, but the interpretation of that Gospel in its canonical content may be something else. The possibility, suggested by Ernst Käsemann, that the Gospel of John was accepted precisely because in the passage of time it was misunderstood cannot be ruled out a priori.[9] But if that is the case, is the interpretation of John in the church of necessity the continuation of that misinterpretation? On these terms a positive answer to this question can scarcely be avoided, at least in principle, but the sharpness of the question and the alternative it implies (historical or churchly exegesis) will be mitigated somewhat if it can be shown that the purpose and character of John are a function of historical circumstances different from those of the Synoptics, rather than of a fundamentally antithetical theological insight or intent.

Jesus in the Johannine Milieu

A consideration of the origin of the distinctive Johannine presentation of Jesus is therefore germane to this question. It has frequently been proposed that John relies upon sources, otherwise unknown, which are different from, although not altogether unrelated to, the Synoptic Gospels.[10] In all probability he does, but this hypothesis only pushes the question of the Johannine milieu, and the influences shaping the Fourth Gospel, back one step farther. What sort of Christian community, subject to what influences, produced the substance, as well as the present form, of the Gospel of John?

The answer that this document is the product of a community of Christians who had undergone a traumatic exit or expulsion from the synagogue goes a long way toward explaining the distinctive character of the Fourth Gospel, if it does not answer every question about its provenance and purpose.[11] The miracles are signs, if not proofs, of Jesus' messianic dignity, and the discourses and dialogues of the first half of the Gospel concentrate upon the question of Jesus' identity and role. Just such a fixation upon the christological question fits the proposed church-synagogue milieu. That milieu in turn helps explain the eristic character of the first half of the Gospel especially, as well as its intense concentration on Christology. Jesus himself is portrayed as the origin of the dispute between Christians (Christ-confessors) and the synagogue, and his affirmations about himself become the warrant and justification for the Christian community's claims for him.

Doubtless those very claims are, in John, cast in the terminology of the Johannine community's confession. Yet at the same time, that community would insist that the christological claims and confession are rooted in and derive from Jesus himself.[12] (In this John is like each of the other evangelists, but he goes far beyond them in attributing explicit Christology to Jesus.) Whether that position is defensible is a good question, and one scarcely answerable in terms of whether or not Jesus actually said such things. Probably he did not.[13] The real question is whether John's presentation of him in these terms is on any grounds legitimate. Certainly it is not if one is seeking an "objective historical account," whatever that may be. It is understandable and legitimate only from a distinctively Christian perspective, that is, only on the confessional position that Jesus is the Christ. On that basis John's presentation is legitimate and becomes enlightening and suggestive. From any other perspective it is offensive, just as in the Gospel Jesus' claims for himself are offensive to those who do not share the belief of his followers.

That belief, its implicated hopes and uncertainties, becomes transparent in the so-called farewell discourses and final prayer (chapters 13–17). There the presupposition of a community of his followers surviving more than a generation after his departure, with all the problems attendant upon their perilous situation in the unfriendly world, is plainly evident. It is such a community, with its peculiar traditions and history, which through one of its gifted members has produced the presentation of Jesus found in the Fourth Gospel.

The possible influence of Gnosticism or Qumran upon the Fourth Gospel is certainly not to be discounted.[14] The evangelist and his community were as much influenced by the surrounding culture as were the authors of any number of other ancient documents one might mention. Yet the similarity of outlook and terminology between John and some Gnostic and Essene writings may be as much a derivative of a similarity of perspective on the community and outsiders as the expression of an actual direct influence, much less literary relationship. John, the Gnostics, and the Essenes shared a similar sectarian attitude toward themselves and the world. This clear distinction between those who are in and those who are not, and the history of that distinction, is as much as anything else characteristic of the Fourth Gospel and determinative of its nature.[15]

John's Unique Metahistorical Presentation of Jesus

The historical circumstances which produced the Johannine presentation of Jesus are important for understanding it, but they do not really "explain" it, nor can they be substituted for it. John's presentation of Jesus comes alive in the narrative itself. He is the Jesus of the past who lived and worked in first-century Palestine among his fellow Jews. His conflicts with his contemporaries have been overlaid, but not lost, in the portrayal of him as the origin of his community's struggle with the synagogue.[16] His miraculous deeds are no longer harbingers of the power of the in-breaking kingdom of God, or even signs of the eschatological crisis precipitated by Jesus' ministry, much less deeds of love and mercy, but are signs of Jesus' messiahship and sonship. Yet in both cases the present role of Jesus and his followers is understood as based upon the historic work of Jesus of Nazareth, interpreted and refracted in the community's tradition and in the Gospel. Moreover, the death of Jesus, portrayed as the work of his Jewish opponents, was nevertheless a real event. Although John's portrayal represents a common early Christian tendency to blame "the Jews" for Jesus' death, at the same time it contains ample evidence pointing in alternative directions.[17]

The Jesus of the Fourth Gospel is also the Jesus of the church's present and future. He is the source of the Spirit-Paraclete who abides with the church in its witness and especially in its adversity. Even as Jesus is depicted as present in the conflict with the synagogue which produced the Johannine community, so he is portrayed as the source of unity, stability, and purpose in the community's continued existence in the world. This presence of Jesus is not only given in the contemporary Johannine community, that is, contemporary with the author; it is given as an abiding assurance to the community about its own future: Jesus will continue to come to, and dwell among, his disciples.

The Spirit or Paraclete as the mode of Jesus' abiding with his disciples seems to be a felt reality, a presence regarded as given rather than imagined.[18] It is not, in other words, a mere theological idea of the evangelist or of his community. Exactly how the Spirit-Paraclete makes the presence of Jesus known and felt in the community is never stated in so many words. That is, the exact mode of his activity, the phenomenology of his presence, is not described, although his function is clear enough. Especially, the emphasis on the Spirit's bringing to recollection and expanding upon Jesus' own teaching suggests that the Spirit-Paraclete worked through the leadership or ministry of the Johannine community. This does not necessarily mean that an ordained ministry of the Johannine church administered or dispensed the Spirit. Quite possibly the gift of the Spirit, especially in the functions described, authenticated the leadership of the church. The leadership of the Johannine church mediates the presence of Jesus to the congregation through the Spirit. But does the choice of leadership determine who shall possess the Spirit? In all likelihood the other way around; the intervention and work of the Spirit determined the leadership of the church. Yet it is clear that the Spirit alone cannot authenticate itself (cf. 1 John 4:6). If the Spirit is nothing other than the continuing presence and revelation of Jesus to his followers, any continuation of that presence or revelation must bear a positive relation to the historical figure.[19] John's Jesus is intended to do just that, despite his Christian theological dress.

The conviction that this Jesus, who lived and died a half century or more before and in his exalted state returns through the Spirit to abide with his church, is more than an important historical personage of continuing significance and memory is expressed in the recurring references to his pre-existence, heavenly abode, and descent and ascent to and from the world of humankind. To say that these "mythological" concepts are exhausted in their meaning by their existential significance, that is, their expression of the importance of Jesus for the believer or the community, may be an unwarranted truncation of their scope. Such an assertion, however, is certainly not without foundation. Hazardous as it may be to claim that the evangelist did not take the language of pre-existence and accompanying phenomena literally, it is nevertheless unnecessary to attribute to him the crudest kind of understanding of this constellation of mythological concepts. Surely he shows evidence of some sophistication, whether literary or theological, throughout his Gospel. If an existentialist, or other modern, interpretation of this Johannine language runs the risk of reading too much into the Gospel, or excluding certain dimensions of its meaning, it is not therefore necessarily wrong in principle. The simple, yet mysterious, character of Johannine language invites the reader to inquire about and explore its meaning.

The presentation of Jesus in the Fourth Gospel is multidimensional. He is still the Jewish man of Galilee. But he is also the spiritual presence with, and head of, the community of disciples which we may safely call his church. He has been with the church in its past struggles and will continue with it into the foreseeable future. His nature is, however, never understood until his origin and destiny with God are truly comprehended. He and the Father are one; he goes forth from the Father and returns; not only he, but his followers as well, will abide with the Father for all eternity. There is no major aspect of this Johannine presentation of Jesus which is absolutely unique or foreign to other strains of early Christianity, even to the Synoptic Gospels.[20] What is uniquely Johannine is the way these aspects of, or perspectives on, Jesus are made to coalesce into a single narrative so that each is always present in almost every part of the narrative. For example, in the prologue the reader is reminded of the historical figure as well as of the Jesus Christ who is the origin of grace and truth. In the account of his deeds one is similarly aware that the worker of signs is more than a miracle worker out of the past. In the account of his death one is, on the one hand, made cognizant of the overarching cosmic and historic frame in which that death is overcome, and, on the other, not allowed to forget that it was a real, historic death of a human being.[21] The farewell discourses are words of the exalted one; but he is still recognizably the person whose ministry has just been recounted, and the shadow of his death now looms in the foreground. It is the genius of the Fourth Evangelist to have created a Gospel in which Jesus as the representative of the world above visits and really lives in this world without depriving it of its verisimilitude and without depriving life here of its seriousness.

A Concluding Reservation

Yet the presentation of Jesus in the Fourth Gospel should not be represented as the culmination of a development in the New Testament, or among the Gospels, of such a sort and magnitude as to render all that came before it or stands beside it superfluous. If John Calvin rightly saw in the Fourth Gospel the key to the others, he did not for that reason regard it as rendering the others unnecessary.[22] The uniqueness of the Gospel of John and, indeed, its theological worth, is enhanced when it is placed alongside the other Gospels and seen with them. Apart from the Synoptics the Johannine portrait of Jesus specifically, as distinguished from other characters such as the man born blind, the woman of Samaria, and Nicodemus, loses much of its depth and color. In fact, if we had had no Synoptics, the Johannine portrait of Jesus would doubtless have produced a rather different configuration of Christian belief than has actually emerged historically. Whether or not John should be described as incipiently docetic,[23] whether or not it is in part the product of gnostic influence, it is nevertheless the case that there is not in that Gospel a depiction of the man Jesus fully capable of standing guard over his genuine humanity. That depiction is present in the Synoptic Gospels, whether because of or in spite of the intentions of their authors.

Moreover, the valid spirituality of the Fourth Gospel would have been jeopardized if Jesus' statement that his kingdom is not of this world had been allowed to stand unbalanced by the Synoptics' presentation of the kingdom as a reality breaking into this world. That Johannine statement about the kingdom is not wrong, even by synoptic standards, but standing alone and in the Fourth Gospel it opens wide a door to the temptation to make of Christianity a thoroughly otherworldly religion. In its canonical context, however, the potential thrust of such a statement is balanced, yes, blunted, by other statements about the relationship of God's kingdom (and Christ) to this world. Indeed, such statements do not really contradict the theological intention of the Fourth Evangelist, who portrays Jesus praying to the Father not to take his followers out of this world, but to protect them from the Evil One.

7

Jesus Tradition in the Gospel of John

Are John's Differences from the Synoptics Coincident with Their Historical Value?

For the purposes of this chapter, *Jesus tradition* refers to material or data that may stem from Jesus of Nazareth or from the period and places of his activity and death. Without claiming comprehensiveness, I intend to give an indication of its maximal extent in John. At the outset two matters related to the existence and character of such tradition should be noted: first, the Gospel's apparent claim to be written by or based upon the testimony of an eyewitness (21:24; cf. 19:35); second, its relation to, and differences from, the Synoptic Gospels.

Both the eyewitness claim and the authorship claim demand further scrutiny. What is said at the conclusion of the Gospel (21:24) is only that the one who is testifying and his testimony are true. But this statement in the narrative context (21:20) clearly implies an eyewitness claim (cf. 19:35). At best, the claim of 21:24 does not necessarily mean that the Gospel was itself written by the disciple whom Jesus loved (21:20). He is designated as the one who "testifies to these things and has written them" or "caused them to be written" (cf. 19:1 NRSV for an analogous translation: *emastigōsen* is properly translated "had [him] flogged"). With either translation the truth claim should be taken seriously, although not at face value.[1]

John's differences from the Synoptic Gospels are far-reaching, but like them John purports to narrate the career of Jesus in early-first-century Palestine. In fact, the name *Iēsous* occurs much more frequently in John (237 times) than in any of the others (Matthew 150; Mark 81; Luke 89). The issue and its implications for the historical value of John can be put simply. If John is totally dependent on the Synoptics for its knowledge of Jesus, then the question of Jesus tradition in John is already answered. Presumably there would be none, for wherever John departs from the Synoptics, it would depart from history. This resolution of the matter is not basically different from the position that dominated criticism until P. Gardner-Smith proposed that John was written independently of the Synoptics.[2] In that case every difference from the Synoptics becomes a case to be decided on its own merits. Independence opens a range of possibilities, but no individual case proves historicity in general. My procedure will be to give precedence to the question of Jesus tradition in John, without deciding in advance the question of John and other Gospels. Yet the question of Jesus tradition in John will often hinge upon cases in which the Fourth Gospel differs from the Synoptics.

Where John differs widely from the Synoptic Gospels, such differences have been thought to speak against John's historical reliability and value:

1. John's narrative of Jesus' ministry differs widely in sheer content. Simply put, most of what is found in John does not appear in the Synoptic Gospels, and vice versa. Only John's Passion Narrative offers an extended parallel to the Synoptics.

2. John differs in chronology and geography. Whereas in the Synoptics Jesus' ministry appears to span a year or less, and he is in Jerusalem only once, to attend the final Passover feast, in John it lasts between two and three years, as three different Passovers are mentioned. In John he is frequently in Jerusalem (or Judea), attending Tabernacles (7:2) and Hanukkah (10:22), as well as more than one Passover. Thus Jesus' ministry is of significantly longer duration and seems centered in Jerusalem and Judea rather than in Galilee, as in the Synoptics.

3. John's account of Jesus' miracles is also significantly different from that of the Synoptics. Matthew and Luke for the most part take up the miracle stories of Mark and also categorize Jesus' deeds as *dynameis,* "mighty works" or "deeds of power." John, however, calls them *semeia,* "signs." They signify who Jesus is, and are often discussed at some length. Moreover, John's miracle stories are to all appearances not about the same events as Mark's or the Synoptics', except for the feeding of the five thousand (John 6:1–15), the only miracle recounted in all four Gospels. At the same time, there are many fewer miracles in John than in the Synoptics, and there are no demon exorcisms or leper cleansings. How are such differences to be accounted for?

4. Finally, the Gospel of John's presentation of Jesus' own message is radically different from what is found in the Synoptics. He speaks and argues with opponents about himself, his status and role. The "I am" sayings (for example, John 6:35: "I am the bread of life") are typical of the Fourth Gospel. There is little that is comparable in the others, in which Jesus proclaims not himself but God's kingdom or rule. He teaches about many specific subjects (for example, purity, giving alms,

prayer, and the expression of piety), often using parables, of which the Fourth Gospel is virtually bereft.

Probably Jesus' self-proclamation is the chief factor in John's having been largely set aside in modern Jesus research, the quest of the historical Jesus. Albert Schweitzer credits David Friedrich Strauss with the demonstration that John's Gospel is not a historical source to be placed on the same level as the Synoptics.[3] John's presentation, Strauss had argued, is dominated by later church Christology, as is most clearly evident in the discourses of Jesus. Strauss's view was to prevail, against liberal as well as conservative theologians.[4] The Johannine portrait of Jesus as God striding about the earth is not the product of Jesus' own self-consciousness but of the evangelist's theology.[5] Strauss's devaluation of John as a historical source has had a lasting effect and is reflected in books as diverse as those of John Dominic Crossan and E. P. Sanders,[6] as well as in works by authors, such as N. T. Wright, with more explicitly theological interest in the study of the historical Jesus.[7] Wright's statement is representative of the latter. He says of his own work that it is "largely based on the synoptic gospels" and that "the debate to which I wish to contribute in this book has been conducted almost entirely in terms of the synoptic tradition."[8]

Yet at least two recent and important investigations of the historical Jesus diverge significantly from this consensus: Paula Fredriksen, *Jesus of Nazareth, King of the Jews,* and John P. Meier, *A Marginal Jew.*[9] Similarly, John played a prominent role in Raymond E. Brown's *The Death of the Messiah,* which deals only with the Passion Narratives.[10] There have also been efforts to address historical Jesus questions from the Johannine side. The most noteworthy of these is C. H. Dodd's *Historical Tradition in the Fourth Gospel,* a work published in the 1960s and not likely soon to be superseded.[11] Nevertheless, the view that the Johannine Jesus is the Christ of the church's faith, while the Jesus of the Synoptic Gospels and their strands of tradition represents much more accurately the historical Jesus, continues to prevail.

The Johannine christological terms and concepts, which likely arose in bitter sectarian conflict, in time became common coinage among Christians who did not understand their origin, and played a fundamental role in the development of the great creedal formulations of the fourth and fifth centuries.[12] But the controversies as represented in the Gospel are also those of a later, postresurrection, time. Certainly Jesus engaged in controversy. Yet Jesus' own controversies with opponents did not center on Christology as that set of doctrines developed in the postresurrection church. That the two levels of controversy were integrally related is, however, a premise upon which the Gospel is based, as has been eloquently argued by J. Louis Martyn, *History and Theology in the Fourth Gospel.*[13] Martyn is, however, concerned with the controversies and conflict of a Johannine community that looks to a Jesus present to his disciples through the Spirit (Paraclete) rather than the *einmalig* level of the historical figure of Jesus.

What then may be historical Jesus tradition in John, and how may one make a determination? Elements or items in John deserve consideration as possibly historical that: (1) without reproducing the Synoptics accord with the picture of Jesus found in them; (2) do not advance the distinctively Johannine Christology; and (3) are historically plausible in the time, place, and setting of Jesus' ministry.[14] Not all these general criteria need come into play at any one point. Any treatment of the subject divides itself naturally into three parts: the Johannine narrative versus the Marcan; sayings tradition in John; and John's purportedly factual information. Perhaps not surprisingly, the narrative and related issues loom largest.

The Johannine Portrayal of Jesus' Ministry versus the Synoptic

Itinerary and Chronology

Justified skepticism about the historicity of the Johannine portrait of Jesus has affected historical judgments about other aspects of the Gospel. The acceptance of the priority of Mark was at first accompanied by the widespread assumption that the Marcan narrative is basically historical. But the view that the priority of Mark warranted the acceptance of the historicity of the Marcan narrative framework began to dissipate with William Wrede, against whose "thoroughgoing skepticism" Schweitzer struggled, presenting his own "thoroughgoing eschatology" as the only viable alternative.[15] Schweitzer had seen the historical inadequacies of the Marcan narrative structure, and Jesus' itinerary, as had Wrede. Yet, as in the case of the theories he so effectively criticized, it was Schweitzer's own imagination that actually supplied the glue (knowledge of Jesus' eschatological intention) to hold the narrative together. With the rise of form and redaction criticism, Wrede's view of Mark and the Synoptics generally has prevailed. Thus Mark's narrative framework is now taken to be a theological and literary product, not a historical, in the sense of chronological, account of Jesus' ministry and itinerary.

Moreover, Paula Fredriksen makes the simple but significant observation that in contrasting John and the Synoptics, it is not a case of one against three, but one against one, since in their narrative frameworks Matthew and Luke generally follow Mark.[16] Thus she proposes that John's longer ministry, with periodic journeys to Jerusalem, is inherently more plausible. The Gospel narratives, which portray Caiaphas and Pilate as having a sense of the character of Jesus and his intentions, require some explanation of why this might be so. It becomes readily understandable if Jesus had been something of a public figure, whose words and deeds were known not only in Galilee, but also from his not infrequent pilgrimages to the Holy City, which John reports. Thus, Fredriksen maintains, he was not unknown to the principal Roman and high priestly authorities. Pilate did not hunt down his followers because he already knew they were not political revolutionaries. He put Jesus to death because his crucifixion would be an example to those who might be. At the same time, Caiaphas and the chief priests viewed Jesus as a potential rabble-rouser, a threat to the concordat they had worked out with the governing Roman authorities, someone they would gladly dispense with.[17]

A longer ministry not limited to Galilee would also help explain or accommodate other aspects of John's narrative, which are arguably historical, such as John's account of Jesus' continuing relationship to John the Baptist. The Baptist material is a structural feature of the evangelical narrative of Jesus' ministry. John, as well as the Synoptics and a couple of the missionary speeches in the Book of Acts (10:37; 13:24), makes clear that the ministry is to be reckoned as following upon Jesus' encounter with John the Baptist.

Jesus' Relationship to John the Baptist

In his comprehensive study, *A Marginal Jew,* Meier portrays John as Jesus' mentor. Was Jesus at one time a disciple of John? Meier's answer is that he was, but that apart from John chapters 1 and 3, no one would suggest this, that is, not on the basis of Q and Marcan tradition.[18] In John Jesus makes his debut not in Galilee (cf. Mark 1:9) but in Bethany beyond the Jordan, where John was baptizing (1:28), that is, in John's territory. Moreover, "the Fourth Gospel's indication that Peter and other disciples first met Jesus in the circle of the Baptist's disciples may well be true."[19] Decades ago Rudolf Bultmann suggested that John's sending his disciples to Jesus (1:35–42) implied that Jesus drew disciples from the Baptist, and that perhaps the evangelist himself had once belonged to Baptist circles.[20]

Jesus' relation to John (never called "the Baptist" in the Fourth Gospel) does not end with the call stories. In Q (Luke 7:18–36, esp. vv. 18–23; Matt 11:2–19) the Baptist is in touch with Jesus through his own disciples from prison. In John, however, Jesus and the Baptist are portrayed as working contemporaneously, for (contrary to the Synoptics) "John had not yet been thrown into prison" (3:24). What is more, not only John, but Jesus also, is engaged in baptizing (3:22, 26; 4:1). Then as if someone has caught a slipup, not Jesus but only his disciples are said to be baptizing (4:2). Yet in the Synoptics there is also no record of his disciples' baptizing. (Many commentators understandably take 4:2 to be a later editorial note.) Moreover, in the Marcan story line there is a sharp demarcation between the time of the Baptist and that of Jesus (1:14–15), which allows for no interval in which Jesus might have been a member of the Baptist's following or working alongside him. John's account gives support to those who, with Eusebius of Caesarea (*Historia Ecclesiastica* III. 24. 7–13), thought that John wrote about events that took place before the imprisonment of John the Baptist, while the other Gospels dealt only with matters coming after his imprisonment. For this reason alone John allows a greater time span for Jesus' ministry.

The basic historicity of the scene(s) in which Jesus and John appear as baptizing rivals is supported by the criterion of embarrassment.[21] Even Jesus' baptism by John was an embarrassment to early Christians. Therefore, John does not explicitly mention it, and Matthew has the Baptist offer a solution that relieves the embarrassment (Matt 3:14). The *Gospel of the Nazareans* (Fragment 2) and the *Gospel of the Ebionites* (Fragment 3) reflect a similar embarrassment.[22] It is unlikely that John the evangelist would have created a scene that actually works against his effort to keep the Baptist in his proper place (cf. 1:6–8, 15, 19–23, 31; 3:30). Their relationship is much more complex than in the Synoptics, and the character of that complexity suggests we are learning something about its historicity not conveyed in the Synoptics.

The Feeding of the Five Thousand

While most of John's miracle stories are basically similar to the synoptic type, one affords a clear parallel, the Feeding of the Five Thousand (6:1–15). The Feeding of the Four Thousand is omitted by Luke, as well as by John, apparently reflecting the fact that it is a doublet. As such it seems to be a secondary addition to an earlier tradition that contained only one feeding story. Luke also omits Jesus' walking on the water (John 6:16–21), along with all of Mark 6:45–8:26.

As in the Synoptics, and Mark particularly, the feeding story (or stories) constitutes a pivotal point in the narrative. In Mark, of course, the Confession of Peter (8:27–31) follows hard upon the second feeding and introduces the crucial central portion of the narrative in which Jesus' opponents' hostility and his own death are increasingly foreshadowed. Something similar happens in John. Although the sharp hostility of "the Jews" has already emerged in chapter 5, it becomes unremitting after chapter 6. John chapters 5 and 6 constitute a turning point in the Fourth Gospel, just as Mark 8 (or Mark chapters 6 and 8) constitutes a turning point in that Gospel. In John also a version of Peter's confession (6:67–71) follows upon the feeding story, as well as the departure of many of Jesus' disciples (6:60–66). Such a withdrawal at this turning point of Jesus' ministry might well have happened, although no other Gospel reports it. Their departure actually suggests that this is a turning point of the ministry. In any event, we see here either John's rather remote imitation of Mark or a parallel pattern of Jesus' ministry.

At the conclusion of the feeding narrative, there are a couple of remarkable statements not found in the Synoptics. First, Jesus is said by the people to be "the prophet who is coming into the world" (v. 14; cf. 4:19), probably the prophet of Deuteronomic expectation (Deut 18:15–22). Then, "When Jesus realized that they were about to come and take him by force to make him king, he withdrew again to the mountain by himself" (v. 15 NRSV). Jesus is also king (that is, Messiah). The fact that this statement leads nowhere in John's narrative already suggests that it is older tradition, and possibly stems from a situation in Jesus' ministry. That Jesus has conducted a messianic banquet suggests that he is the Messiah, or king. As the king of the Jews, Jesus was executed by the Romans. The people's desire to acclaim him as king, which John so vividly portrays, may then have some historical basis, and suggests the possibility that this feeding episode is not only a turning point in the narrative, but also in Jesus' ministry.[23] In other words, if John 6:14–15 is for the author a given, and not his redaction (as seems probable), this bespeaks the existence of a traditional narrative pattern, one common to John and Mark, in which the feeding played a pivotal role.

In addition, John's divergent placement of the feeding on the other (Transjordanian) side of the Sea of Galilee is odd (6:1; *peran tēs thalassēs*). But while Mark presumes it takes place on the western side (where the traditional site of Tabgha is situated), Luke has it at Bethsaida, halfway between, so to speak (Luke 9:10). Commentators struggle to understand why John has moved the feeding, since he must then somewhat awkwardly describe how everyone got back to the Capernaum side (John 6:17, 24, 59). Without claiming too much for history, the exegete should note the possibility that John is here dealing with a traditional given. Moreover, Mark's account of Jesus' sea voyages also presents problems. In John at least the disciples' departure in a boat (John 6:17) is explained: they are going to the other side for what must happen in Capernaum, Jesus' bread discourse (6:59). According to Mark (6:45) they are going "to the other side" (Gr. *eis to peran*) to Bethsaida, which is not exactly across the sea from Tabgha on the western wide. (Thus p45 with some reason deletes the phrase.) The point is not that John must be historically correct, but that just the Gospel's awkwardness suggests we are dealing with something other than the evangelist's own composition or redaction of Mark.

The Portrayal of the Disciples

Perhaps related to this narrative pattern, in which there is a kind of revelatory point, and turning point, in Jesus' public ministry, is the portrayal of the disciples in both John and Mark. It is noteworthy that only after the feedings does Mark have Jesus predict his coming death openly and explicitly (Mark 8:31; 9:31; 10:33), although the disciples nevertheless cannot grasp his meaning. In John, allusions to his death in this context, while real, are more subtle (for example, John 6:15, 51, 71). The disciples' failure to understand in Mark is an aspect of Mark's messianic secret. There is no specifically messianic secret in John, for Jesus' identity is revealed from the beginning of the narrative. Yet there is also in John a pervasive inability on the part of the disciples to understand

Jesus and what is transpiring, even at the end of their final conversation with him (16:29–33). They will know only in retrospect after his death and resurrection (2:17, 22; 12:16; 13:7). Wrede was aware of this Johannine version of the messianic secret and observed that John is in this respect closer to Mark than are Matthew and Luke.[24] We are confronted with a similar or analogous motif in these quite different Gospel narratives, namely, the ignorance of the disciples despite Jesus' self-revelation. Does John adapt what he has read in Mark or does the kinship lie more deeply embedded in the early Christian tradition? In other words, is the messianic secret earlier than any of the Gospels (as Wrede himself thought)?

Among the disciples, Peter plays a leading role, as in the Synoptics, but figures in different narratives. (For example, John 13:1–20, esp. vv. 6–9; 20:2–6, and the whole of chapter 21 are without clear parallel in the Synoptics.) The disciples are twelve in number (6:67, 70–71; 20:24); they were chosen by Jesus (6:70); but there is no list of the Twelve in John and no account of their appointment (cf. Mark 3:13–19). Those who are named as Jesus' disciples are for the most part known from the lists in the Synoptics and Acts.

Yet some disciples (other than Peter) who are named play a larger role in John than in the Synoptics. This is particularly true of Thomas (11:16; 14:5; 20:24–28; 21:2), but also of Philip (1:43–48; 6:5, 7; 12:21–22; 14:8–9) and Andrew, Simon Peter's brother (1:40, 41; 6:8; 12:22), as well as Nathanael (1:45–49; 21:2), who is not named in the Synoptics. (In John 1:44 Simon Peter and Andrew, as well as Philip, are said to be from Bethsaida, apparently contradicting Mark for no obvious reason.) The role of such disciples is all the more striking since James and John, the sons of Zebedee frequently mentioned in the Synoptics, are never called by name in the Fourth Gospel (not even in 21:2)—and yet this Gospel is later ascribed by tradition to a John, presumably the son of Zebedee.

To what extent does this naming of disciples and assigning them different or distinctive roles represent ancient, possibly historical, tradition? We may instance two positive examples worth consideration. First, the risen Jesus' meeting with Peter (21:1–14) and the subsequent conversation with him (21:15–22) is probably historical with respect to two elements: it may be the surviving narrative of Jesus' first resurrection appearance (cf. 1 Cor 15:5; Mark 14:28; 16:7), and it also portrays Peter's recovery and restoration after his denial and desertion of Jesus. While it is scarcely the protocol of a conversation, it portrays a historical reality in narrative and conversational form. Second, the prominence of Thomas is not insignificant. We now possess a gospel attributed to him, which in itself bespeaks the existence of a Thomas tradition. Although it is composed mainly of synoptic-like tradition, its gnosticizing character is reminiscent of John. Moreover, the role played by Thomas in the Gospel of John is not purely negative. At one point he expresses the kind of loyalty to Jesus that

Peter eventually lacked (11:16); he raises a crucial question with Jesus at the beginning of the farewell discourses (14:5); he demands to see as others have before he will believe (20:24–29). This demand is routinely viewed negatively by exegetes, probably because of Jesus' concluding blessing of those who have not seen (v. 29), which refers to the Gospel's audience (cf. 17:20). Thomas is, however, present with those who see the risen Jesus by the sea, where he is named immediately after Simon Peter (21:2). Does the Thomas tradition of John also bespeak his historical role? This may be too much to claim, but some anterior, historical connection between Thomas traditions and Johannine traditions remains a factor to be reckoned with.[25]

Miracle Traditions

The gospel genre and structure was in its inception and development closely related to the narration of Jesus' miracles, his deeds of power according to the Synoptics or signs (*semeia*) according to John. The Johannine miracle traditions differ from those of the Synoptics in that they are for the most part simply different stories. These *semeia,* while markedly fewer, are usually followed by extensive discussions and discourses in which their significance is brought out, even as skeptical opponents call them into question. The issues that emerge here are of a piece with the refutation of Jesus' explicit christological teaching by "the Jews" elsewhere in John. Not surprisingly in this Gospel, three of the miracles occur in Jerusalem or in nearby Bethany (chapters 5, 9, and 11), whereas in the Synoptics no Jerusalem miracles are narrated (although they are mentioned in Matt 21:14–15). In most cases in John, however, a narrative nucleus can be isolated that is similar in form to synoptic-type miracle stories. Arguably, these narratives are more likely to be historical, in the sense of going back to the historical figure of Jesus, than the Johannine Jesus' discourses.[26]

Accordingly, in his detailed examination of the Johannine miracle stories, Meier concludes that most have a traditional, and therefore possibly a historical, basis. In his view only two clearly do not represent historical events: the wine miracle at Cana (2:1–11) and Jesus' coming to the disciples walking on the sea (6:16–21). The latter, of course, has a traditional basis. John did not simply depend on Mark for this story, but John may have composed the wine miracle himself.[27] Meier also notes, in connection with the man born blind (chapter 9), "the tendency of the Gospel of John to heighten the miraculous element in miracle stories."[28] The raising of Lazarus may have grown on the basis of a story about Jesus' healing a mortally ill Lazarus. Meier sees difficulties in deriving it from the Lazarus parable of Luke 16:19–31.[29] Nor does he derive it from the so-called Secret Mark. That Jesus was thought to have raised the dead is reflected in the double-tradition saying in which "the dead are raised" (cf. Luke 7:22; Matt 11:5). The Isaiah passages to which this saying is related (29:18; 35:5–6; 42:18–20; 61:1) routinely mention healing of the deaf, the blind, and the lame, but not the resurrection of the dead (but see 26:19). Perhaps "the dead are raised" actually originated with Jesus himself.[30]

Doubtless Jesus was a miracle worker, and the differences between the synoptic and Johannine miracle stories should not obscure this fact. In Mark and John particularly, healings and other wonders seem to be the principal public activities of Jesus. They drew attention, and possibly also followers, to him. This is already evident from the Synoptic Gospels, particularly Mark, but it is clearly stated in John (2:11; 2:23–25). Thus there is a line of continuity from Jesus through the Synoptics to John. That later Jesus' followers are said to have joined in such activity (14:12; 1 Cor 12:9–10; 2 Cor 12:12) probably underscores this fact.

Whether there were pre-gospel collections of miracle stories will probably remain a disputed issue, but some evidence in John suggests that there were: the perplexing numbering of the first two signs only (2:11; 4:54); the seemingly inappropriate characterization of Jesus' entire activity as signs, even after the resurrection (12:37; 20:30); the tension within the Gospel itself between the importance of seeing and believing signs (2:11; 4:48; 12:37), and the recognition that sign faith alone is inadequate (2:23–25; 3:1–10).

We have examined structural and thematic elements in John which are evidently traditional and arguably historical. There are two other themes or motifs that are not insignificant historically, or theologically, but less central to the development of the gospel genre: Jesus' relation to his natural family and his relationship to women.

Jesus' Relation to His Natural Family

The portrayal of Jesus' relationship to his natural family in John is congruent with the Synoptics, but differs in ways that are historically plausible.[31] First of all, Joseph is twice specifically named as Jesus' father (1:45; 6:42), in the latter case as a means of explaining his human existence in contrast to his immediately preceding claim of having come down from heaven (6:41). Otherwise Joseph is mentioned only in the infancy stories of Matthew and Luke, but not at all in Mark. John, of course, has no infancy stories, nor does the Gospel seem to contemplate Jesus' birth in Bethlehem. From John we would infer he was born in Nazareth (7:40–44), and this is historically more probable.[32] Also, on the basis of what John writes, there is no reason to doubt that he understands Joseph to be Jesus' natural, biological father.

Mark clearly suggests that Jesus' family had severe reservations about his conduct (3:21) and may have thought he was beside himself.[33] Their attitude then explains Jesus' own statement about his true mother, brothers, and sisters (3:31–35), as well as his enemies' charge that he was in league with Beelzebul the ruler of demons (3:22; cf. John 10:20). John does not pick up these statements, if he knew them, but clearly describes his brothers as unbelievers, whose advice Jesus will not take, even though he ends up doing what they suggest (7:1–9, 10).

With Jesus' mother (never called Mary in John) matters are put differently than in Mark. She seems to know what he will do (2:1–5), even though he rebuffs her. Then she, with three other women, presumably followers, stands at the foot of the cross (19:25–27). Few critical exegetes regard this episode as historical, but the chief reason seems to be its absence from the Synoptics. That family should appear at the foot of the cross is not historically implausible, nor is a dying son's effort to provide for his mother. (There is also the presence of the Beloved Disciple, whose identity and historical reality remain the subject of debate.)

The role of Jesus' mother is much more important in John than in Mark, or the other Synoptics apart from the infancy narratives. She appears at the beginning and end of his ministry. Theologically, her prominence may have something to do with the humanity of Jesus (cf. also 6:42). Perhaps John assigns her a more positive role than she actually played during Jesus' ministry (but see Acts 1:14). Yet there are reasons for not too quickly dismissing the possible historical basis of the Johannine presentation of the mother of Jesus. Her role is prominent, but just the fact that its theological significance is not entirely clear suggests that John may be dealing with a given rather than composing de novo. Obviously Jesus' relation to his own family is a historical datum in the tradition to which John independently attests.

Jesus' Relationship to Women

Other women also play significant roles. Jesus' encounter and conversation with the Samaritan woman at Jacob's Well (John 4) is, of course, unique to the Fourth Gospel and brings out Johannine themes. But here the Johannine Jesus also manifests typically human characteristics such as tiredness and thirst. That Jesus should initiate a conversation with a woman, much less a Samaritan woman, is out of keeping with contemporary Jewish custom, as the story eventually indicates (4:9, 27), but this state of affairs does not necessarily speak against the historicity of the incident. Indeed, Jesus' approach to the Samaritan woman, his apparent openness to her, is congruent with and complements the synoptic, especially the Lucan, picture of Jesus (cf. Luke 8:1–3; 10:38–42). Of course, given the Johannine language and themes, one would be hard pressed to argue that John presents an account of an actual conversation between Jesus and this woman.

The sisters Mary and Martha of Bethany appear in John and Luke (10:38–42), but only in John are they said to be sisters of Lazarus also and to reside in Bethany. In John as in Luke they play host to Jesus and thus appear as his friends (11:5, 11). In John only this Mary anoints the feet of Jesus and wipes them with her hair (12:1–8; cf. Luke 7:36–50, where the woman is not named). In John the apparent personal relationship between Jesus and this family in Bethany is the basis of a theologically important narrative: Jesus raises their brother Lazarus from the dead. But whatever one makes of this episode, it scarcely calls into question the reality of the relationship. It is, of course, possible that John has here taken up the sisters from Luke (10:38–42), made the Lazarus of the Lucan parable (16:19–31) their brother, and constructed the narratives we now read in his Gospel. But such a proposal involves the larger question of the relationship of Luke to John, which presents its own difficulties, inasmuch as the distinctive Lucan material is not found in John.

Mary Magdalene, in John as in the other Gospels, appears at the cross and at the empty tomb. In John she becomes the first witness of an appearance of the risen Christ (20:11–18). (This is also the case in Matt 28:9–10, although there she is one of two women, and her role is not stressed.) Certainly John has ascribed a larger role to Mary Magdalene, who now stands out along with the mother of Jesus, the Samaritan woman, and the sisters Mary and Martha as a prominent figure in the Fourth Gospel. It is unlikely that John, in his social and theological setting, enhanced their roles because of nascent feminist interests. Rather, in ways different from the Synoptics, he portrays Jesus' actual relationships with women, who were among his friends and followers. Here John nicely complements Mark and the Synoptics generally, but does not require any or all of them in order to be understood.

The Passion Narrative

In the Passion Narrative the parallels between John and Mark (and the Synoptics generally) become pervasive. With the entry into Gethsemane (called only "a garden" in John 18:1) and the arrest of Jesus the Johannine and Marcan narratives begin to run quite closely parallel. But even from Jesus' entry into Jerusalem (Mark 11:1–10; John 12:12–19) or the Johannine narrative of the priests' (and Pharisees') plotting (11:45–53; cf. Mark 14:1–2), there is a remarkable series of parallel accounts, mostly in the same order.

Prelude to the Passion

John's Prelude to the Passion[34] beginning with the plotting of the priests, is relatively much longer than the comparable part of the Synoptics because of the farewell discourses (chapters 14–16) and Jesus' high priestly prayer (chapter 17). Clearly this segment is the composition of the evangelist, who at points obviously drew on earlier traditions or sources.

The priests' plotting in John (11:45–53) finds a parallel in Mark 14:1–2, whether or not John drew directly on Mark. Jesus then withdraws (11:54) so that the multitudes may gather in Jerusalem to await his advent (11:55–56), even as his enemies, the Pharisees, make ready to seize him (v. 57). Then comes the traditional story of the anointing of Jesus (12:1–8; cf. Mark 14:3–9; Luke

7:36–50), followed in John by Jesus' triumphal entry into Jerusalem (12:12–19), found in all the Synoptics (Mark 11:10 par.). The note about Lazarus and the plot against his life (vv. 9–11) is by all odds a Johannine composition, inasmuch as in John the raising of Lazarus leads to Jesus' condemnation rather than the cleansing of the temple (Mark 11:15–19), which in John has long since occurred (2:13–22).

Now anticipating his destiny, at the approach of the Greeks (12:20) Jesus responds that the hour of his glorification has come (v. 23).[35] From this point to the end of the chapter Jesus is speaking, and enunciating Johannine theology, although his speech contains traditional elements. After the soliloquy of 12:44–50 Jesus withdraws from any further contact with this world, whose representatives he will henceforth encounter only as he goes to his death.

With full knowledge that he has taken leave of this world to go to the Father (13:1–3), Jesus begins to wash his disciples' feet (13:1–20) as his first act at the Last Supper. This humble deed displaces the institution of the Lord's Supper in the Johannine account (cf. Mark 14:22–25 par.), and, as an expression of Jesus' love for his disciples, forms an inclusio with the love commandment (13:34). Jesus also foretells Judas's betrayal (13:21–30) and Peter's denial (13:36–38) as he does in all the Gospels. If John is following Mark his omission of the Words of Institution is deliberate and startling. It may be relevant to observe that the oldest eucharistic text outside the New Testament also does not place the institution of the Eucharist on the night Jesus was betrayed (*Didache* 9–10). Yet the *Didache* may reflect knowledge of the Synoptics, particularly Matthew, but not John. Possibly John and the *Didache* represent the earliest form of the Last Supper and eucharistic traditions, but such a view is nevertheless precarious, since Paul already knows the traditional Words of Institution and sets them on the night Jesus was betrayed (1 Cor 11:23–26, esp. v. 23). John clearly knows eucharistic language (6:52–58)[36] and presumably practice; possibly also the Pauline-synoptic version of the Words of Institution. He also knows the tradition of a Last Supper.

John's account of Jesus' revelation of Judas's betrayal (13:21–30) is more highly developed and detailed than the others and serves also to introduce the disciple whom Jesus loved, who, of course, appears only in John (cf. 19:25–27; 20:2–10; 21:7, 20–24; perhaps also 18:15–16; 19:35). As to its historical basis, any judgment will be negative that rejects the Gospel's claim to reflect the eyewitness testimony of an individual. However that may be, the scene is apparently a literary development based either on the synoptic tradition or something similar. Interestingly, the Synoptics have Judas betray Jesus to the chief priests before the Last Supper, while John presumes he will do so afterward. John's version is historically credible also, although there is little basis on which to decide between them. Jesus' prediction of Peter's denial is much briefer, and quite similar to Mark and Luke, although it is introduced with the distinctly Johannine theme of "afterward" (13:36; cf. 2:22; 13:7), meaning after Jesus' glorification.

John's farewell discourses, which begin as the disciples are still at table with Jesus (cf. 14:31), play a role similar to Jesus' apocalyptic discourse in the Synoptics (Mark 13 par.), which takes place shortly before the supper rather than after. In John, however, apocalyptic eschatological language is reinterpreted (14:22–24; cf. 11:24–25). Jesus' final, high priestly prayer (chapter 17) follows the discourses immediately and precedes his departure into "a garden" for his arrest. In Gethsemane, not mentioned by name in John, Jesus also prays (Mark 14:32–42 par.), but quite a different prayer. In John he prays for his disciples (but cf. John 12:27), in the Synoptics for his own deliverance. Obviously, the synoptic version is more primitive. (Yet John 12:27 seems to reflect knowledge of the Gethsemane episode, as does Heb 5:7–8).

Although John 11:45 through chapter 17 is the composition of the evangelist, the narrative episodes are mostly, although not entirely, in the same order as in Mark. The cleansing of the temple has, of course, occurred a couple of years earlier in John (2:13–22), but the plotting of the priests comes just before the anointing of Jesus, as in Mark. In John only the triumphal entry comes immediately after the anointing (12:12–19), but that event marked the beginning of Jesus' visit to Jerusalem and its environs in Mark (11:1–10). John's biggest differences by far, however, occur in the discourse portions: what Jesus has to say when approached by the questing Greeks (12:20–50); at the Last Supper (chapter 13); during the farewell discourses (14–16); and in the final prayer (17).

With John 18:1 the Passion Narrative proper begins. The narratives of all four Gospels contain the same episodes, with few exceptions, such as the death of Judas (Matt 27:3–10), Jesus before Herod (Luke 23:6–12), and the piercing of Jesus' side (found in John 19:31–37, but not in the other Gospels).

John could be following Mark, perhaps influenced by Luke and less so by Matthew. Sometimes John's differences from Mark can be understood as deliberate alterations due to John's exalted Christology. Thus at his own arrest (18:1–11) Jesus is in control; he is not even kissed by Judas. Jesus carries his own cross to Golgotha (19:17), needing no help from Simon of Cyrene (Mark 15:21), who is not mentioned. There is no cry of dereliction ("My God, My God, why hast thou forsaken me?") and no loud cry at his death (Mark 15:34, 37). Jesus is equal to the occasion and in complete control, at the end saying only, "It is finished" (19:30).

Yet in the same context John would have omitted details given by Mark that seem to accord with his purposes. There is no darkness at noon (Mark 15:33), no rending of the curtain of the temple (Mark 15:38), and no Roman centurion to declare him truly a son of God (Mark 15:39). The darkness fits the

Johannine light-darkness dualism; Jesus as new temple is an important Johannine theme (2:21; cf. 1:14); Son of God is the most characteristic title of Jesus in John. These dramatic, even supernatural interventions in Mark are less likely to be historical—to have actually happened—than the Johannine version that does not contain them.

This specific state of affairs is typical of the Passion Narrative as a whole. In some cases the absence of a Marcan (or synoptic) item from John's account is understandable as a deliberate omission, but in others not. Such instances of John's variations from Mark are particularly noteworthy when, as in the cases just noted, they actually fail to support John's portrayal of Jesus or his distinct point of view. The most striking of such instances are related to John's alleged anti-Judaism and his obvious tendency to place the responsibility for Jesus' death on those he calls "the Jews."

A Jewish Trial?

The Johannine account of Jesus' appearance before the Jewish authorities after his arrest (18:19–24) is remarkably spare and inconclusive in comparison with the Marcan version (14:55–65). In John Jesus is taken to the house of Annas, the father-in-law of Caiaphas, who is said to have been high priest "in that year" (18:13). Yet in the narrative that follows immediately, it is the "high priest" who questions Jesus, and that in context must be Annas, who is then said to send Jesus to Caiaphas the high priest (18:24). There is in John no account of a hearing, much less a trial, before Caiaphas. Indeed, the reader is left to imagine—or supply—what happened.

The Marcan account of the arraignment of Jesus before the high priest (presumably Caiaphas) and the council or Sanhedrin amounts to a full-scale trial concluding with a guilty verdict (14:55–65). Witnesses appear who claim that Jesus threatened the destruction of the temple (14:58). Nevertheless, their testimony is said not to agree (v. 59). Under further questioning Jesus admits his claims to be the Messiah (14:61–62). Moreover, in his direct question to Jesus the high priest has described the Messiah as "the Son of the Blessed" (cf. Matt 26:63: "Son of God"), and Jesus responds to the question, "I am" (*egō eimi*). After Jesus has continued with the Daniel 7:13 quotation, the high priest declares that he has uttered blasphemy and asks the Sanhedrin to decide his fate, whereupon they all condemn him to death (14:62–64). Thus the condemnation seems to be unanimous. This account presents serious historical and related problems, as we shall see (below, 96). Yet, amazingly, it fits exactly John's view that the Jews or Jewish authorities found Jesus' claims for himself blasphemous (10:33–36)—not to mention the fact that he was viewed as a threat to the temple (11:48). Conceivably, this final condemnation would be redundant in John (after chapter 10; 5:17–29); and John after all reports that Jesus was taken to and from Caiaphas (18:24, 28). Yet the difficulty is not easily dispensed with. Why, if John had Mark before him, did he omit the trial and leave his own narrative in such an incomplete and disordered state? The character of the whole Johannine narrative (18:12–27, esp. vv. 19–23) is itself problematic. Its awkwardness—Who is the high priest?—and relatively inconsequential results do not suggest that John composed it as a substitute for the trial before Caiaphas and the Sanhedrin. Rather, the Annas scene seems to be a given with which he was dealing.

Moreover, Luke also lacks the nocturnal Sanhedrin trial found in Mark and Matthew. Although he retains elements from Mark in an early morning scene (Luke 22:66–71), there are no witnesses and no formal verdict. Luke thus omits the specifically juridical elements of Mark. Is Luke influenced by John? Alternatively, do they share a common, more primitive, source or tradition?[37]

The historical difficulties, or improbabilities, presented by Mark's version of a Sanhedrin trial are well known. First of all, what source of information would have been available to Mark or his tradition? The problems for the Marcan and Matthean narrative posed by the later Mishnaic tractate *Sanhedrin* (albeit a later and perhaps idealized formulation) are numerous: capital cases were not to be tried on a feast day or at night; a verdict of condemnation should not be rendered on the day the trial began; two or more witnesses had to agree, but Mark observes that they did not (14:55, 59); all judges might not argue for conviction (cf. Mark 14:64: "they all condemned him as deserving death"). Moreover, the sheer prospect of assembling the Sanhedrin on a Passover Eve would have been mind-boggling.[38] The apparent condemnation of Jesus for having claimed messiahship and divine sonship, as if the two went together (14:61–64), sounds suspiciously Christian. It would not have been blasphemy to claim messiahship, even if the claim were proved wrong, and messiahship did not entail divine sonship. Precisely the aspects of the account that fit John's understanding of the conflict between Jesus and the Jews render it suspect historically. Yet it is not found in John, but in Mark.

So it is difficult to understand John's omission of this episode—or his radical reduction of it to the confusing Annas scene—had the evangelist been using Mark. Probably the trial scene is itself a Marcan composition.[39] But if it is a Marcan composition, and if John agrees with Mark in framing the account of Jesus' appearance before Jewish authorities with the account of Peter's denial (John 18:13–18, 25–27; cf. Mark 14:53–54, 66–72), is it not still likely that John was writing with Mark in view?[40] If so, John seems to have adopted the narrative framing of Mark, but not the theologically pregnant trial account itself. Such a redactional procedure is hard to fathom.

In contrast, John's account of a brief hearing before Annas, and no Sanhedrin trial at all—also no witnesses, no verdict, no condemnation for (christological) blasphemy—has a much better claim to historicity than Mark's elaborate scene with its theologically loaded concluding verdict. Whether or not John knew Mark, John's disagreement with Mark on this point is striking. John differs from Mark in ways that are likely to be more accurate historically.

The Priests' Plotting

John has a Sanhedrin scene, if not a trial, in 11:45–53. Such an informal meeting before the Passover feast would be more likely to have occurred than a formal trial on the very eve of the feast. Moreover, there is here another parallel with Mark, namely, Mark's brief account of the priests' (and scribes') plotting that inaugurates the Passion Narrative proper (Mark 14:1–2). In a noteworthy variation from Mark's order, the priests' plotting in John occurs before Jesus has entered Jerusalem (12:12–19), in Mark well after the entry (11:1–10). Mark's version would seem more likely historically, unless as in John Jesus had previously visited Jerusalem.

Although John scarcely presents the people called the Pharisees and chief priests in a positive light, he does make their actions intelligible, for he gives a much more extensive account and explanation of their plotting. If John 11:47–53 is to be understood as an expansion upon Mark 14:1–2, there remain features of the briefer Marcan account that are strangely absent. Mark is in several respects actually more specific than John, describing the chief priests and scribes as seeking to arrest Jesus by stealth and kill him (14:1). Moreover, in Mark the authorities plot to carry out the deed "not during the feast, lest there be a tumult of the people," and therefore presumably before it (14:2). Although this chronology actually agrees with John's, where Jesus is executed before Passover, nothing is said of that aspect of their planning in the Fourth Gospel. Of course, no scribes are mentioned, which is typical of John, but instead the Pharisees, along with the chief priests (11:46). In any event, John's account is scarcely an expansion of Mark's.

In John the council (*synedrion*) is genuinely perplexed and apprehensive that Jesus' popularity will bring the Romans down on the place, presumably the temple, and the nation (11:47–48). ("Signs" may be mentioned because of the immediately preceding Lazarus episode, scarcely the actual cause of Jesus' death.) Perhaps this fear is to be seen in the context of the popular move to make Jesus king after the feeding of the multitude (6:15). Apparently Jesus is seen as a threat to the priestly, temple authorities and to their concordat with the Romans. Caiaphas's prophecy (11: 49–50) can then be read either as expressing cynical self-interest or as reflecting a genuine concern for the welfare of the people: "You know nothing at all; you do not understand that it is better for you to have one man die for the people than to have the whole nation destroyed." In any event, a cynical reading is not the only one possible. Here John probably comes closer than any other evangelist to identifying accurately a motivation of certain Jewish (priestly) authorities to get Jesus out of the way.

In any event, the grounds for Caiaphas's recommendation and the Sanhedrin's condemnation are prudential rather than theological. In this fundamental way John differs from Mark's rendering, and in a surprising direction.

The Trial before Pilate

Obviously John has elaborated the trial scene (18:28–19:16a) to bring out his theological interests and to underscore the guilt of the Jewish, particularly high priestly, authorities. Probably John had at his disposal a simpler, briefer account, like Mark, if not Mark itself. Perhaps John's theological and related interests in blaming "the Jews" prevented his seeing the incongruity between the Roman attitude as suggested before Caiaphas (11:47–48) and that manifested by Pilate in the trial scene he created. In the one case, Roman power itself is perceived as the danger; in the other, Pilate the Roman governor seems reluctant to exercise his power over Jesus (19:10) and must be persuaded by "the Jews."

The Johannine variations from the Marcan account of Jesus' trial before Pilate move for the most part along the lines of John's recognizable theological interests. Initially "the Jews" seek a death sentence against Jesus from Pilate because they themselves do not have authority to put anyone to death (18:31). When Pilate questions Jesus about his kingship, Jesus' answer is thoroughly Johannine (18:36–37). Pilate's question, "What is truth?" (v. 38), betrays his cynicism, but then the first of his three proclamations of Jesus' innocence occurs (18:38; cf. 19:4, 6). In the face of Pilate's anticipated clemency, "the Jews" seek Jesus' death all the more and even question Pilate's loyalty to Caesar (19:12). Although they eventually get their way (19:16), Pilate has the last word (19:19–22).

Yet in John's account there is a rather curious anomaly. Early on Pilate says to Jesus (18:35), "Your own nation and the chief priests have handed you over to me," which suggests that "the Jews" in this scene are the people generally or the crowds (*ochloi*) that figure in the Synoptic accounts. Yet in the Johannine narrative itself crowds as such do not appear, and "the Jews" alternates with the "chief priests" in such a way as to suggest they are identical (19:6–7). Thus Jesus responds to the chief priests and police (NRSV), but "the Jews" answer. When read alongside the Synoptics, with John's knowledge and use of them assumed, the entire Jewish people's participation in the condemnation of Jesus is implied. (By inference from the Synoptics they constitute the crowds.) When John is read alone, without reference to the Synoptics, this is not as obvious. "The Jews" seem to be the chief priests rather than the crowds or the Jewish people.[41] This does not mean that John exonerates the Jewish people, but his position becomes more ambivalent than is usually thought, and may reflect the historical fact that it was the high priestly authorities who pursued the case against Jesus. After Jesus' death, when, according to Acts, Jesus' disciples reassembled in Jerusalem, their opponents and harassers were the chief priests and Sadducees (Acts 4:1, 5, 23; 5:17, 21, 24), not the Pharisees with whom Jesus had debated. John here creates a fictional or fictionalized scene, but the chief historical protagonists (Jesus, Pilate, the chief priests) appear in it.

The Date of the Crucifixion According to the Jewish Calendar

John has already presented a two- to three-year ministry, in contrast to the Synoptics' ministry of one year or less. Another striking chronological contradiction appears in the Passion Narrative. In the Synoptics, the Last Supper is the annual Passover supper, but in John Jesus dies the afternoon before the Passover. In fact, John seems to go out of his way to emphasize that Jesus died before Passover eve, not on the first day of the feast (13:1; 18:28; 19:14, 31).

Meier, in his treatment of the chronology of Jesus' career, argues that a stronger case can be made for the Johannine chronology than for the synoptic.[42] The lynchpin of his argument is that it is inconceivable that the events of Jesus' arrest, trail, and death should have occurred on the evening when the Passover meal was eaten. It is highly improbable, he writes, that "at the time of Jesus, the supreme Jewish authorities in Jerusalem would arrest a person suspected of a capital crime, immediately convene a meeting of the Sanhedrin to hear the case (a case involving the death penalty), hold a formal trial with witnesses, reach a verdict that the criminal deserved to die, and hand over the criminal with a request for execution on the same day—all within the night and early hours of Passover day, the fifteenth of Nisan!" "Yet," he continues, "this is what the Synoptic passion chronology and presentation of the Jewish 'process' basically demand."[43]

Meier goes on to observe that the Johannine account is far more plausible historically. In fact, the synoptic, the Marcan account, does not demand a Passover eve setting if two notices are removed, namely 14:1, and especially 14:12–16, which specifically indicates the Last Supper will be a Passover meal.[44] Moreover, the caution of Mark 14:2 ("Not during the feast lest there be a tumult of the people.") actually agrees with the Johannine chronology that places the arrest, trial, and execution before the eating of the Passover. Interestingly, in Paul's references to the Last Supper there is no indication that he knew it to be a Passover meal.[45] Furthermore, Paul's statement (1 Cor 5:7) that "Christ, our paschal lamb, has been sacrificed" seems on the face of it to assume, and support, the Johannine chronology.[46] In his commentary Brown argued in favor of the Johannine chronology, as he would continue to do in *The Death of the Messiah*.[47]

Two relatively early extracanonical sources, one Christian, the other Jewish, also agree with John's dating of Jesus' crucifixion. In the apocryphal *Gospel of Peter* Jesus is delivered "to the people on the day before the unleavened bread, their feast." A brief trial scene (3:6–8) and the crucifixion (4:10–5:20) then follow, obviously on the same day. Also, in Baraitha Sanhedrin 43a it is reiterated, that "on the eve of Passover they hanged Yeshu."[48]

Possibly John has shaped the narrative so that Jesus will die when the Passover lambs are slain (cf. John 1:29 and the scripture quotation of 19:36, which refers to the Passover lamb). Yet the fact that John describes Jesus as the Lamb of God who takes away the sin of the world and applies paschal biblical texts to him (Exod 12:10, 46; Ps 34:21; Num 9:12) does not in itself prove that John has changed the chronology. It is equally possible that John is assuming such a chronology as factual and interpreting it. As we have seen, the acceptance of the Marcan chronology poses serious historical problems. (Mark may reflect an early interpretation of the Last Supper as the first Christian Passover.) Jesus' death in the Gospel of John is indeed a vicarious death (chapter 10), but it is not otherwise presented as analogous with the death of sacrificial animals. Such cultic terminology and conceptuality is more characteristic of Paul, Hebrews, Revelation, and even 1 John (1:7, 9; 2:2) than of the Fourth Gospel.[49]

Another chronological discrepancy in the passion account concerns only the time of day, not the date. According to John, at the sixth hour, noon according to Jewish reckoning, Jesus was still before Pilate (19:14). But according to Mark, who tolls off the times and the hours (Mark 15:1, 25, 33, 42), Jesus has already been crucified at the third hour (Mark 15:25), nine in the morning. It seems more reasonable to think that Jesus stood before Pilate at noon than that the entire procedure described in Mark 15:1–24 took place so early. Moreover, Mark's tolling of the hours could represent the disciples' earliest commemoration of the events of Good Friday. Who would have been keeping time on the actual day? The point is not that John is more accurate, but that John's vagueness may more accurately represent what was known, or not known.

While not every item or detail of the Johannine Passion Narrative is historically preferable to the synoptic, some are, and the several we have singled out are quite significant. Probably John knows a passion tradition different from Mark's (or the Synoptics'), which at points is historically preferable. Whether this tradition existed already in written form is less certain, but quite possible. Paul, writing to the Corinthian Christians about the conduct of the Lord's Supper sets its institution by Jesus "on the night he was betrayed" (1 Cor 11:23). This bare statement assumes knowledge of Jesus' betrayal (his "being handed over"), perhaps the identity of Judas (although he is never mentioned by name outside the Gospels and Acts), certainly Jesus' death, probably the fact that those in authority had put him to death (1 Cor 2:8).[50] Paul's reference to this special night assumes his own knowledge of these events in a narrative context, and probably that of his hearers.[51]

The Demonstration of Jesus' Death

Only in the Gospel of John is there an episode between the death of Jesus and his burial: the crurifragium, not of Jesus but of the two others crucified with him, and the piercing of Jesus' side. Breaking the legs of the crucified victim was a merciful act, causing him to die quickly of asphyxia (cf. *Gospel of Peter* 4:14). According to John, Jesus' legs were not broken, because he had already died. But perhaps to make sure, his side was pierced instead, resulting in an efflux of water and blood. The question of who might have seen this transpire is answered in 19:35—presumably the Beloved Disciple (cf. 21:24) who had been standing at the foot of the cross (19:25–27).[52] The identification of the eyewitness is not gratuitous, however, but links this event to the attestation of the Gospel's validity at the end (21:24). Did the crurifragium and the piercing of Jesus' side take place? If there were no attestation by the witness and no scripture quotations (Exod 12:46; Zech 12:10), exegetes might be more inclined to accept this scene as something that likely happened. It would not be unprecedented. Moreover, the discovery that Jesus had already died, sooner than expected, fits what is said in Mark by Pilate (15:44–45), who seems surprised that Jesus was "already dead." Apparently John confirms Mark, and vice versa. In fact, John 19:30, although highly stylized, with Jesus remaining in control until the end, also implies that Jesus died quite suddenly.

The final demonstration of the reality of Jesus' death was his burial ("crucified, dead, and buried"). The Johannine account of the burial is distinctive in that Nicodemus reappears (cf. 3:1–10; 7:50–52) to participate along with Joseph of Arimathea. John seems to have added Nicodemus to the story, which he received either from Mark or a parallel tradition. Interestingly, John's unique description of Joseph fits Nicodemus ("a disciple of Jesus, but secretly, for fear of the Jews"). The detailed description of Jesus' burial (19:39–40), "as is the burial custom of the Jews," and the explicit indication of the reason for haste (v. 42) are unique to John. It has been customary to lay John's differences in detail to his literary and theological purpose, because of the character of the Fourth Gospel, but where traditional data end and theological interpretation begins is often a question difficult to decide.

Resurrection Appearance Narratives

Each canonical Gospel narrates the discovery of an empty tomb by women who believe they are going to visit Jesus' tomb. Beyond that point, the agreement that has extended through the Passion Narrative ends. There are variations among the accounts of the discovery of the empty tomb, John's being the most extensive and significant in that he has Peter and the Beloved Disciple run to the tomb to check it out at the behest of Mary Magdalene (20:2–10). The judgment that this is a Johannine addition to a traditional narrative looks probable, and the exegete would scarcely think otherwise were it not for the testimony of Luke (24:12, 24), which somewhat complicates matters. Luke 24:12 has Peter alone go to the tomb, and although missing in some ancient manuscripts (D) is found in most (p75, Sinaiticus, Vaticanus, and so on). Also Luke 24:24 seems to agree with, and to summarize, John 20:2–10. This instance involves the broader issue of the relation of John and Luke. What dependence, or which way does it run? It is often and understandably assumed that Peter, having denied Jesus, fled immediately to Galilee (cf. John 21:1–3). This is a reasonable surmise, but not a certainty. Yet it remains likely that only the women found the tomb empty. It would have then been entirely natural to include the male disciples as the tradition developed.

Mark, in its oldest extant form, has no appearance narrative. Both John and Matthew report an appearance to Mary (John 20:11–18) or the two Marys (Matt 28:9–10) just outside the tomb. Otherwise, the appearance stories of the Gospels differ as to locale: Galilee (Matthew and John 21; cf. Mark 14:28; 16:7) or Jerusalem and its environs (Luke and John 20, with noteworthy parallels between Luke 24:36–43 and John 20:19–23, as well as 20:24–29). Yet John 21, usually taken to be a later editorial supplement, although it is contained in all known Greek manuscripts, is based on a Galilean resurrection appearance narrative that has clear affinities with the unique Lucan call story of 5:1–11. This appearance to Peter, the Beloved Disciple, and five other disciples by the Sea of Tiberias (Galilee) seems to be a first resurrection appearance (despite 21:14). The disciples were returning to fishing, that is, to work. Moreover, the extant fragment of the *Gospel of Peter* breaks off just at the point where Peter declares that he, his brother Andrew, and Levi the son of Alphaeus took their nets and went to the sea, after they, with the rest of the twelve disciples, had gone home in grief. Clearly the narrative in the *Gospel of Peter* presupposes a *first* appearance by the Sea of Galilee, as does the putative original form of John 21:1–14 (minus vv. 1 and 14). Surprisingly, John 21:1–14 is the appearance story that Mark 14:28 and 16:7 lead the reader to expect. What might have been expected in Mark is found in John, if not also in the *Gospel of Peter*.

A survey of the narrative elements of Jesus' public ministry in the Gospel of John does not reveal a complete narrative structure that is an alternative superior historically to the Marcan. Yet the Marcan narrative is clearly not governed by purely historical, in the sense of chronological, considerations or data. John presents chronological and geographical divergences from Mark that are worth taking seriously as possible alternatives. At the same time, the Johannine narrative lacks the driving literary unity that characterizes Mark. It gives the impression of a broken, perhaps at points truncated and at others emended, narrative. John's narrative of Jesus' public ministry may be an unfinished symphony that defies narrative clarification or reconstruction. This is not true of the Johannine Passion Narrative and the prelude to it (chapters 13–17), in which the narratives run parallel to Mark and the Synoptics generally, but do not seem to be derived from them, and sometimes suggest more likely historical scenarios. There one finds a narrative continuity missing in John's account of Jesus' public ministry. Classical form criticism arrived at the conclusion that the Passion Narrative(s) came into being before narratives of Jesus' ministry were composed (Dibelius, Bultmann, Jeremias). After nearly a century, this still seems probable.

Does John then simply construct an account of Jesus' ministry to precede the Passion Narrative, as Mark apparently did, proceeding de novo? Or were there narrative elements and a narrative framework prior to the passion, that is, existing before John wrote and known to him?[53] John and Mark have several important narrative items in common before the Passion Narrative. Jesus' ministry begins with his encounter with John the Baptist. Jesus comes on the scene as a miracle worker, as well as a teacher, and immediately gains followers, some of whom were women. (Both Mark and John leave the distinct impression that his miracle-working activity set Jesus apart.) Not surprisingly, he met with a mixed reaction from his home folks and family. At some point during this public activity there was a turning point, centering on his feeding of a multitude, after which opposition mounted. Eventually he decided to go up to Jerusalem for Passover and (whether or not by his intention) his death.

Sayings Traditions in John

The discourses attributed to Jesus in John are quite different from the sayings tradition in the Synoptics, in that he speaks at length, carries on conversations with opponents and disciples, most of which concern his own dignity and role, and tells few, if any, true parables. Some sayings of Jesus with obvious synoptic parallels appear in parallel narrative episodes, where they might be expected to occur. Many of these are therefore in the Passion Narrative (chapters 18–19) and in the Prelude to the Passion (especially chapters 12–13). For example, in the anointing in Bethany, Jesus says, "For the poor you always have with you, but you do not always have me" (12:8), which is closely paralleled in the same context by Mark 14:7 (cf. Matt 26:11), except that Mark adds "and whenever you wish you can do them good" (which Matt 26:11, like John 12:8, lacks).[54] At the Last Supper, in the betrayal scene, Jesus says (John 13:21): "Truly, truly I say to you, one of you will betray me." Except for the typical double *amen* in John this saying is exactly paralleled in Mark 14:18 and Matt 26:21. In John 18:33, as in all the Synoptics (Mark 15:2; Matt 27:11; Luke 23:3), Pilate's question to Jesus is the same: "Are you the king of the Jews?"

In the significantly similar Johannine version of the Feeding of the Five Thousand (6:1–15) there are many similarities of detail (for example, five thousand men; five loaves and two fish; the insufficiency of two hundred denarii's worth of bread, the twelve baskets full of left over fragments). The naming of the disciples Philip and Andrew, however, as well as the presence of the small boy who has the five barley loaves and two fish, are distinctive of John.[55] Also in the immediately following story of Jesus walking on the sea there are similarities of detail. Here the apophthegm is a word of Jesus: "It is I; fear not" (John 6:20; Mark 6:50; Matt 14:27; no parallel in Luke). With this notable exception, the two similar synoptic and Johannine stories lack extensive or significant instances of verbatim agreement in words of Jesus. The same may be said of the cleansing of the temple (John 2:14–22; cf. Mark 11:15–17; Matt 21:12–13; Luke 19:45–46). Precisely the climactic word of the Johannine Jesus (2:16; alluding to Zech 14:21) differs from the synoptic (Mark 11:17 par., in which Jesus quotes Isa 56:7 and Jer 7:11). The disciples then (or later) remember Ps 69:9 in John 2:17 only.

The most extensive verbatim agreements in sayings that are significantly implicated in a narrative occur in John 1:23–34. These are not sayings of Jesus, however, but of John the Baptist, and they closely parallel parts of Mark 1:2–11. While in Mark the evangelist is the narrator throughout, in the Gospel of John the Baptist becomes the narrator, testifying, as he is looking back, in retrospect (1:23, 26–27, 30–34). He testifies to Jesus' superiority to himself (vv. 26–27, 30), and to seeing the descent of the Spirit upon Jesus (v. 32), who will baptize with the Spirit (v. 33); and finally he summarizes his own witness to Jesus as Son of God (v. 34). He knows better than anyone in the narrative who Jesus is. In the Gospel of John nothing is said of the Baptist's clothing or diet (Mark 1:6), or of the relation of his preaching to repentance and forgiveness (Mark 1:4–5). John is predominantly a witness (1:31, 32, 34). Not surprisingly, his role as an apocalyptic prophet (cf. Matt 3:7–10; Luke 3:7–9) is also missing. Nothing is said in John about Jesus' having been baptized, but the Baptist's statement about the purpose of his baptizing ministry, "that he might be revealed to Israel" (1:31), implies knowledge of this fact.

John's similarities to the Synoptics are so striking that Bultmann assigned this material (that is, John 1:19–34) in its present form to a later redactor, who attempted here, and at some other points, to bring John into line with the Synoptics.[56] Certainly the Johannine version, and particularly the words of John the Baptist, can readily be understood as an adaptation based on the Marcan narrative. John's words, and the description of the Baptist, have been shaped so that he becomes a witness only, rather than a prophet in his own right.

There is also a striking verbatim agreement between John and Mark that is ingredient to a healing narrative of each and functions comparably within it; but the narratives are different. In John 5:8 (cf. Mark 2:9, 11 par.) Jesus says to the healed man, "Rise, take up your pallet, and walk," which is the same as his command in Mark 2:9. But while the Johannine narrative is set at the pool of Bethesda (or Bethzatha) in Jerusalem, the Marcan is set in

Capernaum. Aside from these words of Jesus and the common motif of the relationship of sin and sickness (Mark 2:5–8; John 5:14) or misfortune, which appears elsewhere in the Gospels (for example, Luke 13:1–5; John 9:2–3), the narratives have little in common. One might suppose that if, as a broad spectrum of gospel tradition has it, Jesus healed sick persons, he said something like this more than once.

There are other less exact instances of such agreements. Jesus' saying in John 12:27 reflects knowledge of his anguish in the synoptic Gethsemane story, although it comes before the Last Supper rather than after as in the Synoptics. There is no Johannine narrative, no reference to Gethsemane, and no extensive verbatim agreement, but in both John and Mark (followed by Matthew) Jesus speaks of the condition of his soul (*psychē*) as "troubled" (John 12:27; cf. Ps 6:3) or "very sorrowful, even to death" (Mark 14:34) and of the anticipated time of his coming death as "the hour" (*hōra*). John may be reflecting Mark's narrative, but Heb 5:7–8 seems to know of such an episode of Jesus' anguish, and also without any reference to Gethsemane or trace of the Gospel of Mark. Perhaps John independently attests Jesus tradition.

John also contains a number of other sayings with clear synoptic counterparts, which occur in contexts different from those in the Synoptics. For example, John 4:44: "For Jesus himself bore witness that a prophet has no honor in his own country." This saying finds a parallel in each of the Synoptics (Mark 6:4; Matt 13:57; Luke 4:24), as well as in the *Gospel of Thomas* (#31) and the Oxyrhynchus Papyrus (lines 31–33). The Marcan context is somewhat different, although there Jesus has gone to his "hometown" and the reaction of his compatriots is ultimately negative (Mark 6:3). In John his compatriots, the Galileans, welcome him, but his own country (as the context requires, not "hometown") is not Galilee (or Nazareth) but Jerusalem. In the extracanonical sources, there is no narrative context. In Luke it is specifically the synagogue in Nazareth (4:16, 24). Conceivably, John has taken the saying from its Marcan context and used it for his own distinctive purposes. In any event, in John it has a different geographical point of reference. The narrative contexts are different, but the meaning—rejection of Jesus by his compatriots—is the same.

Again, John 12:25: "The one who loves his life loses it, and the one who hates his life in this world will keep it for eternal life." The saying sounds entirely Johannine. One might never suspect that it was not composed by the evangelist, if there were not significant Marcan and Q parallels. What is recognizably the same saying is found in Mark 8:35 (cf. Matt 6:25 and Luke 9:24). Moreover, there is another version in Q, the double tradition (Matt 10:39 and Luke 17:33). So this saying about the meaning of discipleship is found in Mark, Q, and John. In Mark 8:35 par. it follows the saying about taking up one's cross and following Jesus. In a slightly different vein, John 12:25 is followed by what could be a veiled version of the cross-bearing saying (12:26): "If anyone serves me, he must follow me; and where I am, there shall my servant be also; if anyone serves me, the Father will honor him." This pair of sayings occurs in Mark (par.) immediately after Peter's confession, Jesus' first passion prediction, Peter's rebuke, and Jesus' remonstrance. In John the context is different. Jesus is already in Jerusalem, but, as in Mark, he is looking toward his death, which is even closer than in Mark.

In John's Last Supper scene there are several sayings with synoptic parallels in different contexts. (Jesus' prediction of his betrayal has been noted above.) There is, most notably, the distinctive version of Jesus' love commandment in 13:34 ("love one another"; cf. John 15:12, 17; 1 John 3:23; 2 John 5). Yet the synoptic (Mark 12:33 par.; Matt 5:43 and Luke 6:27) and Pauline versions are characteristically different, with Paul not referring the commandment to Jesus, but only quoting Lev 19:18 (Rom 13:9; Gal 5:14; cf. Jas 2:8). John 13:20 ("whoever receives one whom I send receives me") is closely paralleled in Matt 10:40, although the Greek verbs are different, perhaps suggesting an underlying Aramaic (cf. also more remote parallels in Mark 9:37 par. and Luke 10:16). Jesus' saying about a servant's not being greater than his master (13:16) is paralleled in Q (Matt 10:24; Luke 6:40), although in John Jesus is called Lord (*kyrios*), while in Q he is teacher (*didaskalos*). At the meal episode's apparent conclusion in John, Jesus says (14:31), "Rise, let us go hence." After they have already departed the supper room, at the conclusion of the Gethsemane scene (Mark 14:42), Jesus says, "Rise, let us be going."

The binding and loosing saying of Jesus in Matt 16:19 and 18:18 is found in a different form in John 20:23, where it is the risen Jesus who says to the disciples: "Of whomever you forgive the sins they are forgiven them, of whomever you retain the sins they are retained." The Johannine version, in a quite different context, gives the meaning of the more enigmatic Matthean version for church discipline (obviously its meaning context in Matt 18:18). This is more likely a saying of the risen Christ (John) than of the earthly Jesus (Matthew).

There are other similar sayings in different contexts. At the temple cleansing itself the Johannine Jesus alludes to the destruction of the temple (2:19; cf. Mark 14:58 par.; Mark 15:29 par.; also perhaps Mark 13:2 par.). In John 3:3 and 5 Jesus speaks of the necessity of being born again, or from above, in order to see or enter the kingdom of God. In the comparable Matthean saying (18:3) it is only a matter of turning and becoming like children in order to enter the kingdom. In his farewell discourses, Jesus several times promises the fulfillment of prayer in his name (14:13–14; cf. 15:7, 16; 16:23–24), a promise which seems to echo several synoptic sayings (Mark 11:22–24 par.; Matt 7:7–11; 18:19; 21:22) although these are not identical. Likewise, the fate of the recalcitrant branches (John 15:6) in the parable of the vine recalls John the Baptist's threat (Matt 3:10; Luke 3:9), as well as Jesus' own word in the Sermon on the Mount or Plain (Matt 7:16–20; Luke 6:43–44).

In most such cases it is arguable that the Johannine version is based on, or a midrash upon, the synoptic. Yet the Johannine context is almost always different. That John relied upon the Synoptics is not impossible, although this reliance would be minimal. Alternatively, John drew upon parallel Jesus sayings tradition, even if he was acquainted with other canonical Gospels. The existence of such tradition is suggested also by the *Gospel of Thomas*.

Distinctive Factual Information

There are a number of instances in which John seems to be possessed of factual information different from, or going beyond, what is found in Mark or the Synoptics. Specifically, John conveys purportedly factual knowledge about Judaism, whether in Jesus' day or his own, about the land of Israel, and about Jesus himself.

John emphasizes that Jesus was from Nazareth, a humble village, about which no great expectations could be entertained: "Can anything good come out of Nazareth?" (1:46). Jesus himself had just been introduced by Philip to Nathanael as "Jesus son of Joseph from Nazareth" (1:45; NRSV). Moreover, Jesus' origin in Nazareth, not Bethlehem (cf. 7:42), is emphasized. There is, of course, no physical description of Jesus in any Gospel, but several clearly human traits appear in John alone. Jesus gets tired and thirsty (4:6–7). He has friends other than his disciples: Lazarus (11:11, 35), and presumably Lazarus's sisters Mary and Martha as well. When Lazarus is reported to have died, Jesus weeps out of love for him (11:36–37), a normal human reaction. Jesus has learning, is literate, although he has never studied formally (7:15). Obviously, he is able to carry on a discussion about the meaning of scripture. Luke gives Jesus' age as about thirty at the beginning of his ministry (3:23). One adds the three or so years of his ministry according to John's account, and reaches the traditional thirty-three years. Yet in John Jesus is said to be not yet fifty (8:57), which jibes with the forty-six years that the temple, which turns out to be the temple of his body (2:21), has been under construction. John hardly intends to inform the reader of Jesus' age, but he may be playing on presumed factual data, that is, Jesus was in his late forties.

John mentions a number of places not found in the Synoptics: Bethany beyond Jordan, where John baptized (1:28; cf. 10:40); Aenon near Salim, another place where John baptized (3:23); the city of Sychar (4:5–6); a mountain of Samaria, presumably Gerizim (4:20); the city of Ephraim (11:54). That many such places can no longer be located with certainty does not necessarily mean that they did not exist. In Jerusalem John knows the Sheep Gate Pool (5:2) and the Pool of Siloam (9:7), which can still be identified. He says that Pilate sat in judgment "at a place called The Stone Pavement" (19:13; NRSV). He knows that Jesus was crucified near the city (19:20; Cf. also Heb 13:12: "outside the city gate"). The other Gospels show no explicit knowledge of this.

The traditional cite of Golgotha, the Church of the Holy Sepulchre, is outside the city wall of Jesus' day. John also indicates that he has specific knowledge of the temple. For example, in Jesus' day it had been under (re)construction for forty-six years (2:20). (It is impossible to say whether the forty-six years apply to Jesus only, to the temple, or to both.) John anticipates the destruction of the temple by the Romans (11:48), which had probably already occurred when he wrote. There seems to be some knowledge of the plan of the temple: the treasury (8:20); Solomon's porch (10:23). Also he asserts that Jesus frequently taught there (chapters 7, 8, 10; 19:20; cf. Mark 14:49).[57]

John tells us that *rabbi* meant teacher, as it probably would have in Jesus' day (1:38; cf. 3:26). He knows that the Pharisees were the leading teachers (3:1, 10), in his own day, if not in Jesus.' John knows Jewish feasts other than Passover (5:1; 7:2; 10:22), and he knows that Jesus went up to Jerusalem for other feasts. He knows exodus traditions (6:31–53). He knows that jars made of stone were used in Jewish rites of purification (2:6). Perhaps most important, John knows about the God of Israel, whom no one has seen (1:18; cf. Exod 33:20; Deut 4:12, 15), although Jesus, who can be seen, is also called *theos* (1:18; 20:28). Thus John understands that Jesus, and the claims made for him, can be seen as a threat to Jewish, and biblical, monotheism (5:18; 10:33). Yet Jesus is called a Jew by someone other than Pilate ("King of the Jews"), that is, by the Samaritan woman in 4:9, and he can say that "salvation is from the Jews" (4:22).

Judas (not an uncommon name) is denigrated more in John than in any other Gospel (cf. 6:70), as he is mentioned more frequently. His name is given more fully than elsewhere in 6:71 as "Judas son of Simon Iscariot" (RSV, NRSV), although Iscariot may indicate the village of Judas's origin (for example, Kerioth-hezron in Josh 15:25). Even as Judas is named as the one objecting to the woman's (in John, Mary's) using expensive ointment to anoint Jesus' feet (12:5), he is said to be the (thieving) keeper of the money box (12:6). But again Judas is called the keeper of the money box in 13:29, with no negative insinuation. Perhaps the accusation of his thievery is inserted in order to deal with an awkward fact, that he was known to have been the treasurer of the group. Although it has sometimes been suggested, because of his name, that Judas (Greek, *Ioudas;* Hebrew, *Yehudah*) personified "the Jew," this is nowhere stated or implied in this, or any, Gospel. He is never numbered among the *Ioudaioi.*

Finally, John's knowledge of Judaism is not an artificial construct to serve as a foil for his own theology. There is a difference between traditional Judaism and the beliefs of Jesus' disciples and followers, but John does not caricature the one in presenting the other.[58] One cannot say that John presents the beliefs of "the Jews," who oppose Jesus and his disciples' belief in him, in a favorable light. Yet he does not basically misrepresent them. Even in John chapter 8, where the polemic is fiercest, what "the Jews" say to Jesus is understandable on the basis of their premises, and not more derogatory than what Jesus is made to say to them; in fact, it is less so. It is not clear that Jesus has the better of the arguments, unless one accepts his claim to bring a new, and determinative, revelation. And that is precisely his claim. Moreover, it is a claim, and not proof, exegetical or otherwise. This is the offense of any claim to revelation. It can only be explained, or defended, after the fact.

Conclusions

In conclusion it may be useful to rank on a scale from almost certain to inconceivable aspects or items of John's portrayal of Jesus and his ministry, particularly with respect to points at which the Fourth Gospel differs from the Synoptics, especially Mark, or presents or omits items found in the latter.[59] In the ranking below *historically preferable* means that an item or instance in John is more likely to represent accurately the historical figure of Jesus or events or circumstances related to him.

I. John is almost certainly historically preferable:
1. in presenting no formal trial of Jesus before Jewish authorities, that is, the Sanhedrin, and in its explanation of the reasons for opposition to Jesus on the part of the chief priests (11:47–53);
2. in implying that Jesus was at first a disciple of John the Baptist and therefore conducted a concurrent baptizing ministry.
II. John is probably historically preferable:
1. in spreading Jesus' ministry or a period of public activity over a period of more than one year rather than less;
2. in maintaining that he made more Jerusalem visits (for Passover or other festivals) than the one Passover visit reported in the Synoptics;
3. in placing Jesus' crucifixion and death during the day immediately prior to the evening Passover meal rather than the day after.
III. John is conceivably historically preferable:
1. in placing the occurrence of the temple cleansing at an early (or earlier) point in Jesus' ministry;
2. in suggesting Pilate's suspicion, if not contempt, of the motives and goals of the chief priests.
IV. John's presentation is inconceivable historically in its representation of:
1. Jesus' proclamation of himself as Son of God and his use of the "I am" phrase to introduce himself and his role;
2. Jesus' disputes with his opponents over his own dignity and role (but not necessarily in disputes over other teaching and miracle-working activity);
3. Jesus' opponents as "the Jews," in apparent distinction from himself and his disciples, and the tendency to equate them with Pharisees;

4. Jesus' proclamation absent the imminent (or future) advent of the
   kingdom of God;
5. Jesus' teaching absent his characteristic parables;
6. Jesus' distinctively Johannine language and conversational style;
7. Jesus' death as resulting from his raising Lazarus from the dead.

The last category above (IV) recalls by way of John's distinctiveness or difference major aspects of the synoptic portrayal of Jesus. The consensus of modern criticism that the Synoptics and the synoptic tradition are in important
respects closer to the historical figure of Jesus is not wrong. My qualification of
that view is not a denial of it. Rather, I maintain that in a number of specific
instances John, while differing from the Synoptics, affords access to historically
significant Jesus tradition. The Jesus research of Meier and Fredriksen, cited
above, strikingly illustrates this fact. Finally, to return to the issues noted at the
beginning: What is the source of the authority of John's witness? What is the
relation of John to the Synoptic Gospels?

The Gospel claims to be based on the testimony of a truthful witness
(21:24), apparently one who has seen what he has testified to (cf. 21:20; 19:35).
(Also 1 John 1:1–4, while probably not written by the evangelist, indicates how
the Johannine witness was first understood.) The sharp debate over the historicity of this Gospel a century ago, which has not yet died out, presumes the
seriousness of this claim, whether to affirm or deny it. The debate is, of course,
integrally related to the question of whether the Beloved Disciple is a historical
figure or the personification of the true witness. Traditionally, this disciple has
been assumed to be a historical figure, ultimately identified with John. This
assessment of Jesus tradition in the Gospel of John must, however, leave the
issue of the identity of the Beloved Disciple unresolved.

There is, finally, a certain antinomy or tension in this assessment. On the
one hand, the distinctive Johannine portrayal of Jesus, his opponents, and controversies does not accurately represent the historical figure of Jesus or his
milieu. Its several aspects are virtually unique to John; they do not match with
the criterion of dissimilarity; they do not cohere with what is said about the
earthly Jesus elsewhere in the New Testament, not only in the Gospels, but also
in Paul.[60] While Paul shares with John the belief that God sent his Son, and
that he therefore descended to earth and ascended to heaven, he does not
understand Jesus' ministry as the manifestation of his glory (cf. John 1:14;
2:11), but of his humiliation (Phil 2:7–8). The earthly Jesus was for Paul a Jewish man (but cf. John 4:9), a human being "born of woman, born under the
law" (Gal 4:4). Paul did not think explicitly in terms of incarnation. On the
other hand, John's narrative, as distinguished from the portrayal of Jesus, often
appears quite plausible historically just at those points at which it differs from

Mark or the Synoptics. Arguably, John presents factual data that are irrelevant to his theological purposes or even contravene them.

The tension between the portrayal of Jesus and the possibly factual data in the narrative of his ministry is understandable if one discerns the two levels of John's Gospel: the historical past, what happened in the time of Jesus, and the historical present, what was going on with Jesus in the community in which the Gospel was written. This Jesus of the historical present is the exalted Christ who continues to address and guide his followers through the Spirit, the Paraclete. The Spirit-Paraclete holds the two levels together.[61] Is it not reasonable to suppose that the guidance of the Spirit began quite early in the history of the Johannine community of Jesus' disciples? Thus they were emboldened to make astounding christological claims and to defend them when they came under attack. Yet John 21:24 and 1 John 1:1–4 imply that the Spirit does not overrule the testimony of the eyewitness generation.[62]

As to the question of John's relation to the Synoptics, the peculiar sense of spiritual authority that produced this Gospel already suggests a basis for its apparent independence from the others. John represents a unique evangelical development based on the same person and events, and on related tradition, but reflecting a different life setting and experience of the work of the Spirit. It is then unnecessary to suppose that John had no knowledge of the existence or content of the other Gospels, but they were at most at the periphery of his vision. John is an independent Gospel, and its claim to be based on an independent witness is worth taking seriously.

Redaction Criticism, Genre, Narrative Criticism, and the Historical Jesus in the Gospel of John

Does John Also Enshrine a Separate Memory?

In the recent Prague-Princeton Symposium on the historical Jesus (held at Princeton Theological Seminary, April 18–22, 2007) members were asked to reflect on the question of the historical Jesus in the respective Gospels by considering questions of redaction criticism, genre, and narrative criticism. This seemed a worthwhile and productive way to proceed. At least it was for me as I considered the question of the value of the Fourth Gospel for knowledge of the historical Jesus and therefore for Jesus research. In the immediately preceding chapter, "Jesus Tradition in the Gospel of John," I have attempted to survey and present the evidence for such tradition, which seemingly exists independent of, and sometimes in contradiction to, the Synoptic Gospels. My original intent was to reduce and summarize that piece for the symposium, but that seemed ultimately unworkable—it would have resulted in a summary of a survey. Instead, the rubrics provided for our section of the symposium program gave me the opportunity to reflect on the evidence assembled earlier.

Redaction Criticism

Can redaction criticism of John get to the historical roots of that Gospel? Redaction criticism of Matthew and Luke proceeds on the assumption that they used Mark as a principal narrative source. Their parallel and overlapping material is attributed to a sayings source (Q, which may have contained more than sayings), and their distinctive materials to their special sources (M, L) or to their creative redaction. With Mark, the problem is more difficult, because we do not have the evangelist's sources. Nevertheless, tradition and redaction can be separated with some degree of confidence. Mark has put together the units of tradition in a literary and theological framework of his own creation. This is the common wisdom of our discipline. With John the situation is different, and prospects of redaction criticism seem less hopeful at the outset. What is the baseline? Or, what are the necessary or appropriate assumptions? What was John's relation to the Synoptics? Did he know and use them? Did he know them but deliberately ignore them (Hans Windisch)?[1] Did he write without knowledge of them (P. Gardner-Smith)?[2] On what basis should redaction criticism proceed? Those who believe that John did not know or use the Synoptics often propose narrative sources that are in the nature of the case hypothetical. Those who believe he knew and used the Synoptics often argue for the superiority of this position because it posits extant and known sources and does not invoke hypothetical ones.[3] Yet their redaction-critical interpretation may itself seem hypothetical in that the whys and wherefores of John's use of the Synoptics are not nearly as obvious as Matthew's or Luke's use of Mark.

A good example of the difficulty, or complexity, of redaction criticism of John in light of the Synoptics is afforded by John's treatment of the Baptist (always called simply John in the Fourth Gospel). First of all, John portrays the Baptist as uttering the same passage from Isaiah (40:3) found in all the Gospels, along with other words attributed to the Baptist in the Synoptics (John 1:23, 26–27, 31–34). Because of their almost verbatim similarity, Rudolf Bultmann assigned their appearance in John to the work of the ecclesiastical redactor, who, among other things, had attempted to reconcile John with the Synoptic Gospels.[4] One might ask, however, why the redactor made such an adjustment here and not elsewhere in a Gospel replete with differences and divergences from the Synoptics. Or, alternatively, why the evangelist did so, if he was the one responsible.[5] Incidentally, the attribution of the title Son of God to Jesus originates in the Fourth Gospel from the Baptist rather than from the voice from heaven. In this Gospel the Baptist always gets it right about Jesus, surpassing Jesus' disciples in knowledge of who he is.

Yet immediately thereafter (1:35–37) the evangelist portrays the Baptist as sending his disciples to Jesus. Here Bultmann suggested, quite plausibly, that some disciples of Jesus came over from among the Baptist's followers.[6] Such an origin would explain the importance of the role assigned to the Baptist in the Fourth Gospel. He is so important that he himself must emphasize that he is not the Christ (1:20; cf. 1:8), who ranks before him although he came after him (1:15, 30). Thus he emphasizes the distinction between them.

Not surprisingly perhaps, Mark (1:14–15) makes a sharp delineation between the time of the Baptist's work, ending with his arrest, and the beginning of Jesus' ministry. This sequence is often taken to be historical, and it comports with the rest of the Marcan narrative and that of the other Synoptic Gospels. John is different, however, in that their ministries overlap, even as Jesus, not unexpectedly, demonstrates his superiority (see esp. 3:22–23, 36; 4:1). Jesus and John are portrayed as rivals in their baptizing ministries, and the oddity of this state of affairs must be ameliorated by noting that John had, obviously, not yet been put in prison (3:24) and, as a kind of afterthought, that not Jesus but his disciples were baptizing (4:2). (Of course, nothing is said elsewhere in any Gospel about the disciples' baptizing.) What is one to make of this? Clearly the Baptist's protestations of his subordination (for example, 3:27–37) are Johannine compositions, but against what background? Perhaps the Synoptics, but John the Evangelist produces a picture of rival ministries of baptizing, which clearly contradicts Mark's sharp delineation of two periods that draws suspicion of being theologically rather than historically based. Is John's version grounded in knowledge of the actual history, however it may have been conveyed to him?[7]

The view that John is independent of the Synoptics seems more congenial with its possible historical value than the alternative. If John knew and used the Synoptics, however, this does not necessarily imply that all Jesus tradition, historical tradition, in John is simply derivative from them (contra Maurice Casey[8]). The problem comes to a head in the passion narrative, in which John is obviously narrating the same events and in much the same order. There John's differences, large or small, are sometimes understandable as his creations or corrections of the synoptic narratives: Jesus carries his own cross. He does not need Simon of Cyrene to help him. Sometimes John's departures are more perplexing. Although Mark's narrative of the trial before the Sanhedrin (Mark 14:55–65) has Jesus condemned to death for the exact reason that he is condemned in John, namely blasphemy (cf. 10:33), John omits this account, which would have been a fitting culmination after Jesus' arrest.[9] John also gives a different chronology, or dating, of Jesus' death according to the Jewish calendar. Could this date be based on a different witness or tradition rather than springing from his theological agenda?[10] Even if the dating fits John's theological agenda, and that is subject to some exegetical dispute, might not the theological development derive from the traditional dating, rather than vice versa?

Gospel Genre

Is the gospel genre distinctive? If so, what is its origin? Did Mark invent or inaugurate it? Are the Gospels *bioi* (lives), in an ancient, if not modern, genre? It is often supposed that if John did not rely on Mark or the Synoptics in general for his material content, he must at least have known about Mark in order to have undertaken to write such a document in the first place, since Mark created this distinctive genre. Yet is this necessarily the case? Biographies or lives of famous religious figures were not unknown in antiquity, from Philo's *Moses* to Philostratus's *Life of Apollonius of Tyana,* not to mention the David narratives in 1 and 2 Samuel (1 Sam 15:35–2 Sam 20:22). Contemporary readers, if they took up and read a Gospel, would likely assume they were reading a *bios* (life, or biography) of a religious leader.[11]

Yet the canonical Gospels are distinctive among such *bioi* in the way they all culminate in extensive accounts of Jesus' final visit to Jerusalem, arrest, trial(s), crucifixion, death, and burial. In every case his tomb is found empty. In other words, they conclude with a passion narrative, with sequence and content that are remarkably similar (Matt 21:1ff.; Mark 11:1ff.; Luke 19:28ff.; John 12:12ff.). One can thus distinguish this period from a so-called public ministry (where John differs widely from the others). Is this common two-fold division, which is not a feature of other *bioi*, the result of literary dependence (the others on Mark) or tradition (the prior existence of a passion narrative or narratives)? An earlier, form-critical, perspective decided for the latter. Passion narratives were generated early because of the importance of Jesus' death for worship (a passion liturgy?) and preaching, out of which theology developed.[12] Is this not still the most likely hypothesis? The gospel genre would in that case be, in important respects, a development of tradition rather than the creation of an individual author.

What are the implications of the question of genre for the historical value of John? If gospel genre is a development of tradition, the Johannine trajectory becomes, in the nature of the case, a more likely source of historical tradition than if John were a spin-off of Mark or the Synoptics generally. This applies, *mutatis mutandis*, to the passion narrative. Moreover, if John's passion narrative differs from Mark and the Synoptics not only in ways that might have been anticipated as his redaction, but also in others (for example, no Sanhedrin trial; the dating of Jesus' death according to the Jewish calendar), this may reflect knowledge of earlier tradition rather than sheer literary dependence.

Narrative Criticism

All the canonical Gospels are narratives of Jesus' ministry that contain important common elements. They have his ministry begin with Jesus' encounter with John the Baptist and end with his crucifixion and burial. In the midst of his ministry there is an apparently pivotal series of events centering on Jesus' feeding of a multitude. Beyond that, he teaches, performs deeds of power (Synoptics) or signs (John), and debates with other Jews. Some other extant ancient writings denominated "gospel" do not share these narrative features. Indeed they are not narratives. Perhaps this is what we might have expected of the Nag Hammadi, presumably gnostic, writings, such as the *Gospel of Thomas* and the *Gospel of Truth*. Otherwise, gospels such as the *Gospel of the Hebrews* and the *Gospel of Peter* were narratives, but do not reveal dependence on Mark, although we know little enough of what they actually contained. The dependence of Matthew and Luke upon Mark, so often taken for granted, is a unique and surprising fact.

The narrative character of the canonical Gospels implies their historical character, but does not of course prove it. In fact, both Matthew and Luke seem to be dependent on Mark's narrative. (Thus in comparing John with the Synoptics it is not one against three, but one against one.[13]) A colleague of mine in the English department of Duke University, Reynolds Price, characterizes Mark as the most compelling narrative ever written.[14] Mark moves in a way that Matthew and Luke do not, with the question of the identity and role of Jesus ever in the foreground. John is another matter entirely. There is a sense in which this Gospel does not move at all, in that the protagonist's character does not unfold within the narrative. Jesus remains the same: "God striding across the earth."[15] Whether or not John knew Mark, John did not depend on Mark. John is the less compelling, more fractured narrative—not only not dependent on Mark, but perhaps even prior to it as well? (Incidentally, John's depiction of a public ministry of more than two years, much of it spent in Judea and Jerusalem, is not intrinsically improbable.)

In considering the narrative character of gospels, another matter might be considered. What is the relationship of narrative to memory? We remember our own lives in narrative form, or as narrative. Yet in gospel study one is accustomed to viewing the tradition as originally fragmented (with the exception of the passion narrative already noted), and assembled only by the evangelist, presumably Mark. Was it K. L. Schmidt who used the metaphor of a string of pearls? Yet what if narrative is intrinsic to memory? Thus we think about ourselves and others as having stories. "What's your story?" (Does *not* having a "story" suggest psychological abnormality?) Needless to say, the narrative quality of memory does not sanction the historicity of gospel narratives. It does, however, suggest the likelihood that Jesus was remembered in a narrative, or as a narrative. And if so, then it is quite conceivable that there was more than one narrative rendering of the Jesus story, with roots going back to Jesus. One is found in Mark, another in John, perhaps another in Q (or proto-Luke). Could there have been others, now forever lost from view?

A case in point might be the brief narratives of Jesus' ministry presented in the summaries of the early Christian missionary preaching found in the Book of Acts (for example, 2:14–39; 3:13–26; 10:36–43; 13:17–41).[16] Apparently they represent Luke's view of this preaching, and perhaps also the practice in his own day. Rather than embodying early tradition or practice, they may represent it, not as verbatim reports, of course, but as instances of what must have gone on. What sense would the proclamation of Jesus' death and resurrection have made apart from some narration of his deeds and words? Yet our earliest source, the Apostle Paul, in his summary of the preaching tradition handed on to him, makes no reference to the deeds and teaching of Jesus (1 Cor 15:3–8). Interestingly enough, Paul never speaks of Jesus' miracles or healings. He does, however, attest the occurrence of such phenomena among his followers (1 Cor.

12:9–10, 28), as well as by his own hand (2 Cor 12:12). Why are they occurring, and why does Paul speak of them, unless they are considered a continuation of Jesus' own work, as is suggested in Acts (2:43; 3:1–16)? Paul also knows of words of Jesus (for example, 1 Cor 7:10–12), and probably a narrative of his passion (1 Cor 11:23: "on the night when he was betrayed"). This reference is followed by the Words of Institution of the Lord's Supper (11:24–26), which interpret Jesus' death. Is it not likely therefore that he presupposes a known narrative framework, acknowledged if unspoken—or at least unwritten?[17]

Historical Jesus

Doubtless the purpose of this rubric from the Prague-Princeton Symposium is to suggest the relevance of the other items named (redaction criticism, genre, and narrative criticism) for historical Jesus research and to provide the opportunity to consider, however briefly, why John has not figured more significantly in this research.

The first reason is the compartmentalization of our discipline. From Albert Schweitzer[18] to E. P. Sanders[19] Jesus research has been carried forward by scholars who have focused on, and made contributions to, synoptic scholarship. This includes those with as diverse interests and conclusions as John Dominic Crossan and N. T. Wright.[20] Thus, where John and the Synoptics conflict, so much the worse for John, or so it is assumed. Yet within the present generation the situation has been changing, as the works of Paula Fredriksen, John P. Meier, and Raymond E. Brown, among others, attest.[21] Of course, nearly a half century ago C. H. Dodd in his magnum opus *Historical Tradition in the Fourth Gospel* made a case for the historical value of a distinctly Johannine tradition, and he was not alone among Johannine scholars.[22] Yet it has been only relatively recently that those engaged in Jesus research have begun to take account of the Johannine tradition as a serious historical resource.

A second reason is the portrayal of Jesus, and particularly the speeches of Jesus, in John. We know that Jesus was a Jew and did not talk Christology. But what Jesus, or whose Jesus, is speaking in John? He looks like the Jesus of Christian doctrine, or, better: the Jesus who was to become the subject of Christian doctrine. Yet this is the Jesus who promised the Paraclete-Spirit of Truth, who already speaks in and through the story of Jesus in the Gospel of John to his followers in the church (cf. John 14:26; 16:12–15, especially). Perhaps because the Gospel of John seems to give too wide latitude to the authority of anyone claiming to be the voice of the Spirit, or a spirit, 1 John denounces false prophets, who wrongly claim spiritual authorization. Moreover, the author emphasizes what was from the beginning, namely Jesus (1:1), and speaks of an old commandment prior to the new (2:7–8). A vital and fundamental interest in what happened in the past, with Jesus, is alive and well in the Johannine community.

Moreover, the Jewish roots of the Gospel of John also suggest something about its historical value. The Johannine Jesus may be emerging from Judaism, but he has been deeply embedded in a Judaism that is clearly recognizable in the Gospel, although it is rejected even as it rejects Jesus as the Messiah. In delineating two levels in the Gospel, J. Louis Martyn focused upon the level of the Johannine community or church and its preaching. At the same time, he also maintained that this level of the narrative stands in a dialectical relationship to an *einmalig* level that purports to reach back to old tradition and ultimately to Jesus.[23] That level invites further investigation. After all, the Gospel of John claims to be based on an eyewitness to Jesus, in contrast to the explicit disavowal of such a claim in Luke (1:1–4), who refers to his many predecessors (1:1). Was John one of them?[24]

The rubrics provided for our discussion in the Prague-Princeton Symposium have provided an appropriate means of access to the question of the search for the historical figure of Jesus in John's Gospel. *Redaction criticism* does not prove John's independence of the Synoptic Gospels, but at least suggests that at many points John may know alternative traditions that are arguably historical. John need not have depended upon Mark (or the Synoptics) for the gospel *genre* itself. (In any event, the term *gospel* was not applied to the documents until later.[25]) There was ample precedent in lives of ancient religious leaders and other figures. Here a passion narrative, common to the four canonical Gospels as well as the *Gospel of Peter,* is a crucial factor. In my view still, the existence of such passion narratives was the product of church life, worship, and therefore tradition, rather than dependence on Mark's creativity. John's gospel *narrative,* sophisticated as it may in some respects seem, is not derivative from, or a spin-off of, Mark's. Does the narrative character of memory suggest the likelihood of more than one narrative track of the story of Jesus? I think probably so. Finally, the way in which the Gospel of John situates Jesus within Judaism is suggestive of a meaningful historical dimension. Jesus stands over against "the Jews" although he himself is a Jew (John 4:9). His forerunner and witness, John the Baptist, is never called a Jew, although, in his baptizing mission he is to reveal Jesus to Israel (1:31). (Here the distinction between "Israel," always used in a positive sense in the Gospel, and "the Jews," usually used in a negative sense, comes into play. Jews who believe become Israel.) There is a history underlying the narrative's presentation of Jesus, but the historical figure of Jesus does not lie on the surface, but underneath, and has to be mined out, so to speak. This is a task for literary and historical criticism, not theology. It may have theological relevance, but that is a question for another occasion.[26]

The Historical Figure of Jesus in 1 John

Jesus at the Beginning Giving a Commandment for the Future

In recent years the Gospel of John has gained increasing credibility in Jesus research. It figures as a significant historical source in John P. Meier's definitive *A Marginal Jew,* as well as in Paula Fredriksen's *Jesus of Nazareth.*[1] There is now a John, Jesus, and History Group in the Society of Biblical Literature. Brill's compendious *Handbook of the Study of the Historical Jesus,* in progress, will contain an article on Jesus tradition in the Gospel of John.[2] Given this resurgence of interest in the historical value of the Fourth Gospel, one thinks also of 1 John, in which the historical figure of Jesus plays an important role.[3]

In anticipating this article, I assumed that the subject of Jesus in 1 John would have been treated already in articles, if not in monographs. Yet a survey of the bibliographies of recent scholarly commentaries on the Johannine Epistles (Raymond E. Brown, Rudolf Schnackenburg, Georg Strecker, and John Painter) turned up few works with "Jesus Christ" in the title, much less "the historical Jesus," or "the historical figure of Jesus."[4]

Of course, every serious commentator must address the question of the meaning of beginning (*archē*) in 1 John 1:1 and thereafter. In verse 1 the subject is not "Word" (*logos*) as in the opening of the Gospel, but "that which was from the beginning" (as RSV translates *ho ēn ap'archēs*). NRSV translates "We declare to you what was from the beginning," but in doing so obscures the fact that "beginning" (*archē*) stands out at the very beginning of the document.

Interestingly enough, both RSV and NRSV capitalize "Word" in the prologue of the Gospel but not in the Epistle. Nor does either capitalize "life" (v. 2) which becomes the subject and is clearly the equivalent of "that which was from the beginning" (v. 1). Neither is taken to be a title of Jesus. Yet both are (in vv. 1, 2) said to have been seen, looked at, heard, and touched (only v. 1). Apparently "from the beginning" signifies the beginning of the community's proclamation of Jesus, which constituted it as church (a term that does not appear in the Johannine Epistles until 3 John 6), and also the historical appearance of Jesus himself.

In his justly famous article, "Was von Anfang war," in the 1954 Bultmann *Festschrift*, Hans Conzelmann keenly observed that while in 1 John the vocabulary, particularly the theological vocabulary, is quite similar to the Gospel's, a *Verschiebung*, or shift, of meaning has occurred.[5] In 1 John *archē* no longer means just the primordial beginning, as in the Gospel, but has in view already the appearance of Jesus and the beginning of the proclamation about him, which now must be defended in the face of erroneous teaching. The Johannine letters are thus in effect "Johannine Pastorals" in their emphasis on right doctrine and their incipient distinction between orthodoxy and heresy (terms that, at least in my view, are at this point in history no longer anachronistic). In his brief article, Conzelmann is obviously more concerned with the Johannine trajectory's moving forward toward early Catholicism than with its backward reference to Jesus, which he acknowledges but does not emphasize. That backward reference is closely related also to the identity of the author, and his relationship to the evangelist, as well as to Jesus himself. In this discussion, however, I want to prescind from the authorship question in order to examine simply the role of the historical figure of Jesus in 1 John, primarily by looking at the occurrences and meaning of *archē*.

Jesus the Beginning

Is "*archē*," despite its importance for church tradition and doctrine, pregnant with 1 John's conception of the historical figure of Jesus, together with his fundamental importance for distinguishing true teaching from false? The word occurs eight times in 1 John and twice in 2 John, taken together more than in any other New Testament book. There are eight occurrences also in the Gospel of John, but it is a document about six times as long as 1 John and 2 John combined. Obviously, *archē* is very important in the Epistles. Do the occurrences in 1 John and 2 John point back to Jesus, even if they are not in each instance simply identical with Jesus? (The one obvious exception is 1 John 3:8, where it is the devil who has sinned "from the beginning.") Significantly in John 15:27 Jesus says to his disciples: "You also are bearing witness [or testifying], because you are [or have been] with me from the beginning." Here *ap'archēs* (from the beginning) refers to Jesus' ministry, as it clearly does in 16:4: "I did not say these things to you from the beginning (*ex archēs*) because I was with you." Here *archē* is virtually a technical term referring to Jesus' historic manifestation and ministry, and this should be borne in mind as we examine instances of its occurrence in 1 John.

In 1 John 1:1 "what was from the beginning" (NRSV) or "that which was from the beginning" (RSV) is, of course, neuter gender. Is the antecedent really then the message about the Son rather than the Son himself? Obviously, neuter implies the message, but seeing, hearing, and touching (vv. 1 and 2) imply the messenger as well. The life that was made manifest (v. 2) was more than the message. It is the bearer and embodiment of the message. The simple language of 1 John is replete with ambiguities, sometimes inherent in the Greek. Here is a striking example. Although neuter gender implies the message, the one who embodies the message, and is the message, is clearly in view also.

In 1:5 the message described is the message heard "from him." From whom? From the Father or from his Son Jesus Christ (v. 4)? The two are even more closely related, or even identified, in 1 John than in the Gospel. Therefore in 1 John there is often a question of which, the Father or the Son, is the antecedent. This is a perennial and difficult problem, but as a kind of exegetical experiment I am going to choose Jesus, the Son, wherever possible and see how that works out. In verse 5, the message proclaimed is about God, and God would seem to be distinguished from the source of the message ("from him"). So the "we" of verses 1, 3–4 proclaim a message about God that they have heard from Jesus (v. 5). It is about Jesus' message. This works well, however, only as far as verse 7. "He is in the light" (v. 7) might point to Jesus, except for the immediately following reference to "the blood of Jesus his Son." So it may be—at this point seems to be—God. But can God be "in the light," when just previously (v. 5) he is said to be light. Moreover, in 1:7 "we," now including the readers as well as the writer, are to walk in the light. Later in 2:6 their walking in the light is clearly an imitation of someone else's walking in the light. That would necessarily be Jesus, rather than the Father. Meanwhile "Jesus Christ the righteous," the advocate with the Father has already been mentioned (2:1) and therefore becomes the implied subject, whose commandment or words are to be kept (vv. 3–5) and whose walking is to be emulated by believers (v. 6), who are implicitly his followers.

Actually, *follow* is used frequently of the disciples' relation to Jesus in the Gospel of John (1:37–43), as in all the Gospels, but does not occur in the Epistle. (Discipleship is "followship.") In fact, in the New Testament aside from the Gospels, *to follow* (*akolouthein*), does not occur in the sense of "following as disciples" except in Revelation (14:4; cf. v. 13 and 19:14). Yet the concept of following, if not the term, is central to 2:6.

In 2:7 *archē* appears again as one reads of the commandment that is not new, but old, the one "you have had from the beginning." This is obviously a play on the new commandment of John 13:34. Jesus there gives his disciples a new commandment, with no reference to an old one. In 1 John the commandment is first old, but then new (v. 8). In the Gospel this is, of course, the famous love commandment. It is not yet repeated in 1 John, but from the discussion of hatred and love that follows (2:9–11), it is clear that the love commandment is in view. Moreover in 2 John 5, the message heard from the beginning (*archē*) is explicitly said to be "that we should love one another." So the love commandment is that old commandment, "which you have had from the beginning."

In 2:12–14 the writer addresses little children, fathers, and young men, with reasons given for addressing each. In the case of fathers only (who are of course the eldest) it is "because you know him who was from the beginning" (*ap'archēs;* 2:13, 14). In the context of 1:1, in which *archē* clearly means the beginning of the tradition, the one (masculine singular) who is from the beginning is Jesus rather than God. It is the fathers, who are the oldest group named, who would be in a position chronologically to know the one man who was from the beginning, namely, Jesus. (This is said twice.) Presumably, the young men, or even the young children, would have been in as good a position to know God the Father, but not Jesus. Only the fathers go back that far.

Twice in 2:24 "what you have heard from the beginning" obviously refers to what has been proclaimed (1:5) rather than to the historical figure of Jesus himself. It is the message from or about Jesus. But in any event, the message originates with Jesus. In 3:11 this message (*angelia*) heard from the beginning is the love command, "that we should love one another." The same is true of 2 John vv. 5, 6. There the play on old and new leads to the repetition of the love commandment (John 13:34), "that we love one another" (v. 5). Following Jesus' commandments (plural) is to love (v. 6). As in the Fourth Gospel his commandments boil down to the one, love commandment. (As we have observed, the actual reference to the love commandment does not occur in 2:8–11, but the repetition here in 2 John 5–6 confirms it is in view. Indeed, this is true of 3:11, except that it is called the message rather than the commandment.)

It is certainly arguable, and I think correctly so, that everywhere in 1 John (except 3:8) *archē* implies, if it does not denote, Jesus. With the possible exception of Hebrews (2:14–18; 4:14–5:10), in no New Testament book beside the Gospels is the reality and character of the historical figure of Jesus as a human being more important than in the Johannine Epistles, particularly 1 John.

Jesus in the Fourth Gospel

The historical figure of Jesus is, of course, central to the Gospel of John. Otherwise, why was a gospel written and not a theological treatise like the *Gospel of Truth*? [6] Yet on the question of the role of the Jesus of the past, the historical figure of Jesus, there is a curious difference between the Gospel and the Epistles in the roles of the past Jesus. In the Gospel emphasis falls upon the accessibility of Jesus in the present time, that is, the time following his death and resurrection appearances. There are numerous indications of this, but none more central or explicit than the so-called Paraclete sayings (14:15–17, 25–26; 15:26–27; 16:7–15). Through the ministry of the *paraklētos,* the one called to the side of, the Advocate (NRSV) or Counselor (RSV), Jesus' presence is felt among his disciples, and he continues to guide them.

Jesus has taught his disciples to love one another (13:34), and that this love should have no limits, even as Jesus' love has been limitless. Such love entails the willingness to lay down one's life for one's friends (15:12–13). This is what Jesus teaches his disciples. Obviously the Spirit will guide them in how to implement obedience to Jesus' command. Perhaps the crisis situation that produced the Gospel resulted in the distillation of Jesus' teaching to this one command. The disciples' obedience to Jesus replicates Jesus' obedience to the Father: "As the Father has sent me, so I send you" (20:21; cf. 17:18).

This narrowing of the content and focus of Jesus' teaching, unique in its simplicity and consistency, is not, however, paralleled in simplicity by the Fourth Gospel's presentation of his ministry. John's account is episodic, broken, with startling omissions that are recognized by the author or final editor (20:30; 21:25). It does not have the narrative force or compelling power of Mark's. Perhaps it was never completed, and therefore was supplemented and published by a later editor. At the same time, John may well be right about some significant historical data, even as his narrative differs from the Synoptics: Jesus, as a follower of the Baptist, himself conducted a baptizing ministry for a time (3:22, 26; 4:1–2); his ministry lasted more than one year rather than less; he was never formally tried before the Sanhedrin (cf. Mark 14:53–65; cf. John 18:12–23); he was crucified on the eve of Passover rather than the day after; therefore, the Last Supper was not a Passover meal. John also cries out to be supplemented from the other Gospels, but it is less than clear that this was the evangelist's intention. He wrote a parallel, but competing, account.

Obviously, the Epistles (1 John particularly, and also 2 John) look to the same historical figure of Jesus. His historicity, that he was really human, is of fundamental importance, as are his teaching and his death (1:7; 2:2; 5:6–8). They presuppose the gospel narrative, apparently the Gospel of John, although no details of John's narrative apart from the crucifixion are required to make sense of the Epistles. More important, however, is the Epistles' emphasis that Jesus' teaching is encapsulated in the command to love, an emphasis that fits the portrayal of the Gospel of John far better than any other Gospel. With good reason Gospel and Epistles have been regarded as the work of the same author. Probably they are not. But they share theological and ethical axioms. God's love is fundamental and prior. The proper response to God's love is (the disciples') love for one another.

Yet while the evangelist emphasizes the present accessibility of Jesus, particularly through the Paraclete, the Holy Spirit, the author of 1 John has recognized the danger in any appeal to the authority and authorization of the Spirit alone (1 John 4:1–3). The importance of Jesus as a real human being is, moreover, underscored by the condemnation of christological heresy in 4:1–3. Who is from God (or "of God") and who is not? Obviously, the crucial criterion is confessing that Jesus has come in the flesh, which means as a real human being. Denial of the humanity of Jesus is the heresy that has divided the community (cf. also 2:18–25), and such denial cannot legitimately claim the support of the Spirit (4:1–3). Interest in the historical figure of Jesus is not academic. The interest is not in history per se, but in doctrine, but the doctrine depends on the historical reality of a human being. Right doctrine is an overriding criterion. But that doctrine is not given in the present. It derives from Jesus, the *archē*—what he taught and who he was. Thus in 1 John there is a surprising point of contrast with the Gospel. While the Gospel presents the "isness" of Jesus, particularly by way of reassuring the disciples that they have not been left alone in a hostile world, 1 John, by way of contrast, emphasizes his "wasness." Certainly the author of the Epistle does not want to imply that believers have been left alone to fend for themselves. The Spirit continues to be the source of reassurance (3:24). Yet the Spirit is no longer identified with the Paraclete (cf. 2:1; "Advocate"), as in the Gospel. Rather the identity of Jesus as a figure of the past is emphasized. His pastness is crucially important.

Thus, 1 John makes clear what the Word's becoming flesh (John 1:14) means. The Epistle is more explicit on this point than the Gospel, although it is a proper interpretation of the Gospel, for which the humanity of Jesus is a basic ingredient.[7] Rarely is Jesus spoken of as the son of Joseph in the Synoptic Gospels, but Philip introduces him to Nathanael as Jesus son of Joseph from Nazareth (John 1:45). After Jesus has referred to himself as the bread from heaven (6:41), the Jews, who are apparently his fellow Galileans, say "Is not this Jesus, the son of Joseph, whose father and mother we know? How does he now say 'I have come down from heaven'?" Jesus is a human being whose natural origins are known. His claims, taken literally, are inconceivable, and therefore presumably false. But they are not to be taken literally. They must be demythologized, as the evangelist has demythologized the myth of the descending and ascending redeemer. For Gospel as for Epistle, the humanity and historical reality of Jesus are basic. At the risk of seeming a bit precious, however, one might say that as the Gospel of John makes explicit what is only implicit in the Synoptics, so 1 John makes unmistakably explicit what is already found, but not as prominently and unambiguously, in the Fourth Gospel, namely, the humanity of Jesus.

The Disappearance of the Jews

Conzelmann observed that there are real and significant differences between 1 John and the Gospel, but he was not the first to note them.[8] Most striking in my observation, however, is the difference in designating those cast as Jesus' opponents. In the Gospel they are "outsiders," "the Jews" or "Pharisees" (and in the passion narrative "the Jews" or "the chief priests.") At the same time, of course, Jesus is also a Jew (cf. 4:9).[9] But at many points "the Jews" identify themselves as such by rejecting Jesus. The polemic between "the Jews" and Jesus at times becomes exceedingly acrimonious.

In 1 John (and 2 John), however, the opponents are "insiders," not Christ-deniers but Christ-confessors. Baldly put, they are not Jewish but Christian. Moreover, we would never suspect from the Johannine Epistles alone that Jesus himself was Jewish, much less that his opponents were. In 1 John the opponents, who have separated from the community (2:18–19), are heretics. They get it wrong about Jesus, even though they may profess to be his followers (2:22–23). They have departed from what the community has heard from the beginning (2:24). They deny the fleshly reality of Jesus (4:1–3; cf. 2 John 7).

It is usually thought that 1 John is later than the Gospel of John and pre-supposes it, and the Gospel's precedence fits with the change in opponents as one moves from Gospel to Epistles.[10] Jesus' contemporaries and countrymen were Jews, as was Jesus himself. It is not necessary to decide whether Jesus was Torah observant, although he seems to have been. He differs with other Jews, particularly scribes and Pharisees, over matters of interpretation, but not over the centrality of the law and the importance of obedience to it. In the Gospel of John Jesus can speak to the Jews of "your law," as if it were of no concern to him or his followers. Yet he presumes that he is on the side of Moses, or better, that Moses is on his side and that scripture cannot be broken (10:35). It is not the case that older traditions are abandoned in John's Gospel because of Jesus, but they are reinterpreted. To put matters simply, in the Gospel Jesus is deeply embedded in Judaism even as he appears to stand out from it. This is quite different from 1 John, which, moreover, contains only one scriptural reference, the case of Cain's murder of Abel his brother (3:11–17; esp. vv. 12–15; cf. Gen 4:1–16).

Probably the author of 1 John realized that Jesus was Jewish, but this seems to have been of little theological importance for him. For the author of the Gospel, however, his Jewish milieu was of central importance, and the Gospel is replete with scripture and Jewish tradition, even if these have been subjected to distinctive and radical reinterpretation.[11]

In the Gospel, the beginning (*archē*) can mean the period of Jesus' ministry, or even the beginning of his ministry (15:27; 16:4), but whichever, that beginning is not necessarily definitive or complete, that is, in its revelatory or normative value. Accordingly, the disciples, when left alone without Jesus after his death or departure, can expect the Holy Spirit, the *paraklētos,* who will teach them, remind them, and guide them into all the truth (14:26; 16:13). Probably the Gospel itself is to be regarded as the literary deposit of the work of the Spirit-Paraclete.[12]

Here is an important difference from the Epistles, particularly 1 and 2 John. In them, the beginning, the *archē,* Jesus in his true humanity (flesh; 4:2) and teaching, which the disciples have had from the beginning (2:7; 3:11), has a uniquely normative role. The author is, to use the words of another Epistle, contending for "the faith once for all entrusted to the saints" (Jude 3). Jude, like the Johannine author, was also confronted by those who claimed to be disciples, but taught false doctrine (v. 4). The similarity across the board with the Pauline Pastorals is clear (cf. 1 Tim 4:1–5; 6:20–21). The distinctiveness of the Johannine Pastorals lies, however, in the basis or norm to which they appeal: the beginning, that which was from the beginning, the old commandment (to love one another), finally, Jesus Christ come in the flesh. The norm is Jesus, the one who was from the beginning, who set the movement on its course, and gave it direction and meaning. As the passage of time carries the community farther and farther from Jesus, its source, Jesus, becomes increasingly important.

As I have observed, according to the majority view 1 John presupposes the Fourth Gospel or something very much like it. Yet what 1 John actually presupposes is the theology of the Gospel (with the differences that have been noted) and particularly the narrowly focused teaching of Jesus himself, which is thoroughly commensurate with that narrative. Does 1 John presuppose the narrative of events in the Gospel?

There is an unambiguous answer to this question: Except for the crucifixion, it does not. Yet none of the other writings in the New Testament reflects knowledge of the Gospel narratives per se. At most they reveal knowledge of Gospel traditions (for example, 1 Cor 7:10–11; 11:23–26; Heb 4:7–8; 13:11–12). Yet Christian readers have readily seen in these texts the natural continuation of the Gospels' story. The same may be true of the relationship between the Gospel of John and the Johannine Epistles, except that the Epistles have an obvious literary and historical connection with the Gospel (with the Revelation to John standing, so to speak, on one side), even though they are probably not the work of the same author.[13] A near analogy may be the relationship of the Epistle of James (or the *Didachē*) to the Gospel of Matthew. Yet in that case the similarities are not nearly as close, and while the possibility of some relationship at the level of Jesus tradition certainly exists, obviously James (or the *Didachē*) does not depend on Matthew in the way that the Johannine Epistles seem to depend on the Gospel of John.

The Second and Third Epistles are so brief that their lack of evidence of knowledge of the Fourth Gospel's narrative is scarcely significant, but 1 John is a different matter. It is worth asking why 1 John, if its author knew the Gospel, does not seem to reflect greater knowledge of the Fourth Gospel's narrative(s). The answer may be that the Epistle is rather narrowly focused because of the conflict that has emerged within the Johannine community. For in 1 John it is the teaching, not the deeds embodied in narrative, that is important. Schismatics, claiming the authorization of the Spirit, have espoused a docetic Christology. (Quite possibly they accepted the signs of Jesus but misconstrued the teaching.) It is a very significant early Christian document, but it might never have been written apart from this conflict. Therefore its focus is quite narrow.

The nature of 1 John's conflict distinguishes it from the Gospel, in which the antidocetic element is less obvious—so much so, in fact, that its existence continues to be the subject of debate.[14] It is obvious, however, that the conflict between Jesus' followers and (other) Jews has left heavy tracks in this Gospel. And although the content and nature of that conflict is anachronistically portrayed in the Gospel as a conflict about Christology, it was doubtless rooted in Jesus himself and the Palestinian-Jewish setting of his ministry. At the very least, this is the Johannine community's perception, and the sine qua non of its existence. This conflict with "the Jews" moves the Gospel's narrative forward, in the sense that it is the motivating force. Since that conflict has disappeared and is no longer the setting or motivating force of 1 John, there is no reason for the Epistle to take up or reflect aspects of the Gospel's narrative. Jesus seems to have been wrenched from his Jewish context and placed in an altogether Christian context, indeed, one defined by intense, presumably bitter, controversy about the nature and meaning of Jesus himself. Yet the intelligibility of the Jesus who is the object of the faith of the community, in which 1 John was written, requires something like the Gospel's presentation, which we know only in narrative form.

The Composition and Narrative of the Fourth Gospel

Our present, canonical version of John betrays marks of the process of its composition, including hints that it was edited or emended (6:52–58; the possible reversal of chapters 5 and 6 in its original form; the addition of chapters 15–16[17]; the addition of chapter 21). Moreover, the long discourses and conversations in which Jesus is a participant are entirely unique to John, in both form and content. They illuminate the narrative, but usually are not required by it. Theories about whether or in what form such materials antedated the composition of the Gospel are not lacking. The same may be said of its narrative framework (for example, Was there a Gospel of Signs?). Necessity is the mother of invention. Not the tendency to multiply entities beyond necessity, thus inviting the application of Occam's Razor, but the nature of the material itself, leads to the formation of hypotheses about the composition and order of the Fourth Gospel.

First John, with its recurring references to "the beginning" (*archē*), presumes a living tradition, and tradition history, about the historical figure of Jesus. (Otherwise, it is entirely fraudulent, which, although possible, is unlikely because it is an unsatisfying historical hypothesis.) Given the existence of such a historical tradition, one may ask in what form it likely existed. Individual stories? Individual discourses or sermons? An extended passion narrative? Were each and all of these separate units? Quite possibly. In the Gospel of John, unified as its individual parts may be, we see signs of its composite character. If the research of the past century has taught us anything, it is that there were in the beginning such discrete entities, formed and transmitted for use in Christian communities. Critical orthodoxy has seen in Mark, an anonymous genius of the late 60s or early 70s, the author who first put it all together in written form, but forty or so years after the death of Jesus. Mark was indeed a genius. (In fact, a distinguished Duke colleague, whose field is English literature, characterizes Mark as the most original narrative writer in history.[15]) The evangelists Matthew and Luke took up his narrative and expanded it. John did not. He may have known Mark, but to try to explain John as a new edition of Mark is an unlikely and largely hypothetical enterprise. But that John without relying on Mark produced (or was in the process of producing) a narrative broadly similar to Mark's, but with many differences and departures, should not surprise us. John was an independent Gospel.[16] More than likely then, the author of 1 John knew it, although quite possibly in some precanonical form.

We remember our own lives in narrative form, as well as the lives of friends and family. Jesus gathered his own family of disciples (cf. Mark 3:31–35), who doubtless shared memories of him. Is not memory a universal human trait, indeed, one not confined to humans? Perhaps narrative memory is a distinctively human property. Be that as it may, is it more reasonable to believe that the memory of Jesus was from the beginning fragmented, with no narrative context, or that a narrative context would have been ingredient to any memory? The latter was the case at least in the passion narrative. It is not possible to develop a theory about the relation of tradition, narrative, and memory. But given the existence of 1 John, given the existence of the Gospel of John, given the close contact (if not agreement) between them, and furthermore the Epistles' insistence on the importance of "the beginning," it is reasonable to suppose that the letter writer knew a pre-existent Johnnine tradition in narrative form and that he therefore knew a document approximating the Fourth Gospel of the New Testament.

Conclusion: Jewishness or Docetism?

There is a continuum running from the Judaism, which the Gospel of John presupposes, through the Johannine Epistles, 1 John in particular. The Gospel of John itself represents a stage in which the circle of Jesus' disciples has moved away from its Jewish milieu in an unfriendly separation. So in it Jesus is distinguished from "the Jews," although he is still sometimes presented as a Jew (4:9). The First Epistle does not represent the next stage, but presupposes at least an intervening stage after the Gospel in which the historical figure of Jesus has been transposed into an object of faith without discernible Jewish roots, who at the same time becomes more than human. Seemingly, the non-Jewish Jesus has become a nonhuman Jesus. Jesus' humanity is integrally related to his Jewishness. In the Epistles, 1 John and 2 John particularly, the denial of Jesus' true humanity, docetism, is strongly resisted, but without any reference to his Jewishness. One might say that in the Fourth Gospel Jewishness is already departing. Among the schismatics, whom the Epistle writer(s) resist, it is gone, together with his humanity. The Epistle writer insists upon Jesus' humanity, but not his Jewishness.

Perhaps John 21 reflects a rapprochement with the Jewishness of Jesus, represented by Peter, without which his humanity would be in jeopardy. Johannine Christianity, in moving away from a Jewish Jesus, was moving toward docetism. That was a movement that 1 John (and 2 John) tried to stop, whether successfully or not, we do not know. Is it possible that in a reconciliation with Petrine Christianity, which included Mark and the Synoptic Gospels, the Jewishness and humanity of Jesus were rescued? (John 21:25 implies its author's acknowledgment of other Gospels.) With that reconciliation accomplished, John joins a fourfold Gospel canon, but Johannine Christianity per se disappeared.[17]

Part Three

John among the Gospels

From Synoptic Jesus to Johannine Christ

Historical Considerations—Choosing between Genuine Historical Alternatives

Marinus de Jonge has repeatedly addressed himself to questions of the history and interpretation of the Johannine literature and has published important contributions to Jesus research, *Jesus: Stranger from Heaven and Son of God* (1977) and *Jesus, The Servant-Messiah* (1991).[1] Although in the latter volume he does not deal with the Gospel of John but focuses mainly on Mark and Q, he nevertheless writes that not only material distinctive of Matthew and Luke, but "even individual pieces of tradition recorded only in the Fourth Gospel, may also go back to an earlier date."[2] In an earlier essay, however, de Jonge had dealt sensitively with the important question "Who are 'We'?," taking his direction from the "we have seen his glory" of John 1:14.[3] De Jonge observes that here, as elsewhere in the Fourth Gospel and in 1 John, the apostolic eyewitness is in view, although John's use of the first person plural cannot be limited to that original group.

Questions of Historicity

In resonance with de Jonge's work, in this chapter it is my intention to set the question of historicity in John over against the problem of John and the Synoptic Gospels, not so much with a view to proving John historical, as to suggest that in a number of cases in which John differs from the other Gospels there is not convincing reason for preferring them for historical purposes or on historical grounds. Insofar as John's differences do not seem to be variants from the Synoptics made for theological reasons, they speak on the side of the independence of the Gospel of John, whether or not the evangelist knew, or knew about, the other Gospels.

Over a half century ago, P. Gardner-Smith wrote that critics are not likely "to accept the Johannine account as historical in the narrower sense of the term; the influence of interpretation is too obvious for that; but where the Fourth

Gospel differs from the Synoptics it may henceforth be wise to treat its testimony with rather more respect than it has lately received, and perhaps in not a few cases it may prove to be right."[4] Gardner-Smith's "henceforth" modestly alluded to his own arguments for the independence of the Fourth Gospel of the Synoptics, which heralded a major change in scholarly opinion. With the publication of C.H. Dodd's *Historical Tradition in the Fourth Gospel,* the view that John wrote independently of the other Gospels, basing his narrative on a separate, if related, tradition, seemed well on the way to becoming canonical.[5] The significance of John's independence of the Synoptics for the historical question was, however, variously expressed, as the differences between Dodd and Rudolf Bultmann show. For Dodd the possible historical value of the Fourth Gospel was an important implication of its independence with distinct theological overtones, but for Bultmann, the historicity of the Fourth Gospel had been, apart from its bare-fact claim, negligible and of little theological import. In any event, John's independence could be taken for granted as a beginning point for discussion, and in his efforts to renew the defense of the historicity of the Fourth Gospel, John A. T. Robinson did just that.[6]

For those who follow Johannine scholarship, however, it is scarcely fresh news that John's independence of the Synoptics is no longer taken for granted. Indeed, a later wave of investigation moved in the opposite direction.[7] In light of this more recent movement, I want to examine some of the historical aspects or implications of the problem of the Gospels' relationship. Obviously, if the Gospel of John was wholly dependent upon the Synoptics for its portrayal of Jesus and his ministry, any deviation from them would imply a diminution of John's historical accuracy. Accordingly, the Gospel would be deemed of no value as an independent source. If, however, John was independent of the Synoptics, the question of its historical value would be worth pursuing. In the latter case, of course, nothing would be necessarily implied about its historical truth, for an independent gospel could be historically valueless or specious. But if, or insofar as, the distinctly Johannine materials present or reflect data or situations that are plausibly or arguably historical, they bespeak the independence of John from the Synoptics. While independence does not imply historical value, the attribution of historical plausibility to the distinctive Johannine material does imply independence, although it, of course, does not prove it.

Points at Which John's Account Is Historically Tenable

In all probability, at least two characteristics of the Gospel of John have led historians of Christian origins to regard it as a document of only secondary historical worth—behind the Synoptic Gospels—if it has any such value at all. In the first place, several of the signs of the Fourth Gospel surpass in their sheer miraculousness the mighty works narrated in the Synoptics. They are more spectacular or incredible. The man at the pool of Bethzatha has been ill for thirty-eight years; the blind man in chapter 9 has been blind from birth; the dead Lazarus has been in the tomb four days. Such astounding aspects of Johannine stories seem to be exaggerations based upon the already amazing deeds of Jesus narrated in the Synoptics. If in the Synoptics Jesus supplies ample food for the five thousand from a few loaves and fish (as he does also in John) the Fourth Evangelist portrays Jesus changing water into wine. But, second, even more distinctive than the Johannine Jesus' deeds are his words. In the Synoptics, especially in Mark, Jesus can scarcely be coaxed into talking about himself, whereas in the Fourth Gospel he proclaims his messianic status and argues with opponents about his dignity and role. The familiar "I am" words of Jesus are altogether typical, and distinctive, of the Gospel of John.

Both these characteristics of the Fourth Gospel are understandably, and rightly, regarded as historically suspect, while at the same time they cast doubt upon the historicity of the Johannine portrayal of Jesus and his ministry generally.[8] While the unhistorical nature of such aspects of the Gospel of John has been granted by most critical scholarship in the course of this century, a similar negative historical evaluation has gradually characterized Synoptic exegesis also. Some Johannine exegetes have sought to turn the situation in synoptic studies to the advantage of the Fourth Gospel, and its historical worth, by pointing out that John's theological character scarcely differentiates it from the other canonical gospels.[9] This is certainly true, but from the standpoint of one who values historical trustworthiness it may be small consolation!

Obviously, it does not enhance the historical value of John just to devalue the other three. Yet there are a number of points at which it may be argued that John represents, or reflects more accurately, the historical situation or events of Jesus' ministry, even if his purpose is not to narrate something we call history or biography. If one seeks criteria to identify such points, or justify their consideration as historical, three simple ones may be suggested. Elements or items deserve consideration as possibly historical that (1) without reproducing the Synoptics accord with the portrayal of Jesus found in them; (2) do not advance the distinctively Johannine Christology; and (3) are historically plausible in the time, place, and setting of Jesus' ministry. I want to point to such elements or items with brief justification, by way of inventory, without drawing any firm conclusions. For our purposes it is neither necessary nor appropriate to presuppose John's independence in the sense of his ignorance or deliberate ignoring of the Synoptics. It is obvious enough that the evangelist goes his own way. I intend simply to point to certain data and leave the conclusions up to the reader. Nothing of what I say will be entirely new. Gathering and quickly surveying the data in view of the question of John's relation to the Synoptics may, however, be worthwhile.

First, there is the chronology of Jesus' ministry. The traditional three-year ministry is, of course, an inference from the Fourth Gospel, for the Synoptics seem to presuppose a ministry of one Passover and of a year or less. John, in contrast, speaks of three distinct Passovers (2:13; 6:4; 11:55). We commonly say that the three-year scheme of the Fourth Gospel accommodates the evangelist's interest in Jesus' replacement of Jewish festivals.[10] This may be the case, but that fact alone would not necessarily mean that there is not something historically correct about John's time frame. Moreover, the synoptic (that is, Marcan) framework is generally acknowledged to be literary and theological rather than historical. Did Jesus gather disciples, teach, gain fame as a miracle worker, and arouse opposition that led to his death in less than a year? Possibly, but the traditional, longer (Johannine) time frame makes considerable sense, particularly if we take into account a period in which Jesus worked under the influence of John the Baptist, as the Fourth Gospel may imply. The ancient and traditional way of harmonizing the Gospel accounts by accommodating the other three to the Fourth Gospel was an obvious and practical apologetic procedure, but not for that reason necessarily wrong.

Another chronological consideration is, of course, the matter of when, according to the Jewish calendar, Jesus celebrated the Last Supper with his disciples and when he was put to death. According to the Synoptics the Last Supper was a Passover meal, and Jesus was tried and put to death during the feast. According to John, however, Jesus' last meal was at most a proleptic Passover feast, for it occurred the evening before Nisan 15. He was then tried and crucified before the feast (cf. Mark 14:2), so that the Jewish authorities wanted his body taken down quickly (John 19:31). In favor of the synoptic chronology it is argued that John makes an alteration to have Jesus die while the Passover lambs are slain. Odd that he should make this juxtaposition and not mention it or otherwise indicate why he has done so. Moreover, one would then expect Jesus' expiatory, salvific death to play a larger role, as it does in Paul and even 1 John. Of course, there have been elaborate efforts to explain John's deviation from the Synoptics by recourse to theories about John's midrashic character or diverging Jewish calendars. But is not the simplest explanation that the Synoptics succumb to an understandable pressure to make of the Last Supper a Passover meal, while John represents a more primitive phase in which that had not yet occurred?[11]

Closely related to the three-year Johannine chronology or itinerary of Jesus' ministry is the geographical locale, which has Jesus appearing frequently and for long periods of time in Judea and Jerusalem. Again, Johannine theological interests are apparently at work. Jerusalem is the headquarters of "the Jews." Yet if, in fact, Jesus' ministry went on for two or three years, is it not intrinsically probable that he made more than the one Passover pilgrimage to Jerusalem that the Synoptics report? The three Passover visits reported by John become a probability, even though they advance Johannine Christology. One might also note that Mark (14:49) has Jesus say to the arresting party that he was daily (*kath'hēmeran*) in the temple teaching, a statement that fits the Johannine chronology and setting better than the Marcan, according to which Jesus could have only been there a few days. Jesus' seeming familiarity with persons or places in Jerusalem, reflected precisely in the Marcan account of the preparation for the Triumphal Entry (11:3) or the Last Supper (14:13–17), bespeaks a longer acquaintance with the capital city than Mark's narrative seems to allow.

The whole question of Jesus' relationship to the Baptist (always called simply John) is handled more elaborately in the Fourth Gospel than in the Synoptics. For example, in the Fourth Gospel the Baptist goes out of his way to make sure that his own temporal priority to Jesus is not misconstrued (1:15, 30). The one who comes after—Jesus—was before, in the sense of prior to, or greater than. Bultmann, following Matthew Black, suggests the possibility that the "coming after" (*erchesthai opisō*) means following in the sense of discipleship.[12] Thus Jesus would at one time have been a disciple of John, and this was then all the more reason for the evangelist to make their actual, theological relationship clear.[13] If, indeed, Jesus himself baptized, as John more than once states (3:22, 26; 4:1), he clearly identified himself with the movement of which the Baptist was the head. The statement that only Jesus' disciples, not Jesus himself, baptized (4:2) seems a lame afterthought and correction. Moreover, this entire scene (3:22–4:3) portrays Jesus and the Baptist as working, if not side by side, at the very same time.[14]

Thus it became necessary to note, probably in light of the contradiction with the Synoptics, that John had not yet been cast into prison (3:24)—again a sort of afterthought.[15] In the Synoptics, of course, John is already out of the way, in prison, before Jesus begins his ministry (Mark 1:14). Here there is a rather strange agreement between John and Luke only, for while Luke notes that Herod imprisoned John (3:19–20), he does not make the sharp dichotomy between John's ministry and Jesus', which we might have expected of him (that is, he omits Mark 1:14). One suspects that John (with Luke) knows something, namely, that John the Baptist's ministry did not end before Jesus' began, that they were for a while contemporaries, and that John would have appeared the originator and leader of a movement Jesus joined. Thus the Fourth Evangelist needs to set matters straight theologically because he knows the somewhat embarrassing history! Certainly John's historical assumptions about the relation of Jesus and John do not serve his Christology nearly so well as the Marcan premise of the clean sequence of Jesus and John, with no overlap, would have. Yet given the conditions of first-century Palestinian Judaism, the more complex relationship predicated by the Fourth Evangelist seems entirely reasonable. What is missing from John's Gospel, of course, is the apocalyptic character of John's preaching, as well as that of Jesus, which we know so well from the Synoptics. But this is exactly what we would expect in John. Furthermore, just that apocalyptic outlook would explain the close relationship of John and Jesus, which the Fourth Gospel describes more fully than do the others. John strongly implies that Jesus was a baptist, and I am inclined to agree!

Moreover, it is arguable that John the Baptist's statement, "I did not know him" (John 1:33), reflects the historical fact that John had not known Jesus prior to this encounter. In Matthew (3:14), however, it is clearly presumed that John had prior knowledge of Jesus and of who he was. Although Mark does not state that John had such prior knowledge, Matthew may have inferred it from Mark 1:7–8. While Luke does not go beyond Mark in this narrative, he had earlier described Mary as a relative of John's mother Elizabeth (1:36), leaving the reader to presume John's knowledge of Jesus, to whom he would have been related. In the Fourth Gospel John comes to know who Jesus is, but only by virtue of the descent of the Spirit (1:33–34).

The portrayal of Jesus' relationship to John the Baptist raises the question of Jesus' own disciples, inasmuch as the Fourth Evangelist has two of them sent to Jesus by John the Baptist. That this happened in the way, and with the words of introduction (1:29, 36) John reports, is unlikely. Yet that some of Jesus' disciples had been attracted to, or were followers of, the Baptist is altogether probable, given the similarities between them. Moreover, the Johannine account is, as interpreters have noted for centuries, better motivated. In Mark (followed by Matthew) Jesus calls disciples who apparently have never before seen him, and they follow. Traditional harmonization has explained this implausible sequence by proposing that Mark's (and Matthew's) narrative assumes John's. As unlikely as this may be, it is a way of taking account of the problem and acknowledging that John supplies an answer to an important question that Mark leaves unanswered—and unasked.

Moreover, while assuming the existence of the Twelve, John clearly acknowledges that Jesus had other disciples, indeed, some who deserted him (6:66). Is it likely that John would have fabricated such a scene had he not known it, or at least the fact of their desertion, as a given?[16] Of course, we now tend to look first at John's own situation to explain and identify such deserters, but if the evangelist had such contemporaries in mind, he could easily have had Jesus predict their desertion in the farewell discourses rather than insert them into his Galilean ministry.

John not only knows that there were disciples who deserted Jesus. He also knows that the loyal disciples did not understand Jesus during his earthly ministry, but only after his crucifixion and resurrection.[17] Mark, of course, knows this as well. But John differs from Mark in his presentation of this state of affairs. In Mark, Jesus clearly predicts his coming death (and resurrection) and seemingly holds the disciples accountable for their failure to understand. John, however, regards the disciples as unable to understand, because the crucial events have, after all, not occurred, and the Holy Spirit or Paraclete has not yet come. Although John's presentation of Jesus is in some ways highly anachronistic—and much more so than the Synoptics'—John does not have Jesus predict his own death so openly; rather he alludes to it obliquely (3:14–15; 12:32), and the disciples are not clearly and culpably obtuse for not understanding. In this respect John seems closer to what must have been the actual situation of Jesus' disciples during his ministry. They did not understand because as yet they could not. Incidentally, in this connection Peter's confession in John does not betray that disciple's failure to understand and his culpability as it does in Mark, and John otherwise shows no particular desire to elevate or exonerate Peter. (Chapter 21 might be regarded as an exception, but even there Peter is subordinated to the Beloved Disciple, who as one who all along does understand in that sense at least represents the postresurrection church.)

Perhaps less important than Jesus' relationship to his disciples, but nevertheless interesting, is his relationship to his family—mother, brothers, and father. Suffice it to say that, as in the Synoptics (Mark 3:21, 31–35), Jesus puts distance between himself and his mother and brothers in incidents that are, however, distinctive of the Fourth Gospel (2:1–11; 7:1–10).

Another of Jesus' relationships that stands out as significant involves the women who appear in the Fourth Gospel.[18] Jesus' mother (never called Mary in the Fourth Gospel) plays a larger and more positive role in the Johannine narrative than in the synoptic, but one that is not contradictory to the synoptic accounts. Jesus' encounter and conversation with the Samaritan woman at Jacob's Well (chapter 4) is, of course, unique to the Fourth Gospel. (Luke shares an interest in Samaria, as well as in Jesus' female followers, with the Fourth Gospel, but without sharing the same narratives.) But here the Johannine Jesus manifests typically human characteristics. He is tired from the journey in the heat of the day, as well as thirsty, and strikes up a conversation with the approaching woman, asking her for a drink. That Jesus should initiate a conversation with a woman, much less a Samaritan, is out of keeping with Jewish custom, as the story eventually indicates (4:9, 27), but this state of affairs does not necessarily speak against the historicity of the incident. Indeed, Jesus' approach to the Samaritan woman, his apparent openness to her, is congruent with and complements the synoptic, especially the Lucan, picture of Jesus. *That* Jesus might have behaved in this way. The reader may be pleasantly surprised, but he is not confused. The conversation that develops is, of course, replete with Johannine theological themes and reflects the style and vocabulary of the Fourth Evangelist. One would be hard pressed to argue that John presents an account of an actual conversation between Jesus and this woman.

The sisters of Lazarus, Mary and Martha of Bethany, appear only in John (11:1–45; cf. 12:1–18) and Luke (10:38–42). But only in John are they said to be sisters of Lazarus and to reside in Bethany. In John as in Luke they play host to Jesus and thus appear as his friends. In fact, Jesus is said to love them, even as he loves Lazarus (John 11:5). In John only, of course, this Mary anoints the feet of Jesus and wipes them with her hair (12:1–8; cf. Luke 7:36–50, in which the woman is not named). In John the apparent personal relationship between Jesus and this family in Bethany is the basis of a theologically important narrative: Jesus raises the brother Lazarus from the dead. But whatever one makes of this episode, it scarcely calls into question the verisimilitude of the relationship. Obviously, verisimilitude is not the same as historical factuality, but it is its sine qua non. That Mary and Martha appear also in Luke in a somewhat different narrative enhances the credibility of the Johannine notices. It is, of course, possible that John has here taken up the sisters from Luke, made the Lazarus of the Lucan parable (16:19–31) their brother, and constructed the narratives we now read in his Gospel. (But such a proposal involves us in the larger question of the relationship of Luke to John, which presents difficulties for it, that is, the distinctively Lucan material or L, is scarcely paralleled in John.)

Then there is Mary Magdalene, who in John, as in the other Gospels, appears at the cross and at the empty tomb. (In Luke she is not named at the cross, but only Luke indicates that she had an earlier relationship with Jesus; cf. 8:2.) In John she becomes the first witness of an appearance of the risen Christ (20:11–18). This is also the case in Matt 28:9–10, although there her role is not stressed. Again, it is possible that John has taken a small item from Matthew and enlarged it greatly, but again we encounter the problem of explaining John's larger relationship—or lack of it—to the other Gospel.[19] Certainly John has ascribed a larger role to Mary Magdalene. She now stands out along with the mother of Jesus, the Samaritan woman, and the sisters Mary and Martha as one of the prominent people of the Gospel story. Is it more reasonable to believe that John in his social and theological setting enhanced their roles because of his nascent feminist interests or that he reflects here, albeit in ways different from the Synoptics, Jesus' actual relationships with women who followed him?

The Johannine Passion Narrative contains a number of interesting divergences from the Synoptics. We have already noticed the flagrant difference in the dating of the Last Supper and Jesus' crucifixion. The other most striking Johannine departure is the omission of any trial before the Sanhedrin following Jesus' arrest. Ironically, John's dating of the arrest before the feast lightens one of the major objections to the historicity of such a trial. Obviously, there is also an element of confusion in John, for Jesus is sent to Annas the father-in-law of the high priest Caiaphas (18:12–13), but subsequently in the same episode Annas is referred to as high priest. At the end Jesus is sent off bound by Annas to Caiaphas the high priest, but nothing is said about what happened there. Is the Marcan (and Matthean) account of the trial to be assumed in reading John? Apparently Luke did not assume it; at least he moves the whole

Sanhedrin scene to the morning after and at the same time removes its juridical elements (22:66–71). How is John's omission to be explained? On the one hand, we are told that the Jewish trial scene is superfluous in John, because all along Jesus has been on trial before the Jews.[20] Moreover, a Jewish verdict against Jesus seems to be presumed in the trial before Pilate (18:30–31), but whether it is based on the verdict of a missing trial scene or the conclusion of the case against Jesus made throughout the Gospel is hard to say. On the other hand, John's omission of the trial is a problem for the exegete because its inclusion would seemingly have fulfilled his purpose and design so well. Jesus is condemned because he finally claims to be the Messiah, the claim that has gotten him in trouble with the authorities since the beginning of his ministry in the Fourth Gospel. Of course, the Marcan episode presents severe historical problems as to its time, execution, and verdict—much more so than the Johannine. Whether John knew Mark or not, his version is to be preferred on historical grounds.[21]

Other distinctive elements of John's account are historically plausible. A (Roman) cohort is involved in Jesus' arrest (18:3). Overkill perhaps, but Roman involvement, especially at Passover, might be expected. After his condemnation, Jesus leaves for the place of execution, bearing his own cross (19:17), the usual procedure in a crucifixion. Of course, in the Synoptics (Mark 15:21 par.) Simon of Cyrene is impressed to carry Jesus' cross. Traditional exegesis has long combined the two; Jesus starts out as in John but subsequently needs help, as Mark describes.[22] This is, in fact, quite possible, although we can scarcely get beyond conjecture in the matter. Only John tells of the intention to break the legs of the three crucified men in order to speed their death, again a common practice. The soldiers in the detail dispatched to do this found Jesus already dead, and this finding agrees with what we read in Mark, namely, that Pilate was surprised to learn that Jesus had already died (15:44). Again, we have to be content with the observation that John's report of the crucifragium could be historically true. That it was invented to provide fulfillment of scripture (Ps 34:21; cf. Exod 12:46 and Num 9:12; Zech 12:10) is possible, but I think less likely than that those passages were used to interpret a historical event, or at least one conveyed as such by tradition. (Such Old Testament testimonia in the Fourth Gospel seem to be traditional rather than the composition of the evangelist, because they frequently have synoptic or other New Testament parallels.)

Missing from the broader Johannine passion is, of course, the cleansing of the temple, which had already taken place on Jesus' first Passover pilgrimage to Jerusalem. Traditional Christian exegesis has resolved the seeming contradiction between John and the Synoptics by having Jesus cleanse the temple twice—an unlikely solution. Robinson's proposal that the Fourth Gospel is correct on this point and the Synoptics wrong has found few takers because of Robinson's other views, but it is by no means outlandish.[23] Most of us have preferred to think that Jesus' action in the temple led directly to his arrest and execution at the same Passover. But it remains possible that Jesus' action at an earlier Passover caught the attention of the temple authorities and caused them to lie in wait for him on his return. (Such a scenario is all the more credible on the basis of E. P. Sanders's view that the displacement of the old temple with a new one was a central item of Jesus' eschatological agenda.[24]) However that may be, it remains arguable and perhaps even likely, that John's departures from the Synoptics·in the passion narrative reflect a more accurate view of what actually took place.

Turning briefly to the resurrection narratives, we find a new and different situation, for here as nowhere else in the Gospel all John's episodes have synoptic parallels, whether close or remote. The arrival of the Beloved Disciple and Peter at the empty tomb, probably a Johannine composition, seems to be the outstanding exception, but even that is already suggested by Luke (24:12, 24). At this point in the narrative, if anywhere, John's account appears to be clearly secondary to the Synoptics. I have already observed that in the Fourth Gospel Jesus' initial resurrection appearance is to Mary Magdalene, but even here John's dramatic account can be viewed as a development of Matthew's rather brief and colorless notice of Jesus' appearance to Mary Magdalene and the other Mary at the tomb.

The most striking and original Johannine resurrection account is, however, in the epilogue (21:1–14). This story, paralleled only in the call narrative of Luke 5:1–11, is presented as the third resurrection appearance of Jesus (21:14), although it is actually the fourth, counting the one to Mary Magdalene. In part because of the Lucan parallel, it has been understood by some exegetes, preeminently Robert T. Fortna, as a sign story that has been transferred to the resurrection period.[25] But the Gospel of Mark and the *Gospel of Peter* anticipate a Galilean resurrection appearance of Jesus. Indeed, *Peter*'s account seems to anticipate just such a scene by the sea as we find in the Fourth Gospel. John's narrative is on the face of it more likely to be a traditional resurrection narrative than the rather obviously Matthean composition that concludes the First Gospel. In fact, this appearance narrative is exactly the one that Mark's Gospel leads us to expect, even to the extent that Peter plays a leading role. (The women are told in Mark 16:7 to tell Jesus' disciples and Peter.) One might facetiously suggest that the lost ending of Mark's Gospel somehow became the appendix to John's! I am not going to suggest that, but, more soberly, that the narrative of John 21:1–14 may well be the earliest account of Jesus' appearance to his disciples that we possess.[26]

Conclusion

If this rather brief survey of the Gospel of John seems to confirm the impression of John's independence with which I started, that should come as no surprise. I have, in effect, been spelling out the basis for that impression. In conclusion, I return to the question of John and the Synoptics, which has hovered in the background all along. What conclusion may be drawn by way of summary? Simply, that where John possesses, reflects, or advances data or a point of view different from, or at odds with, the Synoptic Gospels or tradition, its statements or narratives deserve serious consideration as quite possibly historically superior to the Synoptics. The distinctive Johannine Christology, however, is usually found in the discourses and dialogues of Jesus, which on other grounds seem to be compositions of the evangelist. They scarcely represent the utterances of the historical Jesus.

Are we then to infer that John is independent of the Synoptics? Not necessarily, particularly if independence means ignorance. But if independence means not being determined or even overly influenced by the Synoptics, John certainly seems to live up to that standard, especially in his use of an array of historical data concerning which there is little reason to prefer the Synoptics. Indeed, as we have seen there is often good reason to prefer John.[27]

This chapter closely parallels chapter 7, "Jesus Tradition in the Gospel of John," and that is not coincidental. In the process of preparing this piece, I developed questions and possible conclusions about issues subsequently set out in chapter 7. Moreover, at that earlier time a number of important and relevant works had not appeared: Paula Fredriksen's *Jesus of Nazareth: King of the Jews,* John P. Meier's *A Marginal Jew,* and Raymond E. Brown's *The Death of the Messiah.* Of course, all of these are now cited in "Jesus Tradition in the Gospel of John."

II

The Question of Gospel Genre

Did Mark Create the Genre?

The relationship of the question of gospel genre to the problem of John and the Synoptics is a fascinating one. It has often been assumed that if John got little else from Mark directly, Mark was his inspiration and pattern for writing a gospel in the first place.[1] The purpose of this chapter is not so much to argue against the assumption as to set it in the context of twentieth-century scholarship. Especially, I want to show why the contrary assumption, namely, that John need not have derived the notion to write a gospel from the Synoptics specifically seemed a natural one given the state of scholarship at mid-century. By the same token, the view that John adopted (and adapted) the gospel genre from Mark (or the Synoptics) is in some measure a reflection of a change in emphasis or perspective in gospel scholarship that has been going on for some time.

The issue of whether all the canonical Gospels belong to the same genre could detain us for some time. *Genre* itself, as used in English, means kind, sort, style, category; specifically, "a distinctive type or category of literary composition" (*Webster's Unabridged*, Third Edition). When applied to literary works, the term implies that the works fall into groups distinguished by style, purpose, and form (*Webster's Unabridged:* genre is "applied especially to works of literature or art as falling into distinctive groups with respect to style, form, purpose, etc.").

Clearly the canonical Gospels all consist of narratives of Jesus' ministry, beginning with his encounter with John the Baptist and ending with his execution and the discovery of his tomb empty. They all portray Jesus as working miracles, teaching, and engaging in controversy with opponents, who are often said to be scribes and Pharisees (except that scribes are not mentioned in John). These common characteristics and others are shared by the Fourth Gospel as well as the Synoptics. John and Mark are with reason said to be more intensely christological or kerygmatic than the other two in that they lack the traditional teaching material of Jesus, usually associated with Q, M, and L. Yet when compared with such documents as the *Gospel of Thomas,* not to mention the *Gospel of Truth* or the *Gospel of Philip,* John is much closer to any of the Synoptics whether in form or in content. One may argue that Matthew is a kind of Christian manual of discipline or that Luke is ancient religious biography, and there is significant truth in these judgments. Yet they are both certainly closer in content, and also in form and structure, to Mark or John than to any other documents of antiquity.

Patricia L. Cox has, however, emphasized that "form, or structure, is only one aspect of genre, and thus should not be equated with it. Genre is a broader concept, best defined as an association of qualities that are standard features of the works under consideration." These qualities "include structure, formal literary units, sources, types of characterization and motifs, as well as social setting and the author's attitude and intention."[2] On the basis of such parameters the canonical Gospels do seem to exhibit a similar genre. Obviously in the case of the Synoptics there is considerable similarity of content and form. From the probability that both the evangelists Matthew and Luke, by absorbing much of Mark's narrative, including its form and style, intended to displace it in church usage, one can infer a similar, if not identical, function and purpose. John is another matter, particularly with regard to style. Yet even John possesses similarities of content, form, and purpose (see John 20:31), elements which would of necessity be ingredient to any reasonable understanding of the concept. If those similarities do not seem obvious to all, they have been and continue to be to most.[3]

Granted such similarities, did the idea for, or the genre of, the gospels develop more or less independently along more than one track? Or must the genre have been bequeathed to John in much the same way as Mark apparently bequeathed it to Matthew and Luke? (Of course, a minority of Lucan scholars would argue that Luke had already composed—or received—a primitive gospel, that is, Proto-Luke, before he knew Mark, and some scholars suspect there was a primitive, perhaps Aramaic, form of Matthew that antedated Mark). This question gets us to the heart of modern discussion about the genre, or character, of the canonical Gospels. Was it implicit in the (oral) tradition all along, so that the emergence of a gospel should be no surprise, but what might be expected given the "laws" of traditional development? Or was the creation of a gospel, presumably by Mark, an epoch-making and unprecedented achievement? To cast the alternatives that sharply should contribute to the clarity of the discussion. The implications for Johannine-synoptic relations are strongly implied by, if they do not follow inevitably from, either alternative.

The Character of the Gospels

Fundamental to the discussion of the character of the gospels, and therefore of gospel genre, has been the work by Karl Ludwig Schmidt, "Die Stellung der Evangelien in der allgemeinen Literaturgeschichte," originally published in the

Festschrift honoring Hermann Gunkel in 1923.[4] Schmidt undertook in this long essay to characterize the place of the gospels in literary history and therefore to give an account of their genre. Interestingly enough, he begins his discussion by noting the earlier (1915) treatment of the American Clyde Weber Votaw, then a professor at the University of Chicago.[5] Votaw had championed the view that the gospels can be understood and interpreted as biographies, albeit ancient biographies.[6] Schmidt would take an opposing view. It will be germane to our purpose to review Schmidt's position and his criticism of Votaw.

Votaw did not set forth his position without an awareness of the distinctiveness and religious character of the gospels. Although, as Schmidt makes clear, Votaw's work is not encumbered with any *Auseinandersetzung* with the scholarly literature; it is not simply naive or uninformed in its approach. Schmidt agrees with Votaw's characterization of the gospels as special and popular writings "of the people, by the people, and for the people." (Whether Schmidt caught the allusion to Abraham Lincoln's Gettysburg Address, we shall never know!) Votaw knows the gospels are not inspired by the historical impulse and method, but are "propagandist writings of this early Christian movement."[7] To the question of whether the gospels are biographies, Votaw must answer both no and yes, depending on what is meant by biography. If one means a work based upon research and criticism, then obviously the gospels are not that. But if one means by biography "any writing which aims to make one acquainted with a historical person by giving some account of his deeds and words, sketchily chosen and arranged, even when the motive of the writer is practical and hortatory rather than historical," then the gospels also are biographies.[8] The name cannot be denied them.

There were comparable biographies, particularly of Greek philosophers, in antiquity. Votaw selects for closer examination and comparison Philostratus' *Life of Apollonius of Tyana,* and the presentations of Socrates in Plato's dialogues and in Xenophon's *Memorabilia.* Apollonius, a Pythagorean philosopher whose life spanned most of the first century, was like Jesus in that he was an itinerant teacher who never committed his own teaching to writing. Miraculous deeds were attributed to Apollonius also. Philostratus' work was, however, written in the third century and was largely based on a chronicle of Damis, one of Apollonius' followers. The comparison of the biographies of Jesus with those of Socrates is even more difficult because of the obviously different character of the sources; Plato or even Xenophon and the evangelists are hardly to be compared. Yet Votaw is obviously struck with, and makes a great deal of, the parallels between the work and impact of Socrates and Jesus on Greek and Jewish life respectively. He speaks of Socrates' "ministry," and in effect compares the search for the historical Jesus with the search for Socrates.[9] Moreover, there is some similarity in the character of the sources. For example, the later Platonic dialogues are remotely comparable to the Gospel of John, for in both we see primarily the thought of the author rather than his subject.[10] While Votaw makes many correct observations, as Schmidt allows, he sometimes misconstrues the character of the gospels for the sake of a positive comparison. For example, of Philostratus' *Life of Apollonius* and the gospels, Votaw says they were similar in that "the purpose in each case was a practical one, to promote morality and religion by eulogizing and commending the great teacher in his message and in his example."[11] What is correct in this comparison is as obvious as what is missing, namely the kerygmatic and theological dimension of the gospels, as well as their cultic function and setting.

Schmidt correctly observes that there are great differences among the ancient biographies with which Votaw purports to deal. He is also correct in seeing that their authors taken together differ sharply from the evangelists; they are *Schriftstellerpersönlichkeiten,* writes Schmidt. Yet in this way, despite correct beginnings, we come to no literary-historical appreciation of the gospels.[12] Votaw has in his enthusiasm overstated the similarities, while nevertheless recognizing differences. At the same time, Schmidt's description of the Greek biographers of Socrates, Apollonius, et al. as "literary personalities" already reveals his own attitude toward the evangelists. They are not authors with literary identities and aspirations. (That judgment may be correct, but a later generation will ask whether Schmidt has not unduly minimized the creative role of the evangelists.)

Gospels, according to Schmidt, are from the very beginning not high literature (*Hochliteratur*) but popular literature (*Kleinliteratur*), not the accomplishment of individual authors, but folkbooks, not biographies, but cult legend.[13] Schmidt's essay is then devoted to making this case through a variety of arguments and comparisons (with Faustus legends, lives of monks, their apophthegmata, medieval lives of St. Francis, and so forth). Among other things, his indebtedness to the newly attained insights of form criticism, of which he was a pioneer, is clear. It will be worthwhile to spell out in some detail the character of this indebtedness.[14]

Form Criticism

As is commonly known, form criticism (form history) took its rise from certain basic insights, which were applied to the biblical materials initially by Gunkel. First of all, in contrast to *Hochliteratur,* in which the self-consciousness of the author and his literary purpose are primary, much of the biblical material shares with popular writings or books (*Volksbücher*) an anonymity which is alien to literary interests. Second, such popular writings or traditions have their origin not with individual authors, but with a community (*Gemeinde*). They are rooted in the life of that community or cult, answering to its interests and needs. Third, the stories and sayings were spoken and transmitted orally before having been written down. Fourth, individual units of (oral) tradition are the primary material out of which the gospels were composed. We deal first with stories of Jesus before coming to the story of Jesus. These insights and perspectives about the gospel are established mainly by comparison with other popular materials, which of course have ultimately been written down and collected in books. The dates of such popular materials are of little significance, because we are dealing with a widespread phenomenon of popular cultures that manifests itself in remarkably similar ways among different peoples in various periods.

For Schmidt, the correctness of this approach and perspective was confirmed by his own work on the framework of the story of Jesus, *Der Rahmen der Geschichte Jesu,* which revealed that the ancient Jesus tradition is enshrined in the individual pericopes.[15] The general narrative framework which lends unity and coherence to the material—that is, that makes it a story—is redactional. His own work, while adumbrating the rise of redaction criticism, finds corroboration in, and corroborates, the rather different form-critical works of Rudolf Bultmann and Martin Dibelius. Their view of the character of the gospels, like Schmidt's, arises out of their fundamental assessment of the nature of the stuff of the gospels. Most importantly, there is continuity between the material of the gospels and their final form.

In oft-cited statements Dibelius makes this form-critical consensus clear: "The literary understanding of the synoptics begins with the recognition that they are collections of material. The composers are only to the smallest extent authors. They are primarily collectors, vehicles of tradition, editors."[16] "What took place previously was the formation and growth of small separate pieces out of which the gospels were put together. Even these little pieces obey the laws of Form-construction. They do it all the more as in the development of *their* form the individuality of an original writer played no real part. To trace out those laws, to make comprehensible the rise of these little categories, is to write the history of the Form of the Gospel."[17]

The law which governed the formulation of the tradition was to be found in missionary purpose, which was the cause, and preaching, which was the means "of spreading abroad that which the disciples possessed as recollections."[18] To say preaching is tantamount to saying oral tradition. Thus we already see in Dibelius the emphasis on the nonliterary, oral, communal, and fragmentary character of the material which we found in Schmidt. One finds, of course, a closely allied position in the work of Bultmann.[19] Bultmann differed from Dibelius who, he thought, confined the originative, germinal matrix of the tradition much too narrowly to preaching. But both Dibelius and Bultmann saw in the passion narrative the only exception to the rule that the gospel material was originally transmitted in the form of individual pericopes, stories or sayings. Bultmann observed, however, that the passion narrative too was made up of individual pieces and was not in its totality an organic unity, although he defended the existence of a core narrative into which individual stories such as the Last Supper and the Garden of Gethsemane had been fitted.[20]

For both Dibelius and Bultmann the line of development from oral tradition to written gospel was a direct one, as the title of the English translation of Dibelius's form-critical work indicates: *From Tradition to Gospel.* The evangelists in collecting the tradition also became interpreters of tradition, but there is no sharp line of demarcation. On the one hand, Bultmann heartily endorses Dibelius's characterization of Mark as "the book of secret epiphanies."[21] Mark has combined the Hellenistic Christ-kerygma with the Jesus tradition. Yet, on the other hand, Bultmann regards this development as a logical extension of forces already at work in the tradition. It is not sufficient, however, to see the writing of a gospel simply as the natural result of the fact that the tradition concerned a historical person. Bultmann writes:

> But this consideration by no means suffices to explain the peculiar character of the Synoptic gospels. Indeed, their lack of specifically biographical material, their lacunae in the life story of Jesus are due to their presentation being based on the then extant tradition. But their own specific characteristic, a creation of Mark, can be understood only from the *character of the Christian kerygma,* whose expansion and illustration the gospels had to serve. . . . The Christ who is preached is not the historic Jesus, but the Christ of the faith and the cult.[22]

When Mark writes, he does something original, but the originative impulse arises out of the tradition and the cult; Mark receives the one and lives within the other. Bultmann goes on to say that "the *Gospels are expanded cult legends.*"[23] He speaks as if there were a certain inevitability in Mark's accomplishment, despite the fact it was Mark who first did it. For Bultmann the gospels as a whole grew "out of the imminent urge to development which lay in the tradition fashioned for various motives, and out of the Christ-myth and Christ-cult of Hellenistic Christianity."[24] The gospel genre is thus more "an original creation of Christianity" than of Mark.

We have then before us the classical form-critical view of the gospels and of gospel genre, represented preeminently by Schmidt, Dibelius, and Bultmann. The gospels are *von Haus aus,* as the German so graphically puts it—community, church documents. The stuff of the gospels, from beginning to end, in whole or in part, is cultic and communal; it is not the product of individual literary effort and achievement.

In England this perspective and method were embraced by no less prominent a scholar than C. H. Dodd. He perceived the gospels as a whole as defined by tradition, and not only in the ways suggested by his German colleagues. In his view, the brief kerygmatic formulations of Paul, and especially Acts, based as they were on preaching, grew and reached their proper fulfillment and expression in the composition of the gospels themselves, particularly Mark and John.[25] In other words, the general gospel structure, not just the stuff of the gospels, is defined by tradition. Bultmann had also suggested that the gospel resulted from the coming together of the Jesus tradition and the Christ kerygma, but Dodd wants to see in that kerygma more than a catalyst. It is the structuring principle on which the gospel genre developed (although Dodd does not use the term *genre*). Thus there was a unity of perspective among major New Testament scholars, a unity which had emerged in the 1920s and 1930s but was not recognized and exploited until after World War II.

If we ask what is the relationship between this state of affairs and Johannine scholarship, some intriguing, if subtle, connections come to light. In the first place two of the four scholars who figure largely in our discussion, Bultmann and Dodd, wrote major works on the Fourth Gospel. Neither felt John's use of the Synoptics was a hypothesis necessary to explain the text. Indeed, Dodd's *Historical Tradition in the Fourth Gospel*[26] has as its major conclusion that John did not base his narrative on the Synoptics but on an independent, probably oral, tradition. Bultmann's monumental commentary sets out a literary theory in which use of the Synoptic Gospels per se figures peripherally and only in the very last stage, although there were earlier contacts with synoptic, or synoptic-like tradition.

Before Dodd or Bultmann, P. Gardner-Smith had already (1938) offered as one justification of the view that John was independent of the Synoptics the insights of form criticism into the oral character of the most primitive Christian tradition, and his linking of the two was entirely reasonable.[27] In an early church in which traditions were formed and transmitted orally according to certain laws, it would be entirely likely that parallel but different traditions of the same events or words of Jesus would be transmitted, with the result that they would surface independently in different gospels. Thus, for example, John's story of the ruler's son (4:46–54) or his saying about a prophet not being without honor except in his own country (4:44) might quite naturally turn up there without that implying that the Fourth Gospel was necessarily dependent on any or all of the other three.[28]

Moreover, the perception of form critics that the forces that governed the tradition were also at work in the formation of the gospels was entirely amenable to, if it did not require, the view that gospels of a generally similar sort might emerge quite independently of one another. Such gospels might have similar content and form, given the nature and shape of the material, and all the more so if there were independently formed passion narratives circulating among Christians. Martin Kähler's description of the gospels as passion narratives with extended introductions applies particularly to Mark and John.[29] Given the form-critical view of the development of primitive passion narratives, it would be easy to conceive of more than one rendition of a passion narrative serving independently as core and catalyst of more than one gospel. Indeed, just those gospels which Kähler's description seems to fit best become conceivable as independent of one another. Indeed, apart from the passion and related narratives and material, Mark and John have little enough in common.

Redaction Criticism

The post–World War II period in New Testament scholarship, of course, saw the rise of redaction criticism, which accepted the results of source and form criticism but sought to move beyond them by paying attention to the compositional work of the evangelists. They were now no longer seen as the final increment in a process, but as significant, theologically imbued figures who shaped the material they received in accord with their distinctive insights and purposes. Form and source criticism of course provided the means of identifying redaction over against sources (Mark, Q, or tradition) and thus of performing the redaction-critical task. Redaction critics such as Hans Conzelmann and Willi Marxsen took form critics to task, not so much for having erred in what they did as for having failed to perceive what they should have, namely the creative role of the evangelists.[30] So now the *Schriftstellerpersönlichkeiten* whom Schmidt kicked out the front door seem to be coming in the back! It is probably safe to say that redaction criticism as a mode of interpretation has dominated gospel exegesis until the present. Yet questions of whether one ought to concentrate attention so heavily upon the redactional elements at the expense of the tradition, when the distinction between them is not always so obvious or certain, have certainly arisen. Principal questions as to what really is, or should be, the object of interpretation—the last redactional layer or the text as a whole as it stands—have not been wanting either. Nevertheless, the preeminence of the redaction-critical mode and method of analysis and interpretation in the period since World War II is more or less self-evident.

We must now ask what further implications this state of affairs has had for Johannine scholarship and especially the question of John and the Synoptics. It is well worth observing that Bultmann himself adopted this exegetical method in his own commentary, even though *Redaktionsgeschichte*, as it has since come to be called, had not yet been baptized or named.

Bultmann's interpretation of the Fourth Gospel is really his probing of the evangelist's thought and mind, carried out by examining his use and interpretation of the putative sources which he employed. (Not surprisingly, in the period after the war, redaction criticism flourished especially among Bultmann's disciples.) Although Robert T. Fortna radically revised and simplified Bultmann's analysis, his interpretative program was in principle the same, that is, to come to an understanding of the evangelist's intention and message by analyzing his use of sources and his own distinctive commentary upon them.[31] In the case of Bultmann, Fortna, and others, interpretation has meant exegesis by means of redaction-critical analysis. Significantly, the base of this analysis has generally been provided by a hypothetical traditional source or sources other than the Synoptic Gospels.

By and large, the redaction criticism of John has, since the inception of the art, developed along with the view that John did not know, or at least did not use, other canonical Gospels. It cannot be claimed that anything is thereby proven, but it may be significant that, as applied to John, redaction-critical method and perspective tended to reinforce the view, largely formed in light of form criticism, that the Fourth Gospel is independent of the Synoptics. Johannine redaction criticism had to begin by reconstructing the Gospel source(s), and that source has not seemed to be Mark or one of the Synoptics. By way of contrast, synoptic redaction criticism flourishes under the aegis of Marcan priority and the two-document hypothesis. Matthew and Luke independently have Mark as their source. It is certainly interesting and probably significant that the scholarly reading of John apart from the Synoptics had been on the rise since the development of form criticism and at first burgeoned with the development of redaction criticism. Is it now the case that as serious challenges have been raised against the form-critical method and as the adequacy of conventional redaction criticism (with its sharp distinctions between tradition and redaction) has also been called into question, especially insofar as it presupposes oral tradition or sources,[32] certainty about John's independence of the Synoptics has diminished? Both things have been happening. Form and redaction criticism are no longer sacred cows, and John's use of the Synoptics is again asserted. How closely are the two related?

A Primitive Passion Source

To begin with, a crucial element in the form- and redaction-critical consensus was the continuing belief that Mark had used a primitive passion source similar or parallel to the basic narrative of John. (Possibly Mark had also used sources elsewhere in his narrative, for example, in the feeding narratives of chapters 6 and 8, which have a parallel in John 6.) During the 1970s, however, and on both sides of the Atlantic, the view that John had used such a source began to erode. In Germany the work of Eta Linnemann, among others, heralded the demise of heretofore rather solid agreement about Mark's use of such a continuous source.[33] If Mark had composed the rest of his Gospel out of isolated pieces of tradition, why not the passion narrative as well? In England, E. J. Pryke's London University dissertation on Marcan redaction reduced the extent of what can be ascribed to Mark's passion source, even though he continued to speak of it as though it existed.[34]

Among Perrin's students the work of John Donahue and Werner Kelber has been particularly important in this connection. In his Chicago dissertation, Donahue questioned the necessity of predicating a continuous source for Mark's

trial narrative (14:53–65).[35] Would it not be just as satisfactory, if not more satisfactory, to think of Mark's having himself composed a passion narrative out
of isolated elements of tradition? Perrin himself pointed to the juxtaposition of
Peter's denial with the trial scene in both Mark and John as evidence of the latter's dependence upon the former.[36] Kelber, whose skepticism about the existence of a Marcan passion source had already become evident, in his major
work *The Oral and the Written Gospel* rejected the still widely held view that the
historical verisimilitude of Mark's passion story said anything about its tradition origins, much less its historicity.[37] Mark is simply a skillful narrator who
creates the illusion of historical reality.

Moreover, Kelber is representative of a growing skepticism towards the
recovery of oral and traditional materials of which there is no evidence save the
written documents alleged to embrace them. We might in this connection
mention also the literary-critical approach of Stephen Moore, who has left
source- and tradition-critical questions far behind.[38] These and other scholars,
taken together, represent a movement away from the generally held assumptions of form criticism and the older redaction criticism that simply took form
criticism's approach and general results for granted. Now its validity and results
are instead called into question. Kelber and Güttgemanns are unwilling to
grant that one can make inferences from a gospel text backward to its form and
function. Therefore the form of an *Urtext* behind the Gospel's passion narrative, much less its kerygmatic function, is at best a figment of the informed
scholarly imagination, but it is scarcely an assured result of scientific criticism.

Now to draw together the implications of such recent criticism for the
question of John and the Synoptics. In the first place, the growing recognition
of the freedom and scope of the evangelists' work, especially Mark's, had led
to an increasing recognition of the extent to which individual imagination
has been at work in the process of composition, even in the passion narrative.
(Thus, in a sense, the return of *Schriftstellerpersönlichkeiten*!) By the same
token, while there has been a diminution in confidence in our ability to reconstruct whatever source an evangelist used, it has not seemed necessary to pred-
icate a source, much less a continuous source narrative, at every point in the
narrative. On these terms the case for a primitive passion source seems to many
much less compelling than it once did.

In the second place, the more recent critics, of whom Kelber and Erhardt
Güttgemanns are representative, have not been willing to take for granted a traditioning process that began with the oral formulation of materials, individual
narratives, and resulted in the writing of a gospel or gospels. In other words,
they have rejected the view that the emergence of gospels was a logical or natural culmination of the forces at work in the traditioning process. Indeed,
something quite to the contrary is the case. For example, with Kelber it is precisely the point that writing down the gospel launches an entirely new era in

which the written text, far from continuing the oral tradition, so that we might easily move from one to the other, stands over against it. The living, burgeoning vitality of orality is, so to speak, placed under the iron hand of textuality, which constrains it and, in effect, changes the very nature of the subject matter.

Conclusions

The conclusion can be rather simply stated. In an era in which the perspectives and methods of form criticism were dominant, the possibility of the emergence of more than one gospel, as well as the existence of various renditions of the passion narrative, was taken for granted. Redaction criticism, assuming the results of form criticism, did not at first alter this picture. Yet with the advent of redaction criticism there was already an increased emphasis on the compositional work and even the creativity of the original author and less upon the shaping and staying power of tradition. One consequence was a growing uncertainty about the shape of preliterary tradition and our ability to recover it. Another consequence was an increased emphasis on the importance and epoch-making character of the composition of gospels in the first instance. Previously the tradition had been fragmentary and the growth of tradition had created a centrifugal force. Now the dominant force was unitary and centripetal. Thus the first evangelist, presumably Mark, took a bold and creative step in writing a narrative gospel, one that the previous development of tradition scarcely prepared for, much less made inevitable. His work was a break with tradition, not a continuation of it. On these terms, the likelihood increased that subsequent gospels would be derivative from the first, that is, that John would be dependent on Mark for the genre of the gospel itself, if for relatively little else compared with Matthew and Luke.[39] Moreover, there was, given this state of affairs, a growing uncertainty about the shape of any preliterary tradition, much less our ability to recover it.

Obviously, what is at stake here is the climate of scholarship from one generation to the next, so to speak, rather than direct influence of one scholar upon another. Naturally, other important factors have also changed the climate of opinion on the question of the relationship of John to the Synoptic Gospels, particularly the close exegetical work of Frans Neirynck and his Louvain colleagues. Such work is not directly influenced by the present climate of scholarship that I have described, as far as I can see. Nevertheless, in that climate, which distances the gospel literature from earlier tradition and encourages the investigation of intertextuality, the view that John must have been dependent on the Synoptics—at least for its genre—gets a friendly reception. The principal implication of my thesis, if valid, is that the question of John and the Synoptics should evoke a consideration, or reconsideration, of the question of gospel genre, particularly as it relates to the origin of gospels. Was the writing of gospels a break with tradition rather than its natural culmination? This has been roundly stated and therefore made the working hypothesis of some exegesis, but is it an assured result of criticism? On the question of the positive relation of the growth of the tradition to the writing of gospels, were both Bultmann and Dodd wrong? While their agreement on John's independence of the Synoptics was not explicitly tied to their view of the development of the gospel genre out of the tradition, the one made very good sense in the light of the other.

John and the Apocryphal Gospels

Was John the First Apocryphal Gospel?

Within the past several decades there has been increasing scholarly interest in the existence, character, and significance of the so-called apocryphal gospels. I have specified apocryphal gospels rather than noncanonical gospels in order to narrow the field. Thus such hypothetical documents as Q or the Gospel of Signs fall outside my purview. I want rather to deal with documents whose existence is a certainty, such as the *Gospel of Peter*, the *Gospel of Thomas*, or the *Gospel of the Hebrews*. In what ways is their relationship to the canonical Gospels parallel to the relationship of John to the Synoptics, and how is this relationship to be accounted for in the one case and the other?

Revival of Interest in the Apocryphal Gospels

Particularly in North America, there has been a marked revival of interest in the apocryphal gospels,[1] accompanied by a growing conviction that they should not simply be set aside as secondary and derivative documents, wholly dependent on the canonical Gospels for any tradition or historical data they may contain. As far back as the 1920s, however, P. Gardner-Smith, who was to espouse the cause of the independence of the Gospel of John, argued that the *Gospel of Peter* was not dependent on, or derivative from, the canonical Gospels.[2] Quite recently, in his *Introduction to the New Testament*, Helmut Koester, in discussing apocryphal gospels alongside the canonical, has shown no inclination to regard the latter as antecedent to, and the source of, the former.[3] Indeed, if anything, the opposite seems to be the case, especially as far as such documents as the *Gospel of Thomas* and the *Gospel of Peter* are concerned. Moreover, John Dominic Crossan has argued that the *Gospel of Thomas*, Egerton Papyrus 2, the *Secret Gospel of Mark*, and the *Gospel of Peter* are independent witnesses to the forms of early Christianity they represent, not to be explained on the basis of the canonical Gospels, as if they were derivative from them.[4] Somewhat surprisingly, he has suggested that the *Gospel of Peter* embodies the earliest Passion

Narrative of all, and later wrote a full-length book on the subject.[5] (Of course, his proposals have been subjected to thorough analysis by Raymond E. Brown, as well as by Frans Neirynck, both of whom have expressed severe reservations about them.[6])

Complicating the problem for Crossan is the fact that he cannot argue that the fragment of the *Gospel of Peter* that we possess is, in its present form, the most primitive passion narrative. At some points its dependence on the canonical Gospels is too obvious. Rather, he must maintain that it is possible to identify that primitive passion narrative within a narrative that has obviously been supplemented from the canonical Gospels. The original source comprises the crucifixion and deposition of the body (1:1–2; 2:5b–6:22); the tomb and the guards (7:25; 8:28–9:34); the resurrection and confession (9:35–10:42; 11:45–49). It has been supplemented from the canonical Gospels, so that we now read about Joseph of Arimathea's involvement in the burial (6:23–24); the women's encounter with a youth at the tomb (12:50–13:57); and apparently the beginning of an account of the appearance of the risen Jesus to disciples beside the sea (14:60). By certain redactional additions an editor has prepared the way for the introduction of the canonical materials. Thus Joseph begs the body of Jesus from Pilate before the crucifixion (2:3–5a); Peter describes the mourning of himself and the other disciples after Jesus' death (7:26–27); and the entrance into the tomb of a man, who will later be seen by the women, is also recounted (11:43–44). (The reader should be aware that in the *Gospel of Peter*, verse enumeration runs consecutively from beginning to end, without regard to chapters. Thus our fragment of the Gospel comprises sixty verses in all.)

Insofar as Mark and the other canonical evangelists use this primitive narrative—which is highly tendentious, anti-Jewish, and mythological, based not on historical observation, but on biblical exegesis—they modify it in the direction of making it more historically plausible, giving it a certain verisimilitude. In other words, the movement is not, as we once thought, from history to interpretation, but from the interpretation of a bare fact (the crucifixion of Jesus under Pontius Pilate) to a narration that has the appearance of history, but is not.[7]

Is a beginning of such a passion narrative in the *Gospel of Peter* and a development in the direction of the canonical Gospel narratives really likely? On such a view the antiquity of the kind of scriptural interpretation found in the *Epistle of Barnabas* (especially chapter 7) becomes a prime consideration. But that such exegetical work antedated the canonical narratives is at best a debatable position. Aside from this and other more specific criticisms which Brown and Neirynck have raised, is it thinkable that the tradition began with the legendary, the mythological, the anti-Jewish, and indeed the fantastic, and moved in the direction of the historically restrained and sober? Brown has pointed to

a series of historical errors or implausibilities in *Peter's* passion that render at
least its early and Palestinian origin unlikely (for example, that Herod was exer-
cising a kingly role in Jerusalem).[8]

For the independence of the sayings tradition in *Thomas* more could be
said;[9] also, to a lesser extent, for Egerton Papyrus 2,[10] although we possess so
little of that document it is difficult to render a judgment. The *Secret Gospel of
Mark* presents its own set of problems.[11] Nevertheless, in each case, the arguments for independence from, as distinguished from priority over, the canonical Gospels have a certain plausibility, and Crossan is by no means the first or
only scholar to advance them.

Yet I think it is not unfair to suggest that we have seen a willingness or
propensity to credit the independence and antiquity of the apocryphal gospels
that is somewhat surprising in view of what is allowed in the case of the canonicals. This is, of course, not the same as crediting them as historical reports. As
far as the scholars in question are concerned, neither the apocryphal gospels nor
their canonical counterparts would qualify well on that score. But it is rather a
tilting in the direction of affirming their traditional and churchly roots as giving them an equal standing with the canonical Gospels, which, so to speak,
won out over them in the struggle that gave birth to the New Testament canon.
Despite reservations about specific positions taken, I believe that this effort to
see the origins of the canonical and apocryphal gospels together, as one process,
is a useful one. It puts them on the same trajectory, by which their relationships
may be observed without our ignoring their differences.[12]

Implications for John's Relation to the Synoptics

The general implication of this state of affairs for the question of John's relation to the Synoptics ought to be plain enough. If the apocryphal gospels had
access to tradition that circulated independently of the canonicals, how much
more might John have had the same? Or, if John might have been edited or
augmented to bring it into line with the Synoptics, how much more might the
Gospel of Peter have been augmented and edited to bring it into line with the
canonical Gospels—as Crossan believes happened? (In fact, Crossan, in laying
a basis for his own proposal about interrelationships between *Peter* and the
canonical Gospels, quotes a statement of mine about John's having been so
edited.[13]) The fact that Gardner-Smith, a dozen years before his famous monograph on John and the Synoptics, put forth a similar thesis on the independence of *Peter* is pertinent to the point we are making. Both Gardner-Smith and
some more recent scholarship reflect a way of viewing early Christianity and
the gospel traditions that takes it as highly probable that traditions originally
existed in oral form, and the writing down of the Synoptic, or canonical,
Gospels, did not exhaust them. Such traditions would thus have been taken up
into the Gospel of John or the *Gospel of Peter,* however the case may be. The

problem in making such a claim is that it cannot be demonstrated, as likely as it may seem.[14] Oral tradition, as real as it may have been, is uncontrollable and ephemeral unless it survives for us in written form.

In the case of the apocryphal gospels, the presumption had been that they are later than, and therefore derivative from, the canonicals. They are, of course, notoriously difficult to date. Looking through the introductions to them in the standard *New Testament Apocrypha,* one is struck with how often an apocryphal gospel is said to date from the latter half of the second century.[15] Is such a dating based on their affinities with, and seeming derivation from, the canonical Gospels, which were only collected and circulated (with or without the Fourth Gospel) in the middle or latter portion of the second century? In other words, is dating inferred from a dependence on the canonical Gospels that is presumed? If dependence is not presumed, then at least on that basis a later dating is not demanded, and the apocryphal gospels could be dated much earlier. This is exactly what happens when Crossan or Koester date the original form of the *Gospel of Peter* or the *Gospel of Thomas* to the latter part of the first century.[16] Needless to say, a crucial exegetical issue is whether the presumption of dependence is warranted.

Another factor on the side of late dating and derivative origin is that much of the material we know from the apocryphal gospels appears to be less than serious historically or theologically and therefore peripheral and secondary. I suppose it is partly a matter of taste or judgment. If Herod addresses Pilate as "Brother Pilate" (*Gos. Pet.* 2:5) or Jesus comes out of the tomb with a cross following him and his head overpassing the heavens (*Gos. Pet.* 10:39), we regard such reports as legendary or mythological embellishments. If Jesus says that his mother, the Holy Spirit, took him by his hair to Mount Tabor (*Gos. Heb.,* Fragment 3), we can hardly suppress a smile. When the boy Jesus stretches a bedrail that is too short (*Inf. Gos. Thom.* 13:2), we are mildly amused. If Jesus says that he will make Mary a male so that she may become a living spirit (*Gos. Thom.* 114), we laugh, or more recently, become infuriated. And if he encourages his disciples to take off their clothes and tread upon them (*Gos. Thom.* 37), how can that be taken seriously? Our initial perception is that such materials are historically incredible or bizarre and theologically vacuous, and therefore derivative and late. That such features are patently unhistorical and imply a naive miracle faith I would agree, but such considerations alone do not necessarily date the texts, or put them into a secondary, derivative, relation to the canonical Gospels. On the basis of historical judgments and theological criteria derived ultimately from the canonical Gospels (or the New Testament generally), the content of apocryphal gospels often seems at best an embellishment, at worst a corruption, but in any event derivative and later. They appear not to represent the original narrative or preaching, but at most, or at best, to presume them.

Martin Kähler's famous dictum seems apposite for the canonical Gospels: "all the biblical portrayals evoke the undeniable impression of the fullest reality, so that one might venture to predict how he [Jesus] might have acted in this or that situation, indeed, what he might have said."[17] Most of us would be inclined to agree, or at least to sympathize, even as we remained historically skeptical, particularly with regard to the Fourth Gospel. Such a statement, however, does not seem appropriate to the apocryphal gospels, or at least not to those features of them we have just instanced. They scarcely embody the gospel message or any traditional churchly role or function, much less the historical Jesus, in a form that we can easily imagine or deduce. The instinctual judgment that they are late, peripheral, perhaps not entirely serious, relegates them to the second century or later.[18]

I am not prepared to argue that the apocryphal gospels are important theologically and early, but there is one significant observation that should be made about them. They apparently come from a time when the tradition—and legend—were still developing freely. They reflect no strict canonical control over what could be said about, or attributed to, Jesus. They are precanonical, not in the sense that they predate the canonical Gospels individually, but in the sense that the apocryphal gospels predate the establishment of Matthew, Mark, Luke, and John as an authoritative canon of scripture. It was possible for the authors of the apocryphal gospels to speak and write about Jesus without scriptural or canonical restraint. We are here still living in a time in which the tradition is developing, perhaps sometimes in a wild and uncontrolled manner. But just in this regard there may be an important point of contact with the Fourth Gospel. Certainly most—if perhaps not all—the apocryphal gospels were written at a time when the now canonical Gospels had come into existence and were circulating.[19] (I would want to grant that, while at the same time guarding against the tendency to attribute what seems to us an aberration to a late date.) But obviously they were not yet everywhere functioning as canon in the sense that they had put an end to the writing of other gospels, or caused any other gospels written to conform to them.

Was John the First Apocryphal Gospel?

By the same token, the Fourth Gospel does not conform to the pattern of the other three that would in time be acknowledged as canonical, or holy scripture. By way of contrast, the Synoptic Gospels manifest a significant similarity of pattern, content, and even wording, in which the Gospel of Mark is the middle term. It is perhaps a bit much to say that Mark functioned as a canonical book, as holy scripture. Yet given the Marcan hypothesis, Mark did command a certain respect. Despite the fact that Matthew and Luke obviously used the Marcan material and structure for their own purposes, they nevertheless came to terms with Mark in a way John and the apocryphal gospels did not. The field of Marcan influence creates what we call the Synoptic Gospels. John, with the so-called apocryphal gospels, falls outside that canonical field. Thus John bids fair to be called the first apocryphal gospel. We cannot be sure that it was written before some unknown gospel that did not make the canon. But it is the one such gospel that survived, and that the church affirmed and preserved. Of course, the question of whether, or to what extent, John falls outside the canonical field based upon Mark is itself a much debated one, but the sheer difference of content is on any reckoning immense. We shall return to this question toward the end of the chapter.

The other palpably nonsynoptic gospels failed to survive, or were intentionally suppressed or ignored, only occasionally to turn up in modern times. We know, for example, how Bishop Serapion of Antioch in the late second century on first look gave somewhat halfhearted approval to the *Gospel of Peter*, which later, on closer inspection, he withdrew.[20] We have a fairly large number of references to the apocryphal gospels in the writings of the church fathers. On the whole, their comments about these gospels range from neutral to negative, from toleration to rejection. It is not a matter of chance that the canonical Gospels held the center of the stage and were preserved, copied, and transmitted.

It is instructive to study the way in which gospel tradition is quoted and cited during the course of the second century. Of course, we must keep in mind that we would be reading mostly the orthodox fathers, whose writings have been transmitted—or preserved—for us. Characteristically, most quotations are from the Synoptic Gospels or tradition, but are not cited according to their specific gospel source. In fact, it is arguable that they are not cited from the Synoptic Gospels directly, but from memory or oral tradition.[21] The influence of the Fourth Gospel, or its tradition, can be seen here and there (for example, in Ignatius and Justin), but not as prominently. To what extent do the apocryphal gospels or traditions known from the apocryphal gospels figure? This is a tricky question, because, on the one hand, traditions found in the apocryphal and canonical Gospels may overlap, and, on the other, we do not know the contents of most of the apocryphal gospels, of which we have in most cases only fragments or scattered quotations. It would be a fair guess that in the orthodox writers the Gospel of John comes in somewhere between the Synoptics and the apocryphal gospels.[22]

As the second century goes on, the Fourth Gospel, as the Gospel of John, gains a status equal to the Synoptics, but not without some opposition. The fact that the Valentinian Heracleon had written in Rome a commentary on John doubtless raised questions in orthodox circles.[23] Rejection of the Fourth Gospel may have been motivated by its use by Montanists as well as Valentinian Gnostics, but was based on its differences from the other, Synoptic Gospels. Irenaeus's arguments for the necessity of four gospels may amount to a covert defense of the Gospel of John. Clement's explanation that John, taking cognizance of the other three, wrote a spiritual gospel, offers a neat explanation of why John differs from the other gospels and yet harmonizes with them. John interprets spiritually their more prosaic accounts. It was a good defense that worked in antiquity and still makes sense today. A decade or so later Hippolytus would write a *Defense of the Gospel of John and Revelation* against the presumably orthodox Roman presbyter Gaius, who evidently led the opposition against them.[24]

I find it interesting, and perhaps significant, that the Gospel of John was opposed in Rome by a presbyter against whom Eusebius had nothing negative to say. Gaius was an "ecclesiastical man," a church man.[25] Perhaps his problem was that he was conservative; he wanted to stick with the old rather than embrace the new. Apparently his argument against the Gospel of John centered on its disagreements with the Synoptics, especially at the beginning of Jesus' ministry. It is a short step from this fact to the observation or inference that, whereas Matthew and Luke could be reconciled with Mark, John posed an impossible or, at least much more difficult, task. Was it the case that Mark had originally occupied a position of preeminence in the church of Rome?[26] Such a preeminence accords with much patristic testimony[27] and would go a long way toward explaining the opposition of Gaius, the conservative (if we may so style him) elder of the Roman church. Interestingly enough, the Muratorian canon, presumably representing the situation in Rome at the end of the second century,[28] presents a rather elaborate description of how the Gospel of John was written with the cognizance, if not the participation, of the apostles. This description looks like a defense of its apostolicity, perhaps against old-fashioned Roman Christians who still preferred the Gospel of Mark, or the Synoptics generally.

Be that as it may, Gaius, if he had had the authority, would have barred the Gospel of John in the way Serapion of Antioch barred the *Gospel of Peter* from church usage. But he lost, and history's winners determine the canon of the church as well as the writing of its history. Thus the Gospel of John makes the New Testament and the *Gospel of Peter* fails. That is doubtless a bit too simple, but the point is that the establishment of the gospel canon obviously involved the rejection and suppression of gospels other than the canonical four. *Suppression* is perhaps too strong a word, inasmuch as we are not talking about book burning or that sort of thing. Rather, it was a question of which gospels were to be sponsored for reading in the church's worship, which is where the generality of Christians heard the gospel read.[29] John was ultimately adjudged fit to be read alongside Matthew, Mark, and Luke, even though it was so obviously different from them. It was the preeminent gospel that did not fall within the Marcan field of influence.

Like the other, apocryphal, gospels, John's content differed from the Synoptics more than it was similar, or parallel, to them. John was not written with the other canonical Cospels in view in the way that Matthew and, to a lesser degree, Luke were written with Mark in view. John was not constrained by the Synoptics or, as we have said, he seems to fall outside the Marcan canonical field. At the risk of seeming banal, let me now summarize what we all know. John simply differs from the Synoptic Gospels: Jesus' ministry lasts more than two years; it is mostly in Jerusalem or Judea; none of the Johannine healing stories reproduces Mark's; Jesus utters no true parable; he teaches and argues about himself rather than the kingdom of God.

Of course, the degree of difference between John and Mark, or John and the Synoptics, is considerably reduced as we near the end of the Gospel account. Beginning with the arrest of Jesus (Matt 26:47–56; Mark 14:43–52; Luke 22:47–53; John 18:2–12) and the passion narrative proper, John is closely parallel to Mark and the other Synoptics in content, order, and even wording, although John does not have the extensive verbatim agreements that the Synoptics manifest among themselves, and sometimes differs widely in the description of an episode. Yet it could be argued that Luke (for example, in the trial before Jewish authorities) is already rewriting Mark, and John continues this process and takes it further. John also adds incidents (the piercing of Jesus' side in 19:31–37); but so do Luke (the hearing before Herod in 23:6–12) and Matthew (the placing of a guard at the tomb in 27:62–66). But whereas the Lucan or Matthean accounts can be reconciled with Mark, or with each other, without great difficulty, John presents more serious problems in this regard. The most startling and obdurate difficulty is, of course, that Jesus is crucified on the afternoon before, rather than after, the Feast of Unleavened Bread (Nisan 14 rather than 15). Scarcely less surprising is the omission of any formal trial before the Sanhedrin, although John at least has a place for it (18:24, 28). (In his account of Jesus before Jewish authorities, Luke seems to stand, so to speak, between John and Mark.) Just at this point, John also leaves the unknowing reader in some confusion as to whether Annas or Caiaphas is high priest. The trial before Pilate is quite different as well, but here Jesus' conversation with Pilate can more readily be understood as a Johannine adaptation of the Marcan (or Synoptic) account, as can the sovereign words of Jesus at his arrest and death. In the prepassion material, however, it is less easy to understand why John should have omitted the institution of the Lord's Supper and thus provided a continuing puzzle for exegesis. John's divergences from the Marcan account, as well as the difficulties they will cause the reader, are obviously much greater than in the case of Matthew and Luke.

In the resurrection-appearance narratives there is a different state of affairs, in that each Johannine account, with the exception of the risen Jesus' conversation with Peter (21:15–23), has a synoptic parallel, whether close or remote. (John's "conflation" of appearance accounts bears a remote similarity to Mark 16:9–20.) In 20:11–18 John may simply elaborate upon the story of Jesus' appearance to the women outside the tomb (Matt 28:9–10). In doing so, he of course gives Mary Magdalene a prominence she attains in no other Gospel. In John's rendition of Jesus' encounter with the Twelve in Jerusalem (20:19–29), we have a distinct parallel with Luke (24:36–43), in which the point is clearly the physical character of Jesus' resurrection body. This is, of course, not the point or emphasis of John's account (20:29), although Christians have often read John in light of Luke instead of the other way around. John's account of Jesus' appearance by the sea (21:1–14) has a parallel in Luke 5:1–11. Yet John leaves the reader bemused over why an event that in one rendering begins Jesus' ministry in his own should end it.[30]

My point is not that John did not know the synoptic accounts. He may have, and in any event I do not know how one would go about proving he did not. Rather, the point is that John is not constrained by the Marcan, and synoptic, accounts in that he creates difficulties for anyone reading his narrative alongside theirs, difficulties which he offers little help in resolving. Moreover, the divergences are of a different sort and magnitude than those found among the synoptic accounts, even where, as in the passion and resurrection narratives, John is more closely parallel to them.

The apparent unconcern with which John differs from the Synoptics is matched by the account of Jesus' passion that we find in the *Gospel of Peter*. In fact, in tone and content *Peter's* account is, if anything, more remote from, or independent of, the Synoptics (or the canonical Gospels, including John). I am not convinced that the author of the *Gospel of Peter* had access to more primitive, as well as independent, tradition in composing his passion narrative, although it seems to me quite possible that like John he knew a primitive account of Jesus' appearance to disciples beside the Sea of Galilee.[31] However that may be, *Peter,* like John, presents an alternative account of what we can recognize as the same or related events that we read about in the Synoptics. At the same time, if "Peter" had read the synoptic, or canonical, accounts, as he probably had, he was influenced but not constrained by them. On the other hand, while Matthew and Luke are not limited to the Gospel of Mark, they are constrained by its account in a way Peter and John are not, in that they offer narratives that are much more easily readable and reconcilable with it. As far as we can see, the other apocryphal gospels are, with *Peter* and John, similarly unconstrained: Egerton Papyrus 2; the *Gospel of Thomas; Secret Mark,* if you will; as well as traditional apocryphal gospels known only through quotations in later Christian writers.

We might say that the apocryphal gospels have in common that they do not conform to or follow the Gospel of Mark, the Synoptics, or the canonical Gospels generally, and John has in common with them that he too is not constrained by Mark or the Synoptics. Is John then the first apocryphal gospel? By this definition, of course, it is. Quite obviously, it has been canonical since the end of the second century. That is simply a historical fact. But has the Fourth Gospel proved itself canonical in another, more substantive, way?

In a real sense the Gospel of John is controlled, determined, or guided by a distinct theological position and perspective which sets it apart from the apocryphal gospels that we know. The *Gospel of Peter*, for example, manifests a virulent anti-Jewishness, some possibly docetic tendencies, and an obvious flair, or weakness, for the miraculous—all characteristics similar to the Fourth Gospel—but no serious and consistent theological point of view. The debate over whether the *Gospel of Peter* is docetic evidently began in the late second century and continues today. There are, of course, tensions in Johannine thought, but few will dispute the Gospel's theological seriousness. Perhaps only the *Gospel of Thomas*'s obviously gnostic and encratic interests match the Gospel of John in their consistency and pervasiveness, if not in sophistication. Because the other noncanonical gospels are available to us in such small fragments or fragmentary quotations, we cannot say much with certainty about their theology, except that we possess nothing to indicate that we have in any of them a rival of John. The judgment that the evangelist John was a theologian is not misplaced, and perhaps the best testimony to this fact is the degree that the Fourth Gospel has stimulated other great theological minds, from Origen to Bultmann, both of whom trod at the borders of orthodoxy in order to express in a fresh and relevant way the truth of the gospel, as perhaps did the evangelist also. Yet such theologians, and the weight of church opinion, have deemed John to express in a profound way the truth which the other gospels and early New Testament writers want to attest. In fact, John reads well after, and alongside, the other gospels, as well as Paul and Hebrews. Distinctive and different as it may be, the Gospel of John presents a Jesus who makes a certain theological sense of the Jesus of the other gospels, and the New Testament generally. In canonizing the Gospel of John, the church affirmed that this Jesus is the same Jesus, and indeed the real Jesus Christ who is God's Son and his Word. Whether the Gospel of John stands in the New Testament because of a human error through which God has worked is a question that lies outside the competence of historical or exegetical science. The history of exegesis within the church, however, testifies that its inclusion was not a mistake. John alters or influences the shape or emphases of the New Testament, but maintains a positive contact and continuity with its other witnesses. In this deeply substantive sense its presence in the canon is not only a historical fact but a theological blessing, as well as an exegetical challenge.

13

The Problem of Faith and History

*Common to Both John and the Synoptics,
and Peculiar to Neither*

The relationship of John to the Synoptic Gospels is probably the oldest historical-critical problem in the history of the church. Already at the end of the second century, if not earlier, it was proving troublesome. Very likely, the rejection
of the Fourth Gospel in some Christian circles had to do not only with its association with Gnostics but also with its obvious divergences from the Synoptics.[1] The acceptance of John in the church, and in the emerging canon, went
hand in hand with its attribution to the Apostle John and with a developing
formula or mode of reconciling its differences with the Synoptics.

Thus John was thought to have been written to supplement the other
Gospels or to provide a more spiritual perspective on the ministry of Jesus.
Some such way of reading the Gospel of John not only survived but was dominant, also among critical scholars, into the twentieth century. Even as acute a
scholar as B. W. Bacon did not break with the ancient consensus in this
respect.[2] Obviously, the question of John and the Synoptics has important
implications for broader questions of faith and history, a fact that has been recognized from antiquity. Ancient efforts to reconcile John with the Synoptics
had as their presupposition that it was intolerable for authoritative witnesses to
the earthly ministry of Jesus to contradict one another about matters of historical fact. Gaius of Rome and any *alogi* who rejected the Gospel of John may
have found the contradictions intolerable. On the other hand, Origen acknowledged them gladly, and goaded the "conservative" church exegetes who
were attempting to assimilate John to the Synoptics on the historical level.[3]
While himself not committed to the view that history must undergird faith in
such a prosaic way, Origen was a sufficiently sharp critic to see that the developing modes of reconciling John to the Synoptics were fundamentally suspect
historically.

After Origen, however, churchly exegesis generally took the position that John was written in light of the other Gospels in order to interpret them theologically and/or supplement them historically. The earlier modern criticism for the most part accepted this view, but not necessarily the traditional assumption that John was a historically accurate account, if, indeed, it was a historical account at all. The purpose of this chapter is to sketch the course of later, twentieth-century investigations of the relation of John to the Synoptics and to reflect upon the problem of faith and history in the light of the issues thereby raised.

The Twentieth-Century Consensus

The brief but important monograph of Hans Windisch, *Johannes und die Synoptiker* (1926), broke with the ancient and traditional view of their relationship in that the author argued that John wrote with the purpose of displacing the other Gospels, which he took to be inadequate theologically.[4] Since Windisch, the problem has come full circle, so to speak: John's knowledge of the Synoptics has been fundamentally questioned (P. Gardner-Smith), but is now strongly reaffirmed with more thorough consideration of the consequences than were entertained in antiquity (Frans Neirynck).

Windisch proceeded on the traditional view that John knew and was familiar with all the Synoptic Gospels, but because they were inadequate representations of the gospel as John understood it, he wrote a gospel to supersede them and in doing so found most of their content useless. This explains why John, while knowing the other Gospels, differed so sharply from them. Although Windisch's solution to the problem of John and the Synoptics seems radical, there is a sense in which it is entirely reasonable, given the seriousness of the problem. That is, if the differences between John and the Synoptics are really not amenable to solution on the basis of the traditional view that John intended only to supplement, interpret, or mildly correct the other three—and Windisch argued vigorously and persuasively that they were not—the problem of explaining their relationship assumes a considerable magnitude. Why did John write such a different gospel without accommodating his narrative to the others? A profound problem that was more or less swept under the rug in antiquity demands a thoroughgoing and searching answer.

Gardner-Smith's thesis begins from and argues for a contrary working hypothesis, maintaining that there is no convincing evidence that the Fourth Evangelist knew and used the other Gospels at all.[5] If one considers the large amount of disparity and the relatively small amount of agreement, particularly verbatim agreement, it is not at all obvious that John must have known any or all of the Synoptics. Once it is conceded that oral tradition was an important factor in early Christian tradition, the relatively small areas of agreement, even the word-for-word agreements, are rather easily accounted for. The extensive departures are—if John did not know the Synoptics—no problem to be explained. As it stands they represent a conundrum. The fact that they have not been seen as a problem, as exegetes have fixed upon the agreements, does not make them less of one. Gardner-Smith and Windisch agree in one central respect: conventional and traditional exegesis has not adequately taken account of, and accounted for, the differences between John and the Synoptics.

Gardner-Smith did not deal with Windisch or even mention his book. His work stands on its own as an alternative way of coming to grips with the same perceived problem. It had no immediate impact on the Continent, largely because of the onset of World War II only a year after its publication. But a compatible thesis was soon set forth in Germany. Shortly after the outbreak of war, which was to put an end to scholarly interchange between English- and German-speaking scholars for nearly a decade, Rudolf Bultmann's enormously influential commentary on the Fourth Gospel appeared.[6] Although the explanation of Johannine-synoptic relations was not a central concern of the commentary, Bultmann's work had a significant impact on the discussion of that problem in subsequent scholarship. Bultmann did not find John's dependence on the Synoptics a necessary presupposition for exegesis. Instead, his literary, source-critical analysis led repeatedly to the conclusion that John was not based upon the Synoptics, but rather on an analogous tradition which had already been fixed in written sources, principally the *semeia* (sign) and passion sources. Bultmann's developed position on this issue had, however, already been adumbrated a decade and a half earlier, when in a review of Windisch he had expressed doubts as to whether John knew the Synoptic Gospels at all.[7] His subsequent exegesis obviously confirmed this sense of doubt. Certainly Bultmann's view of John's independence was not advanced in the service of any attempt to defend the historicity of the Fourth Gospel. (Interestingly, Windisch frequently refers to earlier espousals of John's independence as "conservative.") Only in a highly distinctive and rarefied sense is Bultmann's John interested in history's relation to faith. Revelation intersects history, but is not contained in it so that revelation could be obtained or clarified through historical study or research. Nevertheless, this intersection was important for Bultmann, in whose view John represents what has become a classic understanding of incarnation as the presence of God in fully historical, fully human existence in Jesus.

Meanwhile in England particularly, Gardner-Smith's influence and impact were being felt directly, but also indirectly through the subsequent work of C. H. Dodd.[8] Dodd's own studies of the Fourth Gospel confirmed in his mind the correctness of Gardner-Smith's insights. In North America the appearance of Raymond E. Brown's widely used commentary had a similar effect. For in his own exegetical study Brown found little reason to think that John had drawn on the Synoptics directly, and certainly not in the Gospel's originative stages.[9] Of course, unlike Bultmann, both Dodd and Brown found the Fourth Gospel a potentially valuable source of historical tradition about Jesus, at the same time recognizing the considerable extent to which that tradition is refracted through the Gospel's theological interests and, particularly in the case of Brown, its traditional and literary stages. Thus, in the mid-1960s there was already forming in diverse quarters a considerable body of scholarly opinion at odds with the traditional view that John had known and used the other Gospels.

I had observed this consensus in 1964.[10] About a year later Josef Blinzler contested the accuracy of my observation.[11] A decade after the appearance of Blinzler's *Johannes und die Synoptiker,* Neirynck corroborated my judgment about the consensus but expressed a strong demurral from it, signaling his own program of demonstrating John's use of the Synoptic Gospels, which is still very much in progress.[12] In this respect and others, Neirynck came to be known as the head of the Louvain School (for Louvain, or Leuven, University).

Passion Narratives

A number of North American scholars, particularly those associated with the late Norman Perrin of Chicago, had expressed their doubts that John was independent of the Synoptics. To a large extent their contention grew out of the redaction criticism of the Marcan passion narrative.[13] John Donahue, one of Perrin's students, showed the extent of Marcan redactional activity in the trial scene (Mark 14) and raised the possibility that in the passion narrative as well as in the narrative of Jesus' public ministry Mark had worked with independent units of tradition which he was the first to incorporate into an extended narrative.[14] A similar questioning of the existence of a pre-Marcan passion narrative had already found expression on the Continent in the work of Eta Linnemann.[15]

Whether Mark had such a passion narrative before him is a question still debated. The outcome has implications for research into Johannine-synoptic relations, but is probably not as decisive as is sometimes assumed. If Mark knew no earlier passion narrative, but composed his own, it is reasonable, but actually not imperative, to think that John must have relied on Mark's Gospel for his own account. John's account still differs from Mark's in ways that are not so easily explained, and it is not inconceivable that John and Mark should have independently constructed continuous accounts of Jesus' passion out of individual elements of tradition. Thus the finding that Mark had no earlier continuous passion narrative—if correct—does not *eo ipso* mean that John must have relied on Mark. But whether individual units of passion tradition would have existed apart from some general narrative framework is, on the face of it, doubtful. If there were traditions of Jesus' arrest, trial, and so forth, their preservation and transmission would have presupposed some narrative sense of how they fit together. This consideration speaks on the side of some sort of pre-gospel tradition of the passion as a whole (cf. Paul's reference to the institution of the Lord's Supper on the night Jesus was betrayed in 1 Cor 11:23–25).

John and Mark

The question of John's relation to the Synoptics is not simply interchangeable with that of John's relation to Mark, although there is a great overlap between them, and for good reason. A survey of scholarly opinion would doubtless show that of the scholars who think that John knew the Synoptics the largest number would agree that the Fourth Evangelist knew Mark. The reasons for this are clear enough. First of all, since most still adhere to the Marcan hypothesis, Mark figures as the earliest of the Synoptics and, for whatever reason, the gospel known to Matthew and Luke independently. Moreover, the pattern of agreements between John and the other Gospels comports with a fundamental or primary agreement with Mark. Those episodes or pericopes which John has in common with Mark he has, by and large, in the same order as Mark. John does not agree in order with Matthew or Luke against Mark. The verbatim agreements between John and the Synoptics are basically agreements with Mark. There are few verbatim agreements of several successive words with Matthew or Luke that are not also verbatim agreements with Mark.

John and Luke

Strangely, many of the more prominent verbatim agreements between John and Mark are not found in Luke. This is particularly puzzling because of the rather extensive agreements of other sorts between Luke and John. For example, Luke refrains from describing explicitly Jesus' baptism by John, contains no account of a nocturnal trial of Jesus before the Sanhedrin, has the risen Jesus appear to his disciples together in Jerusalem, portrays Jesus as interested in Samaria and Samaritans, and in many other respects shows affinities with John rather than Matthew and Mark. Not surprisingly, a major, and to some extent separate, aspect of the question of John and the Synoptics has been the relationship of John and Luke.

Interestingly enough, almost a century ago Julius Schniewind argued that their affinities were based on the use of common traditions rather than John's use of Luke, although at the same time he continued to assume that John wrote with an awareness of the other Gospels.[16] Subsequent scholarship has tended to move along similar lines, emphasizing common tradition rather than a direct relationship. This is true, for example, even of J. A. Bailey, who nevertheless contends that John also knew Luke directly.[17] For obvious reasons the hypothesis that Luke knew John has not attracted many adherents. Yet Lamar Cribbs was able to point to a number of instances in which Luke seems to follow John, or at least to waffle a bit, precisely when John contradicts or departs from the Matthean-Marcan line.[18] Even Cribbs did not go so far as to suggest that Luke knew John—a possible logical implication of this state of affairs—but contented himself with the reasonable hypothesis that among Luke's sources was an earlier stage of the Johannine narrative.

In any event, John's affinities with Luke remain a major and distinct factor to be understood and explained, differing as they do from the Fourth Gospel's direct parallels in wording and order with Mark. Probably because Luke so often lacks verbatim parallels with John, often precisely those that are found in Mark (and usually also in Matthew), few scholars have thought that John knew only Luke. Just because Luke's distinctive affinities with John seem diffuse and indirect—although quite real—in comparison with Mark's, attempts to explain the relationship as mediated through tradition rather than based on John's use of Luke have flourished.

Thus Anton Dauer extended to the distinctive relationships between Luke and John a thesis he had first applied to the gospel passion narratives.[19] Because he finds some Johannine parallels to Lucan redaction (that is, parts of Luke which on other grounds are judged to be from the Third Evangelist's own hand), but cannot derive other basic aspects of the Johannine reports from Luke (or Mark), Dauer proposes a new kind of resolution of this seemingly contradictory situation. Luke has influenced John via the continuing oral tradition (just as Matthew and Luke have both influenced John in the passion— the point made in his earlier work). Because by and large the evidences of Lucan influence fall within material which Dauer, in agreement with a number of other scholars, would assign not to the evangelist but to the pre-Johannine tradition or source, Dauer theorizes that this oral influence must have already affected that pregospel level of development. That is, Luke's Gospel has influenced the oral tradition that shaped John's sources.

Developing Complexity

Dauer's position typifies a development in Johannine-synoptic investigations which began to appear during the 1970's. Increasingly, the relationship is seen to be more complex than was once thought. Possibly the most elaborate theory of Johannine-synoptic and other gospel relationships has been advanced by M.-E. Boismard.[20] Boismard's complex interweaving of ancient traditions and other, earlier modern theories of gospel origins is at the very least a masterpiece of scholarly ingenuity. For example, the ancient opinion that Matthew was the first gospel is preserved in the thesis of a Document A (which might be called primal, as distinguished from both intermediate and final, Matthew). Document A has influenced Document B (primal Mark) as well as intermediate Mark. Intermediate Mark was then a primary source of both final Matthew and final Luke (Marcan hypothesis). Each Gospel, except for Luke, has a primary, intermediate, and final (canonical) recension. Luke begins, so to speak, at the intermediate level with Proto-Luke, composed under the influence of Q (also used by intermediate Matthew), Document B, and Document C. With Document C we arrive at the primary source of John's Gospel (John I), which underwent two redactions at the hands of the Fourth Evangelist (John II-A and II-B) before being subjected to a final redaction (John III) by a later editor. At the level of the second redaction by the evangelist (II-B) elements from the Synoptic Gospels were incorporated. Thus John the Evangelist, not just the final, later redactor, knew all the Synoptics in the form in which we have them.

But as complexities are introduced, either in method or in result, agreement and consensus among scholars decline. Windisch proposed that John knew but rejected the Synoptics; Gardner-Smith, that he never knew them at all. Brown, like Bultmann, allowed for John's betraying some knowledge of the Synoptic Gospels at the final redactional stage.[21] Boismard's theory posits gospel sources with various interrelationships lying behind our canonical Gospels, including the Gospel of John. Moreover, the Fourth Evangelist at the point of his own final redaction of the Gospel knew and made use of the Synoptics. Neirynck counters with an application of Occam's razor to source criticism: if John is parallel to the Synoptics at points, it is better to explain these parallels on the basis of a direct literary relationship than to multiply source- and tradition-critical hypotheses unnecessarily. The positions of Windisch, Gardner-Smith, and Neirynck have the advantage of simplicity, clarity, and forthrightness. This does not mean that one or more of them must be true. Indeed, they all could not be, although it would be possible to combine Windisch's position with a version of Neirynck's, as we shall see.

Neirynck's response to Boismard is as understandable as it is clear.[22] If at the final redactional stage John knew all the Synoptic Gospels, is such an intricate theory of sources necessary in order to explain the Fourth Gospel? Inasmuch as Boismard's stylistic, contextual, and other evidence and arguments for the existence of earlier literary strata are not unambiguous, why not begin with the hypothesis that those other Gospels, which we have and know, and which Boismard agrees John finally knew, are the basis for the Fourth Gospel? Then the exegetical, redaction-critical task is to explain how John understood and altered his sources to produce the canonical Fourth Gospel. Over against Boismard, whose thesis is a kind of synthesis of all plausible hypotheses combined into one, Neirynck's desire to restore simplicity comes as a breath of fresh air, and in character if not in content similar to Gardner-Smith.

Neirynck's proposal carries with it the strengths of both simplicity and tradition. There is no airtight argument that can prevail against it. What may count against it, however, are, first, the vast differences of content and structure of the Fourth Gospel from the others, unless they can be made intelligible; and, second, the problem of understanding the small differences between John and the Synoptics where, in fact, they run parallel. But there is another consideration, one that bears upon the question of faith and history, as it has been traditionally understood. On such terms as Neirynck has proposed, the Gospel of John is, by implication, an embellishment or midrash, however extensive and sophisticated, upon the Synoptic Gospels. It ceases to be an original source of historical tradition, as much as the evangelist may insist on the importance of the events of Jesus' ministry and his (or someone's) own witness (or eyewitness testimony).

John's Setting

As we earlier observed, the major differences between John and the other Gospels have traditionally been understood in terms of supplementation. Either John was to supplement the other Gospels, or vice versa, or both. Windisch has shown the difficulties of that perspective once the protective aura of canonicity is allowed to fall away. (By aura of canonicity I mean the implication, tacitly drawn from the canonical status of the other Gospels, that John would have accepted their adequacy and authority.) In light of recent research, however, it is not too much to imagine within the Johannine community, or at its boundaries, the need for a gospel very different from the Synoptics to underscore the divine origin of Jesus or to set him in opposition to Judaism, or both.[23] In such a setting, if the Synoptics were known, they likely would not have been regarded as sufficient or definitive, whether or not John sought to displace them. (*Supplementation* is too weak a term to describe the relationship, although *displacement* may be too strong.) Such a position carries with it at least two significant, and related, implications.

First, if John regarded the other, synoptic, Gospels in this way, Windisch's description of his purpose and intention will not have missed the mark entirely. It should be observed, of course, that such affinities of recent research with Windisch's view are not arguments against Neirynck's general position on John's dependence. One would have to ascribe to John neither the negative assessment of the Synoptics entailed in Windisch's approach nor, obviously, ignorance of the Synoptics in order to subscribe to the view that for the evangelist and the Johannine community they were inadequate and incomplete. John could have known the Synoptics but for good reason departed from them to go his own way. A further implication perhaps carries with it more troublesome consequences, perhaps particularly for Neirynck's approach. If John does not reject the three other Gospels, but knows them and largely leaves them on one side, it then becomes problematic to interpret the Gospel of John, or even to analyze individual passages, with the Synoptics primarily in view. In other words, it becomes less than a safe assumption that the Synoptics provide the base line against which the Fourth Gospel is to be measured and understood. Therefore, interpretation so based loses persuasiveness, however deftly and diligently it may be pursued.

Patterns of Agreement

Another consideration relevant to the assessment of the problem of John and the Synoptics is the possible significance of patterns of their agreement. It is a commonplace that as one approaches and enters the passion narrative, the agreements or parallels become more numerous. This is, of course, true, although there are perplexing disharmonies also. With respect to the resurrection narratives an even more striking phenomenon may be observed. On the one hand, every Johannine resurrection narrative has a synoptic parallel. On the other, the discovery of the empty tomb aside, no synoptic resurrection narrative has a parallel in another Synoptic Gospel. There is an interesting general analogy between the Johannine resurrection narratives and the specious longer ending of Mark (16:9–20). That longer ending seems to gather together and summarize what is reported in the other canonical Gospels. John's resurrection narratives could be viewed as a conflation and/or expansion of those found in the Synoptics. Even John 21:1–14 has a nonresurrection parallel in Luke 5:1–11. Yet that episode also answers to the anticipation of a resurrection appearance in Galilee raised by Mark 14:28 and 16:7. Mark, of course, contains no such story.[24] To be sure, John 20:26–29 has no synoptic parallel, but it is probably a doublet of 20:19–23 (par. Luke 24:36–43). John 21:15–23 also appears to lack any synoptic parallel, but it may be viewed as the Johannine continuation of 21:1–14. Moreover, it corresponds to the expectation aroused by the singling out of Peter in Mark 16:7, as well as to the clear indication of the restoration of Peter and his task in Luke 22:31–32. Thus on the basis of the resurrection narratives alone there would be some reason to think that John is a conflation of the Synoptic Gospels.

Such a position is less easy to support in the passion narratives, although the parallels between John and any one Synoptic Gospel are greater here. Yet why does John omit the Lord's Supper from the prepassion tradition, change its calendar date and that of the crucifixion, and omit an actual trial before Jewish authorities? These kinds of problems multiply as one moves backward into the public ministry. Then only chapter 6 and the meeting with John the Baptist at the outset represent strong agreements between the Fourth Gospel and any one of the Synoptics. Indeed, the entire Johannine Galilean ministry of Jesus (with the exception of the Cana miracles, which have either no synoptic parallel [2:1–12] or a parallel only in Q [4:46–54]) is found in chapter 6. As is common knowledge, typical acts and forms of speech from Jesus' synoptic ministry are missing from John: no cleansing of lepers, no demon exorcisms, no parables, no apocalyptic-prophetic words, and no pronouncement stories.

One could go on. For the position that John knew the Synoptics and, at least in part, based his narrative upon them, especially in the passion and resurrection and in certain other pivotal points, there are obvious arguments, as well as problems. Less obvious are the reasons for John's having abandoned the synoptic framework and narratives in the public ministry, that is, before the final visit to Jerusalem. Nevertheless, the resurrection appearance narratives, particularly with the epilogue (chapter 21), strongly support some knowledge of the Synoptics at a late redactional stage (cf. 21:25, especially the allusion to the books that could be written).

Still problematic, however, are the narratives in which John is clearly parallel to the Synoptics, whether in the passion or elsewhere. It is these narratives that Gardner-Smith studied, arguing that the similarities of John to the Synoptics, even the verbal agreements, could be explained as the result of common oral tradition. Such agreements are in any case not very numerous or extensive. Stories are told somewhat differently. Apparently related sayings appear in different forms and contexts. While it is possible to contend that in these cases John based his account on the Synoptics, it is not so easily possible to understand why John changed what he changed and did not alter other things. Not all the divergences from the Synoptics represent Johannine theological interests, nor do they fall into a distinct pattern or patterns. In other words, on these terms John's redactional policy is not easy to understand.

We find here a certain similarity to the problem advocates of the Griesbach-Farmer hypothesis encounter in attempting to understand Mark as a conflation of Luke and Matthew. In that case it is simply difficult to imagine or conceive of the purpose of Mark's redaction. The problem is even more difficult with respect to the entire Gospel than in the case of individual pericopes. Concerning the relation of John to any one, or all, of the Synoptics, there is a similar situation, yet in one sense it is different. In a general way John has been and remains intelligible as a distinct theological interpretation of the Jesus who stands at the center of the Synoptic Gospels and tradition. It becomes more difficult, however, to discern how John's apparent purpose is served by many of his specific departures from the Synoptics. If at this point Windisch's thesis is invoked, one may also observe that if John wrote to displace the Synoptics, it is still not obvious why the evangelist adopted what he included from the Synoptics while omitting some things that might have been of use to him, and created pointless discrepancies and contradictions. Aside from the consideration that the interpretation of specific Johannine texts on the assumption that the Fourth Evangelist had one or more of the Synoptics in view is more often than not problematic, it is difficult to conceive of an author's presupposing the very texts he intends to displace. More likely, he simply goes his own way to write a Gospel relevant to the needs of his community.

Perhaps the most fundamental options remain those represented by Gard-ner-Smith and Neirynck. Each proceeds from a reasonable and, to my mind, right-headed insight or instinct, opposed though they may be. Thus Gardner-Smith insists that the evangelical tradition was not in the beginning limited to, or entirely incorporated within, our canonical Gospels, and there is therefore now no reason to think John's similarities to the Synoptics must have been derived from them, particularly in view of the many and puzzling differences. Neirynck, in contrast, refuses to multiply hypothetical sources and traditions when the points of contact and similarity suggest as the primary possibility John's use of the Synoptics. Both beginning points are reasonable, but they obviously come into conflict. New Testament scholars are inclined to think that such conflicts can only be resolved exegetically, but, in this case, presupposi-tions and predispositions are crucially important.

The Question of Faith and History

It is obvious, as Dodd clearly discerned, that Gardner-Smith's position leaves open the possibility of isolating and assessing the Johannine tradition with a view to its historical worth, that is, as an independent witness to the historical Jesus. By the same token, on Neirynck's view (as also on Windisch's) the scope or range of this possibility is radically reduced, if not nullified. From such a per-spective, John's principal interest in history as the horizon of revelation need not be denied. Nevertheless, over against such an evaluation of the Fourth Gospel as an entirely secondary gospel, the claims of the implied author to be a distinctive and authoritative witness (19:35; 21:24; cf. 1:14) ring rather hollow.

With Neirynck we can see that a curious change of fronts has taken place in the history of criticism. In antiquity and through most of the history of exe-gesis, John's knowledge of the Synoptics was deemed compatible with the his-torical accuracy and value of the Fourth Gospel. In sum, John knew more or better than the other evangelists. But with the rise of higher criticism and the questioning of the tradition of apostolic authorship, John's differences from the Synoptics began to count against its historical reliability as the Fourth Gospel was increasingly regarded as a secondary document, going beyond the Synop-tics in ways that were basically ahistorical. Reflecting on the criticism of the late nineteenth and early twentieth centuries, Windisch could characterize the view that John was independent of the Synoptics as conservative. It was becoming the refuge, or at least the correlate, of a more positive evaluation of John's historical worth, as the still dominant view that John wrote last and with knowledge of the others more and more implied its secondary and "unreliable" character.

With Bultmann one encounters a positive valuation of history as the arena of revelation, a view ascribed to the evangelist without attributing to him much by way of utilization of historical knowledge or tradition. Obviously, Bultmann's evaluation of John as a historical witness or source in the usual sense is rather low, although he grants that John employed elements of a tradition independent of, and parallel to, the Synoptics. The same may apparently be said of Neirynck, the implications of whose view of John as mainly dependent on, or derivative from, the Synoptics would seem to be clear. Neirynck's position takes up and continues the tradition of the late nineteenth and early twentieth century as represented, for example, by B. W. Bacon in North America.

Obviously, then, a negative evaluation of John as a historical source for Jesus and his times is presently congenial with either John's independence of the Synoptics or his dependence upon them. It is, however, probably a correct observation that, except in very conservative circles, those who value the Fourth Gospel as a significant source for our knowledge of Jesus regard it as independent of the other canonical Gospels. A moment's reflection will reveal why this is so. The most impressive and central divergence of John from the Synoptics is its impressive, christologically elevated portrait of Jesus, which no critical scholar any longer takes to depict the way the historical Jesus presented himself. If, on the one hand, those aspects of the narrative that are parallel to the Synoptics are taken to be derivative from them, one will conclude that when John moves away from the Synoptics, he departs from historical reality. If, on the other hand, the parallels with the Synoptics are understood as derivative from substantially related but independent sources, the door opens wider to investigate possibly historical bases of the distinctive Johannine material. For example, in John 4:44, 12:25, and 13:16 we encounter words of Jesus with clear synoptic counterparts. Do such sayings represent the tip of an iceberg of Johannine tradition, or are they only a few odd variants, sayings derived from the Synoptics?

In conclusion, we should observe that the question of the historical dimension of the Fourth Gospel, particularly in relation to the Synoptics, has aspects that are scarcely touched by the evaluation of the Johannine narrative or sayings tradition on historical-critical grounds. In the first place, the Gospel of John alone among the canonical Gospels attests its own reliability as a historical report (19:35; 21:24; cf. 1:14). Doubtless the synoptic evangelists maintained a similar attitude, but only Luke indicates explicitly the importance of historical reliability (Luke 1:1–4; cf. Acts 1:21–23). Does John underscore the reliability of his witness vis-a-vis that of the others? The comparison of John and the Synoptics suggests that question is a relevant one. In any event, the Gospel of John itself does not permit us to put aside as irrelevant the question of whether—or in what sense—it is a valid witness to things that have taken place.

In the second place, the Gospel of John repeatedly emphasizes, as no other gospel does, the importance of remembering, but also the role played by the Spirit in remembering (for example, 2:22; 14:26). Therefore, valid remembering can take place only in light of the cross and resurrection, that is, the exaltation of Jesus. Only then is the Spirit given (7:39). Only from that perspective can Jesus be properly remembered and understood. Any full consideration of the problem of history in John must pay attention to the Gospel's own perception of this problem. Presumably all the evangelists are aware that theologically significant knowledge of Jesus is postresurrection knowledge, but only John makes this crystal clear.

While consideration of historical reliability or worth cannot govern the results of research into the relationship of John and the Synoptics, our survey makes it evident that such concerns hover anxiously around the fringes of this problem, as they have since the second century. Therefore, the relation of John to the Synoptics is likely to remain, or recur, as a pivotal issue in New Testament scholarship.

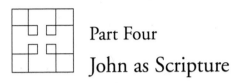

Part Four

John as Scripture

When Did the Gospels Become Scripture?

What Did Their Authors Intend and Their Readers Assume?

In teaching "Introduction to the New Testament," I am fond of saying that the authors of New Testament books would have had no inkling that their writings would become part of something called the New Testament or the Christian Bible, which did not reach exactly its present form until the fourth century. Matthew did not know that his Gospel would begin the New Testament, although he would be happy to discover that it does. It is well suited for that position and purpose. John did not know that his Gospel would stand in the New Testament alongside three other Gospels, and that it would be the fourth, presumably to be read after the others. Some exegetes believe that John was actually written with the others in view, but that premise creates as many problems of interpretation as it resolves.[1] However that may be, the presumption of a historical distance, and consequent difference of purpose, between the composition of the New Testament writings and their incorporation into a canon of scripture is representative of our discipline.

The question "When did the Gospels become scripture?" is certainly not a new one. Understandably, it is ordinarily construed as a question about the formation of the canon, in this case particularly the four-Gospel canon. The matter of the canon is important, interesting, and the subject of relevant discussions. For example, in his subsequently published 1996 Society for New Testament Studies presidential address Graham N. Stanton argued that the four-Gospel canon was formed sooner rather than later in the second century.[2] More radically, David Trobisch has proposed that the entire New Testament as we know it was actually assembled, redacted, and published in the latter half of the second century.[3] John Barton has argued that by that time the principal elements of the New Testament were already functioning as scripture, if not referred to as such.[4] Needless to say, any discussion of canon or scripture stands on the shoulders of such contemporary figures as James Barr, Brevard S. Childs, and James A. Sanders, not to mention Bruce M. Metzger.[5] Their contributions and such proposals as I have just mentioned are significant as well as fascinating to me, but I want to pursue a somewhat different tack.

For the purposes of our discussion I accept the distinction between canon and scripture (as set out, for example, by William A. Graham and now widely accepted).[6] Obviously *canon* presumes *scripture,* that is, the recognition of certain writings as possessing peculiar status or importance. *Scripture* means "texts that are revered as especially sacred and authoritative."[7] *Canon* refers to the delimitation of such texts. Significantly, *canon* (*kanōn*) is not used of sacred writings in the New Testament, but *scripture* (*graphē*) of course is. In most, but not all, cases, *scripture* clearly refers to what Christians call the Old Testament. The existence of scripture as well as canon implies the existence of a religious community that accords status and authority to certain texts. It goes without saying that the community in question believes that such status and authority actually belong to, adhere in, the text because of its subject matter, God in relation to human beings.

The authors of the New Testament books refer to scripture, but—we have assumed—do not think of themselves as writing scripture. We are accustomed to thinking of the Gospels as well as the Epistles as occasional documents generated in specific times and places to address issues of such times and places.[8] Of course, one generally acknowledges that the letters of the apostle Paul were the means of his apostolic presence among his churches, in which they would have been read aloud (1 Thess 5:27; Col 4:16; cf. 2 Cor 10:9–10). Second Peter 3:15–16 suggests that they were regarded as scripture before there was a New Testament. The same may also be true of the Gospels, although that is more difficult to document. From Justin Martyr (*First Apology* 67) we learn that at least by mid-second century "the memoirs of the apostles" (that is, Gospels) were read with the Prophets at Sunday services. Justin's description implies that they were functioning as scripture although neither term (*Gospels* or *scripture*) is used. Quite possibly this practice was established well before the time of Justin. To go back even a step further, G. D. Kilpatrick and Michael Goulder have maintained that the Gospel of Matthew was composed for year-round public reading in the service of worship.[9] Moreover, Philip Carrington has argued a similar thesis for Mark, namely, that it corresponded to a primitive Christian calendar.[10] Obviously, external evidence is lacking, but no less so than in the case of hypothetical gospel sources (Q; the *sēmeia*-source) or earlier traditions (as delineated by form criticism). In fact, the commonly accepted hypothesis that such materials were employed in preaching or catechesis already implies their authoritative character. The leap from such uses in the 50s to the reading of the Gospels in church worship a hundred years later is a reasonable one, even if we cannot document the earlier stages. Probably an intermediate stage would have been the use of only one Gospel as the authoritative document of a particular church (or churches). Thus, as tradition holds, Mark in Rome or John in Ephesus.

If the Gospels were composed for reading in worship services, they were likely intended for concrete church settings. Yet their use year-round would imply that they were conceived to address a general or broad range of needs rather than specific internal crises or issues.

In fact, the generally held presumption that the Gospels, like the Epistles, were written for individual Christian communities to address their specific situations or needs has recently been sharply questioned by Richard Bauckham.[11] He points out that the possibility that any of the Gospels was written for a broader, general Christian audience is seldom entertained, much less embraced, in contemporary Gospel scholarship. Acknowledging that each of the Gospels would have been affected by the circumstances of its origin, Bauckham argues that this does not mean they were addressed to those circumstances primarily. He goes on to suggest that they were intended for Christians generally.

Bauckham raises the question of whether we too easily take for granted the time-and-place-specific purpose and character of the Gospels. His thesis is worth serious consideration, but rather than engage it directly I want to pursue a similar interest and sense of the nature of the Gospels in a somewhat different way by asking the parallel but related question: Did the authors of the Gospels intend to write scripture? To answer that they did would not, of course, imply that they were writing for the New Testament canon, whose existence they could have scarcely foreseen. Whether they did or did not should be approached on the basis of an examination of the form and content of the Gospels, as well as their broader literary and historical context within ancient Judaism and early Christianity. As we shall see, there is no single or simple answer, but the pursuit of the question I find fascinating.

I am well aware that the question of definition—beyond the quite general one offered by Graham—remains largely outstanding. Yet that is one of those questions that, like most important questions, looks simpler at first glance than on close examination. As Graham says, "the term *scripture* is commonly used as though it designated a self-evident and simple religious phenomenon readily identifiable," but in the next sentence he concludes that "*scripture* is a term of considerable ambiguity and complexity."[12]

We do not have a more precise definition of *scripture* ready at hand, although our ancient Christian sources seem to assume that readers know what scripture is. In our own exploration we may be able to see better how scripture was understood in the early church and by certain New Testament writers. I propose now to do two things: first, to look at the Gospels themselves in order to ask how or in what sense they qualify as scripture and, indeed, whether they were intended as scripture; second, to ask whether the results of this survey of the Gospels correlate positively with developments in the Jewish matrix of early Christianity: Was Jewish scripture still being written?

The Gospels as Scripture

We may start with the Gospel of Matthew. Matthew begins with a genealogy that sets Jesus in the context and lineage of the Davidic monarchy. In doing so, Matthew makes clear that Jesus represents the restoration of that dynasty and therefore of the history of Israel and the history of salvation. Thus Jesus continues the biblical narrative. Moreover, the genealogy itself is a biblical genre or form, characteristic of Hebrew scripture, although there are parallels outside the Bible and Judaism.[13] Thus, 1 Chronicles begins with a nine-chapter genealogy. The narrative of Jesus' birth is then punctuated by scriptural prophecies, which, interestingly enough, are not introduced as scripture—as if scripture were in a different category from this Gospel—but as what was spoken by the prophets. (Jesus himself later, and appropriately, refers or alludes to scripture, for example, 21:16; 21:42.) Of course, all the Gospels at one point or another refer to scripture, meaning Jewish scripture or the Old Testament.

That Matthew's Gospel is intended to be a definitive presentation of Jesus, particularly in the five thematic discourses of his teaching, scarcely requires demonstration. Probably those five discourses are intended to correspond to the five books of Moses, as Jesus himself seems to fulfill, or supersede, the role of Moses, whose status is not denied but revised.[14] Moreover, the concluding promise of Jesus covers the history of salvation from his departure to the end (28:20). The definitive revelation has now been given, and nothing new or different is to be expected.

In their International Critical Commentary, W. D. Davies and Dale C. Allison infer from the apparently intentional scriptural analogies, especially the genealogy, that Matthew probably conceived "his gospel as a continuation of the biblical history—and also, perhaps, that he conceived of his work as belonging to the same literary category as the scriptural cycles treating of OT figures." Moreover, *Biblos geneseōs* is the author's deliberate evocation of the Genesis narrative, to which he intends to offer a counterpart.[15]

In describing Matthew to beginning students as an effort to continue the biblical history, one must make clear that it is only one possible continuation of that story, and a distinctively Christian one at that. Another continuation of the biblical story may be found, for example, in 1 Maccabees, whose author also writes in a scriptural style: "In those days certain renegades came out from Israel and misled many, saying, 'Let us go and make a covenant with the Gentiles around us, for since we separated from them many disasters have come upon us'" (1 Macc 1:11). One could cite many other examples. Of course, 1 Maccabees deals with a period nearly two centuries before the appearance of Jesus, so Matthew and 1 Maccabees are not mutually exclusive continuations of the biblical story. (1 Maccabees has accordingly been preserved among Christian versions of the Old Testament.) Nevertheless, 1 Maccabees is far more obviously a continuation of the biblical (Old Testament) story than is Matthew a continuation of the story of the Hasmonean era. First Maccabees hardly anticipates Matthew (as Isaiah may be construed to). The principal point, however, is that 1 Maccabees does continue the biblical story in a recognizably similar narrative genre and style, even as Matthew does. More than one author seems to be writing "scripture" in the postbiblical period.

Something similar could be said of Luke, whose biblical, Septuagintal phrasing has often been noticed.[16] For example, Luke (2:1), like the author of 1 Maccabees (1:11), writes "in those days," in apparent imitation of the biblical style (cf. Judg 21:25). The opening narratives of Jesus' birth and childhood, where Luke is relatively free to compose, are through and through biblical in style and content. Mary's response to the annunciation (1:47–55) is, of course, a recapitulation of Hannah's prayer in 1 Sam 2:1–10. Thus, Luke in ways different from Matthew deliberately imitates or parallels scriptural style. Moreover, Luke, like Matthew, uses the opening, infancy narratives to establish Jesus' continuity with biblical history. Salvation history continues with Jesus. At the end of Luke, on the road to Emmaus, the disciples express the disappointed hope that Jesus was the one to redeem Israel (24:21; cf. Acts 1:6). Needless to say, Luke's intention is taken up and brought to a kind of culmination in the book of Acts, as he extends the narrative beyond Jesus into the mission of the church, which does not contradict, but fulfills, the hope of Israel.[17]

Did Luke intend to write scripture? A recent commentator has put it this way: "Luke sees his writings as a continuation of the scriptural story. . . . The Lukan evangelist is a writer of Scripture, a hagiographer who is proclaiming what 'God has accomplished among us.'"[18] His prefaces (Luke 1:1–4; Acts 1:1–2) may have led us to put him into the same category as Josephus and Hellenistic historians generally rather than the writers of scripture. Of course, Josephus thought of himself as an inspired author,[19] and he rewrites biblical history as well as narrating the postbiblical period. Sirach too begins with a preface (albeit by a later hand) which also accounts for the origin of the book. Probably Luke's preface gives some indication of the situation he faced and the use he anticipated for his own Gospel. Yet it does not necessarily imply that he intended to write history and not scripture.[20] Perhaps he intended to do both. Obviously he intended to supersede Mark, as well as whatever other Gospels, or Gospel-like writings, he knew. Matthew's appropriation of 90 percent of Mark indicates that he had the same intention—to displace Mark. (Evidently, Matthew, as well as Luke, did not regard Mark as scripture.)

But how was Mark by then actually functioning? As scripture? It is remarkable and significant that Mark was used independently by Matthew and Luke, who apparently composed their Gospels in different Christian centers. Quite possibly Mark was read aloud in the churches of Matthew and Luke. Whether or not Mark was written for a general Christian audience, it obviously found such a broader usage. It seems to have functioned as scripture early on.

Arguably, both Matthew and Luke rewrite, augment, and re-present the Marcan narrative to produce documents better suited to function as scripture for Christian audiences generally. Sometimes Matthew and Luke's common omissions of Marcan materials serve such a purpose. Thus they both excise the names of the sons of Simon of Cyrene (Mark 15:21), which evidently were significant for Mark's audience but not for a more general one. They both excise the strange narrative of the young man's fleeing naked in the night at Jesus' arrest (Mark 14:51–52), which may have puzzled them as much as it has puzzled us. They both omit Mark's concluding statement that the women at the tomb said nothing to anyone, for they were afraid (16:8). How then could the narrative continue? And for both Matthew and Luke it is important that this biblical, scriptural narrative continue.

In what sense does Mark think the scriptural (Old Testament) narrative should or would continue? Of course, Mark presents Jesus as the fulfillment of biblical prophecy from the outset of his own narrative (1:2–3).[21] Yet Mark is not nearly so explicit as Matthew and Luke about how Jesus represents the continuation of the biblical story. In fact, it is also much less clear how Jesus' messiahship is understood, despite the importance of the title *Christ* in Mark (1:1; 8:29; 14:61–62). Even, and particularly, the high priest's and the council's reactions to Jesus' positive answer to the question of whether he was the Messiah imply a Christian rather than a Jewish conception of messiahship, that is, Christology rather than messianism. Curiously, despite having been addressed as Son of David (Mark 10:47–48), the Marcan Jesus seems to question the Messiah's Davidic sonship (12:35–37). No doubt Mark believed Jesus was the Messiah expected by contemporary Jews, but he does not place Jesus within the framework of such expectation as carefully as do Matthew and Luke. Thus he does not contribute, as they do, to the articulation of the self-identity of emerging Christianity vis-à-vis Judaism.

To jump ahead for a moment, something similar is happening in the Gospel of John. In John when Jesus' Davidic lineage is challenged by some (7:42), the Fourth Evangelist strikingly allows their objection to go unanswered. Yet John actually pays much more attention than Mark to Jewish messianic hopes or expectations and to whether or in what sense Jesus may be thought to fulfill them. As we have already suggested, both Matthew and Luke also have a great deal more to say than Mark on both counts—that is: (1) on how Jesus and his following represent the continuation of the biblical narrative and (2) on how or in what sense Jesus is the fulfillment of messianic expectations. Thus they remedy Mark's deficiencies and in doing so write narratives that seem better candidates to become scripture.

In this respect the character of Mark is closely related to, perhaps a result of, its apocalyptic, eschatological perspective. Mark's eschatology, which suggests to many exegetes something significant about its setting and purpose, comes to climactic expression in chapter 13.[22] Both Matthew and Luke take up this discourse, but for them it does not occupy so central a role.[23] Moreover, they alter it in significant ways. To put matters succinctly, the centrality and urgency of the expectation of the imminent future revelation of Jesus suggest that Mark does not anticipate a long shelf life for his book. Conversely, Matthew and Luke anticipate longer shelf lives for theirs. Although this state of affairs does not necessarily imply that they intended to write scripture while Mark did not, it is quite congruent with such a purpose. In their tendency to generalize Mark's narrative and thus to presume a broader horizon, both spatially and temporally, Matthew and Luke write Gospels better suited to function as scripture for Christian churches in various places.

Obviously, the eschatology of the synoptic tradition, and that of early Christianity generally, is being revamped in John, who gives explicit indications that this is a conscious, intentional process (11:23–27; 14:22–24; 21:20–23). While their eschatologies differ, neither Mark nor John seems to fit easily into the pattern or shape of scripture understood as the ongoing saga of Israel. Both have obvious roots in, and positive contacts with, that saga.[24] Although both are construable as a continuation of it, neither provides as smooth a transition as do Matthew and Luke.

Continuation of the biblical narrative is not, however, an essential aspect of scripture. Obviously, the canon of both testaments is full of books or parts of books that are not narrative. Nevertheless, the biblical narrative is the backbone of both testaments. Although the narrative of the Tanak does not require the Gospel narrative of the New Testament as its completion, that narrative presupposes what has gone before. Moreover, the early Christian claim that the narrative and prophecies of old are fulfilled and continued in Jesus and the church prefigures, perhaps even demands, the production of more scripture that will explain how this happened. Such scripture is required to explain this not first of all to outsiders but rather to Christians themselves. It becomes an essential part of their identity and self-understanding.

What about John? That the Gospel of John originated in a specific setting of dialogue and conflict between Jews who believed Jesus to be the Messiah and those who denied it with increasing vigor is now one of the more securely established results of Gospel research.[25] Moreover, the clear evidence of the redaction, as well as recensions, of the Gospel, together with the Johannine letters and the book of Revelation (with its distinctive points of contact with the

Gospel),[26] all suggest that the Johannine writings arose out of Christian communities involved in specific and identifiable situations and were in large measure addressed to them. And yet the Gospel of John's purpose and meaning transcend its originative situation. The farewell discourses already suggest this, as they address major, and broader, issues generally relevant to a distinctively Christian community. Certainly the Epistles reflect a different setting, but one in which the Gospel continued to be read as an authoritative document. If Raymond E. Brown is correct, as I think he is, 1 John not only presupposes the Gospel of John, and only John, but is engaged in an exegetical controversy over the correct interpretation of this Gospel.[27] This then implies that some form of the Gospel of John was, for certain circles, already functioning as scripture. That a broader audience is in view is indicated by chapter 21, which reestablishes Peter, and even the authority of Peter, while underscoring the independence of the Beloved Disciple, whose authority underwrites the Gospel. The colophon of the final recension of the Gospel (21:25) then speaks of "the books that would be written" and suggests that the author of chapter 21 knows of the existence of other books, presumably one or more of the Synoptics and perhaps other gospels, which may for him count as scripture. Is there here a hint even of a Gospel canon? That is too much to claim, although the possibility is real. However that may be, the warrant for believing this Gospel as the work of the Beloved Disciple is made clear (John 21:24), and it functions very much like the preface of Luke's Gospel, to assure the reader of the veracity and weight of what is written.

Is it the case that Luke and Matthew incorporated Mark into their Gospels with a view to writing more suitably scriptural accounts? By the same token, has John's narrative been subjected to a similar process, which we can detect only in its redaction history? I think the answer is yes in both cases.

John's final effect and therefore his purpose seem to be somewhat different, however, from Matthew's and Luke's. That John becomes scripture in the same sense, or within the same theological frame of reference, is by no means clear. In John there is no question that Jesus is the Messiah of Israel (1:41, 49), the one "about whom Moses wrote in the law, as well as the prophets" (1:48). Yet such positive assertions are counterbalanced by the several references to "your law" (for example, 8:17), namely, the law of the Jews, and by the blanket opening statement that "he came to his own home and his own people did not receive him" (1:11 RSV). Nevertheless, in John's Gospel Jesus is a Jew (4:9); salvation is from the Jews (4:22); John the Baptist was sent to reveal Jesus to Israel (1:31). This is a complex issue, yet there is hardly the kind of continuity between Israel and Jesus, or Israel and the church through Jesus, that is found in Luke-Acts. John could scarcely have expected his work to become a part of a Jewish Bible. If it is scripture at all, it must become a part of a new covenant or New Testament. With respect to their supersessionism, John and the Epistle to the Hebrews (especially chapter 8) seem to share common ground.

One should at this point ask also about the so-called apocryphal gospels. Did their authors presume to be writing scripture? The fact is that in most cases we do not know enough about their content to say. The best surviving, complete exemplar is the *Gospel of Thomas.* No doubt *Thomas* presents itself as an authoritative work. It is intended to be scriptural in that sense. One could not, in the nature of the case (and because of our lack of knowledge), separate the canonical Gospels from the noncanonical on the basis of whether or not their authors conceived of their works as authoritative and thus scripture. Yet *Thomas* differs sharply from the canonical Gospels in ways that are not only obvious but significant for our question. *Thomas* is not a narrative; it could not, I think by intention, be construed as continuing the biblical story. One might object that *Thomas* is wisdom, a biblical genre, the wisdom of Jesus, not narrative, as was the hypothetical Q source. Yet Q maintains a future, eschatological perspective that is missing from *Thomas.* Moreover, unlike Q, *Thomas* contains no explicit references to scripture.[28] Not only is scripture not cited; there is no indication that any scripture is presupposed. (Saying 66 reflects Ps 118:22 but does not cite it as scripture.) There is no presumed scriptural story for which *Thomas* could present itself as the next chapter.

It is becoming obvious that the answer to the question of whether the evangelists intended to write scripture depends on what is meant by scripture. If we mean by *scripture* an authoritative document for a group of Christians, all the gospels, including *Thomas,* were intended to be scripture. We have, however, narrowed our focus to ask whether gospels show evidence of having been composed as specifically biblical, in the sense of Jewish or Jewish-Christian scripture. We have found reason to think that Matthew and Luke were composed to fulfill such a role. At the other end of the spectrum, apparently *Thomas* was not. *Thomas* was composed not for biblical religion but for another, new, esoteric religion. It presupposes neither the biblical narrative of the Hebrew scriptures nor the narrative of Jesus' ministry. (Is it perhaps telling that Jesus is not called Christ or Messiah in *Thomas?*) John and Mark fall somewhere in between, if for different reasons.

Yet Mark and John have something else in common. To use terminology introduced now a generation ago, they represent parallel trajectories in Gospel development.[29] The Marcan trajectory expands, with Mark's co-option by Matthew and Luke, into the synoptic trajectory. The Johannine trajectory remains within what we now call the Gospel of John. The jagged edges of the Marcan eschatology and Christology are smoothed out into the more scriptural narratives composed by Matthew and Luke. John continues to go a separate way, rooted in the ancient biblical narrative but affirming in ways different from Matthew and Luke that the narrative comes to a theological climax and end with Jesus. Jesus' *tetelestai* from the cross means that the narrative is finished as well. The Johannine tradition, or scripture, stands in tension with the synoptic, even as it was placed alongside it in the developing Christian canon of the New Testament.

Now, as we turn away from specifically Christian developments to look briefly at the contemporary Jewish matrix or milieu against which the emergence of Christian scriptures must be seen, one other observation may be in order. I have dealt only with the Gospels. Of course, the Revelation to John insists on its right to be heard as just that—revelation—as the author warns in advance against any tampering with the authoritative book he has written (Rev 22:18–19). Strangely, or not so strangely, the first and last books of the New Testament present themselves as scripture. That is a story for another day, although it does attest the existence of the idea of distinctively Christian scriptures before the end of the first century. Strikingly, the initial New Testament book is a gospel that begins with a royal, Davidic genealogy and the final one is an apocalypse that characterizes itself as prophecy (1:3; 22:18). Of course, although Revelation has no explicit scriptural citation, it is replete with scriptural, especially prophetic, language. Whether or not some individual planned the New Testament according to this design, the meaning and significance are clear enough. Revelation implies the continuation and culmination of the biblical story.[30]

New Testament Scripture and Intertestamental Judaism

What is happening in the New Testament should not surprise us, however, given what we now know about the production and use of books in intertestamental (and I use the term deliberately) Judaism. We have already noticed the scriptural character of 1 Maccabees. Of course, all the apocryphal or deuterocanonical books can by definition claim recognition as scripture in some religious communities, that is, churches in the Catholic and Orthodox traditions. It is perhaps too much to claim that the pseudepigraphical books by their very ascription to ancient worthies were intended as scripture.[31] Yet the obvious intention of such ascriptions was to lend them authority and weight.[32] Thus 2 Esdras (14:44–47) speaks of ninety-four books of which only twenty-four constitute the Hebrew canon as we know it. (Of course, Jude 14–15 cites *1 Enoch* 1:9, apparently as scripture.) One major preoccupation seems to have been the retelling and rewriting of biblical history. Thus we have *Jubilees* and the *Genesis Apocryphon*. Some books such as the *Testaments of the Twelve Patriarchs* supplement the Bible. Some, the apocalypses, extend the story into the future.

The closing of the Jewish canon (traditionally associated with Jamnia in the year 90) presupposes this penumbra of Jewish books, represented at least in part by the Apocrypha and Pseudepigrapha. The very idea of closing a canon implies the existence of claimants to be denied. By the traditional date of closure Christian Gospels had come into existence, and they—or at least some of them—looked like candidates for incorporation into a Bible as scripture—perhaps also to Jews, who would have rejected them. Whether the Gospels were among such rejected books is a fascinating question, and this has been proposed, but, as far as I can see, adequate evidence is lacking.[33] In any event, the Gospels were written at a time of great literary productivity within Judaism, a time when the continuing production of scripture was not unthinkable in some circles.

It is tempting to describe the postbiblical or intertestamental period as the Age of Scripture—scripture being written as well as fulfilled—and not just for nascent Christianity but for Judaism as well. In this regard the example of the Qumran community is particularly instructive. Over fifty years ago Krister Stendahl noted the important phenomenological parallel between the Essenes of the Qumran community and the earliest church. Both were eschatological sects who believed themselves to be the heirs to scriptural promise and recipients of the coming messianic, eschatological salvation. Stendahl wrote: "We are now for the first time in a position where we can compare the messianic expectation of the Jewish sect called the Christians with another Jewish sect, already on the scene in the time of Jesus."[34] That was in 1957. A few years later Joseph A. Fitzmyer published his analysis, "The Use of Explicit Old Testament Quotations in the Qumran Literature and in the New Testament," in which he demonstrated in detail the close affinities between the use and citation of scripture in Qumran and in the New Testament.[35] It would be convenient to be able to argue that the Essenes were in the process of producing their own "New Testament" when their life was cut short. They had been assiduously preserving and copying scripture and books that might claim scriptural authority. Moreover, their *Hymns* (*Hodayot*) are expressions of a piety comparable to the canonical Psalms. The *Community Rule* is clearly authoritative for the community, although it does not have the breadth and scope of the Gospel of Matthew, which has sometimes been compared with it. From our perspective, the *Community Rule* is not naturally understood as scripture. Unlike Matthew, it does not extend the biblical narrative. It is not written in imitation of scripture, nor does it address itself to Israel generally. Moreover, it does not have the universal applicability of the wisdom books. It is clearly and by intention a sectarian document. The same could be said of the *Damascus Document.* Yet to say that a writing is sectarian does not, of course, mean that it could not be scriptural. (We are here once again coming up against the question of definition.)

Fitzmyer has observed an important difference of outlook that characterizes the New Testament over against the Dead Sea Scrolls: "The Qumran theology is still dominated by a forward look, an expectation of what is to come about in the *eschaton,* whereas the Christian theology is more characterized by a backward glance, seeing the culmination of all that has preceded in the advent of Christ."[36] Perhaps it would be fair to say that the Essenes were on the verge of being able to write their New Testament, for they certainly believed themselves to be recipients of a new covenant.

As Fitzmyer realized, the difference had to do with belief, Christology, but this in turn reflected the difference about where Christians believed themselves to be in the eschatological scheme of things. A new and definitive revelation had occurred. The backward glance of Christians became increasingly a backward stare, as the difference between John's Gospel and Mark's shows. In fact, one could imagine that as Christians, or Jews who were becoming Christians, looked increasingly to the past they more and more felt a need to commemorate and celebrate it in worship. Thus, scripture was needed and was written. If Mark and Q (or *Thomas*) do not look so much like scripture, Matthew, Luke, and the final form of John do.

Obviously, my presumption has been that the earliest development of Christian scripture occurred in a Jewish milieu that was becoming Christian. Such a presumption makes theological and historical sense to the degree that Christian Gospels commend themselves as the continuation of biblical narrative. It is not sheer coincidence that Carrington, Kilpatrick, and Goulder, who see Matthew and Mark as originating in liturgical settings—and therefore in a real sense already scriptural—all maintain that such settings had their roots in the worship of the synagogue.

What Is Scripture?

In conclusion, we return to the question of definition. Over a quarter of a century ago Wilfred Cantwell Smith sharply criticized the guild of biblical scholars for paying no attention to the scriptural status of the literature we study.[37] In a way perhaps somewhat different from what Smith anticipated I have spoken to the broader issue he raised. Smith himself quails before the difficulty of defining scripture and complains that "probably no one on earth today quite knows what scripture is."[38] Yet as he had already observed, "Scripture as a form and as a concept gradually emerged and developed in the Near East in a process of consolidation whose virtually complete stage comes with the Qur'an."[39]

When one casts the net broadly, Graham's "texts that are revered as especially sacred and authoritative" is about as good as we can do by way of definition. When Smith looks at Judaism, Christianity, and Islam, however, he sees this "process of consolidation," which reaches completion in Islam. There the text of the Qur'an *is* revelation. This is different from ancient Judaism or early Christianity, although both of them have of course developed comparable forms of scriptural fundamentalism.[40] In biblical Judaism and Christianity, however, revelation is given in historical events, acts, and words, which are interpreted first orally and then in writing, scripture, as revelation. This,

I think, is for them the central and crucial part of the process to which Smith refers.

In the case of the earliest Christian Gospels we observed already that the initial and fundamental impulse for their composition came with the proclamation of Jesus as the fulfillment of scripture. The use of the Gospels alongside the older, Jewish scriptures in worship, certainly as early as the mid-second century, probably much earlier, was likely a continuation of the use to which the earlier Gospel traditions had already been put. Matthew and Luke particularly, if in different ways, adopted biblical genres and styles as they also continued the biblical story. This is nowhere clearer than in their infancy narratives. In his own independent mode, John rewrites the story of creation from Genesis, like many of his Jewish contemporaries retelling the biblical narrative, but in a revolutionary way.

In looking at the Gospels, I am suggesting, we are already observing an important stage in the process to which Smith refers. If I have made a case for anything it is this: that the intention to write scripture should not be excluded from a consideration of the purpose as well as the result of the composition of the Gospels. Perhaps in purpose as well as effect the Gospels tell us something about what scripture is. Thus they contribute to the resolution of the problem of the definition of scripture.

We began by asking whether the evangelists intended to write scripture. If I had to give a brief answer to that question, I would say that the two Gospels based on Mark were written to function as scripture for the burgeoning Christian communities, whether or not Matthew and Luke thought in those terms. They give not only a narrative of Jesus' career but a substantial representation of his teaching. Because of this neither is as gripping a narrative as Mark. Did Mark intend to write scripture? Perhaps, but I find that a difficult question to answer. It soon became evident, however, that his Gospel, and the gospel genre, met a need for (distinctively Christian) scripture, although at least Matthew and Luke thought Mark needed improvement.

What about John? If John thought he could improve on Mark, he did so by setting Mark aside and starting again. John's Gospel is, in my view, an independent effort to do what Mark had done but to do it differently. When one asks about John, one should probably ask, Which stage of John? At some point, John begins to function as scripture for its community, as 1 John suggests. In its present canonical form it apparently contemplates the existence of other Gospels (21:25, "the books that would be written"), probably one or more of the Synoptics.[41] Did (the redactor of) John think that they were to be regarded as scripture too? With that question we have arrived at the subject of John and the Synoptic Gospels. Did John know them? Accept them? Reject them? To some of us these questions are endlessly fascinating. But let's stop there and leave them for another day!

Four Gospels and the Canonical Approach to Exegesis

Should Their Being Together in the New Testament Make a Difference in Their Interpretation?

Obviously, John's relationship to the Synoptic Gospels is an important issue, with theological as well as literary-historical implications, because they all stand in the same canon of Christian scripture. What their relationship might be if they did not is inconceivable, so closely is their history and interpretation related to their belonging to the New Testament. The historical-critical method of interpretation does not, however, seek to understand the Gospel of John in relation to the Synoptics in the New Testament canon. Rather, historical criticism concentrates upon John, or upon any New Testament book, with a view to understanding it in its own right, that is, with respect to its original setting, purpose, and meaning. On these terms the question of John and the Synoptics is the question of their historic, literary relationship at the point of origin. Usually this question is cast in terms of whether the Fourth Evangelist knew the other Gospels, since it would be exceedingly difficult to understand any of the Synoptics as presupposing, much less derived from the Gospel of John.

The traditional answer to the question of their originative relationship, which was posed as early as the second century, is that John knew and approved of the other Gospels, and presumed knowledge of them as he wrote. Thus he wrote to supplement, mildly correct, or interpret the others. Already Origen saw the difficulty of reconciling the differences between John and the Synoptics on the historical level; their accounts of Jesus' ministry cannot be made historically consistent and coherent. Therefore, he proposed a reconciliation between John and the Synoptics at another hermeneutical level.[1] Thus the justification of Origen's spiritual or allegorical exegesis. In fact, Origen seemed to delight in showing their irreconcilable differences precisely because he wanted to make the hermeneutical move to another level or mode of interpretation. By and large, however, traditional exegesis has throughout most of Christian history sought to minimize the differences between John and the Synoptics. Some exegesis continues along this line, even while working on the basis of historical-critical assumptions. The twentieth century also saw the alternative positions arise as major options: either John rejected the Synoptic Gospels and desired to replace them with his own Gospel, or he did not know them. Such views are only conceivable on the basis of historical-critical presuppositions, that is, on the assumption that John is to be interpreted, and its relation to the Synoptics is to be understood, in relation to its original context, purpose, and assumptions.

Precisely this perspective in interpretation has been sharply rejected as the starting point of exegesis by Brevard S. Childs. In his *The New Testament as Canon: An Introduction,* Childs has specific points to make about the Gospel of John.[2] More basic, however, is his general perspective, which when applied to John, or any New Testament book, has rather far-reaching implications.[2]

For Childs historical criticism cannot be the final arbiter of the meaning of a New Testament writing or text; nor does it afford the initial perspective upon the meaning and shape of a text.[3] In other words, the historical critic asking about a text's origin, historical setting, purpose, and meaning is permitted to have neither the first nor the last word in interpretation. "Historical criticism is an indispensable teacher," writes Childs.[4] But it is a teacher, not judge and jury. Childs does not propose to eliminate traditional historical-critical approaches from the broader task of interpretation, but resists turning over to the historical critic as such the right to say once and for all what a text may mean. To invoke Krister Stendahl's distinction, the historical critic may say what a text meant, but that is not the same as what it means as it now stands in the Christian canon of scripture. But Childs—in his role as churchly, canonical interpreter—will not even agree to allow the historical critic first to say what the text meant, and on that basis take up the further task of stating its theological or canonical meaning.[5] Rather, the canonical shape of the New Testament is the datum with which interpretation *begins.*

Childs on the Fourth Gospel

Obviously, such a position and perspective would become extremely important in the interpretation of the Fourth Gospel as part of the Christian canon of scripture. Interestingly enough, in his chapter on the Gospel of John, Childs concentrates on that Gospel itself, and does not deal extensively with the general question of its relation to the Synoptics or its position in the canon, both of which could have interesting and important implications for interpretation. He wants to insist upon the final, canonical shape of John, including chapter 21 and any other hypothetical later redactional additions, as the proper object of canonical exegesis. Thus his program is, for example, diametrically opposed to that of Rudolf Bultmann, who takes as the object of exegesis the Gospel of John as he has restored it, that is, the Gospel in its original order, freed from its later redactional framing or corruption.[6] (Bultmann did not use such pejorative terms, but that is what his theory of redactional restoration comes to.) Childs's program is more in line with the literary-critical work of R. Alan Culpepper, or the redactional standpoint of Hartwig Thyen, who wants to view the final redactor as the evangelist and to interpret the entire Gospel from his perspective.[7] Yet it is based neither on literary-critical nor on historical-critical grounds, but on the theological and traditional status of the canon as a given for Christian exegesis and interpretation.

While Childs might be interested in John's historical relationship to the Synoptic Gospels, and indeed seems to favor John's independence, his own approach is not governed by his position on this question.[8] On his terms, it could not be, for that would be tantamount to handing over the interpretive task to the historical critic, or, to put it another way, allowing the determination of a historical setting or relationship to guide the course of Christian exegesis. Was John dependent on the Synoptics? Then John should be read in light of them. Was John intended to displace the Synoptics? Then one must choose between them. Was John written in ignorance of the other Gospels? Then they must not be allowed to enter into the exegesis of it. Actually, this final question or position comes closer to representing Childs's own view than the others, but he would not finally embrace it. John after all now finds a place in the canon alongside the other three. Childs rightly calls for more attention to the canonical unity of the Four Gospels.[9] Yet each has its integrity. "No one Gospel is made the hermeneutical key, as would have happened had John's Gospel been constructed into an overarching framework and the three synoptics inserted into its story."[10] Interestingly enough, however, when he deals with the John the Baptist accounts in his canonical harmony of the Gospels, Childs does allow the Fourth Gospel to become the key to the others in a way we would not have anticipated given this earlier general statement. In this connection he remarks that "the Fourth Gospel becomes the key to the new hermeneutical function of the fourfold collection," and goes on to "distinguish between the shape of the Fourth Gospel as a literary composition with a discrete integrity and its function within the canonical collection."[11] Focus upon the latter is primary in exegesis.

Thus the canonical approach to the Gospels would not allow a position on the historical relationship of John to the Synoptics, whether positive or negative, to assume a determinative role in exegesis. On Childs's terms, the question of John and the Synoptics as a historical question of literary and traditional relationships may be interesting, informative, and enriching for exegesis. But it is not the exegetical key, the sine qua non, for the interpretation of the Fourth Gospel. The canonical approach to the Gospel must not begin there. To begin there would, in fact, be to surrender to the historical critic the first, and eventually the last, word. Moreover, it would make what could finally be no more than a hypothesis, a hypothetical construct about origins with accompanying implications for setting and purpose, determinative for exegesis. That is exactly what Childs will on no account allow. Thus he sharply rejects Barnabas Lindars's claim that "the effort to get behind the Fourth Gospel to its tradition and sources is not simply a literary-critical game, but an inescapable task in the process of discovering the real meaning" of the Gospel.[12] Whether behind the Fourth Gospel lie the Synoptics or other traditional sources, be they oral or written, is an interesting question, but one that cannot finally be decisive in interpretation. Canonical John stands on its own, but it stands in relation to the other Gospels.

Not surprisingly then, Childs names Edwyn Clement Hoskyns as posing the crucial hermeneutical question and quotes a decisive statement from Hoskyns's commentary: "The important question is not whether the Fourth Gospel depends upon oral tradition, or upon written documents, or upon both, but whether it is, or is not, a work existing in its own right, and whether it is or is not to be interpreted independently and by itself."[13] Actually, in the extant, posthumously published text of his commentary, Hoskyns does not clearly espouse John's historical and literary independence from the Synoptics, but presupposes that the evangelist knew their tradition in something like the form encountered in them.[14] At the same time he stresses the distinct and in that sense independent theological profile of the Gospel. It is apparently on this latter point of emphasis that Childs so thoroughly agrees with him. When Childs states that "the primary issue turns on the function of the witness to the earthly life of Jesus within the Fourth Gospel,"[15] he is indeed close to Hoskyns. At the same time, the question of the relationship to the Synoptics (or to the substance of the specific witnesses), which Hoskyns dealt with at the level of historical criticism, has been removed by Childs in principle to the level of canonical relationship.

In an interesting way Childs's position on the Fourth Gospel, which he can only outline in the context of a general introduction, is analogous to both Culpepper's and Hans Windisch's. The last two are, of course, pursuing different questions and cannot simply be lumped together. Yet their view of the relation of John to the Synoptics has striking points of similarity. For both, John's Gospel is, on the one hand, independent, in that it is a full and adequate account which is not intended to play a supplementary role and does not require supplementation. On the other, it is clear for both that John presumes knowledge we have from the Synoptics. Culpepper characterizes the Johannine narrative as reliable and sufficient, while at the same time noticing that the implied reader is presumed to know many of the major figures and events of the story already.[16] For example, in the Johannine temple cleansing it becomes apparent that the implied reader knows that Jesus has risen from the dead (as any Christian would). Windisch speaks of the Gospel of John as a commentary without text or a commentary intended to displace the text.[17] Two things are implied: John's independence of the Synoptics, but at the same time his knowledge—and the reader's presumed knowledge—of personages and matters known to us from the Synoptic Gospels. Windisch, of course, believes John's knowledge of people and events came from the Synoptics as well and that he intended to displace the other Gospels in the church's use. Culpepper leaves this matter open. With Childs, John's independence is fundamental, although the question of whether or not he used the Synoptics is finally not crucial. Initially, with Childs, as with Culpepper and Windisch, knowledge of the Synoptics does not seem necessary for understanding and interpreting the Fourth Gospel, which is an independent narrative. Yet in each case, as also with Hoskyns, John is perceived as presupposing the reader's knowledge of either the canonical Gospels or their equivalent tradition. With Windisch and Hoskyns this is a more or less traditional historical-critical judgment. With Culpepper we are in the arena of literary criticism; with Childs canonical criticism. But is there in any case a tension between the affirmation of independence and John's actual relation to the Synoptics? If so, this tension, confirmed from different perspectives, may say something about the character of the Fourth Gospel.

John's Canonicity in Historical Perspective

There are several other matters related to John's canonical status which, although not at the center of Childs's attention, may be of importance for the issues he is pursuing. These have to do with the history and shape of the Gospel canon, and particularly with John's role in that historical development and shaping process. The remainder of this chapter will be devoted, first, to aspects of John's early canonical history that are related to its authority in the church, and then to the matter of the reciprocal roles of John and the Synoptics, particularly Matthew, in canonical interpretation. Perhaps even their relative positions say something about how they may be understood. In this connection some interesting implications for the question of John and the Synoptics—now once again much discussed—may emerge.

The history of the development of the canon is touched on rather briefly by Childs. There is a chapter entitled "The Canon as an Historical and Theological Problem," but the canonical approach to exegesis is not based upon a particular understanding of the history and development of the canon. In a discussion of the canonical place and role of the Book of Acts Childs indicates he does not accept the revisionist view of the formation of the canon identified with A. C. Sundberg and others, which rejects the once generally held position that the core of the New Testament canon had been established by the end of the second century.[18] Nevertheless, the validity of the canonical approach is not tied to any historical view of the origin and development of the canon. In particular, it does not depend upon the relatively early emergence of the canon as distinctively Christian scripture. More specifically, the canonical status or validity of the Fourth Gospel is not related to the process of its becoming a part of the four-Gospel canon.

Childs chides Westcott, Lightfoot, Zahn, and Lagrange for running in the face of the canonical shaping of the Gospel, in which the author's anonymity is preserved behind the veil of the Beloved Disciple, when they seek to defend Johannine authorship. John the son of Zebedee is never mentioned as the author in the Gospel itself (in fact, never mentioned by name at all), and that is certainly not a matter of chance. Of course, these great conservative scholars were in all probability right in thinking that the Fourth Gospel became a part of the developing canon toward the end of the second century only as it was believed to be the work of that apostle. If so, the canonical process, John's becoming a part of the canon, was in fact intimately related to the determination of authorship. Childs successfully divorces the canonical status of John from the question of specifically Johannine authorship on the authority and at the level of the Fourth Gospel itself. Yet the Gospel's canonicity as a historical process and fact was related to the specific claim of authorship (the Johannine) that has become the church's tradition. And as Childs frequently reiterates, the canonical approach is intimately related to the hearing of John, that is, the receiving of it. It was heard and received as John's Gospel.

Of course, the question of John and the Synoptics is related to the formation of the canon too, for a major part of the resistance to John in the early church was grounded in its unaccountable divergences from the other Gospels that were already playing an authoritative role. John comes in alongside the other three as the work of an apostolic figure of peerless authority and as the Gospel intended to supplement and interpret them. Ernst Käsemann pungently and correctly points out that in canonizing John the church domesticated it by divorcing it from its original setting and purpose.[19] For Childs, the questions of canonical authority, as well as canonical interpretation, do not hinge upon reconstructions of historical development or upon the issues which probably played such a large role in the actual unfolding of that development, such as apostolic authorship. Present canonical shape, not reconstructions of the shaping process behind it, is the beginning point and focus of the canonical approach. Nevertheless, these simple observations about the ways in which certain historical and literary questions (authorship and relation to the Synoptics) have played a role in John's gaining canonical status and authority are at least worth bearing in mind. If the canonical approach brackets them out, as well it may, one must recognize that the basis for canonical authority is now somewhat different from what it was in antiquity.

The Canonical Balance of Matthew and John

The actual shape of the Gospel canon as it confronts us in the New Testament is not central to Childs's approach and does not command the center of his attention. He rightly observes that the order of the Gospels has varied historically in canonical lists and manuscripts, although in time the present universally accepted order became firmly established. Because of the flexibility in the process, one should not attach too great importance to the order of the Gospels. Yet the common canonical order of the Gospels, like the canonical shape of the individual books, makes a certain sense. It seems to bespeak an intention. To speak of "intention" in this regard is uncertain or question begging. Whose intention? How conscious was it? We cannot say. Childs is wary of ascribing too much by way of conscious intention to the redactors of books, and wants instead to speak of their canonical shaping in the church. Moreover, he is aware of the obvious analogy with the canon as a whole. One does not want to ascribe too much to conscious intention in the church's preservation, development, and ordering of the Gospel canon.[20] At the same time the character of the final product, including the final ordering, projects a kind of intention that can scarcely be ignored.

The positions of Mark and Luke do not appear to be immediately significant or meaningful, yet one could imagine that Mark, if the earliest Gospel, was displaced from its position at the head of the canon by Matthew, which incorporates ninety percent of Mark and was very likely intended to replace it.[21] Luke, it might be argued, was once intended to be followed immediately by Acts, at least by the author, but they were separated when John was accepted into the canon. All this is plausible enough, but scarcely rises above the level of informed speculation, or at best logical inference from the respective texts.

Turning to Matthew, however, several obvious, but nevertheless substantial and I think more significant, observations may be made. Matthew's Gospel stands at the beginning of the New Testament, where it makes meaningful connections forward and backward. Just the fact that Matthew begins with a genealogy, a well-known and ancient Old Testament genre, seems to link the new with the old in characteristic ways. (We should remember, of course, that neither the Masoretic text nor the Septuagint ends with the minor prophets, and therefore with Malachi.) The genealogy itself puts Jesus of Nazareth into the Davidic royal line. (Contrast Luke, in which Jesus is a son of David, but otherwise not of the kingly line.) Thus the narrative not only of Matthew, but of the entire New Testament as well, is linked to Israel's *Heilsgeschichte,* to the drama of God's calling forth and dealing with a people. This is no less important because it is obvious. The birth of Jesus is then described, principally from the standpoint of Joseph, the father, who accedes to God's will in unusual circumstances in order that all righteousness may be fulfilled. The theme of the fulfilling of righteousness then leads like a red thread into the heart of the Gospel according to Matthew. John baptizes Jesus in order that all righteousness may be fulfilled. That Matthew's emphasis on righteousness reaches a high point in the Sermon on the Mount scarcely requires demonstration: "Unless your righteousness exceeds that of the scribes and Pharisees, you shall by no means enter into the kingdom of heaven" (5:20).

Quite plainly the fact that Jesus begins his ministry by delivering the Sermon on the Mount is typical of what we might call the ethical interests of Matthew. It is both legitimate and important to identify those interests. At the same time, that Jesus in his first public appearance announces God's blessedness upon the poor in spirit, those who mourn, the meek, and those who hunger and thirst after righteousness; that he says "You have heard it said to the people of old . . . but I say to you"; that he tells a parable to exhort his followers to build their lives upon his words—all this is significant not just for the interpretation of Matthew, but for the interpretation of the New Testament, the Christian Bible, and Christianity itself as well. Jesus is defining the righteousness of God. Without overlooking the importance of Christology in Matthew—Jesus is God with us (1:23)—that Gospel's presentation of Jesus establishes at the beginning of the New Testament the importance of the character of Jesus Christ. He not only fulfills messianic prophecy and expectation, but he also defines, and redefines, who the Messiah is. That this definition goes on in close conversation and agreement with the Old Testament and Judaism again makes an important statement. By virtue of Matthew's position in the canon this becomes a statement not only of and about Matthew, but also about the nature of New Testament Christianity.

One could go on at length, but two further instances of the pivotal role of events in Matthew, which take on added significance because it is the first Gospel, will suffice. Only in Matthew's apocalyptic discourse does Jesus describe the last judgment and the standards according to which it will take place (25:31–46). Fundamental is each believer's relationship to Jesus. (That believers come under eschatological judgment is not to be minimized.) This relationship is not, however, defined so much in terms of faith, certainly not faith as belief, as in terms of obedience—that is, the obedience that unknowingly serves Jesus himself by serving his little ones. Again, in Matthew's account of the risen Jesus' appearance to his disciples on the mountain in Galilee Jesus formally commissions them for their mission, which culminates in the concluding injunction about "teaching them to observe all that I have commanded you; and lo, I am with you always, to the close of the age" (28:20). Once again the emphasis is on Jesus' teaching or word; and now also on the promise of his presence. The reader of the New Testament is put on notice that the Jesus about whom he has been informed is not a figure out of the past, but the living and

reigning Lord. Doubtless the Christian reader for whom the Gospel was originally intended would have been well aware of this. Nevertheless, whoever picks
up the New Testament and reads it through is at the beginning apprised of with
what and whom it has to do.

Perhaps enough has been said about Matthew to allow us to turn to John
and put it into clearer focus by comparing and contrasting the two. It is obvious, but nonetheless significant and true, that as Matthew properly opens the
Gospel canon (and the New Testament) John closes it. Matthew makes entirely
clear that the historical and theological roots of the gospel of Jesus Christ lie in
Israel, and what kind of Messiah he is.

As Matthew places Jesus in *Heilsgeschichte,* John places him in creation and
cosmic history. Although both Gospels reflect hostility between emerging
Christianity and its parent religion, Matthew remains conceptually, theologically closer to Judaism.[22] The message of the opening chapters of Matthew is
that the relationship and continuity are close. This impression is due not a
little to the genealogy and to the Old Testament formula quotations that punc-
tuate the birth narrative. In some contrast, John's opening reference to Jewish
history is sharply negative: "He came to his own home, and his own people did
not receive him" (1:11). Despite arguments to the contrary (Bultmann et al.),
that statement is best understood as a reference to Jesus' own nation. With
them are contrasted those who believe in his name (1:12), who are defined by
that faith and not by human origin. The incarnation and its effects (1:14–18)
are then described as events and possibilities available universally. The formula
Old Testament quotations, which are encountered immediately in Matthew,
with one or two exceptions (6:31; 7:42; cf. 10:34), do not appear in John until
the passion narrative and related episodes (12:14–15, 38, 39–40; 13:18; 19:24,
28, 36, 37). Almost certainly their appearance there is to be traced to their existence in the pre-Gospel tradition. In those portions of John which stem from
the evangelist, Abraham, Moses, and other heroes of Israel tend to be presented
as antitypes; and in chapter 8 descendants of Abraham (8:37) are said to be
children of the devil (v. 44), not of God (vv. 42, 47). As J. Louis Martyn
observes, John does not choose to enter into midrashic debate or discussion
with Jewish opponents.[23] Instead, he poses the radical alternative of faith in
Jesus as the one whom God has sent. Precisely that possibility is not the culmination of midrashic debate; it is something that only God can give. In this and
related ways John establishes not an absolute contradiction, but a significant
and creative tension with Matthew. Matthew stands at the beginning of the
Gospel canon relating Jesus positively to the Old Testament, and thus to Jewish expectations. John stands at the end, not denying that Jesus is the fulfillment of those expectations, but quite explicitly affirming that he is more than
this and setting at the center of his portrayal and emphasizing Jewish rejection
of him.

It would be wrong to portray the difference between Matthew and John in terms of a low Christology in one and a high Christology in the other. Matthew does not have a low Christology.[24] He who is "God with us" and who receives "all authority in heaven and on earth" is something more than a young and fearless prophet of ancient Galilee. (Nor should one minimize the obvious tension between Matthew and Judaism.)

But Matthew differs decisively from John in the way in which Christology is filled out or explained. Matthew draws deeply upon the Jesus tradition as it is amply reflected elsewhere in the New Testament, and especially upon the tradition of Jesus' logia. It is the teaching Jesus, who proclaims God's rule and will for all humankind, but particularly for his followers, who is Messiah and Son of God. Moreover, Jesus' teaching is law, not his law, but the definitive expression and interpretation of Torah. John, in contrast, virtually ignores this logia tradition and puts the Jewish law in an ambiguous light. As is well known, there are no parables, no pronouncement stories, no ethical discourses, and no announcements of the imminent in-breaking of God's rule in John. The Fourth Evangelist gives force to Jesus' claim of messiahship and divine sonship in a different way. He has Jesus assert and argue his own case. Thus, as is frequently observed, the Jesus of the Fourth Gospel talks Christology explicitly. In Matthew, as in the other Synoptic Gospels, Christology is very much present, but as the overall framework into which a tradition which obviously arose in Jewish Palestine during Jesus' ministry is fitted. Jesus appealed to Judaism, his fellow Jews, by positive reference to their rich scriptures, traditions, and history. Thus, paradoxically, Matthew's representation of that appeal, which when put alongside John can be seen to be generally true historically, has more than a parochial or ethnic interest. For Judaism, with its national, juridical, and personal, individual dimensions, is paradigmatic of human interests and necessities.

John goes another way entirely. In his narrative framework there are striking similarities to Matthew and to the Synoptics generally: the encounter with the Baptist, the feeding of five thousand, and other incidents about the Sea of Galilee, the events of the passion. The episodes which John shares with Mark, for example, he has for the most part in the same order. It is primarily John's representation of the speech of Jesus, and secondarily of his healing ministry, that is so different. In the one case Jesus speaks only of himself before the public (and later on before his disciples); in the other his very acts of healing are symbolic not of God's kingdom but of his divine sonship. Through word and deed Jesus points to himself as king and seeks to establish the claim through argument, sometimes exegetical (6:31; 10:34), and demonstration of unheard-of supernatural power. The reader either accedes to the claims or is deeply offended. There is almost no way to appreciate what Jesus says and does apart from his imperious claim, for in a real sense that is all Jesus presents. Already within the Gospel of John the Jews, that is, Jesus' or the church's opponents, take offense, and thus Jewish rejection of Christian claims about Jesus is reflected.

Standing at the beginning of the canon, Matthew represents continuity with, affirmation of, and openness to Jewish tradition, despite clear indications of significant hostility and tension with Judaism (for example, Matt 27:25). At the end of the Gospel canon John seems to view these positive relations as mainly terminated (although even, and only, in John we have Nicodemus, the Pharisee and *archōn* of the Jews, who, in my judgment, is still open to and inclined to accept Jesus). Certainly for John allegiance to Jesus means the termination of relations with the synagogue and with Judaism. Discipleship is thus negatively as well as positively conceived. In fact, to say that in John discipleship is conceived positively as believing in Jesus' claims and negatively as separation from the Jewish community may be an oversimplification, but it is not an exaggeration. The basis for discipleship is theological belief, dogma, social ostracism, and a new community identity. Jesus' teaching about love is not unimportant but applies primarily, if not only, within the community of his disciples, and in any case is not the basis of his challenge to believe in him.

Affinities between John and Paul

At this point there is a clear similarity or parallel between John and Paul, neither of whom presents us with a portrayal of Jesus drawn from the tradition of his words or his teaching. To use the common theological parlance, which in this case is meaningful and appropriate, for John as for Paul Jesus Christ is the eschatological event, the appearance in history of God's salvation and judgment. In both cases faith in Jesus initially has no content apart from the acknowledgement that in him, or in the event of his crucifixion, God has acted or spoken and revealed himself decisively in favor of humankind. That is, taken by themselves, Paul and John do not provide a basis in life, history, or tradition for the claim made by Jesus. Thus Bultmann could say—while remaining true to his understanding of Pauline or Johannine theology—that Jesus was not the eschatological or salvation event because he was the Christ; rather he was (understood as) the Christ because he was (experienced or confessed as) the eschatological or salvation event.[25] In other words, for both Paul and John taken alone (or together) the eschatological event requires no traditional or historical accreditation as such. Indeed, the eschatological event cannot tolerate such accreditation, because so to accredit it would be to violate the character of revelation, particularly revelation in Christ, which is *eo ipso* self-authenticating. (This is what is meant by the statement that Jesus is not the eschatological or revelatory event because he is the Christ, he is the Christ because he is—or is the occasion of—that event.)

Probably it is significant, and even crucial, that Bultmann in his work generally, but particularly the *Theology of the New Testament*,[26] lifts Paul and John out from the canon of the New Testament and isolates them as the bearers of this theological insight. In his exegesis of the Pauline letters Bultmann correctly declines to see Paul as presupposing the Synoptic Gospels, which did not then exist, and does not deem their tradition, which Paul knew in some small part, important for his kerygma and theology. (The degree to which Paul knew that tradition is still a matter of debate.) By the same token John is viewed exegetically as independent of the Synoptic Gospels and presupposing other traditions and sources. In this he may be correct. Against Windisch, Bultmann does not believe that John intended to displace the Synoptics, in part because it is doubtful that he knew them; in part because he cannot find evidence that John was negatively disposed toward antecedent tradition.[27] Nevertheless, in this major landmark of New Testament theology, the twin peaks of theological development within the New Testament are seen as relatively independent of the synoptic tradition, which was at most only partially or fragmentarily known to them. Furthermore, theologically relevant interpretation of Paul and John takes them out of the canon, so to speak. We hear them not as a chorus, not even as a duet, but as successive soloists singing the same basic aria, albeit in different keys. Without denigrating the position or insights of Bultmann, it is almost certainly correct and appropriate to observe that we have here a classic instance of the pressing to a logical conclusion of Luther's criterion of what *preaches* Christ as a hermeneutical key. This criterion has been correlated with a particular existentialist anthropology in a way that has now become familiar. Moreover, it is not surprising that Paul and John should emerge as the two chief exponents or representatives, for at least on Bultmann's terms, they are the leading New Testament proponents of Jesus as the eschatological Christ.

The relative isolation of Paul and John from the New Testament canon, and the de facto minimizing of canon as a vehicle of authority is, of course, a telling move. (The Synoptic Gospels as well as the other canonical writings become in Bultmann's *Theology of the New Testament* a part of the development toward that same early catholicism that later produced the New Testament itself.) The canon, if anything, tends to muffle their highest or sharpest notes, for a canonical reading of John or Paul would require that they be attended to among a broader chorus of voices. The canon has a both/and effect, neutralizing theological extremes. Childs has shown quite clearly and well how the framing of the uncontested, genuine Pauline letters with Acts on the one side and the deutero-Pauline letters, particularly the pastorals, on the other has produced a canonical Paul, who stands in a positive relation to, but is not identical with, the historical Paul.

The Effect of Canonicity upon the Reading of the Fourth Gospel

Now if one considers the Gospel of John within the canon, especially the Gospel canon, there is a similar effect. That is, there emerges a canonical John.

Käsemann, with his typical forcefulness and disdain of compromise, has accurately and acutely described how John was accepted in the church when it was read in light of other, more moderate, views, and its sharp edges were honed down.[28] Of course, the inclusion of the Gospel of John with the other three was well calculated to have precisely this effect. It need not, however, be stated in negative terms, as if the theological value or revelatory significance of John lay solely in its uncompromising and distinctive individuality and brilliance. I would be inclined to argue that John makes sense best, and makes proper theological sense, only when it is viewed in light of the Synoptic Gospels. It is the Jesus who presents himself in Matthew, Mark, and Luke who makes intelligible—and I would say legitimizes—the Johannine Jesus.

The canonical status of John, if taken seriously, considerably mitigates the question of John's relationship to the Synoptics. If one assumes that John's intended relationship to the Synoptic Gospels is crucial for understanding and appropriating the theological message of the Fourth Gospel, a great deal may seem to be at stake in arguing that Windisch, or Gardner-Smith for that matter, was mistaken. John did not intend to displace the Synoptics, nor did he write without cognizance of them. On these terms the theological importance of the traditional, churchly or critical position is apparent. John wrote with the Synoptics in view and intended to supplement and interpret what he already knew and accepted. Yet the difficulties of that traditional position are real, as we have already seen. It is still defensible, but certainly not unimpeachable.

In contrast, if the canonical status and position of John are assumed as significant data to be reckoned with theologically, whether or not John was written in positive cognizance of the Synoptics—or in cognizance of them at all—remains an interesting historical theological question, but ceases to require any particular answer. John stands fourth, last, in the Gospel canon, as if it were to be read not only alongside the other three but after them as well. Its traditional position, however arrived at, makes that point rather neatly and clearly. In fact, it is arguable that the traditional viewpoint, that John wrote after the others and in order to supplement and interpret them, is actually related to the usual canonical positioning of John. That is, it reflects an intelligible and intelligent way of reading John as a canonical book, which would have been read back into its historical origin and purpose. Whether this is the case is somewhat beside the point for our purposes and need not be argued here. The point is that this way of conceiving and understanding John represents a kind of canonical approach to that document that is sensible and not valueless. It has its own hermeneutical justification even if it is dubious or even incorrect historically.

Probably the Christian reader, including the Christian New Testament scholar, whatever his or her theological or other leanings, would find it impossible to read John's Gospel and at the same time bracket out completely or effectively the portrayal, image, or *Gestalt* of Jesus formed largely on the basis of the Synoptics. It would be difficult to imagine a picture of Jesus formed solely on the basis of the Fourth Gospel. Whether anyone ever had such a picture is an interesting question, for even if neither John nor his intended audience knew one or more of the Synoptics they apparently knew related tradition which is not conveyed by the Fourth Gospel (John 20:30; 21:25).[29] Indeed, such a picture would be truncated and distorted, defined as it is so exclusively by dogma, and in all probability dogma already deeply colored and shaped by controversy and conflict within, and later with, the synagogue from which the Johannine community emerged. Important presuppositions are lacking for an acceptable reading of John if the other Gospels are not taken into consideration. The picture of an otherwordly, dogmatic, anti-Jewish Jesus can readily be formed on the basis of the Fourth Gospel alone. That such a portrayal or conception of Jesus does, in fact, inform some modern Christian piety, particularly in North America, can scarcely be denied, and is all the more reason for insisting that John not be read by itself but attended to in concert with the New Testament as a whole.

Another danger in reading the Gospel of John in isolation from its canonical context is, however, implicit in the document itself. As in different ways scholars as diverse in their judgments and methods as Windisch, Gardner-Smith, Bultmann, Hoskyns, and Culpepper have argued or shown, John evokes a sense of completeness and adequacy in the reader. It is not necessary to appeal to other writings in order to understand John. Yet what kind of understanding one elicits is another matter. Perhaps the great variety of Johannine interpretations that modern criticism has unleashed says something about the real difficulty of understanding John historically as an independent, self-sufficient witness to, and account of, Jesus. It well may be the case that this difficulty existed from the beginning, as John was claimed by interpreters of various theological perspectives or stripes. Probably Valentinian Gnostics and Montanists early on saw in John a Gospel that had strong affinities with, or justified, their own positions. Raymond E. Brown's effort, in the early 1980s, to understand the early history of the community of the Beloved Disciple led him to view the Johannine Epistles, particularly 1 John, as bearing witness to a pitched battle over the right interpretation of the Fourth Gospel. According to Brown, 1 John is to be understood in relation to its historical context and purpose as a kind of definitive statement, if not commentary, on how the Gospel of John is to be read and understood. Accordingly, the strong emphasis on the flesh and tangibility of Jesus in 1 John (1:1–4) and the polemic against those who apparently denigrate Jesus' fleshliness (4:1–3; cf. 2 John 7) are directed against interpreters within the Johannine community who read the Gospel in a quasidocetic sense.

Childs does not find Brown's thesis entirely helpful in discerning the canonical meaning of the Johannine Epistles.[30] However that may be, Brown's carefully and elaborately worked out historical reconstruction is, unless it is far off base, enormously relevant to the canonical reading of the Gospel of John. That is, it illustrates concretely the problem of the difficulty in reading the Gospel of John outside a canonical setting, and particularly apart from the other Gospels. Brown's thesis implies that John was not yet being read with any of the other Gospels. In fact, he remarks that the fact that the Epistles do not make use of the synoptic tradition or Gospels as affording handholds for the interpretation of the Gospel probably means that the author(s) does not know them.[31] What evidence we have from the first decade or so of the second century does not support the existence of a Gospel canon, even one consisting only of the Synoptics, at that time and thus is consistent with Brown's position. Certainly the ways in which the Gospel of John was interpreted and misinterpreted later in the second century count on the side of Brown's proposal. But perhaps his most significant contribution is to suggest how open the Fourth Gospel was (and is) for divergent and even contradictory interpretation when it is taken alone, outside any ruling theological or literary context. It is perhaps too much to suggest that John invites heretical readings. Nevertheless, there is an interesting parallel between the second-century and modern critical readings of that Gospel. In both cases John has been read and interpreted outside the canon, so to speak, first because there was none, and second because canon has been ruled out of order on historical-critical grounds. In both cases interpretations of the Fourth Gospel have tended to diverge widely.

There is little question that the canonical positioning of the Fourth Gospel, which may or may not accord closely with its historically original purpose and setting, affords an important guide or direction for its interpretation within the Christian community. And, of course, the New Testament canon and the church are close correlatives. We need not involve ourselves in the old chicken-egg question of which came first, the canon or the church. Obviously the church was chronologically prior, although it is equally obvious that in establishing a canon of scripture the church intended to say that its source and historic ground of authority lay beyond itself. The New Testament as canon commands and endorses the authority of the Gospel of John to the church and to Christians. We have the Gospel of John first of all within the canon, and that, as Childs rightly never tires of insisting, is the primary context for interpretation for Christians who are seeking in that Gospel a word from or about God. We may ask how or why it was written, or about its canonical status and context. When, however, we attend to it as apostolic witness, within the New Testament's witness, we acknowledge it as canon and acknowledge the authority and wisdom of the church that gave it to us as such. John cannot in that setting and for purposes appropriate to it be read otherwise. The historical-critical method may, as Childs agrees, be an indispensable teacher, but it is not the final arbiter of meaning. Standing together in the canon, the Gospels shed light on one another. As one legitimately reads John in light of Matthew, and the Synoptics generally, one also reads Matthew and the other Synoptics in the light of John. John may be the key that unlocks the other Gospels, as Calvin confessed, but the other Gospels lay down necessary suppositions and groundwork on the basis of which John is to be read. Of course, those Gospels too are fundamentally determined by the christologies of their authors and communities. Yet they provide both perspectives and data without which one would read the Gospel of John quite differently and, one must say, to the detriment of the faith that the church wishes to attest in and through the New Testament.

16

Toward a Canonical Reading
of the Fourth Gospel

*Canonical Readings from Clement of Alexandria through
Abraham Lincoln to Rudolf Bultmann and C. H. Dodd*

Canonical reading of scripture has always been standard operating procedure
for most people, even sophisticated theologians.[1] Most readers would consider
the historical limitations or constraints under which biblical exegetes now labor
unnecessarily confining.

In the early 1980s John Dominic Crossan wrote a book on Jesus that,
because of the content as well as the title—*The Historical Jesus: The Life of a
Mediterranean Jewish Peasant*—attracted a good bit of attention.[2] In due course
Crossan appeared on the Larry King television interview show, gave a brief syn-
opsis of his work, and answered questions phoned in by viewers, most of whom
of course had not read the book. A good many of them simply wanted to set
Crossan straight. If you really want to know who Jesus was and what he
thought, just read the Bible. Doesn't Jesus say that he and the Father are one
(John 10:30)? Doesn't he say that he is the way, the truth, and the life (John
14:6), and so on? In other words, such questions as Crossan was seeking to
answer through scholarly investigation are already answered in the Gospels,
particularly in the Gospel of John. The callers were interpreting the Synoptic
Gospels' portrayals of Jesus in light of the Gospel of John. "That's theology,"
said Crossan, "but I'm interested in history." We know what Crossan was saying, and would probably agree with him. But the callers were greatly perplexed.
Following the lead of scripture, the canon, they were answering questions arising out of the Synoptic Gospels by drawing upon the Fourth Gospel. That has
ancient precedent! Clement of Alexandria saw in John a spiritual gospel, written in full cognizance of the other three. Calvin professed that he found in the
Gospel of John a key to the other three. The church, in listing the authoritative Gospels and then putting them together into one codex, usually placed the

Gospel of John last, after the other three. The implication was clear enough. John was to be read last, presumably to clarify christological questions the others raised.

John and the Synoptics

The Common Lectionary seems to break with the order of the canon by distributing readings from the Gospel of John through the three years of the lectionary cycle. Yet the effect is to encourage a canonical reading of John in that readings from the Fourth Gospel are interspersed among the other three. John is read and preached not continuously, that is, straight through, as the other Gospels are, but along with them. One wonders what the effect on the preaching of the Gospel of John, and the others, may be.

In teaching a course on preaching from the Gospel of John with a colleague in homiletics, we have found that there is often a tendency for a synoptic-like characterization of Jesus to slip into the sermon based on a Johannine text. (The obverse has also occurred when we teach Mark.) Sometimes it is simply a matter of the historicist assumption—inappropriate enough with the Synoptics—creeping into the interpretation of John. Naturally, my colleague and I frown gently on this when it happens. Often it is simply an expression of naiveté. But it is partly something more or other than that. John, like the Synoptics, tells the story of Jesus, and that story is laid alongside the others in the New Testament. The readers, or preachers, naturally merge the narratives together in their consciousness. In other words, the naiveté of the reader or preacher is the natural result of the shape and character of the canon. It was mainly modern and historical-critical exegesis that taught us to read the Fourth Gospel, and other Gospels, the way we do, independently of one another except when literary-historical considerations dictate otherwise.

Moreover, on one reading of the John-Synoptics relationship, namely the one dominant until the mid–twentieth century, the exegete could legitimately claim that John should be read in light of the others, because it was written in cognizance of them and intended to be so read. This, in fact, became the position of Frans Neirynck and of an increasing number of scholars.[3] Perhaps the most skillful, persuasive, and finely nuanced presentation of this position was set out by Sir Edwyn Clement Hoskyns in his commentary on the Fourth Gospel, which was published initially in the 1930s.[4] Hoskyns took the position that the Fourth Evangelist presupposed, if not the Synoptic Gospels in the form we have them, certainly their substantial content or tradition. There is something essentially correct in this, as most serious readers of John, including Clement and Calvin, will attest.

John's historical and literary relationship to the Synoptic Gospels is, however, complex, and it is difficult to explain because the evidence points in opposite directions. One might simplify the problem in a way that is not misleading by saying that, on the one hand, the theology of John agrees fundamentally with the Synoptics. That is, there are no outstanding contradictions, and for the most part John seems to accentuate, amplify, or make explicit what is found or suggested in the Synoptics. On the other hand, John presents other kinds of problems for the reader who knows the synoptic accounts.

Not only is he alone in portraying a three-year ministry, mostly in Judea, but he also has a different chronology or calendar of the Last Supper and passion. One could go on to enumerate the sheer differences in content as well as in the work and attitude of Jesus himself. Seemingly, in relation to the Synoptics, John creates fewer difficulties for the theologian than for the student of the gospel narratives.[5]

Yet, to say that last is indeed an oversimplification, for at some points John seems to presuppose what we read in the Synoptics. Even the way the name of Jesus Christ is introduced in the prologue (1:17) may suggest that the reader already knows who he is. Actually, *Jesus Christ* occurs only here and in 17:3 in John. To judge from Acts and Paul, it virtually functioned as a proper name. Of course, the prologue prepares for the naming of the name, but the prologue would be particularly meaningful only to one who already knew the story and the name, as we do. (The now increasingly common view that the prologue was added to the penultimate form of the Gospel fits this view of how it would have been read.[6]) If the Fourth Gospel presupposes the Synoptics, the prologue would also be read in light of them. But such a presupposition is not, strictly speaking, necessary. Possibly the prologue was intended to be read against the background of Paul, or of commonly known Christian belief and tradition. Of course, when read for the first time, it unfolds an intriguing mystery. But the mystery is not resolved by the naming of Jesus (1:17), unless one already knows something of who Jesus is.

Canonical Reading

Actually, this discussion of the prologue in John illustrates the problem. If one asks from a historical-critical point of view exactly what is presupposed by the prologue, a definitive answer is scarcely attainable. It makes good sense to view the prologue as a hymn that extols and places in a cosmic setting what is already known, namely, that when the time had fully come, God sent forth his Son (Gal 4:4). This reading of the prologue makes excellent sense, not only in the light of the rest of the Gospel of John, but also in light of the New Testament generally. This is what we mean by a canonical reading. When the prologue is read before a Christian congregation on Christmas Eve or Christmas Day as the appointed reading, this is the way it is heard. Whether or not the evangelist intended it to be heard in this way, I believe he would nevertheless have applauded and approved this reading and hearing.

Now to return to the question of what the Gospel of John actually presupposes historically. At the conclusion of the temple cleansing (2:22), the author refers to Jesus' resurrection as if it were something already known to the reader. The coming of the Spirit is similarly referred to during the narrative of Jesus' appearance at Tabernacles (7:39). The repeated references to Jesus' glory, or the coming hour of his glorification (2:4; 7:39; 12:23), seem to presuppose that the reader knows of Jesus' death and needs to be guided into a more profound understanding of its meaning. Smaller items: Jesus' encounter with the Baptist is recounted in retrospect by John; Mary and Martha are mentioned in 11:1 as if they are already known; the trial before Caiaphas, reported in the Synoptics, is alluded to, but not narrated; in the trial before Pilate the Jewish condemnation seems to be assumed without having been reported. In other words, John appears to presume knowledge of the story of Jesus as well as early Christian tradition. All this comports well with the view that John is the last of the canonical Gospels and written with the others in view. Again, while such a view makes perfectly good sense in many respects, it is not a necessity. But at least the Gospel presupposes knowledge of the Christian kerygma and story, if not necessarily the documents that we have in the New Testament. Yet, the question of a canonical reading does not depend on canonical knowledge, that is, John's knowledge of other canonical books. Canonical reading is a given for us, whatever the intention or knowledge of the author and his intended readers.

A canonical reading of John is now natural for anyone who falls under Christian cultural influence, what used to be called Christendom. Thus Harold Bloom, in the introduction of his edited volume of essays on the literary interpretation of the Gospels, seems to view John as the epitome of what offends, while at the same time stimulates, in the New Testament.[7] As a strong misreading of the Hebrew Bible, John surpasses Paul, although Paul is on the same track, not to mention the other Gospels. This negative canonical reading of John is quite understandable, particularly given the role that the Fourth Gospel has occupied in Christian canonical interpretation of the New Testament.

Canonical reading is also a common phenomenon outside the realm of biblical interpretation. The historian Garry Wills has made us aware of how one document can influence the interpretation of another and thus change or define the course of American constitutional interpretation. (Not coincidentally, the field of constitutional law affords interesting and informative parallels to the field of biblical interpretation.) In a recent article on Lincoln and the Gettysburg Address, Wills maintains that "Abraham Lincoln transformed the ugly reality [of the bloody battle of Gettysburg] into something rich and strange—and he did it with 272 words."[8] Lincoln's immediate purpose was largely practical and political. But Lincoln also "knew the power of his rhetoric to define war aims. He was seeking occasions to use his words outside the normal round of proclamations and reports to Congress."⁹ So his own purposes were more than momentary and local. Lincoln was "a student of the Word," as Wills calls him; he knew and intended that this address should have a broader resonance. Yet, he scarcely could have anticipated its long-term effect.

Lincoln's Gettysburg Address became a kind of canonical event (my word, not Wills's). Afterward, our speech changed and the nation's primary documents were read differently. (For one thing, and perhaps tellingly, after Gettysburg "the United States" became a singular, no longer a plural, term.) Lincoln's theme at the outset was the new nation "conceived in liberty, and dedicated to the proposition that all men are created equal." The speech ended with the hope "that this nation under God shall have a new birth of freedom—and that government of the people, by the people, for the people, shall not perish from the earth." Lincoln, writes Wills, was a revolutionary: "He not only presented the Declaration of Independence in a new light, as a matter of founding law, but put its central proposition, equality, in a newly favored position as a principle of the Constitution"¹⁰ (although the Constitution never uses the word *equality*!). Through his Gettysburg Address Lincoln accorded a new status to the Declaration of Independence and changed the way people thought about the Constitution, much to the annoyance of states' rights advocates and strict constructionists ever since.

Perhaps the Gettysburg Address is best described as a crucial hermeneutical event rather than a canonical one, but the two categories are not unrelated. In fact they are related in important ways. The establishment of the canon was the crucial hermeneutical move shaping the way the early Christian writings that make up the New Testament were to be read. Moreover, the inclusion of the Gospel of John in the canon exerted an important influence on how the other Gospels and the rest of the New Testament were read.

It would perhaps be unwise to argue, or to attempt to demonstrate, that the Gospel of John is to the New Testament as Lincoln's Gettysburg Address is to the Constitution of the United States. For one thing, John is a part of the New Testament in a way the Gettysburg Address is not part of the Constitution. Yet one might consider that the Gettysburg Address is a part of the national canon of scripture, including also the Declaration of Independence and the Constitution, by which the nation thinks to live. As such, it plays a central role in the national consciousness. Similarly the Gospel of John has played a crucial role in Christian consciousness and in defining what being Christian is to countless millions of people who through the centuries have considered themselves followers of Jesus. The words of John and of the Johannine Jesus determine the way Christians understand themselves and their Lord.

The Word became flesh and dwelt among us. (1:14)
God so loved the world that he gave his only Son. . . . (3:16)

You will know the truth and the truth will make you free. (8:32)

I came that they may have life and have it abundantly. (10:10)

I am the resurrection and the life; he who believes in me, though he
die, yet shall he live. (11:25)

I am the way, the truth, and the life, no one comes to the Father but
by me. (14:6)

Whatever else Jesus Christ may mean to Christians, to many if not most of
us he is defined by such sayings as these. The confidence that Jesus in John
brings to full expression what the synoptic Jesus represented, while it cannot
perhaps be demonstrated exegetically, need not be dismissed as simply uninformed. Within the Christian community it can scarcely be dismissed, so
deeply is the historic Christian consciousness imbued with the Gospel of John.
In becoming a part of the canon, John quickly assumed a key role, not only in
determining how believers and preachers would understand Jesus in the other
Gospels, but also how he would be understood in the development of church
doctrine. The language of the Nicene Creed and the issues addressed in the
Creed of Chalcedon hark back to the Gospel of John in remarkable ways.
(Thus John affects not only the canon of faith with regard to its New Testament parallels and antecedents, but also the canon of faith that was instituted
in the creeds.)

The Gospel of John as Central Canonical and Hermeneutical Event

All that we have been discussing seems to point in the direction of the central
role of John as a hermeneutical instrument in the formation of the canon. Even
those modern exegetes who doubt John's dependence on other Gospels or his
knowledge of such germinal predecessors as Paul tend to regard this Gospel as
somehow centrally located in its presentation of the mission of Jesus and the
message of early Christianity. I am thinking, of course, of the two great
mid–twentieth century interpreters of the New Testament, Rudolf Bultmann
on the Continent and C. H. Dodd in England.

It is clear that for Bultmann the Johannine literature (Gospel and Epistles)
represented the essence of the New Testament presentation of the revelation of
God in Jesus Christ. Appropriately, John appears as the third of four major
parts in Bultmann's *Theology of the New Testament;* the final part is devoted to
the development toward early Catholicism. Moreover, Bultmann's theological,
as well as exegetical, magnum opus is his commentary on the Gospel of John.[11]
It is John who understands most clearly that what has happened is precisely revelation, a making known of God as the light and life-giver—and of humankind
in the precariousness of existence before God or nothingness. It would be
wrong to speak of a zenith of the development of New Testament theology, for
Bultmann eschews both the concepts of development and the notion that John

stands on the shoulders of his predecessors. Rather, in retrospect, toward the end of the first century, John presents his pristine understanding of the New Testament preaching with respect to its theology and its inseparably related anthropology. Thus John becomes the canon within the canon. Bultmann has often been criticized for advocating such a view or promoting it, but in this respect he belongs in a venerable tradition of Christian theology and piety.

Something similar could be said, mutatis mutandis, of C. H. Dodd. Dodd's project was perhaps not so explicitly theological as Bultmann's. Yet Dodd turns to the Fourth Gospel at crucial points to confirm his view of the essence of the New Testament message. Thus in his programmatic book *The Apostolic Preaching and Its Developments,* Dodd saw in the Gospel of John not only the culmination of theological development in the New Testament, but the best, and historically most felicitous, view of Jesus' eschatology.[12] Jesus did not announce an imminent, apocalyptic kingdom, but rather the presence of the kingdom in his own ministry. Dodd's assessment of John's importance is also reflected in the weight of his own scholarly publications, which culminated in two monumental volumes, one on the interpretation of John's Gospel, the other on the question of historical tradition in that document.[13] For Dodd, as well as Bultmann, the Gospel of John is an implicit canon within the canon. They are not by themselves, as some other treatments of the theology of the New Testament confirm.[14]

There is another side of the picture, however, and that is the role that the other Gospels, and other New Testament writers may, or should, play in the interpretation of the Fourth Gospel. This role is not something that belongs in the realm of the purely hypothetical or within the ambience of some now passé liberal theology. It has very ancient roots that reach back to the beginning of the process of canonization, in which John was evidently a relative latecomer.

There was no New Testament canon that did not include the Fourth Gospel. At least, we do not have any such canonical list. Yet the very resistance to that Gospel, as represented by Gaius of Rome, and perhaps others, at the end of the second century implies that a gospel canon, consisting of the Synoptics but not John, was establishing itself, however informally. If Matthew and Luke independently used Mark, or even if Luke used Mark and Matthew, such usage implies a nascent canon of the Gospels. There was evolving a "standard" way of treating the mission and message of Jesus that the Fourth Gospel put under severe strain. Polycarp in the 130s and Justin Martyr in the 150s attest the widespread use of the synoptic tradition, probably the Synoptic Gospels, but not the Gospel of John. When Marcion, roughly a contemporary of Justin, formed his canon he chose as his Gospel a version of Luke, not John. (Yet one might have thought Marcion's dualism would have commended the Fourth

Gospel to him.) Only with Tatian's *Diatessaron,* probably to be dated about 170, do we arrive at a "canonical" use of the Fourth Gospel. Interestingly enough, Tatian was a former student of Justin Martyr, who used the Gospel of John rarely, if at all.

When Irenaeus argues for the necessity of *four* Gospels, his arguments from the four winds and the four corners of the earth seem flimsy enough to us. It may be that he is really making a case for the Fourth Gospel which was a relative newcomer to the developing Gospel canon. The evidence for the rejection of, or hesitation about, the Fourth Gospel may be slim, but so is contemporaneous evidence for its second-century use in orthodox circles. That John was used by Valentinian Gnostics is clear enough, as the *Gospel of Truth,* Heracleon's commentary on John, and Irenaeus's polemic against gnostic exegesis of John suggests. That its popularity among Gnostics (and Montanists) slowed its acceptance into the canon cannot be proved, but constitutes a good and informed hypothesis.[15]

The point is that John encounters some resistance because there is already a developing canon with which it is in some respects at variance. It needed to be explained with reference to the Synoptics before it could be used to explain them. Thus, Clement explains it as a spiritual gospel; Eusebius notes that John was composed with knowledge of the others to explain Jesus' early ministry; Origen derides the growing industry with which John was harmonized with the others. Such efforts to explain and justify the Gospel of John bespeak hesitancy or resistance in some quarters. Moreover, modern exegetes from Bultmann to Raymond E. Brown, as well as others, have seen in the final redaction of the Gospel of John evidence of knowledge of the Synoptic Gospels—an indication of an effort to reconcile the synoptic and Johannine traditions.

Decades ago Brown made an important suggestion about the relationship of 1 John to the Gospel that also bears significantly on the question of canon.[16] He views 1 John as not only subsequent to the Gospel but as deliberately designed to guide its interpretation as well. First John's emphasis upon the audibility, visibility, and palpability of the word of life (1:1) underscores and interprets what the evangelist meant when he wrote, "The Word became flesh and dwelt among us." As Hans Conzelmann pointed out, the beginning (*archē*) in 1 John is the beginning of the Christian tradition, not the primordial beginning as in the Gospel. The beginning of the tradition is its defining point. The Epistle was clearly directed against Christian opponents whose Christology verged in a docetic direction (4:1–3). First John cordoned off the road leading to such an erroneous Christology. (Ernst Käsemann's suggestion of a naively docetic Gospel was already anticipated and counteracted by the alert author of the Epistle!) Brown's suggestion is ingenious, and is, of course, argued with erudition and in great detail in his commentary on the Epistles. We cannot here do it justice. But if it is correct, it contributes another important piece in the puzzle of the Fourth Gospel's canonicity. Brown suggests that the Epistles, particularly 1 John, are intended to guide or direct the reading of the Fourth Gospel. One might go beyond Brown, but not, I think, Brown's intention to say that 1 John intends to say what a canonical reading of the Gospel must be like, and before John was customarily read alongside the other Gospels. In other words, there was already coming into being a Johannine canon that anticipated the fuller canon of early Christian writings.

Of course, once the four-Gospel canon had been widely established and accepted—something that was already happening at the beginning of the third century—John was read in concert with the other Gospels. Ernst Käsemann reflects upon the way in which John was harmonized with the Synoptic Gospels —and continues to be—as a necessity, but a necessity fraught with ambiguity.[17] Nevertheless, he presents an interpretation of John that shows why such a harmonization—dare one say a canonical reading?—of John was a necessity for the emerging universal church. The charismatic, naively docetic, dogmatic Gospel of Käsemann's reading was scarcely the Gospel that the emerging catholic church read! It may be an oversimplification to suggest that the naively docetic aspect was abandoned. Perhaps it was developed in terms of the doctrine of the two natures. The charismatic aspect was somewhat domesticated, institutionalized, and channeled. Yet it continued to inspire charismatic activity within the church. The dogmatic aspect was fully embraced, developed, and even made normative in the great ecumenical creeds, especially the Nicene Creed. Thus, Käsemann's heterodox Gospel became, ironically, the criterion of orthodoxy, but only as it was read in correlation with the Synoptic Gospels.

Conclusion

So should a canonical reading of the Gospel of John place it at the center of the canon and allow all the rest to be read in light of it? Understandably, that has frequently happened. But we are also in urgent need of reading the Gospel of John in light of the other Gospels, not to mention Paul. The early resistance to the Fourth Gospel, the Epistles' attempt to guide its interpretation, even the early efforts to harmonize John with the other Gospels, bespeak a sense of the need for reading the Fourth Gospel not alone but in concert. That need may explain theologically the attractiveness of the age-old, and now again more widely espoused, view that John presupposes, if he does not use, the other Gospels. It is not enough for the Jesus of the Sermon on the Mount to be subsumed under the incarnate Logos. Only the Jesus of the Sermon on the Mount adequately justifies or explains why there should be an incarnate Logos, or who the incarnate Logos is. Such a statement as I have just made—provocative as I hope it will be—is intelligible in a consideration of canonical readings. Canonical readings go back to the beginnings of the New Testament, at least to the gathering of the various documents. To discern and perceive them is a legitimate historical task. To appreciate them may be a task of literary criticism. To propose them is the continuing task of theological exegesis.[18]

Notes

Chapter 1: The Gospel of John in Its Jewish Context

1. Books and scholars dealing with the subject of Jesus' Jewishness are too numerous to mention, but still indispensable is E. P. Sanders, *Jesus and Judaism* (Philadelphia: Fortress, 1985). Sanders's knowledge of ancient Judaism matches his knowledge of the Gospels and Jesus tradition. For a more popular but well-informed perspective on the Jewishness of Jesus from a Jewish New Testament scholar, see Amy-Jill Levine, *The Misunderstood Jew: The Church and the Scandal of the Jewish Jesus* (San Francisco: HarperCollins, 2006).

In the first edition of *Anatomy of the New Testament: A Guide to Its Structure and Meaning* (New York: Macmillan, 1969), 5, Robert A. Spivey and I maintained: "Jesus was a Jew. So were his disciples. In fact, the earliest Christians did not think of themselves as members of a new religion separate from Judaism. Yet from the beginning Jesus and his disciples represented something new." In the most recent edition this statement stands, somewhat emended but not basically changed. See Robert A. Spivey, D. Moody Smith, and C. Clifton Black, *Anatomy of the New Testament* (6th ed.; Upper Saddle River, N.J.: Prentice Hall, 2007), 11.

As for the Scrolls, such affinities were long ago observed by James H. Charlesworth, "A Critical Comparison of the Dualism in 1QS 3:13–4:26 and the 'Dualism' Contained in the Gospel of John," *New Testament Studies* 15 (1968–69): 389–418; republished without major alterations in the same author's edited volume, *John and the Dead Sea Scrolls* (New York: Crossroad, 1990), 76–106.

John Ashton, *Understanding the Fourth Gospel* (Oxford: Clarendon, 1991), 235–37, regards Charlesworth's work as basic, but goes beyond him in suggesting that the evangelist was himself an Essene. Ashton has since brought out a revised edition of this work (Oxford: Oxford University Press, 2007) in which he explicitly drops this suggestion. In subsequent citations the proper edition (1991 or 2007) will be noted.

2. In the Synoptic Gospels *the Jews* usually appears when Jesus is referred to as "the King of the Jews" (e.g., Matt 2:2; 27:11). *Ioudaios* occurs only five times each in Matthew and Luke, six times in Mark, but seventy-one times in John (exceeded only by the 79 occurrences in Acts). The relative paucity of references in the Synoptics means that Jesus is viewed almost entirely within a Jewish context. Exceptions are Matt 28:15 and Mark 7:3, which embody a patently postresurrection perspective, similar to that of John.

3. On the similarity between Revelation and the Gospel of John on this matter, see chapter 5 "John's Quest for Jesus," esp. 63–65. Cf. also M. E. Boring, "The Influence of

Christian Prophecy on the Johannine Portrayal of the Paraclete and Jesus," *New Testament Studies* 25 (1978–79): 113–23, esp. 115–16.

4. On the relation of Revelation to the Johannine Writings, see Jörg Frey's essay, "Erwägungen zum Verhältnis der Johannesapokalypse zu den übrigen Schriften im Corpus Johanneum," which concludes Martin Hengel's *Die johanneische Frage: Ein Lösungsversuch* (Wissenschaftliche Untersuchungen zum Neuen Testament 67; Tübingen: Mohr, 1993), 326–429. Prior to that and much more briefly, see D. Moody Smith, "Johannine Christianity: Some Reflections on its Character and Delineation," *New Testament Studies* 21 (1974–75): 222–48, esp. 232–35, 243–44; republished as "Johannine Christianity," in the author's *Johannine Christianity: Essays on Its Setting, Sources, and Theology* (Columbia, S.C.: University of South Carolina Press, 1984), 1–36.

5. On the possible relation of the conflict between Jews and Christians in Revelation to the *Birkath ha-Minim* (Blessing of the Heretics) and thus to the Gospel of John, see C. J. Hemer, *The Letters to the Seven Churches in their Social Setting* (Journal for the Study of the New Testament: Supplement Series 11; Sheffield: JSOT, 1986), 4, 9, 12, 149.

6. In the first and second editions of *Anatomy of the New Testament* (New York: McMillan, 1969, 1974) the Gospel of John, along with the other Johannine writings, was treated at the end of the book, implying that they represent a kind of culmination of the New Testament (although this was not stated). But in the third edition (New York: McMillan, 1982) we moved the Gospel of John forward to treat it with the other Gospels, after the Synoptics. In doing so we acknowledged that John needed to be studied with the other Gospels as a witness to Jesus. At the same time we no longer left the impression that John came later as the capstone of such a "development."

7. Edwyn Clement Hoskyns, *The Fourth Gospel* (ed. Francis Noel Davey; 2d rev. ed.; London: Faber, 1947), 1: "The Gospel according to Saint John is a strictly 'theological' work." At points Hoskyns seems to assume John wrote with the Synoptics in view (e.g., 45, 73). Yet at many other points he is content to posit only a relationship to the synoptic tradition (59–60, 68, 82), particularly its Marcan form. Moreover, John "assumes that all his readers stand where the Jews once stood. He assumes, indeed, that all men, because they are men, occupy this position" (49). John is the clarification and capstone of earlier Christian tradition (82–85).

Ernst Käsemann, *The Testament of Jesus: A Study of the Gospel of John in the Light of Chapter 17* (trans. Gerhard Krodel; Philadelphia, Fortress, 1968), asks, "into which historical situation should the Gospel of John be placed?" By this he means historical situation in the emergence of Christianity. "The theological problems must, after all, point to a specific sector of primitive Christian history and, conversely, we must be able to deduce it from them" (3). That is, theological analysis must yield historical results. Finally, John does not represent the capstone of Christian theological development, however, but a sectarian, charismatic, although dogmatic, offshoot.

8. Rudolf Bultmann, *Theology of the New Testament,* vol. 2 (trans. Kendrick Grobel; New York: Scribner's, 1955), 3–14, esp. 9–10, on the relationship to Paul. Bultmann acknowledges the possibility that John's background was Judaism, probably a pre-Christian gnosticizing Judaism attested by the then recently discovered Dead Sea Scrolls (13).

9. Already in his commentary Bultmann (1941) had taken note of the references to expulsion of Christ-confessors from synagogues and understood them to reflect actual events. See Bultmann, *The Gospel of John: A Commentary* (trans. G. R. Beasley-Murray,

R. W. N. Hoare, and J. K. Riches; Philadelphia: Westminster, 1971), 335 (esp. nn. 5 and 6, on John 9:22–23), 454 (on 12:42), and 555–56 (on 16:2). Yet Bultmann was less interested in the historical circumstances in which the Gospel arose than with the reconstruction of its complex literary development.

10. Martyn's first edition appeared in 1968 (New York: Harper), to be followed by a revised edition in 1979 (Nashville: Abingdon). The current (3d) edition, *History and Theology in the Fourth Gospel* (Louisville, Ky.: Westminster John Knox, 2003), also contains "Glimpses into the History of the Johannine Community" from the author's *The Gospel of John in Christian History* (New York: Paulist, 1978), 90–121.

11. Raymond E. Brown's *The Community of the Beloved Disciple* (New York: Paulist, 1979) appeared only three years after Oscar Cullmann's *The Johannine Circle* (trans. John Bowden; Philadelphia: Westminster, 1975), which had been published in German just the year before. Although Brown discusses Cullmann's work briefly, pointing out his agreements and disagreements (176–78), he obviously was unable to interact with him in the composition of his own work. The same is true of Brown's relation to R. Alan Culpepper's *The Johannine School: An Evaluation of the Johannine-School Hypothesis Based on an Investigation of the Nature of Ancient Schools* (Society of Biblical Literature Dissertation Series 26; Missoula, Mont.: Scholars Press, 1975), which Brown mentions only in a footnote (14, n. 9). Through the study of historical analogies drawn from classical antiquity, ancient Judaism, and early Christianity, Culpepper shows how a Johannine school might have developed and what it would have looked like. Culpepper speaks of a Johannine community and Johannine school interchangeably (287–89) and concludes that "the Johannine community, therefore, was a school" (289).

12. P. Gardner-Smith, *Saint John and the Synoptic Gospels* (Cambridge: Cambridge University Press, 1938).

13. The classical demonstration remains William Wrede, *The Messianic Secret* (trans. J. C. G. Greig; Cambridge: Clark, 1971), published in the original German in 1901. The seventy-year wait for an English translation may be the longest on record, but says something about the enduring value of the volume.

14. Robert T. Fortna, *The Gospel of Signs: A Reconstruction of the Narrative Source Underlying the Fourth Gospel* (Society for New Testament Studies Monograph Series 11; Cambridge: Cambridge University Press, 1970), was originally a dissertation at Union Theological Seminary with Martyn. Fortna followed it nearly two decades later with *The Fourth Gospel and Its Predecessor: From Narrative Source to Present Gospel* (Philadelphia: Fortress, 1988), a considerable elaboration of his earlier work, but not a departure from it.

15. Martyn, *History and Theology* (2003), 101–23, 125–30. Cf. Fortna, *Gospel of Signs,* 230–34, who attributes this insight to Martyn (230, n. 4)

16. C. K. Barrett, *The Gospel according to St. John* (2d ed.; Philadelphia: Westminster, 1978), 61–62, 133–34, tentatively suggests that John the Apostle moved from Palestine to Ephesus and there composed apocalyptic works that one of his disciples incorporated into the canonical Apocalypse. Others of his disciples then wrote the Epistles of John and the Fourth Gospel.

17. Martyn, *History and Theology* (2003), 47, n. 8, citing Barnabas Lindars, *Behind the Fourth Gospel* (London: SPCK, 1971), 47.

18. See below, 47–56, "The Problem of History in John." There I suggest that something like this same pattern also underlies J. M. Robinson's monograph *The Problem of History in Mark* (Studies in Biblical Theology 21; Naperville, Ill.: Allenson, 1957).

19. See the insightful book of Robert Kysar, *John the Maverick Gospel* (rev. ed.; Louisville, Ky.: Westminster John Knox, 1993), still an excellent introduction to this very different Gospel.

20. Bultmann, *Gospel of John,* 108, takes seriously the possibility that this scene is based on the historical fact that disciples of John were among Jesus' early disciples, perhaps joining him when he broke away from the Baptist.

21. See *John among the Gospels* (2001), 205–7, and "Jesus Tradition in the Gospel of John," below, 81–111. The historical relation of Jesus to the Baptist is treated exhaustively in John P. Meier, *Mentor, Message, and Miracles* (vol. 2 of *A Marginal Jew: Rethinking the Historical Jesus;* New York: Doubleday, 1994), 19–233. Meier characterizes John the Baptist as Jesus' "mentor."

22. Bultmann, *Gospel of John,* 86: "The term *Ioudaioi,* characteristic of the Evangelist, gives an overall portrayal of the Jews, viewed from the standpoint of Christian faith, as the representative of unbelief (and thereby, as will appear, of the unbelieving 'world' in general)."

23. See chapter 3, 26–43, below.

24. Wayne A. Meeks, *The Prophet-King: Moses Traditions and the Johannine Christology* (Supplements to Novum Testamentum 14; Leiden: Brill, 1967).

25. Meeks, "The Man from Heaven in Johannine Sectarianism, "*Journal of Biblical Literature* 91 (1972): 44–72, credits Martyn with having "made a major contribution toward locating the kind of milieu in which the anti-Jewish polemic of one stratum of the Johannine materials was formed" (49, n. 16; cf. 40, 77).

26. See chapter 3, below, 26–43. One sees various transliterations of the term, which means "Blessing of the Heretics"; we simply follow Martyn's. It was the twelfth of the Eighteen Benedictions of the Synagogue liturgy and is sometimes referred to as such. The issue between Martyn and his critics hinges on the questions of when and for what purpose this solemn imprecation was instituted.

27. See Ashton, *Understanding the Fourth Gospel,* esp. 107–111. Ashton has issued a new and revised eidtion of this work (Oxford: Oxford University Press, 2007) from which this discussion has been deleted.

28. See R. Bieringer, D. Pollefeyt, and F. Vandecasteele-Vanneuville, eds., *Anti-Judaism and the Fourth Gospel* (Louisville, Ky.: Westminster John Knox, 2001), which contains papers presented at the Leuven (Louvain) conference of January 17–18, 2000, undertaken by the Catholic University of Louvain.

29. *History and Theology in the Fourth Gospel* (2003), 85, 86–89.

30. D. Moody Smith, "John and the Jews," *Interpretation* 23 (1969): 220–23; the quotation cited is on 223.

Chapter 2: Judaism in the Johannine Context

1. This chapter appeared originally as "John," in *Early Christian Thought in Its Jewish Context* (ed. John Barclay and John Sweet; Cambridge: Cambridge University Press, 1996), 96–111. See also D. Moody Smith, "Judaism and the Gospel of John," *Jews and Christians: Exploring the Past, Present, and Future* (ed. James H. Charlesworth; New York: Crossroad, 1990), 76–96, for an exposition of the ancient, historical issues. Note also R. Alan Culpepper, "The Gospel of John as a Threat to Jewish-Christian Relations" in *Overcoming Fear between Jews and Christians* (ed. James H. Charlesworth; New York: Crossroad, 1992), 21–43, as well as Eldon J. Epp, "Anti-Semitism and the Popularity of the Fourth Gospel in Christianity," *Journal of the Central Conference of American Rabbis* (22, 44 [fall] 1995), 35–57.

2. Early and important articles include Raymond E. Brown, "The Qumran Scrolls and the Johannine Gospel and Epistles," in *The Scrolls and the New Testament* (ed. Krister Stendahl; New York: Harper, 1958), 183–207, and James H. Charlesworth, "A Critical Comparison of the Dualism in 1 QS 3:35–4:26 and the 'Dualism' Contained in the Gospel of John," *New Testament Studies* 15 (1968–69): 389–418. The latter article appeared in slightly revised form in Charlesworth's edited volume *John and the Dead Sea Scrolls* (New York: Crossroad, 1990).

3. Most commentators agree. See, for example, C. K. Barrett, *The Gospel according to John: An Introduction with Commentary and Notes on the Greek Text* (2d ed.; Philadelphia: Westminster, 1978), 151; and Rudolf Bultmann, *The Gospel of John: A Commentary* (trans. G. R. Beasley-Murray, R. W. N. Hoare, and J. K. Riches; Philadelphia: Westminster, 1971), 20.

4. In chronological order: William Wrede, *Charakter and Tendenz des Johannesevangelium* (Sammlung gemeinverständlicher Vorträge und Schriften aus dem Gebiet der Theologie und Religionsgeschichte 37; 2 vols.; Tübingen: Mohr, 1933, but originally published in 1903); H. Odeberg, *The Fourth Gospel Interpreted in Relation to Contemporaneous Religious Currents in Palestine and the Hellenistic-Oriental World* (Uppsala: Almquist and Wiksells, 1929); Adolf Schlatter, *Der Evangelist Johannes: Wie er spricht, denkt, und glaubt* (Stuttgart: Calwer, 1930).

5. Brown's suggestion preceded Martyn's full-blown thesis. See Raymond E. Brown, *The Gospel according to John (I–XII)* (Anchor Bible 29; Garden City, N.Y.: Doubleday, 1966), lxx–lxxv. In 1968 Martyn first published *History and Theology in the Fourth Gospel,* which appeared in a revised edition in 1979. The current third edition is published by Westminster John Knox (Louisville, Ky.: 2003). It contains, among other things, an updated version of D. Moody Smith's "The Contribution of J. Louis Martyn to the Understanding of the Fourth Gospel," originally published in *The Conversation Continues: Studies in Paul and John* (ed. Robert T. Fortna and Beverly R. Gaventa; Nashville: Abingdon, 1990), which appears as chapter 3 below.

6. Those who question Martyn's proposal point out that the text of the *Birkath ha-Minim* is not uniform, and the witnesses are at best centuries later than the expulsion of Johannine Christians from synagogues. There is no explicit evidence that the Twelfth Benediction was used for banning Christians from the synagogue, although the Talmudic anecdote about Samuel's forgetting the words (*Berakoth* 28b–29a) and the testimony of Justin Martyr may suggest this. Nevertheless, given the virtual certainty that Johannine Christians felt threatened by exclusion from the synagogue (9:22; 12:42; 16:2), not to mention the tension between early Christian confessors and Jews that is reflected elsewhere in the New Testament (e.g., Acts 7; 2 Cor 11:24), Martyn's decision to search for Jewish evidence of the expulsion of Christ-confessors was appropriate and his solution a plausible one. (See below, chapter 3.) A balanced, well informed treatment is, in my judgment, W. Horbury, "The Benediction of the *Minim* and Early Jewish Christian Controversy," *Journal of Theological Studies* 33 (1982), 19–61.

7. On Martyn's book, see the significant evaluation of John Ashton, *Understanding the Fourth Gospel* (Oxford: Clarendon, 1991), 107: "probably the most important single work on the Gospel since Bultmann's commentary"; cf. 111.

8. Wayne A. Meeks has written a number of important studies. Representative and perhaps most significant are *The Prophet-King: Moses Traditions and the Gospel of John,* (Supplements to Novum Testamentum 14; Leiden: Brill, 1967), and "The Man from Heaven in Johannine Sectarianism," *Journal of Biblical Literature* 91 (1972), 44–72.

9. See Bultmann, *Gospel of John*, 85–86; also his *Theology of the New Testament*, vol. 2 (trans. Kendrick Grobel; New York: Scribner's, 1955), 27–32.

10. Bultmann, "Jesus and Paul," available in Schubert Ogden's English translation in *Existence and Faith: Shorter Writings of Rudolf Bultmann* (New York: Meridian Books, 1960), 183–201.

11. See "Paul," *Existence and Faith*, 111–46, esp. 11–13.

12. *Jesus and the Word* (trans. L. P. Smith and E. Huntress; New York: Scribner's, 1934). The original (German) edition appeared in 1926.

13. Declaration on the Relationship of the Church to Non-Christian Religions (*Nostra Aetate*), section 4: "True, authorities of the Jews and those who followed their lead pressed for the death of Christ (cf. John 19:6); still, what happened in his passion cannot be blamed upon all the Jews then living, without distinction, nor upon the Jews of today." I quote from Walter M. Abbott and J. Gallagher, eds., *The Documents of Vatican II* (New York: Guild Press, 1966), 665–66. The Declaration was promulgated by Pope Paul VI on October 28, 1965. See also R. Brooks, ed., *Unanswered Questions: Theological Visions of Jewish-Catholic Relations* (Notre Dame, Ind.: University of Notre Dame Press, 1988), which contains basic documents, including *Nostra Aetate*, as well as important articles.

14. Epp, "Anti-Semitism and the Popularity of the Fourth Gospel in Christianity," 35.

15. Rosemary Ruether, *Faith and Fratricide: The Theological Roots of Anti-Semitism* (New York: Seabury, 1974), 113.

16. Bultmann, *Gospel of John*, 189, n. 6, simply rejects "salvation is of the Jews" as impossible in John, because "the Evangelist does not regard the Jews as God's chosen and saved people." Barrett, *Gospel according to St. John*, 237, declares that the statement "does not mean that the Jews as such are inevitably saved, but rather that the election of Israel to a true knowledge of God was in order that, at the time appointed by God, salvation might proceed from Israel to the world, and Israel's own unique privilege be thereby dissolved." Interpreted in this way, there is no need to regard 4:22 as a gloss. Interestingly, Wrede, *Charakter and Tendenz*, 42, does not yet advocate excising the statement, but interprets it as "eine historiche Erinnerung, die für die Gegenwart nichts mehr bedeutet."

17. Martin Scott, *Sophia and the Johannine Jesus* (Journal for the Study of the New Testament: Supplements Series 71; Sheffield: JSOT, 1992).

18. On the meaning and significance of the sacramental act, see David K. Rensberger's discussion of 6:51c–58, the controversial eucharistic passage, in *Johannine Faith and Liberating Community* (Philadelphia: Westminster, 1988), 70–80. Rensberger emphasizes the social significance of the Eucharist in setting the followers of Jesus apart as a distinct community separate from the synagogue.

19. This is the basic position of Severino Pancaro, *The Law in the Fourth Gospel: The Torah and the Gospel, Moses and Jesus, Judaism and Christianity according to John* (Supplements to Novum Testamentum 42; Leiden: Brill, 1975). Markku Kotila, *Umstrittener Zeuge: Studien zur Stellung des Gesetzes in der johanneischen Theologiegeschichte* (Annales academiae scientificarum fennicae, Dissertationes humanarum litterarum 48; Helsinki: Tiedeakatemia, 1988), in contrast, undertakes a tradition-historical or source-critical analysis of references to the law, which enables him to resolve tensions in John's attitude to the law by assigning sayings that seemingly affirm or presuppose the validity of the law to an earlier stratum within, or closer to, the synagogue and sayings that

put distance between Jesus and the law (e.g., "your law," 8:17 and elsewhere) to a later stage in which the community of Jesus' followers had separated from the synagogue. Kotila's analysis has the advantages and suffers from the limitations of all such efforts. It resolves tension, but on a basis that must remain hypothetical.

20. See Martyn, *History and Theology* (2003), esp. 123.

21. Ibid., 101–23.

22. I simplify, but I believe not inaccurately, a more complex situation in the Samaritan sources that has been investigated by Meeks (*Prophet-King*, esp. 216–54). Meeks concludes that for the *Memar Marqah* the *Taheb* was Moses (250).

23. See J. Brad Chance, *Jerusalem, the Temple, and the New Age in Luke-Acts* (Macon, Ga.: Mercer University Press, 1988).

24. On the theological significance of the closely related tabernacle motif and its function in the Fourth Gospel, particularly in 1:14, see Craig R. Koester, *The Dwelling of God: The Tabernacle in the Old Testament, Intertestamental Jewish Literature, and the New Testament* (Catholic Biblical Quarterly Monograph Series 22; Washington: Catholic Biblical Association, 1989).

25. See W. D. Davies, *The Gospel and the Land: Early Christianity and Jewish Territorial Doctrine* (Berkeley: University of California Press, 1974), 334; for the Gospel of John see 288–335.

26. Menahem Stern, ed., *Greek and Latin Authors on Jews and Judaism; Edited with Introduction, Translations, and Commentary* (3 vols.; Jerusalem: Israel Academy of Sciences and Humanities, 1974–81).

27. Ibid., 2. 411–12.

28. Ibid., 3. 24–25.

29. "The Dialectical Theology of St. John" in Barrett's *New Testament Essays* (London: SPCK, 1972), 48–69; the quotation cited is on 55.

Chapter 3: The Stressful Tension between Judaism and the Johannine Jesus

1. This essay originally appeared in *The Conversation Continues: Studies in Paul & John in Honor of J. Louis Martyn* (ed. Robert T. Fortna and Beverly R. Gaventa; Nashville: Abingdon, 1990), 275–94.

2. Bultmann, *The Gospel of John: A Commentary* (trans. G. R. Beasley-Murray, R. W. N. Hoare, and J. K. Riches; Philadelphia: Westminster, 1971). The German original, *Das Evangelium des Johannes* (1941), was first published in fascicles, 1939–41, and has been supplemented through the years with several *Ergänzungshefte*.

3. C. H. Dodd, *Interpretation of the Fourth Gospel* (Cambridge: Cambridge University Press, 1953); *Historical Tradition in the Fourth Gospel* (Cambridge: Cambridge University Press, 1963).

4. Hoskyns, *The Fourth Gospel* (2d rev. ed.; ed. Francis Noel Davey; London: Faber, 1947), unlike Dodd's *Interpretation*, is a commentary proper.

5. As well as the commentary, note also Bultmann's *Theology of the New Testament*, vol. 2 (trans. Kendrick Grobel; New York: Scribner's, 1955), 3–92.

6. Bultmann, *Gospel of John*, 716.

7. Bultmann, *Theology of the New Testament*, 2.5.

8. Bultmann's source theory is well known. The evangelist worked with several literary sources: a sign-source, a revelation-discourse source, and a passion source, as well as other more fragmentary sources or traditions. In a real sense he interpreted and even demythologized them as he wove them into the Gospel he was creating. The original

form of this Gospel was unaccountably lost, but it has been the object of at least two serious efforts at restoration. The first was undertaken, according to Bultmann, by the ecclesiastical redactor, but with only limited success. The second was the work of Bultmann himself, who in a real sense created the text he was commenting on. His reconstruction entailed both large-scale and minuscule rearrangements of the traditional text as well as the elimination of some passages (such as 6:51–58; chap. 21), deemed the creation of the redactor. For further details, consult the English translation of Bultmann's commentary, for which a table of contents has been helpfully provided, enabling the reader to locate passages Bultmann has repositioned, or my *Composition and Order of the Fourth Gospel: Bultmann's Literary Theory* (Yale Publications in Religion 10; New Haven: Yale University Press, 1965). In that monograph I call attention to the fact that Bultmann never offers an explanation for the destruction or, indeed, the defective restoration of the text as a deficiency in his work. I have since come to question the significance of such a historically based criticism, given Bultmann's hermeneutic. The text stimulates the interpreter, but the interpreter with the proper *Vorverständnis* then understands better than the (author of the) text what the text is about. Why should the interpreter not then improve upon the text—within the resources provided by the text—to bring its *Sache* to clear expression? I do not seriously suggest that Bultmann actually or explicitly thought in this way, only that such a procedure is the logical extension of his hermeneutical program.

9. Translated as *The Testament of Jesus: A Study of the Gospel of John in the Light of Chapter 17* (trans. Gerhard Krodel; Philadelphia: Fortress, 1968).

10. Käsemann, "Ketzer und Zeuge," *Zeitschrift für Theologie und Kirche* 49 (1951): 292–311.

11. Martyn, *History and Theology in the Fourth Gospel* (New York: Harper, 1968). References in this chapter are to the third edition (Louisville, Ky.: Westminster John Knox, 2003).

12. Ibid., 47.

13. Ibid.

14. Ibid., 59, 64–65.

15. As is well known, Kenneth L. Carroll related *aposynagogoi* to the *Birkath ha-Minim* in his article "The Fourth Gospel and the Exclusion of Christians from the Synagogues," *Bulletin of the John Rylands Library* 40 (1957–58): 19–32. Curiously, Carroll continued to think of the author of the Gospel as a Gentile Christian and did not make his insight productive for an understanding of its setting and purpose. Already William Wrede, *Charakter und Tendenz des Johannesevangeliums* (Sammlung gemeinverständlicher Vorträge und Schriften aus dem Gebiet der Theologie und Religionsgeschichte 37, Tübingen: Mohr, 1903), had observed that the Jews in the Fourth Gospel reflected a Johannine conflict with contemporary Judaism. Shortly after the appearance of Martyn's book, but still independent of it, Göran Forkman, *The Limits of the Religious Community: Expulsion from the Religious Community within the Qumran Sect, within Rabbinic Judaism, and within Primitive Christianity* (Coniectanea Biblica, New Testament—Series 5, Lund: Gleerup, 1972), connected the *Birkath ha-Minim* with expulsion of Christians from the synagogue (90–92) and found that the experiences reflected in John 9:22; 12:42; and 16:2 are in all probability related to its promulgation. Forkman cites as important for his own work the unpublished University of Göttingen dissertation of Claus-Hunno Hunzinger, "Die jüdische Bannpraxis im neutestamentlichen Zeitalter" (1954), also cited by Martyn, which I have not seen.

Forkman does not, however, cite Martyn, nor does he apparently know the works of Carroll or T. C. Smith.

16. See Wayne A. Meeks, "Breaking Away: Three New Testament Pictures of Christianity's Separation from the Jewish Communities," in *"To See Ourselves as Others See Us": Christians, Jews, "Others" in Late Antiquity* (ed. Jacob Neusner and Ernest S. Frerichs, Studies in the Humanities 9; Chico, Calif: Scholars Press, 1985), 93–115; pertinent discussion is on 102. Meeks's contribution began with his important monograph *The Prophet-King: Moses Traditions and the Johannine Christology* (Supplements to Novum Testamentum 14; Leiden: Brill, 1967).

17. See Martyn, *History and Theology*, 60, n. 69, and 61–62, n. 75, for Martyn's summary of discussions with Meeks and Morton Smith.

18. Much more negative, however, is Reuven Kimelman, "*Birkat ha-Minim* and the Lack of Evidence for an Anti-Christian Jewish Prayer in Late Antiquity," in *Jewish and Christian Self-Definition*, vol. 2 (ed. E. P. Sanders et al.; 1981), 226–44; also Stephen Katz, "Issues in the Separation of Judaism and Christianity after 70 C.E.: A Reconsideration," *Journal of Biblical Literature* 103 (1984): 43–76. Peter Schäfer, "Die sogannante Synode von Jabne," in *Studien zur Geschichte und Theologie des Rabbinischen Judentums* (Leiden: Brill, 1978):, 45–55 (reprinted from *Judaica* 31 [1975]), argues that the Benediction was directed as much against political oppression as against heretics, and in any case was not intended to separate Christians from Jews. A balanced treatment with ample bibliographical citation is William Horbury, "The Benediction of the *Minim* and Early Jewish-Christian Controversy," *Journal of Theological Studies* 33 (1982): 19–61. Horbury's judgment, 60 ("The Jamnian ordinance belongs to this more systematized opposition of the late first century, and probably reinforces an earlier exclusion attested in John, although uncertainties of dating leave open the possibility that these two measures may be contemporaneous."), expresses approximately the same proportion of agreement and qualification as do those of Meeks and Morton Smith. But while also allowing for the Johannine persecution to antedate the Jamnian formulation, Horbury is inclined to continue to date the Twelfth Benediction within the first century.

19. See Martyn, *The Gospel of John in Christian History* (New York: Paulist, 1978), 92; see also 103–4.

20. Meeks, "Breaking Away," 95; see also 94–104.

21. Martyn, *Gospel of John in Christian History*, 56.

22. Published in the proceedings of that conference, *Jesus and Man's Hope*, vol. 1 (Pittsburgh: Pittsburgh Theological Seminary, 1970), 247–73.

23. See Robert T. Fortna, *The Gospel of Signs: A Reconstruction of the Narrative Source Underlying the Fourth Gospel* (Society for New Testament Studies Monograph Series 11; Cambridge: Cambridge University Press, 1970).

24. Robert T. Fortna, *The Fourth Gospel and Its Predecessors: From Narrative Source to Present Gospel* (Philadelphia: Fortress, 1988), 224.

25. See W. D. Davies, *The Setting of the Sermon on the Mount* (Cambridge: Cambridge University Press, 1966), 256–315, esp. 275–86.

26. Martyn, *History and Theology*, 118–19.

27. Meeks, "Breaking Away," 94–104, 109, apparently finds both Martyn and Davies largely convincing about the Gospels of John and Matthew respectively.

28. See Brown, *The Gospel According to John (i–xii)* (Anchor Bible 29; Garden City, N.J.: Doubleday, 1966), lxxiv–lxxv.

29. See Brown, *The Community of the Beloved Disciple* (New York: Paulist, 1979); *The Epistles of John* (Anchor Bible 30; Garden City, N.Y.: Doubleday, 1982).

30. See C. K. Barrett, *The Gospel according to John: An Introduction with Commentary and Notes on the Greek Text* (2d. ed.; Philadelphia: Westminster, 1978).

31. Evidently, Barrett's influence does not end with the English-speaking world. A German translation of his commentary, somewhat revised, appeared in 1990 under the title *Das Evangelium nach Johannes* and stands along Bultmann's *Das Evangelium des Johannes* in the Meyer (Kritisch-exegetischer Kommentar über das Neue Testament) series. (Apparently Vandenhoeck & Ruprecht will also keep Bultmann in print, but Barrett's commentary will fill the need for a standard, up-to-date work.) If it would be excessive to say that, through Barrett, Martyn's work has become canonical in Germany as well as in Great Britain, the important point is nonetheless clear. Martyn's thesis has become a paradigm. It is a part of what students imbibe from standard works, such as commentaries and textbooks, as knowledge generally received and held to be valid. For example, in *Anatomy of the New Testament: A Guide to Its Structure and Meaning* (6th ed.; Upper Saddle River, N.J., 2007), 164–69, Robert A. Spivey, Clifton Black, and I present Martyn's thesis as providing historical perspective for the treatment of the Fourth Gospel. Something similar might be said of John Painter's excellent introduction, *John: Witness and Theologian* (London: S.P.C.K., 1975), 13. That none of these works represents original scholarship is exactly the point. Insofar as they are successful in accomplishing their goals, they reflect the state of the art in Johannine research, and Martyn's work rightly stands at their center. One might add that these books are more or less typical of works of this genre.

32. See Klaus Wengst, *Bedrängte Gemeinde und verherrlichte Christus: Der historische Ort des Johannesevangelium als Schlüssel zu seiner Interpretation* (Biblisch-theologische Studien 5; Neukirchen: Neukirchener Verlag, 1981), esp. 30, n. 82.

33. See Martyn, *History and Theology,* 76, n. 100.

34. See Meeks, "Breaking Away," 102–3.

35. Jerome S. Neyrey, in *Ideology of Revolt: John's Christology in Social Science Perspective* (Philadelphia: Fortress, 1988), 3, 9–15, 35, 122–48, 196, 211.

36. David Rensberger, *Johannine Faith and Liberating Community* (Philadelphia: Westminster, 1988).

37. Ibid., 22.

38. Meeks, "Breaking Away," 94.

39. R. Alan Culpepper, *Anatomy of the Fourth Gospel: A Study in Literary Design* (Philadelphia: Fortress, 1983).

40. John Ashton, *Understanding the Fourth Gospel* (Oxford: Clarendon, 1991).

41. Daniel Boyarin, "Justin Martyr Invents Judaism," *Church History* 70 (2001): 427–61. That Martyn continues to stand at the center of discussion is manifest in the article of Colleen M. Conway, "The Production of the Johannine Community: A New Historicist Perspective," *Journal of Biblical Literature* 121 (2002): 479–95, as well as Robert Kysar's 2002 Society of Biblical Literature paper, "Expulsion from the Synagogue: A Tale of a Theory," to which I responded at the meeting.

42. Ashton, *Understanding the Fourth Gospel* (1991), 109, n. 102. Similarly, Stephen G. Wilson, *Related Strangers: Jews and Christians 70–170 C.E.* (Minneapolis: Fortress, 1995), 73: "It is not essential to connect the expulsion from the synagogue with the *Birkat ha-minim.*"

43. Martyn, *Gospel of John in Christian History,* 55–89 (chapter 2: "Persecution and Martyrdom").

44. Ashton, *Understanding the Fourth Gospel* (1991), 167; cf. Brown, *Community of the Beloved Disciple*, 34–54, esp. 36–40, 42–47, 174.

45. Moloney, "'The Jews' in the Fourth Gospel: Another Perspective," *Pacifica* 15 (February 2002): 16–36, esp. 33–35.

46. Reinhartz, *Befriending the Beloved Disciple: A Jewish Reading of the Gospel of John* (New York: Continuum, 2001). Although earlier on Reinhartz mirrors scholarly skepticism about Martyn's thesis (37–40), she later seems to concede that John does reflect the historical fact of separation, probably interpreted quite differently by the opposing parties (96–97). Wilson, *Related Strangers*, 73, also takes the rupture to have been historical.

47. Martyn, *Gospel of John in Christian History*, 56.

48. D. Moody Smith, *The Theology of the Gospel of John* (New Testament Theology; Cambridge: Cambridge University Press, 1995), xi.

49. Cf. Leander E. Keck, *Who Is Jesus? History in Perfect Tense* (Studies on Personalities of the New Testament; Columbia, S.C.: University of South Carolina Press, 2000).

Chapter 4: The Problem of History in John

1. See James M. Robinson, *The Problem of History in Mark* (Studies in Biblical Theology 21; Naperville, Ill.: Allenson, 1957); later republished in Robinson's *The Problem of History in Mark and Other Marcan Studies* (Philadelphia: Fortress, 1982); also J. Louis Martyn, *History and Theology in the Fourth Gospel* (3d rev. ed.; Louisville, Ky.: Westminster John Knox, 2003). Martyn's work first appeared from Harper & Row in 1968. In subsequent editions he entered into discussion with critics, but saw no reason to change his basic position.

2. Ernst Käsemann once addressed this question eloquently: "But if John felt himself under constraint to compose a Gospel rather than letters or a collection of sayings, Bultmann's argument is revealed as very one-sided. For it seems to me that if one has no interest in the historical Jesus, then one does not write a Gospel, but, on the contrary, finds the Gospel form inadequate." See the English-language collection of Käsemann's essays, *New Testament Questions of Today* (trans. W. J. Montague; Philadelphia: Fortress, 1969), 41. The essay appeared originally in the second volume of Käsemann's *Exgetische Versuche und Besinnungen* (Göttingen: Vandenhoeck & Ruprecht, 1964); see 47.

3. See Bultmann's groundbreaking essay, "The New Testament and Mythology," in *Kerygma and Myth: A Theological Debate* (ed. Hans Werner Bartsch; trans. Reginald H. Fuller; London: SPCK, 1957), 1–44.

4. See D. Moody Smith, *John among the Gospels* (2d ed.; Columbia, S.C.: University of South Carolina Press, 2001), where the positions noted here are described in more detail.

5. Maurice Casey, *Is John's Gospel True?* (London: Routledge, 1996).

6. Mgr. de Solages, *Jean et les Synoptiques* (Leiden: Brill, 1979).

7. See P. Gardner-Smith, *Saint John and the Synoptic Gospels* (Cambridge: Cambridge University Press, 1938); C. H. Dodd, *Historical Tradition in the Fourth Gospel* (Cambridge: Cambridge University Press, 1963).

8. D. Moody Smith, "Jesus Tradition in the Gospel of John," in the *Handbook of the Study of the Historical Jesus* (ed. Stanley Porter and Tom Holmen; Leiden: Brill, forthcoming), a four-volume work. It appears as chapter 7, below.

9. Robinson, *The Problem of History in Mark*, 18, and especially n. 1.

10. Ibid., 63.
11. Ibid., 13.

Chapter 5: John's Quest for Jesus

1. As noted by Dennis Nineham in his "Foreword to the Complete Edition" of Schweitzer's *Quest of the Historical Jesus* (ed. and trans. John Bowman and others; Minneapolis: Fortress, 2001), 488 n. 6. This significant new edition includes for the first time in English translation Schweitzer's own additions to his second edition (1913), entitled *Geschichte der Leben-Jesu-Forschung*, as well as revisions of W. Montgomery's translation (1912).

2. On this important point note the work of Leander E. Keck, *Who Is Jesus? History in Perfect Tense* (Studies on Personalities of the New Testament; Columbia, S.C.: University of South Carolina Press, 2000), esp. 2–7.

3. John Painter, *The Quest for the Messiah: The History, Literature, and Theology of the Johannine Community* (2d ed.; Nashville: Abingdon, 1993).

4. J. Louis Martyn, *History and Theology in the Fourth Gospel* (3d. ed.; Louisville, Ky. Westminster John Knox, 2003), esp. 34–45.

5. On the positive role of Thomas in the Gospel of John, see James H. Charlesworth, *The Beloved Disciple: Whose Witness Validates the Gospel of John?* (Valley Forge: Trinity Press International, 1995). In arguing that Thomas is the Beloved Disciple, he rightly emphasizes the important, and even positive, role Thomas plays in the narrative (see esp. 225–87). He also presents a valuable history of the discussion of the problem, indicating the various proposals about his identity (127–224).

6. The NRSV shows a tendency to strive for consistency in translation. Thus "Advocate" is used to translate *paraklētos* in 1 John 2:1 and in the farewell discourses of the Gospel. But in the Gospel "Counselor" (RSV) seems a better translation, because it embraces the juridical aspect of the term as well as the obvious function of the Paraclete in conveying the reality of Jesus to the disciples.

7. As far as I know, this apt term was introduced to prominence by George Johnston, *The Spirit-Paraclete in the Gospel of John* (Society for New Testament Studies Monograph Series 12; Cambridge: Cambridge University Press, 1970), 29–39.

8. This proposal is by no means new. See my own *The Theology of the Gospel of John* (Cambridge: Cambridge University Press, 1995), 139–44. There I cite works that have been seminal for me: M. E. Boring, "The Influence of Christian Prophecy on the Johannine Portrait of the Paraclete and Jesus," *New Testament Studies* 25 (1978–79): 113–23; D. Bruce Woll, *Johannine Christianity in Conflict: Authority, Rank, and Succession in the First Farewell Discourse* (Society of Biblical Literature Dissertation Series 60; Chico, Calif.: Scholars Press, 1981), 109–28; David E. Aune, "The Odes of Solomon and Early Christian Prophecy," *New Testament Studies* 28 (1982): 435–60. Earlier on I had made such a suggestion in "Johannine Christianity: Some Reflections on Its Character and Delineation," *New Testament Studies* 21 (1976): 222–48; note esp. 232–33 and 243–44. Of course, in Ernst Käsemann's famous monograph, *The Testament of Jesus: A Study of the Gospel of John in the Light of Chapter 17* (trans. Gerhard Krodel; Philadelphia: Fortress, 1968), one finds a Gospel that is not only sectarian, incipiently docetic, and fundamentally dogmatic, but also charismatic (esp. 36–38, 45–47), originating in Christian prophecy (38), and subject to the vagaries of Spirit inspiration (47). The dogma of Christ as the Word and the insistence upon following him alone, however, controls the Johannine proclamation.

9. Martyn, *History and Theology*, 136–43, esp. 138–39.

10. Thus Rudolf Bultmann, *Theology of the New Testament* (trans. Kendrick Grobel; 2 vols.; New York: Scribner's, 1951–55), 2.3–92, treats them together: "Whether the Epistles were written by the author of the Gospel himself or simply came out of his 'school' can here be disregarded" (3). For a good discussion of questions regarding common authorship and tradition, see Raymond E. Brown, *The Epistles of John* (Anchor Bible 30; Garden City, N.Y.: Doubleday, 1982), 14–35. He concludes: "I think it very likely but not certain that 1 John was written by one other than the evangelist" (35).

11. As Bultmann already acknowledged (see above, n. 10). Brown, *Epistles of John*, esp. 94–97, distinguishes the Johannine school as the tradition bearers from the Johannine community generally.

12. Jörg Frey's long essay, "Erwägungen zum Verhältnis der Johannesapokalypse zu den übrigen Schriften des Corpus Johanneum," concludes (326–429) Martin Hengel's *Die johanneische Frage: Ein Lösungsversuch* (Wissenschaftliche Untersuchungen zum Neuen Testament, 67; Tübingen: Mohr-Siebeck, 1993).

13. On the sayings of Jesus in Revelation, see David E. Aune, *Revelation 1–5* (Word Biblical Commentary 52; Dallas: Word Books, 1997), 264–65, who cites relevant bibliography.

14. On the priority of the Gospel of John over the Epistles, see Brown, *Epistles of John*, 32–35, whose summation (34–35) I find persuasive. Nevertheless, some commentators before and after Brown are not convinced, most notably recently Georg Strecker, *The Johannine Letters* (trans. Linda M. Mahoney; ed. Harold Attridge; Hermeneia; Minneapolis: Fortress, 1996), xxxv–xlii, 4, and passim.

15. Aune, *Revelation*, lvi–lxx, shows that the evidence for dating Revelation is mixed, and that while the final edition appeared at the end of the first century (Trajan), there was likely an earlier edition to be dated in the 60s, if not earlier. C. K. Barrett, *The Gospel according to St. John: An Introduction with Commentary and Notes on the Greek Text* (2d ed.; Philadelphia: Westminster, 1978), conjectures that Revelation has quite ancient roots that go back to the Son of Thunder, that is, John the Son of Zebedee (Mark 3:17), who may have himself composed apocalyptic works (133–34; also cf. 62).

16. After a finely nuanced discussion, Brown (*Epistles of John*, 342–48) concludes that "it is likely that the author was referring to an *anointing with the Holy Spirit*, the gift *from Christ* which constituted one as a Christian" (348).

17. On the problem of spiritual authority in the early church see also 1 Cor 15:3 and *Did.* 11:7, as well as 1 Thess 5:19–21.

18. Although Brown argues for its originality (*Epistles of John*, 494–96), and thus agrees with Bultmann, most recently Strecker (*Johannine Letters*, 136) rejects it: "It may have entered the text rather late, under the influence of the christological conflicts." He cites also the article of Bart Ehrman, "1 John 4:3 and the Orthodox Corruption of Scripture," *Zeitschrift für die neutestamentliche Wissenschaft und die Kunde der älteren Kirche* 79 (1988): 221–43.

19. For the traditional eschatological enemy, see 2 Thess 2:3–4; Mark 13:5–6, 21–22; Rev 20:7–10. Many other examples could be cited. Yet the term *Antichrist* appears only in 1 and 2 John.

20. Brown argues that the Epistle's prologue is not only modeled on the Gospel's, but would scarcely be intelligible apart from it (*Epistles of John*, 176–80).

21. Brown's discussions are precise and finely nuanced, as he repeatedly attempts to determine with precision what the antecedent in any given case may be (cf. on 3:23–24,

p. 464) and maintains that "regularly 1 John attributes commandments to God." Strecker (*Johannine Letters*, 127) sees, I think correctly, that precision is scarcely to be attained.

22. Strecker has a most helpful discussion of the docetist heresy against which 1 John apparently struggles (*Johannine Epistles*, 69–76), although he is unwilling to see in 1 John an "early Catholicism" that has equated truth with dogma (244–49).

23. To what extent is John 1:14 to be seen against the background of docetic denial of Jesus' humanity, and therefore 1 John's explicit antidocetism? In his famous monograph, Käsemann rejected traditional concepts of incarnation, including Bultmann's, as inappropriate to the Fourth Gospel (Käsemann, *Testament of Jesus*, 9–12, and passim) and described the Gospel as "naively docetic" (26, 66, 70). On this whole problem see Marianne Meye Thompson, *The Humanity of Jesus in the Fourth Gospel* (Philadelphia: Fortress, 1988), republished as *The Incarnate Word* (Peabody, Mass.: Hendrickson, 1993). The historical interest and validity of the Fourth Gospel are reconsidered in D. Moody Smith, *John among the Gospels* (2d ed.; Columbia, S.C.: University of South Carolina Press, 2001), 195–241, "John, an Independent Gospel."

Chapter 6: John's Portrait of Jesus

1. This typology was suggested to Robert A. Spivey and me by a former teacher, Paul W. Meyer, then of Yale Divinity School. Simple though it is, it nicely and rather fully comprehends the Gospels' portrayal of Jesus (see *Anatomy of the New Testament: A Guide to Its Structure and Meaning* [6th ed.; Upper Saddle River, N.J.: Prentice Hall, 2007], 187–238.).

2. Such nomenclature, as applied to miracles, is not entirely foreign to the Synoptic Gospels (Mark 8:11–13; Matt 12:38–39), Acts (2:22), or even the Old Testament (Exod 4:8–9, 17). In the Synoptics, of course, Jesus rejects the desire to see legitimating signs. Precisely such signs are offered in the Fourth Gospel.

3. A view not accepted, or at least not assumed, by Rudolf Bultmann (*The Gospel of John: A Commentary* [trans. G. R. Beasley-Murray, R. W. N. Hoare, and J. K. Riches; Philadelphia: Westminster, 1971], 119 n. 2). Bultmann appears to question whether the historicity of the signs was important to the evangelist.

4. See, for example, the proposal of Oscar Cullmann, which introduces an element of speculation, or so it seems to me, into the otherwise well-argued presentation of his case (*The Johannine Circle* [trans. J. Bowden; Philadelphia: Westminster, 1976], 93–94).

5. Contrast, for example, James 2. Although the author of James is not using the vocabulary of love, most of his examples would fit the exhortations of 1 John 4:7–12, 16–21.

6. On this point I agree with the perspective of Ernst Käsemann, without necessarily endorsing his general view of the death of Jesus in John's Gospel and Johannine theology (*The Testament of Jesus: A Study of the Gospel in the Light of Chapter 17* [trans. Gerhard Krodel; Philadelphia: Fortress, 1968], 19).

7. This is the viewpoint of Hans Windisch who answers, "Ersetzen" (*Johannes und die Synoptiker: Wollte der vierte Evangelist die älterer Evangelien ergänzen oder ersetzen?* [Untersuchungen zum Neuen Testament 12; Leipzig: Hinrich, 1926]). It is also the position of E. C. Colwell, who argues that John seeks to allay objections about Jesus among readers offended by aspects of the synoptic portrayal (*John Defends the Gospel* [Chicago: Willett, Clark, 1936]).

8. Here the seminal work has been P. Gardner-Smith's *Saint John and the Synoptic Gospels*, a slim volume whose size belies its importance (Cambridge: Cambridge University Press, 1938). An impressive array of scholars, including Bultmann, C. H. Dodd, and Raymond E. Brown, has come to share substantially his position. But by no means all agree; C. K. Barrett and Werner Georg Kümmel, among others, remain unconvinced.

9. It was perhaps canonized "through man's error and God's providence." See Käsemann, *Testament of Jesus*, 75.

10. The most significant source theory is still that of Bultmann, *Gospel of John*, passim. Cf. my article "The Sources of the Gospel of John: An Assessment of the Present State of the Problem," *New Testament Studies* 10 (1963–64): 336–51, and book, *The Composition and Order of the Fourth Gospel: Bultmann's Literary Theory* (New Haven: Yale University Press, 1965). Bultmann discerned *semeia* (sign), revelation, and passion sources, among others, in the Gospel. Some more recent source-critical work, while less comprehensive than Bultmann's, is methodologically better grounded. Robert T. Fortna's *The Gospel of Signs: A Reconstruction of the Narrative Source Underlying the Fourth Gospel* is a painstakingly careful and yet bold effort in an area where source criticism is most likely to prove fruitful, that is, the Johannine narratives (Society for New Testament Monograph Series 11; Cambridge: Cambridge University Press, 1970).

11. Certainly the leading proponent of this position has been J. Louis Martyn, *History and Theology in the Fourth Gospel* (3d ed.; Louisville, Ky.: Westminster John Knox, 2003). Before 1966 Raymond E. Brown saw the importance of expulsion from the synagogue as an issue in determining the date and provenance of the Fourth Gospel (see his *The Gospel according to John (i–xii)* [Anchor Bible 29; Garden City, N.Y.: Doubleday, 1966], lxx–lxxv, lxxxv). Fortna's source theory (n. 10, above) is, of course, tied to Martyn's overall view of Johannine origins. The Gospel of Signs is the first gospel produced by the Christians who eventually gave us the Fourth Gospel. Certainly his source-critical work has not been carried out in isolation from other necessary historical considerations.

12. This insistence is implicit in the narrative gospel form itself. On the significance of this point see the sophisticated discussion of Franz Mussner, *The Historical Jesus in the Gospel of St. John* (trans. W. J. O'Hara; New York: Herder & Herder, 1967).

13. The view that he did not is, I believe, essentially correct and compelling, although certainly not universally shared. Cf. the view of Cullmann, *The Johannine Circle*, and the perspective of Leon Morris, *The Gospel according to John: The English Text with Introduction, Exposition, and Notes* (New International Commentary on the New Testament; Grand Rapids, Mich.: Eerdmans, 1971), esp. 45ff. Morris also has recourse to the theory of a private, more esoteric teaching found principally in John.

14. Gnosticism and Qumran frequently figure in discussions of Johannine origins as if they necessarily represented mutually exclusive alternatives, although they do not, as Bultmann already saw. In fact, he claimed that the discovery of the Dead Sea Scrolls supported, rather than refuted, his view of the gnostic antecedents of the Fourth Gospel. See *Theology of the New Testament*, vol. 2 (trans. Kendrick Grobel; New York: Scribner's, 1955), 13; cf. his *Gospel of John*, 23 n. 1. A representative collection of essays on John and Qumran is to be found in a book edited by James H. Charlesworth, *The Dead See Scrolls* (New York: Crossroad, 1990). The gnostic position is not so well represented in the English literature on John, although one may with profit consult, for a

judiciously sympathetic but critical presentation, Rudolf Schnackenburg (*The Gospel according to St. John* [trans. Kevin Smyth; New York: Herder & Herder, 1968], 1.135–52, 543–57). A recent statement of the case for the gnostic origin and, indeed, character of John is Luise Schottroff, *Der Glaubende und die feindliche Welt: Beobachtungen zum gnostischen Dualismus und seiner Bedeutung für Paulus und das Johannesevangelium* (Wissenschaftliche Monographien zum Alten und Neuen Testament 37; Neukirchen-Vluyn: Neukirchener Verlag, 1970).

15. Cf. Wayne A. Meeks, "The Man from Heaven in Johannine Sectarianism," *Journal of Biblical Literature* 91 (1972): 44–72.

16. Martyn does not in his two-level theory about the Johannine episodes emphasize what he calls their *einmalig* dimension, concentrating rather on the later level in which the church-synagogue dispute is reflected. Without unwarrantedly ascribing to him any views on the historicity of the incidents recounted, it is fair to say that on his terms the basic narratives could have been, and presumably were, regarded by the Johannine Christians as accounts of Jesus' actual deeds.

17. To give some obvious examples: It is only the high priest who decides and decrees that Jesus must die, when other Jewish leaders are uncertain what to do about him (11:50); a cohort of (Roman) soldiers participates in Jesus' arrest (18:3); there is in John no account of a trial and condemnation before the Sanhedrin; although it is said that Pilate wished to release Jesus, it is finally he who orders him crucified (19:16, 19–22) and takes responsibility for the execution (19:31, 38); finally, (Roman) soldiers crucify Jesus (19:23 passim).

18. On the Spirit-inspired character of Johannine Christianity and the Johannine community, see George Johnston, *The Spirit-Paraclete in the Gospel of John* (Society for New Testament Monograph Series 12; Cambridge: Cambridge University Press, 1970), esp. 127–48; also Käsemann, *Testament of Jesus,* esp. 36ff.; and Alv Kragerud, *Der Liebingsjünger im Johannesevangelium: Ein exegetischer Versuch* (Oslo: Osloer Universitätsverlag, 1959), esp. 93–112.

19. On Jesus and the Paraclete see Raymond E. Brown, "The Paraclete in the Fourth Gospel," *New Testament Studies* 13 (1966–67): 113–32, esp. 126–32. Cf. also R. Alan Culpepper's interesting observations regarding the parallel functions of the Paraclete and the Beloved Disciple, *The Johannine School: An Evaluation of the Johannine-School Hypothesis Based on an Investigation of the Nature of Ancient Schools* (Society for Biblical Literature Dissertation Series 26; Missoula, Mont.: Scholars Press, 1975), 267–70.

20. Needless to say, however, John has his unique style, vocabulary, and emphases. John's Gospel is in some significant ways a strange and different book. Yet the main lines of his presentation of Jesus seem to be positively related to, even if they are not derived directly from, the portrayal of him which we find in the Synoptics and in other New Testament writings. Edwyn Clement Hoskyns wrote: "The test that we must in the end apply to the Fourth Gospel, the test by which the Fourth Gospel stands or falls, is whether the Marcan narrative becomes more intelligible after reading the Fourth Gospel, whether the Pauline Epistles become more transparent, or whether the whole material presented to us in the New Testament is breaking up into unrelated fragments" (*The Fourth Gospel* [ed. F. N. Davey; London: Faber & Faber, 1947], 133). This test is ultimately theological and cannot finally depend solely upon exegetical conclusions pro or con about literary and historical relationships. It is the question of whether John's presence in the canon makes theological sense.

21. For a balanced presentation of the significance of Jesus' death in John, see J. T. Forestell, *The Word of the Cross: Salvation as Revelation in the Fourth Gospel* (Analecta biblica 57; Rome: Pontifical Biblical Institute, 1974).

22. " I am accustomed to say that this Gospel is a key to open the door for understanding the rest; for whoever shall understand the power of Christ, as it is here strikingly portrayed, will afterwards read with advantage what the others relate about the Redeemer who was manifested" (John Calvin, *Commentary on the Gospel according to John* [trans. W. Pringle; Edinburgh: Calvin Translation Society, 1847], 22).

23. Käsemann, *Testament of Jesus,* 26, 66, 70.

Chapter 7: Jesus Tradition in the Gospel of John

1. See Andrew T. Lincoln, "The Beloved Disciple as Eyewitness and the Fourth Gospel as Witness," *Journal for the Study of the New Testament* 35 (2002): 3–26. Lincoln has been a colleague in the Society of Biblical Literature Consultation, "John, Jesus, and History," presided over by Tom Thatcher, who with Robert T. Fortna has edited a volume of seminal essays, *Jesus in Johannine Tradition* (Louisville, Ky.: Westminster John Knox, 2001). To these and other participants I am indebted for their stimulation and criticism. My thanks also to colleagues E. P. Sanders and J. Louis Martyn, who read and commented helpfully on an earlier version of this essay, as well as to my research assistant Kavin Rowe, who read it meticulously at several stages. They have saved me from embarrassing errors. Needless to say, I am responsible for its final form, as well as for the translation of most of the New Testament quotations.

2. P. Gardner-Smith, *Saint John and the Synoptic Gospels* (Cambridge: Cambridge University Press, 1938).

3. Albert Schweitzer, *The Quest of the Historical Jesus* (trans. and ed. John Bowden and others from the "First Complete Edition" of the German, *Geschichte der Leben-Jesu-Forschung* [Tübingen: Mohr, 1913]; Minneapolis: Fortress, 2001), 80–83.

4. Schweitzer, *Quest,* 59–64, on Friedrich Schleiermacher; also Schleiermacher, *The Christian Faith* (ed. H. R. Macintosh and J. S. Stewart; Edinburgh: T&T Clark, 1928), 85, 474, who takes John 10:30 to be an authentic statement of Jesus.

5. Ernst Käsemann, *The Testament of Jesus: A Study of the Gospel of John in the Light of Chapter 17* (trans. Gerhard Krodel; Philadelphia: Fortress, 1968), 9, n. 6, in which he attributes the imagery to F. C. Baur.

6. John Dominic Crossan, *The Historical Jesus: The Life of a Mediterranean Jewish Peasant* (New York: HarperSanFrancisco, 1991); E. P. Sanders, *Jesus and Judaism* (Philadelphia: Fortress, 1985) and *The Historical Figure of Jesus* (London: Penguin, 1993).

7. N. T. Wright, *Jesus and the Victory of God* (vol. 2 of *Christian Origins and the Question of God;* Minneapolis: Fortress, 1996); Gerd Theissen and Annette Merz, *The Historical Jesus: A Comprehensive Guide* (trans. John Bowden; Minneapolis: Fortress, 1998); James D. G. Dunn, *Jesus Remembered* (vol. 1 of *Christianity in the Making;* Grand Rapids, Mich.: Eerdmans, 2003).

8. Wright, *Jesus,* xvi.

9. Paula Fredriksen, *Jesus of Nazareth, King of the Jews: A Jewish Life and the Emergence of Christianity* (New York: Knopf, 2000); John P. Meier, *A Marginal Jew: Rethinking the Historical Jesus* (vols. 1–3; New York: Doubleday, 1991–94; vol. 4 forthcoming).

10. Raymond E. Brown, *The Death of the Messiah: From Gethsemane to the Grave* (2 vols.; New York: Doubleday, 1994).

11. C. H. Dodd's work, *Historical Tradition in the Fourth Gospel* (Cambridge: Cambridge University Press, 1963), appeared forty-five years ago. It was followed by John A. T. Robinson, *The Priority of John* (London: SCM, 1985), and Craig L. Blomberg, *The Historical Reliability of John's Gospel: Issues and Commentary* (Downers Grove, Ill.: InterVarsity Press, 2001). Blomberg begins by citing Maurice Casey's rejection of the historical value of John in *Is John's Gospel True?* (London: Routledge, 1996) and continues with the Jesus Seminar's similar negative position (17–18). He disputes such negative findings in almost every case. There have been, of course, other studies dealing with historical issues in John.

12. See D. Moody Smith, *The Theology of the Gospel of John* (New Testament Theology; Cambridge: Cambridge University Press, 1995), 173–82, esp. 174–76.

13. J. Louis Martyn, *History and Theology in the Fourth Gospel* (3d ed.; Louisville, Ky.: Westminster John Knox, 2003).

14. D. Moody Smith, *John among the Gospels* (2d ed.; Columbia, S.C.: University of South Carolina Press, 2001), 203. Cf. on criteria Meier, *The Roots of the Problem and the Person* (vol. 1 of *A Marginal Jew;* New York: Doubleday, 1991), 167–95.

15. William Wrede, *Das Messiasgeheimnis in den Evangelien: Zugleich ein Beitrag zum Verständnis des Markusevangelium* (Göttingen: Vandenhoeck & Ruprecht, 1963; unaltered from the 1st ed. of 1901), 101, in which, typically, Wrede emphasizes how the purpose and work of the evangelist Mark should take precedence over historical questions about Jesus. The English translation, *The Messianic Secret* (trans. J. C. G. Greig; Cambridge: Clark, 1971), came seventy years after the work's original publication, a tribute to its enduring importance.

16. Fredriksen, *Jesus of Nazareth,* 34. The Marcan narrative sequence is basic to both Matthew and Luke, although other ancient narratives may have existed.

17. Fredriksen stresses that the Johannine pattern of Jesus' alternation between Galilee and Jerusalem is historically plausible. It would have been normal for a Jewish male to attend the great festivals, and necessary given Jesus' own mission. See *Jesus of Nazareth,* esp. 238–41; cf. 219–20, 244, 251–59.

18. *Mentor, Message and Miracles* (vol. 2 of *A Marginal Jew;* New York: Doubleday, 1994), 116–17.

19. *Companions and Competitors* (vol. 3 of *A Marginal Jew;* New York: Doubleday, 2001), 222.

20. Rudolf Bultmann, *The Gospel of John: A Commentary* (trans. G. R. Beasley-Murray, R. W. N. Hoare, and J. K. Riches; Philadelphia. Westminster, 1971), 108. For an intriguing proposal about the interrelationship of John and Jesus, see Francis J. Moloney, "The Fourth Gospel and the Jesus of History," *New Testament Studies* 46 (2000): 42–58.

21. Meier, *The Roots of the Problem,* 168–71.

22. Wilhelm Schneemelcher, ed., *The Gospels and Related Writings* (vol. 1 of *New Testament Apocrypha,* trans. R. McL. Wilson; Louisville, Ky.: Westminster John Knox, 1991), 160, 169.

23. See John Painter, *The Quest for The Messiah: The History, Literature and Theology of the Johannine Community* (2d ed.; Nashville: Abingdon, 1993), 259–67, for a good discussion of John 6:1–21, and particularly of the meaning of the titles prophet and king in 6:14–15, which Painter regards as "pre-crucifixion" (262). He adds that such an

overtly political motif would not have been added by John or his (Christian) tradition (216). Dodd, *Historical Tradition*, 216–17, had made a similar same case for its antiquity.

24. Wrede, *Messiasgeheimnis*, 179–206.

25. Possible links between the Gospels of *Thomas* and John are discussed by Helmut Koester, *Ancient Christian Gospels: Their History and Development* (Philadelphia: Trinity Press International, 1990), 133–24; cf. Koester, *History and Literature of Early Christianity* (2d rev. ed.; New York: Walter de Gruyter, 2000), 184–85. Koester is careful to point out that the Gospels of *Thomas* and John share a common genre and tradition, without claiming a literary relationship. James H. Charlesworth, *The Beloved Disciple: Whose Witness Validates the Fourth Gospel?* (Valley Forge: Trinity Press International, 1995), contends that the Beloved Disciple is Thomas, but also holds that the antecedents and milieux of the Gospels of John and *Thomas* are closely related (360–89).

26. Meier, *The Roots of the Problem*, 45; also 53, n. 22. In general, Meier is more optimistic about identifying a historical basis of the Johannine miracle stories or traditions than is Michael Labahn, the author of the most thorough study of the Johannine miracle narratives, *Jesus als Lebensspender: Untersuchungen zu einer Geschichte der johanneischen Tradition anhand ihrer Wundergeschichten* (Beihefte zur Zeitschrift für die neutestamentliche Wissenschaft 98; Berlin: de Gruyter, 1999), 466: "Solcher historischer Kern im Leben des historischen Jesus lässt sich m. E für keine der im vierte Evangelium berichteten Wundererzählungen festmachen."

27. Meier, *Mentor Message, and Miracles*, 908–14 (on 6:16–21), 934–49 (on 2:1–11).

28. Ibid., 698.

29. Ibid., 822–31.

30. Ibid., 832–37.

31. On Jesus' family relations in John, whether stated or implied, see Sjef van Tilborg, *Imaginative Love in John* (Biblical Interpretation Series 2; Leiden: Brill, 1993).

32. Raymond E. Brown, *The Birth of the Messiah: A Commentary on the Infancy Narratives in Matthew and Luke* (Garden City, N.Y.: Doubleday 1977), 515–16, remains more tentative in his approach, but grants that evidence for Jesus' birth in Bethlehem is not strong.

33. Joel Marcus, *Mark 1–8: A New Translation with Introduction and Commentary* (Anchor Bible; New York: Doubleday, 2000), 269–71.

34. Dodd, *Historical Tradition in the Fourth Gospel*, 152–73.

35. See Painter, *Quest for the Messiah*, 376–77. As Painter observes, the quest of the Greeks remains unfulfilled. Yet the quest motif appears, quite significantly, at this turning point, when the hour of Jesus' glorification is announced as having arrived.

36. Helmut Koester, "Geschichte und Kultus im Johannesevangelium und bei Ignatius von Antiochen," *Zeitschrift für Theologie und Kirche* 54 (1957): 56–69, esp. 62ff., recognizes this, although he agrees with Bultmann in assigning 6:51c–58 to later redaction.

37. In an important study of the Lucan version of the Sanhedrin episode (22:66–71), David R. Catchpole, *The Trial of Jesus: A Study in the Gospels and Jewish Historiography from 1970 to the Present Day* (Studia Post-biblica 18; Leiden: Brill, 1971), 183–220, decides in favor of a common tradition or source; so also Hans Klein, "Die Lukanisch-johanneische Passionstradition," *Zeitschrift für die neutestamentliche Wissenschaft und die Kunde der älteren Kirche* 67 (1976): 155–86. For a persuasive case that Luke is somehow influenced by the Johannine narrative, see Mark A. Matson, *In Dialogue with*

Another Gospel: The Influence of the Fourth Gospel on the Passion Narrative of the Gospel of Luke (Society of Biblical Literature Dissertation Series 178; Atlanta: Society of Biblical literature, 2001). The starting point of Matson's research was the observation of F. Lamar Cribbs, "St. Luke and the Johannine Tradition," *Journal of Biblical Literature* 90 (1971): 422–50, that Luke's departures from Mark coincide with instances where John either contradicts Mark or is clearly different.

38. As Fredriksen acutely observes, *Jesus of Nazareth,* 223.

39. See John Donahue, *Are You the Christ? The Trial Narrative in the Gospel of Mark* (Society of Biblical Literature Dissertation Series 10; Missoula, Mont.: Scholars Press, 1973).

40. Contra Norman Perrin and John Donahue, who take this position, Robert T. Fortna, "Jesus and Peter at the High Priest's House: A Test Case for the Question of the Relation Between Mark's and John's Gospels," *New Testament Studies* 24 (1977–78): 371–83, shows that this is not necessarily the case.

41. On this issue see the fuller discussion in D. Moody Smith, *John among the Gospels* (2d ed.; Columbia, S.C.: University of South Carolina Press, 2001), 222–24. Also, see Martin Hasitschka, "Beobachtungen zu Chronologie und Topographie der Passionsgeschichte nach Johannes," in *Für und Wider die Priorität des Johannesevangeliums* (ed. Peter Leander Hofrichter; Theologische Texte und Studien 9; Hildesheim: Georg Olms, 2002), 151–59, esp. 154.

42. Meier, *The Roots of the Problem,* 390–401.

43. Ibid., 396.

44. Ibid., 396–97.

45. Pointed out by Günther Bornkamm, *Jesus of Nazareth* (trans. Irene and Fraser McLuskey with James M. Robinson; London: Hodder and Stoughton, 1960), 161–62.

46. See Meier, *The Roots of the Problem,* 1. 428–29, n. 108.

47. Raymond E. Brown, *The Gospel According to John* (2 vols.; Anchor Bible 29, 29A; Garden City, N.Y.: Doubleday, 1966, 1972), 555–56, as well as Brown's *The Death of The Messiah,* 1350–78, esp. 1373.

48. Cited from Morris Goldstein, *Jesus in the Jewish Tradition* (New York: Macmillan, 1950), 22.

49. In her March 17, 2004, Kenneth W. Clark Lecture at Duke Divinity School, entitled "Jesus as Passover Lamb: A Case of Mistaken Identity," Marianne Meye Thompson argued that the Gospel of John does not actually identify Jesus with the Passover lamb, but that this is an interpretive misconstrual of John's references to a lamb.

50. See Gordon D. Fee, *The First Epistle to the Corinthians* (New International Commentary on the New Testament; Grand Rapids, Mich.: Eerdmans, 1987), 103–4, who cites Gene Miller, "ARCHONTŌN TOU AIŌNOS TOUTOU—A New Look at 1 Corinthians 2:6–8," *Journal of Biblical Literature* 91 (1972): 522–28. Also see Richard B. Hays, *First Corinthians* (Interpretation; Louisville, Ky.: John Knox, 1997), 44, who notes the importance of 2:6 as well.

51. Hays, *First Corinthians,* 197.

52. Charlesworth, *Beloved Disciple,* argues that Thomas (John 20:25) wants to see Jesus' side, the lance wound, as well as his hands, because he, and he alone, knows of the lance wound, since he observed it (422–24). He was standing by the cross with Jesus' mother; he is the disciple whom Jesus loved (19:26).

53. On evidence for a continuous narrative in the double tradition (Q) of Matthew and Luke, see Stephen Hultgren, *Narrative Elements in the Double Tradition: A Study of*

their Place within the Framework of the Gospel Narrative (Beihefte zur Zeitschrift für die neutestamentliche Wissenschaft 113; Berlin: Walter de Gruyter, 2002), esp. 350–54. That the Gospel of John developed on the basis of an earlier narrative has been argued by many, notably Robert T. Fortna, who discerns a more primitive Gospel of Signs underlying the present, canonical text. See *The Fourth Gospel and Its Predecessor: From Narrative Source to Present Gospel* (Philadelphia: Fortress, 1988), in which he maintains and refines the position set forth in his earlier monograph, *The Gospel of Signs: A Reconstruction of the Narrative Source Underlying the Fourth Gospel* (Society for New Testament Studies Monograph Series 11: Cambridge: Cambridge University Press, 1970). Yet Gilbert Van Belle, *The Signs Source in the Fourth Gospel* (Bibliotheca ephemeridum theologicarum lovaniensium 116; Leuven: Leuven University Press, 1994), remains unconvinced.

54. See J. F. Coakley, "The Anointing at Bethany and the Priority of John," *Journal of Biblical Literature* 10 (1988): 241–56.

55. E. P. Sanders, *The Tendencies of the Synoptic Tradition* (Society for New Testament Studies Monograph Series 9; Cambridge: Cambridge University Press, 1969), 88–189, examines "Increasing Detail as a Possible Tendency of the Tradition" and sees no clear direction among the Synoptic Gospels. Sometimes details such as proper names are added, but sometimes they are dropped. He does, however, find that in patristic and apocryphal writings there is a tendency to assign proper names to figures who in the Synoptics are anonymous (145, 189). The question of where John would belong cannot be treated here. See D. Moody Smith, "The Problem of John and the Synoptics in Light of the Relation between Apocryphal and Canonical Gospels," in *John and the Synoptics* (ed. Adelbert Denaux; Bibliotheca ephemeridum theologicarum lovaniensium 101; Leuven: Leuven University Press, 1992), 147–62.

56. See Bultmann, *Gospel of John*, 84–97, esp. 85–86.

57. See W. F. Albright, "Recent Discoveries in Palestine and the Gospel of St. John," in *The Background of the New Testament and its Eschatology: In Honour of Charles Harold Dodd* (ed. W. D. Davies and D. Daube; Cambridge: Cambridge University Press, 1956), 153–71; also Martin Hengel, "Das Johannesevangelium als Quelle für die Geschichte des antiken Judentums," in *Judaica, Hellenistica et Christiana: Kleine Schriften II* (ed. Jörg Frey, Dorothea Betz, et al.; Tübingen: Mohr-Siebeck, 1999), 293–34. Both Albright and Hengel note John's apparent knowledge of ancient sites and the Gospel's Jewish context. One must now consult also the most recent canvassing of archaeological evidence in James H. Charlesworth, ed., *Jesus and Archaeology* (Grand Rapids, Mich.: Eerdmans, 2006). Of particular relevance are the articles pertaining specifically to John's Gospel by Urban von Wahlde (523–86) and Paul N. Anderson (587–618).

58. See D. Moody Smith, "John," in *Early Christian Thought in its Jewish Context* (Cambridge: Cambridge University Press, 1996), 96–111, which appears as chapter 2, above.

59. Precedent for this sort of ranking may be found E. P. Sanders, *Jesus and Judaism*, 326–27. Sanders is, of course, focusing upon the historical Jesus as presented principally by the Synoptic Gospels.

60. On Jesus tradition in Paul, see Dale C. Allison, "The Pauline Epistles and the Synoptic Gospels: The Pattern of the Parallels," *New Testament Studies* 28 (1982): 1–32.

61. As Martyn pointed out, *History and Theology,* 140.

62. On this point see the important article of Theo K. Heckel, "Die Historisierung der johanneischen Theologie im Ersten Johannesbrief," *New Testament Studies* 50 (2004): 425–43, esp. 440–43. On the relationship between history and Spirit inspiration in the Gospel of John, see Robert G. Hall, *Revealed History: Techniques for Ancient Jewish and Christian Historiography* (Journal for the Study of the Pseudepigrapha: Supplement Series 6; Sheffield: Sheffield Academic Press, 1991), esp. 209–36.

Chapter 8: Redaction Criticism, Genre, Narrative Criticism, and the Historical Jesus in the Gospel of John

1. Hans Windisch, *Johannes und die Synoptiker: Wollte der vierte Evangelist die älteren Evangelien ergänzen oder ersetzen?* (Untersuchungen zum Neuen Testament 12; Leipzig: Hinrich, 1926), quotes John 10:8 on the back of the title page, along with 2 Cor 5:16, both in the original Greek (perhaps to avoid offending the innocent lay reader).

2. P. Gardner-Smith, *Saint John and the Synoptic Gospels* (Cambridge: Cambridge University Press, 1938).

3. This is the bottom line of Frans Neirynck's arguments, originally set forth in his article "John and the Synoptics" in *L'Evangile de Jean: Sources, rédaction, théologie* (ed. M. de Jonge; Bibliotheca ephemeridum theologicarum lovaniensium 44; Louvain: Louvain University Press, 1977), 73–106. This essay, delivered as a paper at a Louvain conference, was intended to renew the debate on John and the Synoptics in the face of a consensus on the Fourth Gospel's independence. It succeeded in doing so.

4. See Bultmann's *The Gospel of John: A Commentary* (trans. G. R. Beasley-Murray, R. W. N. Hoare, and J. K. Riches; Philadelphia: Westminster, 1971), 83–97, esp. 84–85.

5. See D. Moody Smith, Jr., *The Composition and Order of the Fourth Gospel: Bultmann's Literary Theory* (Yale Publications in Religion 10; New Haven: Yale University Press, 1965), 119–25, esp. 124.

6. Bultmann, *Gospel of John,* 108; cf. Smith, *Composition and Order,* 1.

7. See D. Moody Smith, *John among the Gospels* (2d ed.; Columbia, S.C.: University of South Carolina Press, 2001), 205–7.

8. Maurice Casey, *Is John's Gospel True?* (London: Routledge, 1996); cf. Smith, *John among the Gospels,* 234–35.

9. See Smith, *John among the Gospels,* 216–19.

10. Ibid., 204.

11. See the fundamental work of Richard A. Burridge, *What Are the Gospels? A Comparison with Graeco-Roman Biography* (Society for New Testament Studies Monograph Series 70; Cambridge: Cambridge University Press, 1992), whose survey of ancient documents and modern scholarship is comprehensive. On the gospel genre, see below, chapter 11 ("The Question of Gospel Genre").

12. That the Gospels were composed out of traditional units or narratives (the passion) does not run counter to the perception of ancient readers that they were *bioi* (lives). Did the evangelists intend to write *bioi?* Obviously, this is too big a question to be discussed here. Luke obviously intended to meet contemporary expectations of literate readers, personified by Theophilus, who is portrayed as a believer.

13. A simple point, but one well made and emphasized by Paula Fredriksen, *Jesus of Nazareth, King of the Jews: A Jewish Life and the Emergence of Christianity* (New York: Knopf, 2000), 34.

14. See especially Price's *Three Gospels* (New York: Scribner's, 1996), 17: "Yet a strong argument can easily be made that Mark—whoever he may have been (and we have no

other sure work from his hand)—is the most original narrative writer in history, an apparently effortless sovereign of all the skills and arts of durable storytelling." In a notable essay on Mark in the same volume (37–84), Price also maintains (38) that "Mark has proved the most influential of human books. All other books from four thousand years of epics, plays, lyrics, and biographies have touched human life less potently."

15. Ernst Käsemann, *The Testament of Jesus: A Study of the Gospel of John in the Light of Chapter 17* (trans. Gerhard Krodel; Philadelphia: Fortress, 1968), 9, n. 6, in which he attributes the imagery to F. C. Baur.

16. The classic work of a couple of generations ago, C. H. Dodd's, *The Apostolic Preaching and its Developments* (New York: Harper, 1936), is no longer discussed and probably not much read, but it suggests a line of development from the initial preaching to the appearance of gospels that is plausible if not demonstrable.

17. See Richard B. Hays, *The Faith of Jesus Christ: The Narrative Substructure of Galatians 3:1–4:11* (2d ed.; Grand Rapids, Mich.: Eerdmans, 2002), 33–34, 209 ("Christstory"), 218–20, 274. Hays suggests that Paul represents an early stage in a process that eventually led to the Gospel narratives (218–20), and cites Dodd (218).

18. Albert Schweitzer, *The Quest of the Historical Jesus* (trans. and ed. John Bowden and others, as the "First Complete Edition" of the German, *Geschichte der Leben-Jesu-Forschung;* Minneapolis: Fortress, 2001), 80–83; cf. also 59–64. (The original German second edition appeared in 1913.)

19. E. P. Sanders, *Jesus and Judaism* (Philadelphia: Fortress, 1985); also *The Historical Figure of Jesus* (London: Penguin, 1993).

20. John Dominic Crossan, *The Historical Jesus: The Life of a Mediterranean Jewish Peasant* (New York: HarperSanFrancisco, 1991); N. T. Wright, *Jesus and the Victory of God* (vol. 2 of *Christian Origins and the Question of God;* Minneapolis: Fortress, 1996). See also Gerd Theissen and Annette Merz, *The Historical Jesus: A Comprehensive Guide* (trans. John Bowden; Minneapolis: Fortress, 1998); James D. G. Dunn, *Jesus Remembered* (vol. 1 of *Christianity in the Making;* Grand Rapids, Mich.: Eerdmans, 2003).

21. Fredriksen, *Jesus of Nazareth;* John P. Meier, *A Marginal Jew: Rethinking the Historical Jesus* (vols. 1–3; New York: Doubleday, 1991–2001; vol. 4 forthcoming); Raymond E. Brown, *The Death of the Messiah: From Gethsemane to the Grave* (2 vols.; New York: Doubleday, 1994).

22. C. H. Dodd, *Historical Tradition in the Fourth Gospel* (Cambridge: Cambridge University Press, 1963) was, of course, inspired by Gardner-Smith, *Saint John and the Synoptic Gospels,* cited by Dodd (8, n. 2). Gardner-Smith was mentioned by Dodd already in his *Interpretation of the Fourth Gospel* (Cambridge: Cambridge University Press, 1953), 449, n. 2.

23. J. Louis Martyn, *History and Theology in the Fourth Gospel* (3d ed.; Louisville: Westminster John Knox, 2003). Martyn's exact reconstruction is still much debated, but his situating the Gospel's origin within Judaism is now widely accepted.

24. In an important study of the Lucan version of the Sanhedrin episode (22:66–71), David R. Catchpole, *The Trial of Jesus: A Study in the Gospels and Jewish Historiography from 1970 to the Present Day* (Studia Post-biblica 18; Leiden: Brill, 1971), 183–220, decides in favor of a common tradition or source; so also Hans Klein, "Die Lukanischjohanneische Passionstradition," *Zeitschrift für die neutestamentliche Wissenschaft und die Kunde der älteren Kirche* 67 (1976): 155–86. But for a persuasive case that Luke is somehow influenced by the Johannine narrative, see Mark A. Matson, *In Dialogue with*

Another Gospel: The Influence of the Fourth Gospel on the Passion Narrative of the Gospel of Luke (Society of Biblical Literature Dissertation Series 178; Atlanta: Society of Biblical Literature, 2001). The starting point of Matson's research was the observation of F. Lamar Cribbs, "St. Luke and the Johannine Tradition," *Journal of Biblical Literature* 90 (1971): 422–50, that Luke's departures from Mark coincide with instances where John either contradicts Mark or is clearly different. Did Luke know a Johannine narrative tradition, if not the Gospel on its present form?

25. Helmut Koester, *Ancient Christian Gospels: Their History and Development* (Philadelphia: Trinity Press International, 1990), 24–31.

26. Since this article was originally composed, I have become acquainted with the works of Richard Bauckham, who has recently published two volumes that bear directly on the question under discussion, namely, the value of the Gospel of John for knowledge of the historical Jesus. In *Jesus and the Eyewitnesses: The Gospel of Eyewitness Testimony* (Grand Rapids, Mich.: Eerdmans, 2006), Bauckham considers John alongside the Synoptics, giving proportionally more attention to the Fourth Gospel than to the others (358–471). He also devotes considerable effort to the presentation, assimilation, and evaluation of the nature of memory and its relation to the transmission of tradition and historical knowledge in antiquity. Obviously, he goes far beyond the suggestions about memory made above. *The Testimony of the Beloved Disciple: Narrative, History, and Theology in the Gospel of John* (Grand Rapids, Mich.: Baker Academic, 2007) is a collection of Bauckham's essays on the Fourth Gospel, but it is more than that. Taken as a whole, it is a programmatic statement of the author's thesis and argument, the crux of which is embodied in the title. If one were to infer from these essays that Bauckham believes that the Johannine community of scholarship has largely gone off the rails, that would not be wrong. He proposes to set it right by paying close attention to the Gospel's own data and claims and by canvassing and assessing the considerable body of evidence bearing on this Gospel in patristic sources. This has not been done in a long time, and perhaps never as thoroughly, and with such penetrating critical insight. That Bauckham has a thesis to set out and defend makes his book all the more interesting and important.

Chapter 9: The Historical Figure of Jesus in 1 John

1. John P. Meier, *A Marginal Jew: Rethinking the Historical Jesus,* 3 vols. (New York: Doubleday, 1991–2001); Paula Fredriksen, *Jesus of Nazareth, King of the Jews: A Jewish Life and the Emergence of Christianity* (New York: Knopf, 2000).

2. D. Moody Smith, "Jesus Tradition in the Gospel of John," in *Handbook of the Study of the Historical Jesus* (4 vols.; Leiden: Brill, forthcoming). This essay appears as chapter 7 above.

3. The designation "the historical figure of Jesus" is adopted from E. P. Sanders, *The Historical Figure of Jesus* (London: Penguin, 1993), because it is, in my view, more suitable and less ambiguous than "the historical Jesus." The author of 1 John did not write with the historical Jesus, as moderns may reconstruct or construe him, in view. But he did have in view a historical figure, as much as his conception of him may have differed from any modern reconstruction or construal.

4. In chronological order Raymond E. Brown, *The Epistles of John* (Anchor Bible 30; Garden City, N.Y.; Doubleday, 1982), 131–46; Rudolf Schnackenburg, *The Johannine Epistles* (trans. Reginald and Ilse Fuller; New York: Crossroad, 1992), 303–16, esp. 309–13; Georg Strecker, *The Johannine Letters* (trans. Linda Mahoney; ed. Harold

Attridge; Hermeneia; Minneapolis: Fortress, 1996), xxi–xxvi; John Painter, *1, 2, and 3 John* (Sacra Pagina; Collegeville, Minn.: Liturgical Press, 2002), 108–13. Quite recently, however, there has been an important article bearing directly on the subject: Theo K. Heckel, "Die Historisierung der johanneischen Theologie in Ersten Johannesbrief," *New Testament Studies* 50 (2004): 425–43. Heckel's article, although different from mine, is grounded in the same interest and insight. See also my "John's Quest for Jesus," chapter 5, above.

5. Hans Conzelmann, "'Was von Aufang war,'" in *Neutestamentliche Studien für Rudolf Bultmann* (ed. W. Eltester; Beihefte zur Zeitschrift für die neutestamentliche Wissenschaft 21; Berlin: Töpelmann, 1957), 194–201; esp. the formulation on 201.

6. Ernst Käsemann once addressed this problem eloquently. "But if John felt himself under constraint to compose a Gospel rather than letters or a collection of sayings, Bultmann's argument is revealed as very one-sided. For it seems to me that if one has no interest in the historical Jesus, then one does not write a Gospel, but, on the contrary, finds the Gospel form inadequate." See the English-language collection of Käsemann's essays, *New Testament Questions of Today* (trans. W. J. Montague; Philadelphia: Fortress, 1969), 41. See Käsemann's *Exegetische Versuche und Besinnungen* (Göttingen: Vandenhoeck & Ruprecht, 1964), 47, for the original version of the quotation above.

7. See Marianne Meye Thompson, *The Humanity of Jesus in the Fourth Gospel* (Philadelphia: Fortress, 1988), reissued as *The Incarnate Word: Perspectives on Jesus in the Fourth Gospel* (Peabody: Mass.: Hendrickson, 1993).

8. See, for example, C. H. Dodd, *The Johannine Epistles* (Moffatt New Testament Commentary; London: Hodder and Stoughton, 1946), liii–liv. Dodd noted differences in eschatology, the concept of the atonement, and the work of the Spirit, which were much debated at the time, but have since been widely acknowledged as suggesting a later time and a different author, perhaps of more conservative tendencies, especially in relation to the Fourth Evangelist.

9. "The Jews" in quotation marks indicates that I am using the evangelist's nomenclature without prejudice to the question of who is meant by the author. It is important to note that not "all Jews" is meant, but the people so designated were Jews, as, of course was Jesus, as well as his disciples. The fundamental work remains J. Louis Martyn, *History and Theology in the Fourth Gospel* (3rd ed.; Louisville, Ky.: Westminster John Knox, 2003), of which the original edition appeared in 1968. In subsequent editions (2d ed. 1979), Martyn has taken account of criticism, but has not altered his basic views.

10. See Brown, *Epistles of John,* 32–35.

11. See chapter 2 above.

12. The definitive study remains George Johnston, *The Spirit-Paraclete in the Gospel of John* (Society for New Testament Studies Monograph Series, 12; Cambridge: Cambridge University Press, 1970), which has been published by Cambridge in paperback (2005).

13. On the existence of a Johannine community or school see R. Alan Culpepper, *The Johannine School* (Society of Biblical Literature Dissertation Series, 26; Missoula, Mont.: Scholars Press, 1975), esp. 261–99. More briefly, D. Moody Smith, *Johannine Christianity* (Columbia, S.C.: University of South Carolina Press, 1984), 1–36, esp. 9–22. This opening chapter appeared originally in *New Testament Studies* 21 (1976): 222–48.

14. The leading exponent of the antidocetic character of the Gospel of John is Udo Schnelle, *Antidocetic Christology in the Gospel of John: An Investigation of the Place of the*

Fourth Gospel in the Johannine School (trans. Linda M. Mahoney; Minneapolis: Fortress, 1992).

15. Reynolds Price, *Three Gospels* (New York: Scribner's, 1996), 17: "Yet a strong argument can be made that Mark . . . is the most original narrative writer in history, an apparently effortless sovereign of all the skills and arts of durably convincing story-telling. He is, above all, the first great master of ideal narrative distance—he stands his reader in the ideal position before his subject: The reader sees precisely enough at any moment to induce in him or her a further hunger to see more; and to the very end, that hunger is never surfeited, perhaps never sated."

16. See D. Moody Smith, *John among the Gospels* (2d ed.; Columbia, S.C.: University of South Carolina Press, 2001), chapter 8 (195–241).

17. See the seminal suggestions of Raymond E. Brown, *The Community of the Beloved Disciple* (New York: Paulist, 1979), 145–64, "Phase Four: After the Epistles Johannine Dissolution," esp. 161–62.

Chapter 10: From Synoptic Jesus to Johannine Christ

1. See, for example, the collection of his Johannine essays, *Jesus: Stranger from Heaven and Son of God, Jesus Christ and the Christians in the Johannine Perspective* (Society of Biblical Literature Sources for Biblical Study 11; Missoula, Mont.: Scholars Press, 1977); on Jesus himself, *Jesus, The Servant-Messiah* (New Haven: Yale University Press, 1991).

2. De Jonge, *Jesus, Servant-Messiah,* 2.

3. The essay, entitled "Who Are 'We'?" is found in de Jonge's *Jesus: Inspiring and Disturbing Presence* (trans. J. E. Steely; Nashville: Abingdon, 1974), 148–66. The earlier part of the essay, which concerns us here, was written in 1968 as a public lecture and published in Dutch that same year.

4. *Saint John and the Synoptic Gospels* (Cambridge: Cambridge University Press, 1938), 97.

5. C. H. Dodd, *Historical Tradition in the Fourth Gospel* (Cambridge: Cambridge University Press, 1963), 8 n. 2, refers to Gardner-Smith's work as "a book which crystallized the doubts of many [regarding John's dependence on the Synoptics], and has exerted an influence out of proportion to its size." One may cite, in North America, Raymond E. Brown's important commentary as typical of this emerging position: *The Gospel according to John* (Anchor Bible, 29, 29A; Garden City, N.Y.: Doubleday, 1966, 1970); note especially 1.xliv–xlvii: "To summarize, then, in most of the material narrated in both John and the Synoptics, we believe that the evidence does not favor Johannine dependence on the Synoptics or their sources'"(xlvii). But already in 1941 Rudolf Bultmann had completed his *Das Evangelium des Johannes* (Göttingen: Vandenhoeck & Ruprecht) for the Kritsch-exegetischer Kommentar series, which thirty years later was to be translated by G. R. Beasley-Murray, R. W. N. Hoare, and J. K. Riches G. R. Beasley-Murray as *The Gospel of John: A Commentary* (Philadelphia: Westminster, 1971); in this critically important commentary Bultmann finds John's use of the Synoptics an unnecessary hypothesis and at best a late, redactional phenomenon, peripheral rather than central to John's composition.

6. See Robinson's *The Priority of John* (ed. J. F. Coakley; London: SCM, 1985), in which Robinson begins from the premise of John's independence (cf. 10–23). Robinson's "The New Look on the Fourth Gospel," in his *Twelve New Testament Studies* (Studies in Biblical Theology, 34; London: SCM, 1962), 94–106, was first given as a

paper at the Oxford conference "The Four Gospels" in 1957. It expresses the same point of view more tentatively. At about the same time, A. J. B. Higgins was writing his brief book, *The Historicity of the Fourth Gospel* (London: Lutterworth, 1960), in which John's independence is affirmed.

7. It is represented most impressively by the work of Professor Frans Neirynck and his colleagues at the Catholic University of Louvain. On this most recent turn in the discussion of the problem, see my *John among the Gospels* (2d ed.; Columbia, S.C.: University of South Carolina Press, 2001). The trend is well represented in the papers presented to the Louvain Biblical Collegium 1990 on John and the Synoptics. See A. Denaux, ed., *John and the Synoptics* (Bibliotheca ephemeridum theologicarum lovaniensium 101; Leuven: Leuven University Press, 1992).

8. John Ashton, *Understanding the Fourth Gospel* (Oxford: Clarendon, 1991), 36–38, cites David Strauss and F. C. Baur in documenting the demise of the Fourth Gospel as a historical source in the eyes of nineteenth-century critics.

9. Already Raymond E. Brown effectively made this point in one of his early articles, "The Problem of Historicity in John," *Catholic Biblical Quarterly* 24 (1962): 1–14 (esp. 3). His purpose was broader than ours, namely, to show that John's Gospel should be considered representative of a Palestinian, eyewitness historical tradition in some ways as valuable as the synoptic. Our purpose is simply to argue that at a number of points at which John differs from the Synoptics his account is at least as likely—sometimes more likely—to be historically valid. Perhaps closer to our purpose is Brown's "Incidents that are Units in the Synoptic Gospels but Dispersed in John," *Catholic Biblical Quarterly* 23 (1961): 143–60. Brown's interest in maintaining an important element of historicity at the level of Jesus himself is strongly evident in the first volume of his Anchor Bible Commentary especially, and I think he has never abandoned it, despite the fact that he has later shown greater interest in *The Community of the Beloved Disciple* (New York: Paulist Press, 1979). Likewise, his longtime Union Seminary colleague J. Louis Martyn, who in *History and Theology in the Fourth Gospel* (3d ed.; Louisville, Ky.: Westminster John Knox, 2003) portrays the Gospel as a narrative on two levels, the *einmalig* (putatively Jesus') and that of the primitive Johannine church, nevertheless focuses his attention on the latter level.

10. Cf. already Edwyn Clement Hoskyns, *Fourth Gospel,* 63–64, cited by Bultmann, *Gospel of John,* 122 n. 3. This is, of course, a recurring theme with many variations in the exegesis of the Fourth Gospel.

11. I here follow Dodd (*Historical Tradition in the Fourth Gospel,* 109–11), who assembles the evidence in favor of John's dating. C. K. Barrett, *The Gospel according to St. John: An Introduction with Commentary and Notes on the Greek Text* (2d ed.; Philadelphia: Westminster, 1978), 48–51, makes the case for the historicity of the synoptic dating. Bultmann's indifference to the historical question is typical: "Nor is the historical question, which of the two datings is correct (perhaps the Johannine), of any importance for the interpretation of John" (*Gospel of John,* 465 n. 1).

There is another significant Johannine variant, in that Jesus is said to be crucified at, or after, the sixth hour (19:14), whereas in Mark he is crucified at the third hour (15:25). Assuming the Jewish reckoning of time in both cases, John would put the crucifixion at noon, when the Passover lambs were slain, arguably a theologically motivated timing, which, however, seems more likely to lie in John's tradition rather than in the evangelist's redaction. Moreover, John's twelve noon would seem a more plausible time for the crucifixion to begin than nine in the morning, particularly since the trial before Pilate immediately preceded. (This gets us into such questions as how early in the morning a Roman prefect would have gone to work and whether that is irrelevant because of the unusual circumstances. These matters cannot be adjudicated here.)

12. Bultmann, *Gospel of John*, 75 n. 4.

13. Ibid., 108.

14. Dodd (*Historical Tradition in the Fourth Gospel*, 285–86), takes the representation of Jesus as baptizing to derive from old tradition, if it is not historical. Bultmann (*Gospel of John*, 168) conjures with the possibility that 3:22 is derived from old tradition, but nevertheless views the entire section 3:22–26 as a literary composition of the evangelist designed to show Jesus' superiority to the Baptist.

15. Bultmann (*Gospel of John*, 171) proposes that 3:24 is the insertion of the ecclesiastical redactor, for the evangelist shows no interest in harmonizing his account with the Synoptics. Dodd (*Historical Tradition in the Fourth Gospel*, 279–80) also takes 3:24 to be "an editorial note" but from the evangelist.

16. Dodd (*Historical Tradition in the Fourth Gospel*, 220–21) thinks that 6:66 has some traditional and historical basis.

17. On the disciples' inability to understand earlier, see F. F. Segovia, "'Peace I Leave with You; My Peace I Give to You': Discipleship in the Fourth Gospel," in *Discipleship in the New Testament* (ed. F. F. Segovia; Philadelphia: Fortress, 1985), 76–102 (esp. 92–94); also de Jonge, *Jesus: Stranger from Heaven*, 7–9.

18. See the remarkable essay by Raymond E. Brown, "Roles of Women in the Fourth Gospel," in his *The Community of the Beloved Disciple*, 183–98. Brown underscores the evidence that women are fully, and perhaps uniquely, recognized as disciples of Jesus in the Gospel of John.

19. Brown (*Gospel according to John*, 1002–3), regards Matt 28:9–10 as a later insertion into the Matthean narrative, among other reasons, because v. 8 leads so nicely into v. 11 if it is omitted. Thus John 20:14–18 would be an independent version of the same tradition and not a Johannine development of a Matthean episode.

20. Cf. Barrett, *Gospel according to St. John*, 523–24. Moreover, according to Barrett (524), "there is little in his story that cannot be explained as a Johannine modification of a narrative not unlike Mark's." On the Gospel of John as a juridical proceeding, see A. E. Harvey, *Jesus on Trial: A Study in the Fourth Gospel* (London: SPCK, 1976). In a paper read before the 1990 Louvain Colloquium on John and the Synoptics, A. Dauer argued that John 10 presupposes, or is based upon, a narrative of the Jewish trial similar to, but not identical with, Mark's. See his "Spuren der (synoptischen) Synedriumsverhandlung im 4. Evangelium. Das Verhältnis zu den Synoptikeen," in *John and the Synoptics*, 307–39.

21. As Dodd contends, *Historical Tradition in the Fourth Gospel*, 88–96, 120.

22. Brown (*Gospel according to John*, 899) observes that "serious scholars of the caliber of Dodd and Taylor judge . . . [this] solution a perfectly reasonable interpretation of the evidence."

23. Robinson, *Priority of John*, 127–31, 185–86.

24. E. P. Sanders, *Jesus and Judaism* (Philadelphia: Fortress, 1985), 61–76.

25. Robert T. Fortna, *The Gospel of Signs: A Reconstruction of the Narrative Source Underlying the Fourth Gospel* (Society for New Testament Studies Monograph Series 11; Cambridge: Cambridge University Press, 1970), 87–88. In his more recent *The Fourth Gospel and Its Predecessor: From Narrative Source to Present Gospel* (Philadelphia: Fortress, 1988), 65–79, Fortna maintains his position, but acknowledges its more hypothetical character in relation to his other proposals (66).

26. Bultmann, *Gospel of John,* 705: "The early Easter story, related in vv. 1–14, manifestly originally told of the first (and only?) appearance of the risen Jesus to the disciples." Moreover, "that this story, or a variant of it, formed the original conclusion of Mark (and of the Gospel of Peter) has a certain probability" (705 n. 5). Bultmann is not being facetious.

27. That the Johannine account of Jesus' words and works is a theologically freighted narrative is clear enough, and no longer needs any defense. Yet this fact does not determine, or should not determine, its value as a historical source on specific points. In this regard the statement of R. Pesch, "The Gospel in Jerusalem: Mk 14.12–26 as the Oldest Tradition of the Early Church," *The Gospel and the Gospels* (ed. Peter Stuhlmacher; Grand Rapids, Mich.: Eerdmans, 1991), 116, is very much to the point: "The linkage of theology to history—in subordination to the biblical witness of the canon—is the linkage to the faith-interpreted history of God with his people. . . . The stubbornly factual character of that history and of the concrete speech of the word of God resists the arbitrariness of our willful arrangements—even in the language of legend, which by no means lacks a relationship to history simply because it is not interested in the historical accuracy of the course of events portrayed in the world of the narrative but is very interested in the meaning of the history as faith understands it."

Chapter 11: The Question of Gospel Genre

1. In an otherwise favorable review of my contribution (*John*) to the Proclamation Commentaries series in *Interpretation* 31 (1977): 296–99, Howard Clark Kee took issue with what he described as the "repeated assertion that John need not have known the Synoptics" (298). He continued: "His evidence that John is basically different from the other Gospels is valid, but John must have known the Gospel as a literary genre for him to have seized on that medium for his portrayal of the Word made flesh." A similar observation was made by my colleague Dan O. Via after I had read a paper on John and the Synoptics to a faculty group at Duke University. Earlier, George W. MacRae had said in a private conversation that the peculiar combination of exoteric and esoteric ministries (that is, public ministry and preparation for the passion) must have been derived by John from Mark, if not from the Synoptics generally. There is a certain obviousness and rightheadedness about this suggestion. How could it be otherwise, given the priority of Mark over John? Indeed, the similarity of genre becomes a basis for granting Mark priority over John, unless, of course, one wants to argue the priority of John, a task that few, other than the late Bishop Robinson, would essay (see John A. T. Robinson, *The Priority of John* [ed. J. F. Coakley; London, SCM, 1985]).

2. Patricia L. Cox, *Biography in Late Antiquity: A Quest for the Holy Man* (Transformation of the Classical Heritage 5; Berkeley: University of California Press, 1983), 55.

3. E. D. Hirsch, Jr., in his important essay in hermeneutics, *Validity in Interpretation* (New Haven: Yale University Press, 1967), 68–126, underscores the importance of genre and genre recognition in the interpretation of texts. Hirsch believes "that an interpreter's preliminary generic conception of a text is constitutive of everything that he subsequently understands, and that this remains the case unless and until that generic concept is altered" (74). Thus a reader's initial grasp of the genre of a text will determine his understanding of it and of its content (75). "All understanding of verbal meaning is necessarily genre-bound" (76). From the standpoint of New Testament, and particularly gospel, exegesis, Hirsch's axioms seem unexceptionable. The position of the Fourth Gospel within the canon of Christian scripture, alongside and after the other Gospels, strongly suggests that it is to be understood as belonging to the same genre. It

may be that in antiquity the Synoptics gave the generic clue for the reading of the Gospel of John. In modern interpretation it has more often been the other way around. John, and especially 20:30–31, has provided a valuable indication of the purpose of all gospels and therefore serves as a generic clue as to how they should be read. For a monograph devoted to gospel genre, see Detlev Dormeyer, *Evangelium als literarische und theologische Gattung* (Erträge der Forschung 263; Darmstadt: Wissenschaftliche Buchgesellschaft, 1989). Cf. Dormeyer and Hubert Frankemölle, *Evangelium als literarische Gattung und als theologischer Begriff. Tendenzen und Aufgaben der Evangelienforschung im 20. Jahrhundert, mit einer Untersuchung des Markusevangeliums in seinem Verhältnis zur antiken Biographie,* in *Aufstieg und Niedergang der römischen Welt* 2.25.2 (1984), 1543–1704. Helmut Koester, *Ancient Christian Gospels: Their History and Development* (Philadelphia: Trinity Press International, 1990), puts the development of gospel genre in historical perspective and argues that the concept of gospel as a written document dealing with the career of Jesus arose only after the canonical Gospels had been written and had achieved authoritative status. One may also consult the article by Robert Guelich, "The Gospel Genre," in *The Gospel and the Gospels* (ed. Peter Stuhlmacher; Grand Rapids, Mich.: Eerdmans, 1991), 173–208. (Stuhlmacher's volume was first published as *Das Evangelium und die Evangelien* by Mohr in 1983; German articles have been translated for the English edition). Although Guelich's discussion of the question of genre is more detailed than the one here, with copious references to contemporary discussion and literature, I do not believe there is a basic disparity. In the same volume, see Albrecht Dihle's "The Gospels and Greek Biography," 361–86, in which the classicist approves the use of *biography* for the gospels with the proviso that it says nothing "about their peculiar genre in the strict sense of the word" (361). Moreover, Dihle does not think that ancient Greek biography directly influenced the formation of the gospel genre, different as it was in character, motivation, and purpose.

4. Schmidt, "Die Stellung der Evangelien in der allgemeinen Literaturgeschichte," in *EYXAPIΣTHPION: Studien zur Religion und Literatur des Alten und Neuen Testaments. Hermann Gunkel zum 60. Geburtstag,* 2. Teil (ed. Hans Schmidt; Göttingen: Vandenhoeck & Ruprecht, 1923), 50–134. Since the original publication of this article, Byron R. McCane has translated Schmidt: *The Place of the Gospels in the General History of Literature* (Columbia, S.C.: University of South Carolina Press, 2002).

5. *Place of the Gospels,* 3–4.

6. See Votaw's "The Gospels and Contemporary Biographies," *American Journal of Theology* 19 (1915): 45–73, 217–49. Republished as *The Gospels and Contemporary Biographies in the Greco-Roman World* (Facet Books, Biblical Series, 27; Philadelphia: Fortress, 1970). Page references will be to this edition.

7. Ibid., 5.

8. Ibid.

9. Ibid., 31.

10. Ibid., 62.

11. Ibid., 21.

12. See *Place of the Gospels,* 4.

13. Ibid., 27.

14. In this connection see the brief, but insightful, essay of John Reumann in his introduction to the 1970 republication of Votaw's *Gospels and Contemporary Biographies,* iii–viii, as well as Werner Georg Kümmel, *The New Testament: The History of the Investigation of Its Problems* (trans. MacLean Gilmore and Howard C. Kee; Nashville: Abingdon, 1972), esp. 327–38.

In the post-form-critical era the case for the biographical character (that is, religious biography) of the completed Gospels has been reviewed and carefully argued again by Charles H. Talbert, *What Is a Gospel? The Genre of the Canonical Gospels* (Philadelphia: Fortress, 1977). Talbert's work has been subjected to intense scrutiny and rather harsh criticism by David E. Aune, "The Problem of the Genre of the Gospels: A Critique of C. H. Talbert's *What Is a Gospel?*," in *Gospel Perspectives: Studies of History and Tradition in the Four Gospels* (ed. R. T. France and David Wenham; Sheffield: Journal for the Study of the Old Testament Press, 1981), 9–60. Among other things Aune suggests, with some reason, that while Talbert has focused his attention on the consensus represented by Bultmann, Schmidt's essay actually remains the classic statement of the position that the gospels (and therefore gospel genre) are the unique creation of early Christianity (16).

15. Schmidt, *Der Rahmen der Geschichte Jesu: Literarkritische Untersuchungen zur ältesten Jesusüberlieferung* (Berlin: Trowitzsch, 1919).

16. M. Dibelius, *From Tradition to Gospel* (trans. Bertram Lee Woolf; New York: Scribner's, 1935), 3.

17. Ibid., 4.

18. Ibid., 15.

19. See especially Bultmann's *History of the Synoptic Tradition* (trans. John Marsh; New York: Harper & Row, 1963).

20. Ibid., 275.

21. Ibid., 346.

22. Ibid., 370.

23. Ibid., 371.

24. Ibid., 373–74.

25. C. H. Dodd, *The Apostolic Teaching and Its Developments* (New York: Harper, 1936), esp. 36–56. Although Guelich, *Gospel Genre,* 191–94, points out that Dodd's view has been tellingly criticized in its details, as well as overall, he himself arrives at conclusions about the traditional character of the gospel genre that are not so different form Dodd's (201–2).

26. Dodd, *Historical Tradition in the Fourth Gospel* (Cambridge: Cambridge University Press, 1963).

27. P. Gardner-Smith, *Saint John and the Synoptic Gospels* (Cambridge: Cambridge University Press, 1938).

28. Ibid., 21–24.

29. Martin Kähler, *The So-Called Historical Jesus and the Historic, Biblical Christ* (trans. Carl E. Braaten; Philadelphia: Fortress, 1964), 80, n. 121.

30. Hans Conzelmann, *The Theology of St. Luke* (trans. Geoffrey Buswell; London: Faber & Faber, 1960), 9–12; Willi Marxsen, *Mark the Evangelist: Studies on the Redaction History of the Gospel* (trans. James Boyce et al.; Nashville: Abingdon, 1969), esp. 15–22. Bultmann himself regarded such works as Marxsen's and Conzelmann's as simply continuing the task of the form criticism of the gospels: "But it also studies them as finished works, in order to evaluate the literary activity of the evangelists, and to discover the theological motives that guided them." See his preface to Frederick C. Grant, ed., *Form Criticism* (New York: Harper Torchbooks, 1962), 4.

31. Robert T. Fortna, *The Gospel of Signs: A Reconstruction of the Narrative Source Underlying the Fourth Gospel* (Society for New Testament Studies Monograph Series 11; Cambridge: Cambridge University Press, 1970). See also Fortna's *The Fourth Gospel and Its Predecessor: From Narrative Source to Present Gospel* (Philadelphia: Fortress, 1988).

32. See Erhardt Güttgemanns, *Candid Questions Concerning Gospel Form Criticism: A Methodological Sketch of the Fundamental Problematics of Form and Redaction Criticism* (trans. William G. Doty; Pittsburgh Theological Monograph Series 26; Pittsburgh: Pickwick, 1979).

33. Eta Linnemann, *Studien zur Passionsgeschichte* (Forschungen zur Religion und Literatur des Alten und Neuen Testaments 102; Göttingen: Vandenhoeck & Ruprecht, 1970).

34. E. J. Pryke, *Redactional Style in the Marcan Gospel: A Study of Syntax and Vocabulary as Guides to Redaction in Mark* (Society for New Testament Studies Monograph Series 33; Cambridge: Cambridge University Press, 1978); on the existence of a passion source, see 126.

35. John R. Donahue, *Are You the Christ? The Trial Narrative in the Gospel of Mark* (Society of Biblical Literature Dissertation Series 10; Missoula, Mont.: Society of Biblical Literature, 1973).

36. See Norman Perrin, *The New Testament: An Introduction. Proclamation and Parenesis. Myth and History* (New York: Harcourt Brace Jovanovich, 1974), 228–29. His statement about the intercalation of the trial scene into the denial implying John's knowledge of Mark is repeated in Dennis C. Duling's revision of Perrin's work (New York: Harcourt Brace Jovanovich, 1982, 334). Duling is now able to refer to Werner Kelber, ed., *The Passion in Mark: Studies on Mark 14–16* (Philadelphia: Fortress, 1976), as well as to Donahue's *Are You the Christ?*; but see the criticisms of Robert T. Fortna, "Jesus and Peter at the High Priest's House: A Test Case for the Question of the Relation between Mark's and John's Gospels," *New Testament Studies* 24 (1978): 371–83.

37. Kelber, *The Oral and Written Gospel: The Hermeneutics of Speaking and Writing in the Synoptic Tradition, Mark, Paul and Q* (Philadelphia: Fortress, 1983), esp. 186–91.

38. See Stephen D. Moore, *Literary Criticism and the Gospels: The Theoretical Challenge* (New Haven: Yale University Press, 1989).

39. But if Mark introduced the gospel genre into the early church, and that genre was a Christian expression of the widespread phenomenon of religious biography, it certainly is arguable that what Mark did, another (John?) might easily have done also, and independently. In fact, Talbert in *What Is a Gospel?* (9–10), takes the independence of John from Mark as a reason to open once again the question of gospel genre. He concludes that the canonical Gospels belong to a certain genre of Greco-Roman biography. (By implication the existence of such a genre then helps account for the independent emergence of John and Mark.) Of course, the gospel genre may also be importantly related to historical and biographical aspects of the Old Testament (see Dihle, *The Gospels and Greek Biography,* 367, 380–81, who mentions the David narrative of 1 Samuel 16–1 Kings 2).

Chapter 12: John and the Apocryphal Gospels

1. Representative of this growing interest is the extremely useful bibliography of James H. Charlesworth and James R. Mueller, *The New Testament Apocrypha and Pseudepigrapha: A Guide to Publications, with Excursuses on Apocalypses* (Metuchen, N.J.: Scarecrow, 1987). This work gathers the harvest of modern critical scholarship on the so-called apocryphal New Testament. The standard English edition is *New Testament Apocrypha* (ed. Wilhelm Schneemelcher; trans. R. McL. Wilson; 2 vols.; Louisville, Ky.: Westminster John Knox, 1991–92).

2. "The Gospel of Peter," *Journal of Theological Studies* 27 (1925–26): 255–71. Gardner-Smith argues first that Peter is not dependent on John (256–59); then he considers

Matthew and Luke (259–63); and finally Mark (264–70). He concludes (270): "It is my contention that the similarities which exist between the canonical accounts and this apocryphal gospel can be explained on the hypothesis that all the evangelists, including 'Peter,' collected the floating traditions with which they were familiar and made of them the best narrative they could." In a subsequent article Gardner-Smith dated the *Gospel of Peter* ca. 90 (or between 80 and 110): "The Date of the Gospel of Peter," *Journal of Theological Studies* 27 (1925–26): 401–7. Important for his dating are possible allusions to Peter by Justin Martyr and the now established fact that the author did not know the canonical Gospels. On either basis a date much after 100 becomes increasingly improbable.

3. Koester, *History and Literature of Early Christianity* (2d. ed.; vol. 2 of *Introduction to the New Testament*; New York and Berlin: de Gruyter, 2000), 154–58 (on the *Gospel of Thomas*); 166–68 (on the *Gospel of Peter*), 186–87 (on Egerton Papyrus 2).

4. Crossan, *Four Other Gospels: Shadows on the Contours of the Canon* (Minneapolis: Seabury/Winston, 1985). Typical of the upsurge of interest in the apocryphal gospels is the issue of the journal *Semeia* 49 (1990) subtitled *The Apocryphal Jesus and Christian Origins*. Several scholars offer essays on the *Gospel of Peter* (Arthur J. Dewey) and *Secret Mark* (Marvin W. Meyer), among others, and Crossan responds to these two (155–68).

5. Crossan, *The Cross That Spoke: The Origins of the Passion Narrative* (San Francisco: Harper, 1988). The book is more than four hundred pages long. Crossan's work is adumbrated by a suggestion of Helmut Koester, "Apocryphal and Canonical Gospels," *Harvard Theological Review* 73 (1980): 105–30, esp. 126–30. Some previous research on the *Gospel of Peter* had led to the conclusion that it reflects tradition independent of the canonical Gospels (see Gardner-Smith cited above in note 2). Also the Kiel dissertation of Jürgen Denker, *Die theologiegeschichtliche Stellung des Petrusevangeliums: Eine Beitrag zur Frühgeschichte des Doketismus* (Europäische Hochschulschriften, Reihe XXIII, Band 36; Bern: Lang, 1975), draws somewhat more modest conclusions with regard to the *Gospel of Peter's* independence of the canonical Gospels, dating the present document between 100 and 130. Earlier, Martin Dibelius had argued that at three points at least *Peter's* use of Old Testament texts (Isa 58:2 and 59:9–10; Amos 8:9; Ps 22:18) in relation to Jesus' sitting on a seat of judgment (*Gos. Pet.* 3:7; John 19:13), the time of Jesus' crucifixion (*Gos. Pet.* 5:15; John 19:14), and the dividing of his garments (*Gos. Pet.* 4:12; John 19:23–24) respectively reflected an earlier stage of the development of the tradition than the Gospel of John's. Dibelius's insight is, characteristically, tied to his estimate of the importance of preaching for the tradition, and of the primal role played by scripture in preaching. See Martin Dibelius, *Die alttestamentlichen Motive in der Leidensgeschichte des Petrus- und des Johannes-Evangeliums,* in *Botschaft und Geschichte: Gesammelte Aufsätze* (Tübingen: Mohr, 1953; originally published in 1918 in the von Baudissin Festschrift), 221–47.

Interestingly enough, Crossan's work reaches conclusions opposed to a trend in Marcan studies to see Mark as the creator of the passion narrative. The latter view has had strong representation in the school of Norman Perrin, of which Crossan has been a part. See Werner H. Kelber, ed., *The Passion in Mark: Studies on Mark 14–16* (Philadelphia: Fortress, 1976). In contrast, Étienne Trocmé argues that the Marcan passion is the most primitive, but that it is traditional and not the work of the evangelist; indeed, that it was added to his Gospel only later. Luke and John represent independent recensions of this essentially pre-Marcan narrative that had its originative setting in the Christian Passover celebration of the Jerusalem church. See his *The Passion as*

Liturgy: A Study of the Origin of the Passion Narrative in the Four Gospels (London: SCM, 1983).

6. Raymond E. Brown, "*The Gospel of Peter* and Canonical Gospel Priority," in *New Testament Studies* 33 (1987): 321–43; Frans Neirynck, "The Apocryphal Gospels and the Gospel of Mark," in *The New Testament in Early Christianity: La réception des écrits néotestamentaires dans le christianisme primitive* (ed. J.-M. Sevrin; Bibliotheca ephemeridum theologicarum lovaniensium 86; Leuven: Leuven University Press, 1989), 123–75. Joel B. Green, "*The Gospel of Peter:* Source for a Pre-Canonical Passion Narrative," *Zeitschrift für die neutestamentliche Wissenschaft und die Kunde der älteren Kirche* 78 (1987): 293–301, responding only to Koester's proposals (note 5, above), grants the possibility that *Peter* may reflect noncanonical tradition, but argues that in a number of cases *Peter's* dependence on the canonical versions is the more likely explanation of obvious parallels. Green has himself developed a more conventional view of a pregospel passion narrative. See his dissertation, *The Death of Jesus: Tradition and Interpretation in the Passion Narrative* (Wissenschaftliche Untersuchungen zum Neuen Testament 33; Tübingen: Mohr, 1988), esp. chapters 6 and 7.

7. See Crossan, *Cross That Spoke,* 405–7, for a succinct summary of this position. See also Koester, "Apocryphal and Canonical Gospels," 127–28.

8. Brown, "*Gospel of Peter,*" 338. In the fifth edition of Hennecke-Schneemelcher, 183, Schneemelcher makes a similar point.

9. See Koester, *History and Literature,* 154–58, and his discussion in "Apocryphal and Canonical Gospels," 112–119, in which relevant literature for and against *Thomas's* dependence on the Synoptic Gospels is cited.

10. Koester, *Introduction,* embraces the view that Egerton Papyrus 2 is independent of the canonical Gospels, particularly John; cf. "Apocryphal and Canonical Gospels," 119–23. This was the position taken by Goro Mayeda, *Das Leben-Jesu-Fragment Papyrus Egerton 2 und seine Stellung in der urchristliche Literaturgeschichte* (Bern: Haupt, 1946). Joachim Jeremias and Wilhelm Schneemelcher, *New Testament Apocrypha,* 1:96–97, opt for knowledge of all the canonical Gospels, but only from memory. Schneemelcher rejects Koester's attempt to show that Egerton 2 is independent of the canonical Gospels, referring to Neirynck's demonstration that the text is "post-synoptic," and calls attention to the fact that the early dating of the fragment itself has been questioned (97).

Only after this paper was complete in final draft did I see, through the courtesy of the author, the article of D. Wright, "Papyrus Egerton 2 (the "Unknown Gospel")— Part of the *Gospel of Peter?,*" *Second Century* 5 (1985–86): 129–50. Not only does Wright advance an interesting thesis, but his article is also an excellent source of bibliographical information on the *Gospel of Peter* and the Unknown Gospel. One should note also his other richly documented essays: "Apocryphal Gospels: the "Unknown Gospel" (Pap. Egerton 2) and the *Gospel of Peter,* in *The Jesus Tradition Outside the Gospels* (vol. 5 of *Gospel Perspectives;* ed. D. Wenham; Sheffield: Journal for the Study of the Old Testament Press, 1985), 207–32; also "Apologetic and Apocalyptic: The Miraculous in the Gospel of Peter," in *The Miracles of Jesus* (vol. 6 of *Gospel Perspectives;* ed. Wenham and C. Blomberg; Sheffield: Journal for the Study of the Old Testament Press, 1986, 401–18).

11. See now Stephen C. Carlson, *The Gospel Hoax: Morton Smith's Invention of Secret Mark* (Waco, Tex.: Baylor University Press, 2005), who makes a thoroughgoing case against its genuineness.

12. Koester has long espoused the importance of the apocryphal gospels and deplored the way in which they are usually deemed secondary and of little worth ("Apocryphal and Canonical Gospels," 105–7). In principle his position is affirmed, albeit from a more conservative perspective, by Richard Bauckham, "The Study of Gospel Traditions Outside the Canonical Gospels: Problems and Prospects," in *The Jesus Tradition Outside the Gospels* (vol. 5 of *Gospel Perspectives,* ed. David Wenham; Sheffield: Journal for the Study of the Old Testament Press, 1984, 369–403). He writes (373–74): "Though I disagree with many of Helmut Koester's conclusions on this subject, it seems to me the great merit of his *Introduction to the New Testament* is that he has attempted a broad description of the Gospel tradition in first- and second-century Christianity without isolating the Gospels from this larger context." Bauckham's assessment of the importance of apocryphal and/or noncanonical gospels for understanding the development of the canonical Gospels and gospel traditions seems to me to be judicious and sound. Actually, Bultmann appears to have pointed in somewhat different directions in this matter. On the one hand, he illustrates the development of the tradition by citing material in the apocryphal gospels. On the other, he seems to presume these materials are later. Thus, at the end of *The History of the Synoptic Tradition* (trans. John Marsh; New York: Harper, 1963), 374, he writes that the apocryphal gospels "are but legendary expansions" of the synoptic form.

13. Crossan, *Cross That Spoke,* xii.

14. There is, of course, that famous statement attributed to Papias (Eusebius, *Historia Ecclesiastica* III. 39, 3–4), which concludes: "For I did not suppose that information from books would help me so much as the word of a living and surviving [or abiding] voice." Morton Smith, "Clement of Alexandria and Secret Mark," inveighs against a widespread scholarly ignoring of the reality and importance of oral tradition (453): "Though everybody pays lip-service to the notion of oral tradition, few realize that it constituted a supply of expressions and motifs from which all Christian writers, including the authors of the canonical gospels, independently drew." In this connection he cites the early work of Koester, *Synoptische Überlieferung bei den apostolischen Vätern* (Texte und Untersuchungen 65; Berlin: Akademie Verlag, 1957). That Bultmann inspired this Marburg dissertation gives indication of his later recognition of the importance of extracanonical gospel tradition.

15. For example, in *New Testament Apocrypha,* 221, Wilhelm Schneemelcher writes: "We can only establish that according to the testimony of Serapion the Gos. Pet. must have originated sometime before c. 190. If we assume knowledge of the four canonical Gospels, we shall not place Gos. Pet. too early in the 2nd century. On the other hand the older traditions which can be shown are an indication that it cannot be dated too late. We can scarcely get beyond conjectures."

16. See Crossan, *Cross That Spoke,* 13–15, 407–8, in which the author indicates a preference for an early date, prior to the canonical Gospels, without fixing upon one. This is the logical implication of his position. Similarly, Koester, *History and Literature of Early Christianity,* 167.

17. Kähler, *The So-Called Historical Jesus and the Historic Biblical Christ* (trans. Carl E. Braaten; Philadelphia: Fortress, 1964 [from German original, 1896]), 78.

18. B. A. Johnson, *The Gospel of Peter: Between Apocalypse and Romance* (Texte und Untersuchungen 129; Berlin: Akademie Verlag, 1985), 170–74, has put the matter well (170): "It is common in a discussion of New Testament gospel literature to appeal in the demarcation between canonical and non-canonical literature to the sharp qualitative

distinction between them. The majesty of the canonical gospels and Acts is compared to the near banality of most second and third century gospels and Acts. One can read an entire document such as the Acts of Paul and have the distinct impression that there is little or no relation to actual events. By comparison the canonical Acts manifest a dignified relationship to significant history." Johnson then goes on to point out that such a qualitative distinction exists between the canonical Gospels and the *Gospel of Peter,* but he maintains that although *Peter* is a secondary document in relation to the canonicals, it reflects some knowledge of primary materials or tradition. He instances specifically the empty tomb tradition of *Peter,* which he studied in a doctoral dissertation: Johnson, "Empty Tomb Tradition in the *Gospel of Peter,*" Th.D. dissertation, Harvard University Divinity School, 1966.

19. Brown, "*Gospel of Peter,*" suggests that the influence of the canonical Gospels upon informal oral traditions must not be discounted as a factor in the shaping of the *Gospel of Peter* and similar writings (335–36). At the same time he does not discount the possibility that *Peter,* and other apocryphal gospels, had access to traditions of extra-canonical origin (337). Brown's suggestion that some oral tradition originated in written gospels recalls the proposals of Anton Dauer that the Johannine passion source was influenced by oral tradition derived from the Synoptic Gospels and that Lucan influence upon the Fourth Gospel was conveyed in a similar way. See A. Dauer, *Die Passionsgeschichte im Johannesevangelium: Eine traditionsgeschichtliche und theologische Untersuchung zu Joh 18,1–19,30* (Studien zum Alten und Neuen Testament 30; Munich: Kösel, 1972); also the same author's *Johannes und Lukas: Untersuchungen zu den johanneisch-lukanischen Parallelperikopen Joh 4,46–54 / Lk 7,1–10—Joh 12,1–8 / Lk 7,36–50; 10,38–42—Joh 20,19–29 / Lk 24,36–49* (Forschung zur Bibel 50; Wurzburg: Echter, 1984).

20. Eusebius, *Historia Ecclesiastica* VI. 12.2–6. The most recent discussion is by Crossan, *Cross That Spoke,* 10–12, who does not think that the *Gospel of Peter* was docetic and notes that Bishop Serapion had to have the docetic readings pointed out to him. Of course, Serapion and his contemporaries had the whole gospel, while we have only a fragment. Jerry W. McCant, "The Gospel of Peter: Docetism Reconsidered," *New Testament Studies* 30 (1984): 258–73, vigorously denies that *Peter* is docetic, although he concedes (n. 67) that Serapion had access to the entire gospel, while we have only a fragment. McCant also raises the "interesting question" of whether we have the same gospel that Bishop Serapion banned.

21. As is maintained by Koester, *Synoptische Überlieferung bei den apostolischen Vätern* (Texte und Untersuchung 65: Berlin: Akademie Verlag, 1957). Cf. also Brown, "*The Gospel of Peter,*" 335–36.

22. Koester's survey of the admittedly fragmentary earliest manuscript and citation evidence would seem to indicate that the apocryphal gospels were at one time more strongly represented. See "Apocryphal and Canonical Gospels," 107–112. Peter Pilhoffer, "Justin und das Petrusevangelium," *Zeitschrift für die neutestamentliche Wissenschaft und die Kunde der älteren Kirche* 81 (1990): 60–78, has made a strong case that Justin Martyr knew the *Gospel of Peter;* that would, incidentally, imply a date no later than 130, which agrees with the dating of Jürgen Denker in *Die theologiegeschichtliche Stellung des Petrus-evangeliums.*

23. On the gnostic use of the Gospel of John in Rome and its possible implications for the status of the Gospel there, see the interesting reflections of Walter Bauer, *Orthodoxy and Heresy in Earliest Christianity* (ed. R. A. Kraft and Gerhard Krodel; Philadelphia, 1971 [German, 1934, 1964]), 206–8.

24. See now, as well as Bauer, *Orthodoxy and Heresy*, the work of Joseph Daniel Smith, "Gaius and the Controversy over the Johannine Literature," Ph.D. dissertation, Yale University, 1979.

25. Eusebius, *Historia Ecclesiastica* II. 25. 6.

26. Martin Hengel, *Studies in the Gospel of Mark* (trans. John Bowden; Philadelphia, 1985), has recently revived arguments for a Roman origin of the Gospel of Mark, citing the ancient evidence (1–8, 28–30).

27. Still most conveniently available for the English reader in Vincent Taylor, *The Gospel According to Mark: The Greek Text with Introduction, Notes, and Indexes* (London: Macmillan, 1952), 1–8.

28. Bruce Metzger, *The Canon of the New Testament: Its Origin, Development, and Significance* (Oxford: Clarendon, 1987), 191–201, continues to accept a date "not later than the year 200" (194), despite efforts to call its great antiquity into question.

29. See Paul J. Achtemeier, "*Omne verbum sonat:* The New Testament and the Oral Environment of Late Western Antiquity," *Journal of Biblical Literature* 109 (1990): 3–27.

30. Frans Neirynck, "John 21," *New Testament Studies* 36 (1990): 321–36, argues that John 21:1–14 is dependent on Luke 5:1–11 rather than on an independent, related source or tradition. He has, in my judgment, shown how Luke could be the source of John. But the problems of reading John in light of Luke are not directly addressed. See Robert T. Fortna, "Diachronic/Synchronic: Reading John 21 and Luke 5," in *John and the Synoptics* (ed. Adelbert Denaux: Bibliotheca ephemeridum theologicarum lovaniensium 101; Leuven: Leuven University Press, 1992, 387–99. Fortna responds to Neirynck and asks how much the supposition that John 21:1–14 is based on Luke 5:1–11 contributes to the understanding of the Johannine pericope. He concludes, in my opinion correctly, that such a premise creates as many difficulties in understanding John as it resolves. Fortna's arguments do not prove that John did not know Luke, but they certainly show the magnitude of the redaction-critical task, given this premise. Nevertheless, it does seem to me that the reference to the world's not being able to hold the books that could be written about Jesus' deeds (21:25) presupposes knowledge of other gospels. With most commentators, I take chapter 21 to be a later addition to the Gospel, probably by a different hand.

31. See also Gardner-Smith, "Gospel of Peter," 259. He takes the omission of any mention of a Jerusalem appearance to the disciples in *Peter* to prove that the author had not read John or Luke. This is a bit strong, but the absence of the appearance in *Peter* is striking. On the resurrection in *Peter*, see Johnson, "Empty Tomb."

Chapter 13: The Problem of Faith and History

1. See J. J. Gunther, "Early Identifications of Authorship of the Johannine Writings," *Journal of Ecclesiastical History* 31 (1981): 413–15; and especially Joseph Daniel Smith, Jr., "Gaius and the Controversy over the Johannine Literature" (Ph.D. dissertation, Yale University, 1979), 289–92, 384–91. Smith argues that Gaius's opposition to the Fourth Gospel was motivated by its use among the Montanists whom he opposed (426).

2. See my article, "B. W. Bacon on John and Mark," in *Johannine Christianity: Essays on its Setting, Sources, and Theology* (Columbia, S.C.: University of South Carolina Press, 1984), 106–27, in which Bacon's position, as represented in a number of his works, is set forth in some detail.

3. Origen, *Commentary on the Gospel of John* 10.2–15.

4. Hans Windisch, *Johannes und die Synoptiker: Wollte der vierte Evangelist die älteren Evangelien ergänzen oder ersetzen?* (Untersuchungen zum Neuen Testament 12; Leipzig: Hinrich, 1926).

5. P. Gardner-Smith, *Saint John and the Synoptic Gospels* (Cambridge: Cambridge University Press, 1938).

6. Bultmann's *Das Evangelium des Johannes* (Göttingen: Vandenhoeck & Ruprecht), completed in 1941, is available in English translation as *The Gospel of John: A Commentary* (trans. G. R. Beasley-Murray, R. W. N. Hoare, and J. K. Riches; Philadelphia: Westminster, 1971).

7. *Theologische Literaturzeitung* 52 (1927): 198.

8. Especially Dodd's *Historical Tradition in the Fourth Gospel* (Cambridge: Cambridge University Press, 1963).

9. Raymond E. Brown, *The Gospel according to John* (Anchor Bible 29/29A; Garden City, N.Y.: Doubleday, 1966–70.

10. D. Moody Smith, "The Sources of the Gospel of John: An Assessment of the Present State of the Problem," *New Testament Studies* 10 (1963–64): 336–51, esp. 349; reprinted in *Johannine Christianity,* 39–61.

11. Josef Blinzler, *Johannes und die Synoptiker: Ein Forschungsbericht* (Stuttgarter Bibelstudien 5; Stuttgart: Katholisches Bibelwerk, 1965), 31–32 and passim.

12. Frans Neirynck, "John and the Synoptics," in *L'Évangile de Jean: Sources, rédaction, théologie* (ed. M. de Jonge; Bibliotheca ephemeridum theologicarum lovaniensium 44; Louvain: Louvain University Press, 1977), 73–106, esp. 73–74.

13. See Werner H. Kelber, ed., *The Passion in Mark: Studies in Mark 14–16* (Philadelphia: Fortress, 1976). Cf. Kelber's *The Oral and Written Gospel: The Hermeneutics of Speaking and Writing in the Synoptic Tradition, Mark, Paul, and Q* (Philadelphia: Fortress, 1983), 185–99. In the latter work Kelber advances exegetical and theoretical arguments against a pre-Marcan narrative.

14. Donahue, *Are You the Christ? The Trial Narrative in the Gospel of Mark* (Society of Biblical Literature Dissertation Series 10; Missoula, Mont.: Scholars Press, 1973).

15. Linnemann, *Studien zur Passionsgeschichte* (Forschungen zur Religion und Literatur des Alten und Neuen Testaments 102; Göttingen: Vandenhoeck & Ruprecht, 1970).

16. Schniewind, *Die Parallelperikopen bei Lukas und Johannes* (2d ed.; Darmstadt: Wissenschaftliche Buchgesellschaft, 1958); first published in 1914.

17. Bailey, *The Traditions Common to the Gospels of Luke and John* (Novum Testamentum Supplements 7; Leiden: Brill, 1963).

18. Cribbs, "St. Luke and the Fourth Gospel," *Journal of Biblical Literature* 90 (1971): 422–50.

19. Dauer, *Johannes und Lukas: Untersuchungen zu den johanneisch-lukanischen Parallelperikopen Joh 4,46–54 / Lk 7,1–10—Joh 12,1–8 / Lk 7,36–50; 10,38–42—Joh 20,19–29 / Lk 24,36–49* (Forschung zur Bibel 50; Würzburg: Echter, 1984).

20. M.-E. Boismard and A. Lamouille, *Synopse des quatre évangiles en français* (vol. 3 of *L'Évangile de Jean;* Paris: Editions du Cerf, 1977). Boismard is regarded as the creator of the theory.

21. Brown, *Gospel according to John,* 1.xxxviii.

22. Neirynck et al., *Jean et les synoptiques: Examen critique de l'exégèse de M.-E. Boismard* (Bibliotheca ephemeridum theologicarum lovaniensium 49; Louvain: Louvain University Press, 1979).

23. Some such view of John's purpose is set forth or implicit in the work of many scholars: Peder Borgen, Raymond E. Brown, Wayne A. Meeks, Klaus Wengst, et al. Of pivotal importance in this regard is the work of J. Louis Martyn, *History and Theology in the Fourth Gospel* (3d ed.; Louisville, Ky.: Westminster John Knox, 2003).

24. Interestingly enough, at the point at which our manuscript of the *Gospel of Peter* breaks off (14:60), an appearance of Jesus by the sea (of Galilee) is clearly to be anticipated.

Chapter 14: When Did the Gospels Become Scripture?

1. See the summary of the twentieth century's scholarly discussion and debate in my *John among the Gospels* (2d ed.; Columbia, S.C.: University of South Carolina Press, 2001). Needless to say, the debate goes on, but perhaps at a less frenetic pace.

2. Graham N. Stanton, "The Fourfold Gospel," *New Testament Studies* 43 (1997): 317–46.

3. David Trobisch, *Die Endredaktion des Neuen Testaments: Eine Untersuchung zur Entstehung der christlichen Bibel* (Novum Testamentum et Orbis Antiquus; Göttingen: Vandenhoeck & Ruprecht; Freiburg: Universitätsverlag, Switzerland, 1996). The English translation is *The First Edition of the New Testament* (Oxford and New York: Oxford University Press, 2000).

4. John Barton, *Holy Writings, Sacred Text: The Canon in Early Christianity* (Louisville, Ky.: Westminster John Knox, 1997).

5. The contributions of these scholars are too numerous to enumerate here; I mention representative works that have been important to me: James Barr, *Holy Scripture: Canon, Authority, Criticism* (Philadelphia: Westminster, 1983); Brevard S. Childs, *The New Testament as Canon: An Introduction* (Philadelphia: Fortress, 1985); James A. Sanders, *Torah and Canon* (Philadelphia: Fortress, 1972). For the history of the development of the canon and related matters I rely on Bruce M. Metzger's *The Canon of the New Testament: Its Origin, Development, and Significance* (Oxford: Clarendon, 1987).

6. William A. Graham, "Scripture," in *The Encyclopedia of Religion* (ed. Mircea Eliade; New York: Macmillan, 1987), 13.142.

7. Ibid., 133.

8. "Hence the Gospels, no less than the letters of Paul, are occasional documents, composed in and directed toward specific and local constituencies," writes Harry Y. Gamble, Jr., who in so saying succinctly sums up the widely held assumption on which much Gospel interpretation is based. See his article "Christianity: Scripture and Canon," in *The Holy Book in Comparative Perspective* (ed. Frederick M. Denney and Rodney L. Taylor; Studies in Comparative Religion; Columbia, S.C.: University of South Carolina Press, 1985), 41. But Gamble then adds: "It was somewhat contrary to their actual character as interpretations of the Jesus-traditions that the Gospels came to be valued first as historical records, and not as scripture" (42). He then instances Justin Martyr's references to the Gospels as "memoirs" or "reminiscences" of the apostles (57 n. 16). Moreover, Gamble has evidently continued to reflect on the matter (see below, n. 11). Reflecting on the purpose of the Gospels in his magisterial *Formation of the Christian Bible* (London: Black, 1972), 122, Hans von Campenhausen writes: "As regards the formation of the Canon, the only question of interest is whether, and if so in what way, the authors of the Gospels invested their works with a claim which did not simply assert the independent authority attaching to any genuine tradition but demanded special status for this particular book. In the case of the traditional Four this

never happens. The majority of them are completely silent concerning what it was that made them undertake their task, or the importance and function of their work." Actually, only Matthew and Mark are silent. Luke is quite explicit (1:1–3) and John is scarcely silent (21:24–25).

9. G. D. Kilpatrick, *The Origins of the Gospel according to St. Matthew* (Oxford: Clarendon, 1950), esp. 72–100, "The Liturgical Character of the Gospels"; see also M. D. Goulder, *Midrash and Lection in Matthew* (London: SPCK, 1974), who regards Matthew as a midrashic expansion of Mark, parallel to Chronicles' relation to Kings (esp. 3–9), intended to be read around the church's year (182–83). Both Kilpatrick and Goulder set Matthew against the background of Jewish synagogue worship practice.

10. Philip Carrington argues in detail that Mark was composed as Gospel lections for a church year (*The Primitive Christian Calendar: A Study in the Making of the Marcan Gospel* [Cambridge: Cambridge University Press, 1952]). W. D. Davies does not accept Carrington's arguments, but, referring to Kilpatrick, *The Origins of the Gospel according to St. Matthew,* believes his general thesis regarding the influence of liturgical practice worthy of further consideration ("Reflections on Archbishop Carrington's 'The Primitive Christian Calendar,'" in *The Background of the New Testament and its Eschatology: In Honour of C. H. Dodd* [ed. W. D. Davies and D. Daube; Cambridge: Cambridge University Press, 1956], 124–52, esp. 148). Paul F. Bradshaw rightly emphasizes the paucity of evidence for the first century, or New Testament period, and rejects as without adequate foundation the work of Carrington, Goulder, and Kilpatrick, among others (*The Search for the Origins of Christian Worship: Sources and Methods for the Study of Early Liturgy* [Oxford and New York: Oxford University Press, 1992], 30–56). Certainly he is correct in his judgment that the evidence is too slim and too ambiguous to allow for persuasive reconstructions of earliest worship practice. (This is, as he observes, as problematic for early Judaism as for ancient Christianity.) However, if one asks for what purpose were the Gospels written or what function did they fulfill, one can scarcely exclude public reading in services of worship as a likely possibility, perhaps the most likely possibility in light of the evidence of Justin Martyr and our best estimate of the function of pre-Gospel sources and traditions.

11. Richard Bauckham, "For Whom Were the Gospels Written?" in *The Gospels for All Christians: Rethinking the Gospel Audiences* (ed. Richard Bauckham; Grand Rapids, Mich.: Eerdmans, 1998), 9–48. D. N. Peterson also objects to the assumption that Gospels, particularly Mark, not only arose from, but were also addressed to, a specific early Christian setting. See his *The Origins of Mark: The Markan Community in Current Debate* (Biblical Interpretation Series; Leiden: Brill, 2000). On the wider intended audience of Gospels, see also Harry Y. Gamble, *Books and Readers in the Early Church: A History of Early Christian Texts* (New Haven: Yale University Press, 1995), 102–3, as well as Barton, who contemplates the possibility that John and Matthew were composed as scripture (*Holy Writings,* 25).

12. Graham, "Scripture," 133.

13. See William S. Kurz, "Luke 3:23–38 and Greco-Roman and Biblical Genealogies," in *Luke-Acts: New Perspectives from the Society of Biblical Literature Seminar* (ed. C. H. Talbert; New York: Crossroad, 1984), 169–87; also Gerard Mussies, "Parallels to Matthew's Version of the Pedigree of Jesus," *Novum Testamentum* 28 (1986): 32–47. For the biblical and Jewish milieu, see Marshall D. Johnson, *The Purpose of the Biblical Genealogies: With Special Reference to the Setting of the Genealogies of Jesus* (2d ed.; Society for New Testament Studies Monograph Series 8; Cambridge: Cambridge University Press, 1988).

14. See W. D. Davies and Dale C. Allison, *A Critical and Exegetical Commentary on the Gospel according to Saint Matthew* (International Critical Commentary; 3 vols.; Edinburgh: T & T Clark, 1988–97) 1.423–24.

15. Ibid., 187; cf. 149–55 on *biblos geneseōs* as a title. On the scriptural qualities of Matthew, as well as the other Synoptic Gospels, see E. P. Sanders and Margaret Davies, *Studying the Synoptic Gospels* (London: SCM; Philadelphia: Trinity Press International, 1989), 258–64 (Matthew); 270–75 (Mark); 290–96 (Luke).

16. On Lucan style, see Joseph A. Fitzmyer, *The Gospel According to Luke (I–IX)* (Anchor Bible 28; Garden City, N.Y.: Doubleday, 1981), 107–27, esp. 113–22 on the relation to biblical, particularly Septuagintal, style.

17. See David Ravens, *Luke and the Restoration of Israel* (Journal for the Study of the New Testament: Supplement Series 119; Sheffield: Sheffield Academic Press, 1995).

18. Craig A. Evans, "Luke and the Rewritten Bible: Aspects of Lukan Hagiography," in *The Pseudepigrapha and Early Biblical Interpretation* (ed. James H. Charlesworth and C. A. Evans; Sheffield: JSOT, 1993), 200–201. In a note (n. 73) Evans continues: "Simply put, Luke may have thought that Luke-Acts belongs in the *Old Testament,* not some sort of *New* Testament." See also David P. Moessner, *Lord of the Banquet: The Literary and Theological Significance of the Lukan Travel Narrative* (Minneapolis: Fortress, 1989), 325; as well as William S. Kurz, *Reading Luke-Acts: Dynamics of Biblical Narrative* (Louisville: Westminster John Knox, 1993), 159–66.

19. See David E. Aune, "Charismatic Exegesis in Early Judaism and Early Christianity," in *The Pseudepigrapha and Early Biblical Interpretation* (ed. Charlesworth and Evans), 138.

20. See Loveday Alexander, *The Preface to Luke's Gospel: Literary Convention and Social Context in Luke 1.1–4 and Acts 1.1* (Society for New Testament Studies Monograph Series 78; Cambridge: Cambridge University Press, 1993), whose extensive canvassing of ancient sources calls any such easy generalization into question. She writes: "Once the preface is over, Luke reverts with startling suddenness to a 'biblical' style with which he clearly feels much more at home" (175).

21. On Mark's intentional use of scripture, particularly (Deutero-)Isaiah, see Joel Marcus, *The Way of the Lord: Christological Exegesis of the Old Testament in the Gospel of Mark* (Louisville, Ky.: Westminster John Knox, 1992).

22. The importance of the Little Apocalypse was underscored already by W. Marxsen, *Mark the Evangelist: Studies on the Redaction History of the Gospel* (trans. James Boyce et al.; Nashville: Abingdon, 1969), esp. 151–206.

23. Ibid., 190–206.

24. That exegesis of this saga, its traditions, and literature is not just a postbiblical activity is the central thesis of the important work of Michael Fishbane, *Biblical Interpretation in Ancient Israel* (Oxford: Clarendon, 1985). On the use of scripture within scripture in the Old Testament and intertestamental books, see *It Is Written: Scripture Citing Scripture: Essays in Honour of Barnabas Lindars, SSF* (ed. D. A. Carson and H. G. M. Williamson; Cambridge: Cambridge University Press, 1988), 25–83 (for Old Testament); 99–189 (for later books). The citing of scripture as such begins in the apocryphal or deuterocanonical books but is infrequent until the New Testament and Qumran.

25. The fundamental work remains J. Louis Martyn, *History and Theology in the Fourth Gospel* (3d ed.; Louisville, Ky.: Westminster John Knox, 2003). See the important assessment of Martyn's work by John Ashton, *Understanding the Fourth Gospel*

(Oxford: Clarendon, 1991), who calls it "probably the most important single work on the Gospel since Bultmann's commentary" (107).

26. On the affinities between Revelation and the Gospel and Epistles of John, see the work of Jörg Frey, "Erwägungen zum Verhältnis der Johannesapokalypse zu den übrigen Schriften im Corpus Johanneum," published as an appendix to Martin Hengel, *Die johanneische Frage: Ein Lösungsversuch* (Tübingen: Mohr, 1993), 326–429.

27. Raymond E. Brown, *The Epistles of John* (Anchor Bible 30; Garden City, N.Y.: Doubleday, 1982), in my view still a most persuasive commentary on the Johannine Epistles, is based on this premise.

28. On the influence of scripture on Q there are two important articles from a Louvain colloquium: C. M. Tuckett, "Scripture and Q," and Frans Neirynck, "Q6, 20b–21; 7, 22 and Isaiah 61," both published in *The Scriptures in the Gospels* (ed. C. M. Tuckett; Bibliotheca ephemeridum theologicarum lovaniensium 131; Leuven: Leuven University Press, 1997) 3–26, 27–64, respectively.

29. James M. Robinson and Helmut Koester, *Trajectories through Early Christianity* (Philadelphia: Fortress, 1971).

30. Note the bold, but in my judgment correct, assessment of Revelation by Richard Bauckham: "It is a book designed to be read in constant intertextual relationship with the Old Testament. John was writing what he understood to be a work of prophetic scripture, the climax of prophetic revelation, which gathered up the meaning of the Old Testament scriptures and disclosed the way in which it was being and was to be fulfilled in the last days" (*The Climax of Prophecy: Studies on the Book of Revelation* [Edinburgh: T & T Clark, 1993], xi). See also Bauckham's similar statement in *The Theology of the Book of Revelation* (New Testament Theology; Cambridge: Cambridge University Press, 1993), 5.

31. Roger Beckwith argues that the Old Testament canon was in effect closed by the time of Jesus and the earliest church (by the time of Judas Maccabeus) (*The Old Testament Canon of the New Testament Church and its Background in Early Judaism* [Grand Rapids, Mich.: Eerdmans, 1986], 406) and that the pseudepigraphical books could have had little hope of gaining canonicity. In contrast, James A. Sanders and James C. VanderKam observe the "biblical" character, as well as the ascriptions, of many pseudepigraphical books. See Sanders, "Introduction: Why the Pseudepigrapha?," and VanderKam, "Biblical Interpretation in 1 Enoch and Jubilees," in *The Pseudepigrapha and Early Biblical Interpretation* (ed. Charlesworth and Evans), 13–19 and 19–125, respectively. VanderKam explicitly rejects the view of Beckwith (97).

32. John Barton observes that ascribing pseudonymous works to ancient prophetic or similar figures was a way of claiming authority for them (*Oracles of God: Perceptions of Ancient Prophecy in Israel after the Exile* [New York: Oxford University Press, 1986], 61–62). Otherwise such ascriptions would be pointless.

33. See W. D. Davies, *The Setting of the Sermon on the Mount* (Cambridge: Cambridge University Press, 1966), 273–75, who accepts the arguments of K. G. Kuhn that "books of the *minim*" in rabbinic sources scarcely refers to Gospels.

34. Krister Stendahl, "The Scrolls and the New Testament: An Introduction and a Perspective," in *The Scrolls and the New Testament* (ed. Krister Stendahl; New York: Harper, 1957), 7.

35. Joseph A. Fitzmyer, "The Use of Explicit Old Testament Quotations in the Qumran Literature and in the New Testament," *New Testament Studies* 7 (1960–61): 297–333. It is an interesting fact that, while the mode of scripture citation in the Dead

Sea Scrolls closely parallels the New Testament, that of the Apocrypha and Pseude-pigrapha on the whole does not. See Devorah Dimant, "Use and Interpretation of Mikra in the Apocrypha and Pseudepigrapha," in *Mikra: Text, Translation, Reading and Interpretation of the Hebrew Bible in Ancient Judaism and Early Christianity* (ed. Martin Jan Mulder and Harry Sysling; Compendia rerum iudaicarum ad Novum Testamentum 2/1; Assen, Netherlands: Van Gorcum; Philadelphia: Fortress, 1988), 379–419, esp. 384–400.

36. Fitzmyer, "Use of Explicit Old Testament Quotations," 303–4.

37. Wilfred Cantwell Smith, "The Study of Religion and the Study of the Bible," *Journal of the American Academy of Religion* 39 (1971): 131–40.

38. Wilfred Cantwell Smith, *What Is Scripture? A Comparative Approach* (Minneapolis: Fortress, 1993), 212.

39. Ibid., 47. See also the significant article of W. D. Davies, "Canon and Christology," in *The Glory of Christ in the New Testament: Studies in Christology in Memory of George Bradford Caird* (ed. L. D. Hurst and N. T. Wright; Oxford: Clarendon, 1987), 19–36. Davies articulates the distinctive role of the canon of scripture in Judaism as defining Israel through its history and finds no real parallel in, for example, the role of Homer in Greek history and culture (esp. 27–30). Davies proposes that Christ assumed for Christianity the role of Torah in Judaism (34–36). Interestingly enough, Smith maintains that in Islam the place of Christ is taken by the Qur'an, so that the most fruitful comparison is not between the Qur'an and (Christian) Bible but between the Qur'an and Christ (*What Is Scripture?*, 46). I was also helped by the substantive literature review of Martin S. Jaffee, "Oral Culture in Scriptural Religion: Some Exploratory Studies," *Recherches de science religieuse* 24/3 (July 1998): 223–30, who deals with works of William A. Graham, Barbara A. Holdrege, Susan Niditch, and Mary Carruthers.

40. For the articulation and elaboration of this insight I am indebted to my colleague Bruce B. Lawrence, whose *Defenders of God: The Fundamentalist Revolt against the Modern Age* (San Francisco: Harper & Row, 1989) was republished with a new preface by the author as part of the series Studies in Comparative Religion, ed. Frederick M. Denny (Columbia, S.C.: University of South Carolina Press, 1995).

41. In discussing the scriptural character of the Gospels, we have not considered apostolic origin, which became an important factor in the development and delineation of the New Testament canon, although it had not been in the writing of gospel scriptures. The Gospel of John, however, claims apostolic authorship in its final colophon (21:24), in which it is attributed to the disciple whom Jesus loved. He has borne witness to these things and caused them to be written, and "we" (his circle of disciples?) know that his witness is true. Such a claim of apostolic origin is unique in the Gospels and stands in contrast with John's earlier colophon (20:30–31), which presents the purpose of the Gospel but not its authorization. Apostolic origin is mentioned at just the point that other books, which the world could not hold, come into view (21:25). If these books were other gospels, one would need to know which ones to believe and on what basis.

Chapter 15: Four Gospels and the Canonical Approach to Exegesis

1. *Commentary on the Gospel of John* 10.2–4. On the differences among the Gospels as a problem in antiquity see Oscar Cullmann, "The Plurality of the Gospels as a Theological Problem in Antiquity," *The Early Church* (ed. and trans. by A. J. B. Higgins; Philadelphia: Westminster, 1956), 37–54; also H. Merkel, *Die Pluralität der Evangelien*

als theologisches und exegetisches Problem in der Alten Kirche (Traditio Christiana 3; Bern: Lang, 1978), an extremely useful collection of primary sources with an introduction.

2. Brevard S. Childs, *The New Testament as Canon: An Introduction* (Philadelphia: Fortress, 1984), 117–42.

3. Ibid., 250.

4. Ibid., 45.

5. Ibid., 250.

6. Rudolf Bultmann, *The Gospel of John: A Commentary* (trans. G. R. Beasley-Murray, R. W. N. Hoare, and J. K. Riches; Philadelphia: Westminster, 1971); cf. D. Moody Smith, Jr., *The Composition and Order of the Fourth Gospel: Bultmann's Literary Theory* (Yale Publications in Religion 10; New Haven: Yale University Press, 1965), esp. 244–48.

7. See R. Alan Culpepper, *Anatomy of the Fourth Gospel: A Study in Literary Design* (Philadelphia: Westminster, 1983); Hartwig Thyen, "Johannes 13 und die 'kirchliche Redaktion' des vierten Evangeliums," in *Tradition und Glaube: Das Frühe Christentum in seiner Umwelt: Festgabe für Karl Georg Kuhn zum 65. Geburtstag* (ed. G. Jeremias et al.; Göttingen: Vandenhoeck and Ruprecht, 1971), 343–56, esp. 356.

8. Childs, *New Testament as Canon,* 131.

9. Ibid., 153.

10. Ibid., 155. John Calvin, whom Childs cites often, appears to think otherwise: "The others are certainly not silent on Christ's coming into the world to bring salvation . . . just as John also devotes part of his work to historical narration. But the doctrine that points out to us the power and fruit of Christ's coming appears far more clearly in him than in the others. And since they all had the same object, to show Christ, the first three exhibit his body, if I may be permitted to put it like that, but John shows his soul. For this reason, I am accustomed to say that this Gospel is a key to open the door to the understanding of the others. For whoever grasps the power of Christ as it is here graphically portrayed, will afterwards read with advantage what the others relate about the manifested Redeemer." Calvin adds that John was placed fourth because of when he wrote (presumably last), but reiterates that the Fourth Gospel should be read first. *Calvin's Commentaries: The Gospel of John 1–10* (trans. H. L. Parker; Grand Rapids, Mich: Eerdmans, 1961), 6.

11. Childs, *New Testament as Canon,* 169.

12. Ibid., 122, quoting Lindars, *Behind the Fourth Gospel* (London: SPCK, 1971), 22.

13. Childs, *New Testament as Canon,* 132, quoting Edwyn Clement Hoskyns, *The Fourth Gospel* (ed. Francis Noel Davey; 2nd rev. ed.; London: Faber, 1947), 68.

14. Hoskyns, *Fourth Gospel,* 69: "Yet in spite of the simplicity of its form, the Fourth Gospel is not a simple book. One of the causes of this lack of simplicity is that it does not, in fact, exist in its own right and is not in itself adequate for its own understanding."

15. Childs, *New Testament as Canon,* 134.

16. Culpepper, *Anatomy of the Fourth Gospel,* points out that some events, such as Jesus' calling and commissioning of disciples, are presupposed although they are not recounted in the Fourth Gospel (59). The implied reader seems to know of Jesus, most of the named disciples and other major characters in the story, Jewish groups, and the general geography of the story (213–16). In fact, the story of Jesus himself would seem to be known (222). On the "reliability" of the narrator see p. 32.

17. Hans Windisch, *Johannes und die Synoptiker: Wollte der vierte Evangelist die älteren Evangelien ergänzen oder ersetzen?* (Untersuchungen zum Neuen Testament 12, Leipzig: Hinrich, 1926), 134. On John's independence see also Windisch "Die Absolutheit des Johannesevangeliums," *Zeitschrift für systematische Theologie* 5 (1928): 3–54, which is in the main a response to F. Büchsel, "Johannes und die Synoptiker," *Zeitschrift für systematische Theologie* 4 (1926–27): 240–65.

18. Childs, *New Testament as Canon*, 238.

19. Ernst Käsemann, *The Testament of Jesus: A Study of the Gospel of John in the Light of Chapter 17* (trans. Gerhard Krodel; Philadelphia, Fortress, 1968), 74–76.

20. Childs, *New Testament as Canon*, 172–73.

21. On the evidence of Irenaeus and the Ravenna mosaics for a canonical order of the Gospels in which Mark stood first, see Frederick C. Grant, *The Gospels: Their Origin and Growth,* (New York: Harper, 1957), 65–67.

22. On John see J. Louis Martyn, *History and Theology in the Fourth Gospel* (3d ed., Louisville, Ky.: Westminster John Knox, 2003); on Matthew, W. D. Davies, *The Setting of the Sermon on the Mount* (Cambridge: Cambridge University Press, 1966), esp. 256–315.

23. *History and Theology in the Fourth Gospel,* 122–23.

24. See esp. J. D. Kingsbury, *Matthew: Structure, Christology, Kingdom* (Philadephia: Fortress, 1975).

25. After insisting that faith in the resurrection is the same as faith in the saving efficacy of the cross, Bultmann goes on to add: "The saving efficacy of the cross is not derived from the fact that it is the cross of Christ; it is the cross of Christ because it has this saving efficacy." See "The New Testament and Mythology," in *Kerygma and Myth: A Theological Debate* (ed. Hans Werner Bartsch; trans. Reginald H. Fuller (London: SPCK, 1957), 4.

26. Bultmann, *Theology of the New Testament* (2 vols.; trans. Kendrick Grobel; New York: Scribner's, 1951–55).

27. See Bultmann's review of Windisch's *Johannes und die Synoptiker,* in *Theologische Literaturzeitung* 52 (1927): 197–200.

28. Käsemann, *Testament of Jesus,* 74–76.

29. See n. 16 above.

30. Childs, *New Testament as Canon*, 482–85.

31. Raymond E. Brown, *The Epistles of John* (Anchor Bible 30; Garden City, N.Y.: Doubleday, 1982), 98, n. 226.

Chapter 16: Toward a Canonical Reading of the Fourth Gospel

1. I dedicated this chapter to Frederick Herzog for his seventieth birthday, which he never attained, as a token of esteem, friendship, and gratitude for his stimulation as a colleague and fellow reader of the Gospel of John. His *Liberation Theology: Liberation in the Light of the Fourth Gospel* (New York: Seabury, 1972) raised for me in an acute way the question of how we should read that Gospel and made me aware for the first time of the importance of the question of who is reading.

2. John Dominic Crossan, *The Historical Jesus: The Life of a Mediterranean Jewish Peasant* (New York: HarperCollins, 1991).

3. Neirynck, now Professor Emeritus at Leuven University, has devoted much of his attention to Gospel relationships and especially to the relationship of the Gospel of John to the Synoptic Gospels. His works are too numerous to cite here. Representative

of his position and the present state of scholarship is his *Forschungsbericht,* "John and the Synoptics: 1975–1990," in *John and the Synoptics* (ed. A. Denaux; Bibliotheca ephemeridum theologicarum lovaniensium 101; Leuven: Leuven University Press, 1992), 3–62. Neirynck's paper, along with the others collected in this volume, was presented at the 1990 Louvain Colloquium on John and the Synoptics.

4. Edwyn Clement Hoskyns, *The Fourth Gospel* (ed. F. N. Davey, rev. ed.; London: Faber & Faber, 1947).

5. On the history of the problem of John and the Synoptics, see my *John among the Gospels: The Relationship in Twentieth-Century Research* (2d ed., Columbia, S.C.: University of South Carolina Press, 2001).

6. See, for example, John Ashton, *Understanding the Fourth Gospel* (Oxford: Oxford University Press, 1991), 84, 286–87. The most consistent representative of this position on the North American scene has been Robert T. Fortna. See his *The Fourth Gospel and Its Predecessor: From Narrative Source to Present Gospel* (Philadelphia: Fortress, 1988), 28–29, in which he maintains his earlier position in *The Gospel of Signs: A Reconstruction of the Narrative Source Underlying the Fourth Gospel* (Society for New Testament Studies Monograph Series 11; Cambridge: Cambridge University Press, 1970).

7. See Harold Bloom's introductory article in *The Gospels, Modern Critical Interpretations* (ed. Harold Bloom; New York: Chelsea, 1988), 1–15.

8. Garry Wills, "The Words that Remade America: Lincoln at Gettysburg," *Atlantic Monthly* (June 1992): 57–79. The quotation is found on p. 57.

9. Ibid., 58.

10. Ibid., 79. See also Wills's more extensive treatment of the Gettysburg Address: *Lincoln at Gettysburg: The Words that Remade America* (New York: Simon & Schuster, 1992), from which the *Atlantic* article is largely excerpted. Students of the prologue of the Gospel of John will also be interested in Wills's observation about the form and style of the Gettysburg Address (*Lincoln at Gettysburg,* 172–74). In reproducing the text of the address, he uses bold face, italics, and underlining to show that "each of the paragraphs . . . is bound to the preceding and the following by some resumptive [word or] element." Moreover, "by this reliance on a few words in different contexts, the compactness of the themes is emphasized. . . . The spare vocabulary is not impoverishing because of the subtly interfused constructions. . . . 'Plain speech' was never less artless." All these observations are equally true of the Johannine prologue. Wills elsewhere shows Lincoln's indebtedness to classical and biblical style. One wonders whether the Gettysburg Address was subtly influenced by the prologue of John's Gospel!

11. Rudolf Bultmann, *Theology of the New Testament* (trans. K. Grobel; New York: Scribner's, 1955), 2:3–92 (Part 3: "The Theology of the Gospel of John and the Johannine Epistles"); also, *The Gospel of John: A Commentary* (trans. G. R. Beasley-Murray, R. W. N. Hoare, and J. K. Riches; Philadelphia: Westminster, 1971).

12. C. H. Dodd, *The Apostolic Preaching and Its Developments* (New York: Harper, 1936), 65–78.

13. Dodd, *The Interpretation of the Fourth Gospel* (Cambridge: Cambridge University Press, 1953), and *Historical Tradition in the Fourth Gospel* (Cambridge: Cambridge University Press, 1963).

14. What might be called the canonical dominance of John is reflected in the fact that the Gospel or the Johannine writings are often treated last in books dealing with New Testament theology or interpretation, a practice implying that John represents the perspective from which the whole is to be viewed. See Hans Conzelmann, *An Outline*

of the Theology of the New Testament (trans. J. Bowden; New York: Harper & Row, 1969); W. G. Kümmel, *The Theology of the New Testament According to Its Major Witnesses: Jesus-Paul-John* (trans. J. E. Steely; Nashville: Abingdon, 1973); L. T. Johnson, *The Writings of the New Testament: An Interpretation* (Philadelphia: Fortress, 1986). The earlier editions of R. A. Spivey and D. Moody Smith, *Anatomy of the New Testament: A Guide to Its Structure and Meaning* (New York: Macmillan, 1969 and 1974) followed the same pattern, treating John last. In the third and subsequent editions (Macmillan, 1982, 1989; Prentice Hall, 1995, 2007), however, we broke away from this pattern and simply put John in its place in the Gospel canon.

15. J. N. Sanders, *The Fourth Gospel in the Early Church: Its Origin and Influence on Christian Theology up to Irenaeus* (Cambridge: Cambridge University Press, 1943). Martin Hengel (*The Johannine Question* [trans. J. Bowden; London: SCM; Philadelphia: Trinity Press International, 1989]) disputes "the view, widespread today, that the Fourth Gospel is a semi-'gnostic' Gospel which was first rescued for the mainstream church by the efforts of Irenaeus" (8). This, however, is not the view of the Fourth Gospel that Sanders holds. He regarded it as the effort of an author with access to ancient traditions to state the (orthodox) gospel in terms that would be intelligible to (Alexandrian) protognostics (85) and granted that it had already gained wide acceptance in Asia Minor when Irenaeus received it: ". . . his use of it marks the final stage in its acceptance as scripture, for he challenged the Gnostic interpretation of the Gospel and vindicated it as the *regula veritatis,* a position it has held in Catholic theology ever since" (86–87). See also C. K. Barrett, *The Gospel according to St. John* (rev. ed.; Philadelphia: Westminster, 1978), 123–25, 131, who basically concurs with Sanders.

16. For Brown's position, see his *The Community of the Beloved Disciple* (New York: Paulist, 1979), 93–144, in which he sets out basic historical premises upon which his commentary *The Epistles of John* (Anchor Bible 30; Garden City, N.Y.: Doubleday, 1982), is based.

17. Ernst Käsemann, *The Testament of Jesus: A Study of the Gospel of John in the Light of Chapter 17* (trans. G. Krodel; Philadelphia: Fortress, 1968), 74–78.

18. We have intentionally spoken of canonical reading rather than canonical criticism because canonical reading is, and has been, practiced by Christians who were unaware of canonical—or any other kind of—criticism. Nevertheless, I want to acknowledge the impact and importance of the canon-critical proposal and work of Brevard S. Childs, best known to New Testament students through his *The New Testament as Canon: An Introduction* (Philadelphia: Fortress, 1985). (See chapter 15, above.) Also significant is the more historically oriented approach of J. A. Sanders (see, for example, *Torah and Canon* [Philadelphia: Fortress, 1972]). Only after I had delivered this paper at the 1992 Society of Biblical Literature annual meeting, did I become aware, through the courtesy of the author, of E. E. Lemcio's article, "Father and Son in the Synoptics and John: A Canonical Reading," in *The New Testament as Canon: A Reader in Canonical Criticism,* (ed. Robert W. Wall; Sheffield: Sheffield Academic Press, 1992).

Index of Biblical and Other Ancient Texts

Index of Other Ancient Texts

Index of Modern Authors

About the Author

D. MOODY SMITH is the George Washington Ivey Professor Emeritus of New Testament at the Divinity School, Duke University, where he has taught since 1965. His books include *The Composition and Order of the Fourth Gospel,* *The Theology of the Gospel of John, John among the Gospels,* and the Abingdon New Testament commentary *John.* Smith is also the editor of the Studies on Personalities of the New Testament series published by the University of South Carolina Press.